THE GLOBAL
REVOLUTIONS OF 1968

A NORTON CASEBOOK IN HISTORY

NORTON CASEBOOKS IN HISTORY SERIES

The Global Revolutions of 1968 by Jeremi Suri

Indian Removal
by David S. Heidler and Jeanne T. Heidler

Two Communities in the Civil War
by Andrew J. Torget and Edward L. Ayers

FORTHCOMING TITLES INCLUDE:

1989: The End of the 20th Century
by James Carter and Cynthia Paces

Jim Crow by Jane Dailey

Pirates in the Age of Sail by Robert Antony

Mongols in Global History by Morris Rossabi

THE GLOBAL REVOLUTIONS OF 1968

A NORTON CASEBOOK IN HISTORY

Jeremi Suri

W. W. NORTON & COMPANY

New York / London

W. W. Norton & Company has been independent since its founding in 1923, when William Warder Norton and Mary D. Herter Norton first published lectures delivered at the People's Institute, the adult education division of New York City's Cooper Union. The Nortons soon expanded their program beyond the Institute, publishing books by celebrated academics from America and abroad. By mid-century, the two major pillars of Norton's publishing program—trade books and college texts—were firmly established. In the 1950s, the Norton family transferred control of the company to its employees, and today—with a staff of four hundred and a comparable number of trade, college, and professional titles published each year—W. W. Norton & Company stands as the largest and oldest publishing house owned wholly by its employees.

First Edition

The text of this book is composed in Baskerville MT with the display set in Cloister Openface.

Series design by Jo Anne Metsch.
Composition by ElectraGraphics, Inc.
Manufacturing by the Courier Companies—Westford Division.
Project editor: Lory A. Frenkel.
Production manager: Benjamin Reynolds.

Library of Congress Cataloging-in-Publication Data

The global revolutions of 1968: a Norton casebook in history / [edited] by Jeremi Suri.
   p. cm.
   Includes bibliographical references and index

ISBN-13: 978-0-393-92744-3 (pbk.)
ISBN-10: 0-393-92744-X (pbk.)
      1. History, Modern—1945–1989—Sources. 2. Nineteen sixty-eight, A.D.—Sources.
   3. Radicalism—History—20th century—Sources. 4. Revolutions—History—20th
   century—Sources. I. Suri, Jeremi.

D848.G66 2006
909.82´6—dc22

                                                                                 2006047158

W. W. Norton & Company, Inc., 500 Fifth Avenue, New York, N.Y. 10110-0017
www.wwnorton.com
W. W. Norton & Company Ltd., Castle House, 75/76 Wells Street, London W1T 3QT
1 2 3 4 5 6 7 8 9 0

CONTENTS

Acknowledgments   *viii*

Introduction   *x*

SECTION I: ORIGINS OF THE GLOBAL REVOLUTIONS   *1*
- Nikita Sergeyevich Khrushchev, 20th Party Congress
  Speech (24–25 February 1956)   1
- Martin Luther King Jr., The Rising Tide of Racial
  Consciousness (1960)   10
- Frantz Fanon, Concerning Violence   18
- John F. Kennedy, Address of the Honorable
  John F. Kennedy Accepting the Nomination for
  the Presidency of the United States (15 July 1960)   25
- Young Americans for Freedom, The Sharon
  Statement (11 September 1960)   32
- National Liberation Front for South Vietnam,
  Ten-Point Manifesto (December 1960)   34
- Deng Tuo, The Kingly Way and the Tyrannical
  Way (25 February 1962)   35
- Students for a Democratic Society, The Port Huron
  Statement (1962)   40
- Lyndon B. Johnson, Special Message to the Congress:
  The American Promise (15 March 1965)   50
- Ernesto Guevara, Excerpt from *The African Dream:
  The Diaries of the Revolutionary War in the Congo*   61
- Herbert Marcuse, Political Preface 1966   72

SECTION 2: 1968   *83*
- Mao Zedong, Talk to Leaders of the Centre
  (21 July 1966)   83

v

• Andrei Sakharov, Excerpt from *Memoirs*   86
• Rudi Dutschke, The Students and the Revolution
    (7 March 1968)   118
• Daniel Cohn-Bendit, Interview by Jean-Paul Sartre
    (20 May 1968)   132
• Betty Friedan, The Politics of Sex (Fall 1968)   141
• Ludvík Vaculík, Two Thousand Words for Workers,
    Farmers, Scientists, Artists, and Everyone
    (27 June 1968)   158
• Memorandum of Conversation between Leonid
    Brezhnev and Alexander Dubček (13 August 1968)   166
• Strike Committee of the Faculty of Philosophy and
    Letters of the University of Mexico, The Mexican
    Student Movement: Its Meaning and Perspectives   184
• Mexican Student Poems   198
• The National Strike Committee, For a
    Worker/Peasant/Student Alliance
    (12 September 1968)   200
• Abbie Hoffman, Interview (1969)   206
• CIA Report, Restless Youth (September 1968)   216
• Stokely Carmichael, The Pitfalls of Liberalism
    (January 1969)   238

SECTION 3: REACTIONS AND LEGACIES   *247*
• President Lyndon Johnson, Soviet Ambassador
    Anatoly Dobrynin, and National Security Council
    Advisor Walt Rostow, Summary of Their Meeting
    (20 August 1968)   247
• John Kenneth Galbraith and Henry Kissinger,
    Correspondence (2 July 1969–10 October 1970)   254
• Richard Nixon and Mao Zedong, Memorandum
    of Conversation (21 February 1972)   259
• U.S. Department of State Bulletin, Basic Principles
    of Relations Between the United States
    of America and the Union of Soviet Socialist
    Republics (29 May 1972)   268
• U.S. National Security Council, Memorandum
    of Conversation (6 November 1970)   272

- U.S. Department of State, Memorandum
    (11 July 1975)   278
- Ronald Reagan, Vietnam II (30 November 1976)   280
- Ronald Reagan, Blind on the Left (20 February 1978)   282
- Charter 77–Declaration (1 January 1977)   284
- Mikhail Gorbachev, Excerpt from *Memoirs*   290

SECTION 4: INTERPRETATIONS   *301*
- Paul Berman, The Dream of a New Society   301
- Arthur Marwick, The Consummation of a Cultural
    Revolution   309
- Jeremi Suri, Power and Protest   316

Supplementary Bibliography   *324*
Credits   *330*
Index   *333*

ACKNOWLEDGMENTS

In this book and other writings, I have benefited enormously from the insights of 1960s "veterans" around the world. In addition to the countless documents they left, I have enjoyed hearing them reflect on their experiences, their regrets, and their wishes. I have also benefited from my own late birth. I was born after 1968. I am part of the first generation that can see the period as history. This does not make me or my generation better at analyzing the 1960s, but it does provide a certain perspective, perhaps a little more detached and global than the men and women who were "in the trenches."

My students at the University of Wisconsin, also generally born after 1968, have helped me to understand this period as history. In an advanced undergraduate seminar that I have taught for a number of years, we have analyzed various primary and secondary texts, and argued over origins and legacies. My students and I have also focused on some of the same issues in my large lecture course on the international history of the twentieth century. The selection of documents in this volume reflects the preferences and suggestions of my students.

David Rodriguez, one of my graduate students at the University of Wisconsin, helped me to organize the materials for this book. He offered many valuable suggestions about the documents, especially for Latin America and Africa. David continually reminded me of the need to remain global in focus, without sacrificing analytical depth or accessibility for students. Trudy Fredericks helped to check the page proofs. Her enthusiasm for this project and time period inspires me.

Karl Bakeman, my editor at W. W. Norton & Company, first suggested this project. He has been patient and supportive in all of the ways that an author appreciates. Karl has an excellent eye for both intellectual rigor and undergraduate needs. Rebecca Arata handled the production of this manuscript with superb skill.

As always, my family deserves the deepest thanks for its inspiration, support, and love. Alison rolled her eyes when I told her I was taking on "yet another project," but she helped me in countless ways. Her love sustains me. Natalie added her wonderful smile and laugh, even when she rearranged Daddy's papers. Zachary came into our lives as I was working on this book. His enthusiasm for life has reminded me of the brighter possibilities in human nature, and a moment like 1968.

INTRODUCTION: 1968 AS HISTORY

History is not the same as lived experience. People who lived through the 1960s, and the tumultuous events of 1968 in particular, have an irreplaceable perspective on the period. They witnessed the violence, they exulted in the possibilities of progressive change, and they feared the evidence of social breakdown. Many veterans of the 1960s suffered physically and emotionally for their (often unintended) participation in events.

These "authentic" 1960s experiences are pregnant with valuable insights, but they also have serious limitations for the student of history. The emotion of the street protests, military conflicts, and family struggles makes it very difficult for participants to separate themselves from the politics of the era. They are still fighting many of the same battles in ways that often prohibit a broader perspective. Former civil rights and feminist activists in the United States, for instance, have had trouble recognizing that their political opponents—often young social and political conservatives— also had serious ideals and high-minded convictions.[1] The same critique, of course, applies to the "neo-conservative" writers who condemn the alleged moral decadence of the radical reformers in the 1960s.[2] Some activists have since switched sides in these debates, but the battle lines remain sharp. Old animosities close off avenues of investigation that challenge long-standing assumptions about political legitimacy and social justice.

---

[1] On this point, see Alan Brinkley, "The Problem of American Conservatism," *American Historical Review* 99 (April 1994), 409–29.

[2] For a correction to allegations of moral decadence, see Maurice Isserman and Michael Kazin, *America Divided: The Civil War of the 1960s* (New York: Oxford University Press, 2000), 293–300.

The people who lived through the 1960s also carry a particular geographical vision of the period. The observation that the events of 1968 were global in scope is quite common (almost cliché), but the dominant analytical frame for understanding social and political change remains national in scope. Those who organized local marches against the Vietnam War or worked to ensure law and order have trouble integrating global forces into their perspective. This is especially true for Americans, who are often poorly informed about events in other parts of the world. Although the diffusion of ideas, images, and institutions across national boundaries was incredibly powerful in the 1960s, it frequently escaped the notice of citizens and leaders struggling to cope with the mounting pressures of everyday life.

The local focus of many people during this period was not a reflection of naïveté. A student enraged by the prospect of military service in Vietnam or a police officer provoked by a hostile crowd had little opportunity to reflect on the global conditions that made that moment possible. They had to act, and they had to act quickly. Today their memories of the 1960s remain locked, to some extent, in the intensity of these confrontational moments—a point that becomes evident when more than forty years later, they continue to display raw emotion about their local interpersonal encounters. The personal was political, as many said at the time, but the global was political as well.

This collection of primary documents and historical reflections is designed to guide a post-1960s generation of readers through this period as history. Readers must understand the assumptions that guided politics and social change, but they must also examine the global forces that transformed these assumptions. No one planned for or expected 1968 to become a year of global revolutions. The year evolved as it did because the local divisions and confrontations that built through the decade produced pressures for radical change across political parties, national boundaries, and distinct cultures. Revolutionary impulses expressed themselves in diverse ways around the world and elicited varied responses, but they were part of a common global experience.

To this day, many languages and cultures reserve a special place for the phrase "68 generation" to recognize a turning point in society.

Like the window on a museum display case, the year 1968 separates us—physically and symbolically—from a world that appears appreciably different. Although we can recognize the roots of our present condition in the images and artifacts from before that tumultuous year, we also understand that we are somehow radically different. The pre-1968 past is ever-present in popular memory, but it is incredibly distant from daily behavior. Considering that before the late 1960s many public institutions in the United States legally offered separate and unequal facilities for whites and blacks, as well as men and women, the pre-1968 past feels like ancient history. 1968 divides the "before" from the "after," the world we lost from the world we gained.

The most important and influential events of the 1960s did not occur precisely in a single year, but the worldwide conjunction of disorders in 1968 marked a high point in the growing sense, across nations, that an old political and social order had died. Government leaders lost the legitimacy, and even reverence, that they generally commanded a decade earlier. Inherited paternalistic and racist assumptions about cultural superiority came under siege as they had never been before. Most startling, young people around the world emerged as prominent consumers, political actors, and violent protesters on a scale unimaginable in other times. Particularly in 1968, the global media picked up on the rise of "youth culture" and its challenge to established authority. This became the dominant story of the year and its incessantly reproduced iconography.

The political and social transformations surrounding 1968 affected both government policy makers and ordinary citizens. One of the documents in this volume reproduces an excerpt from an alarmist report prepared by the U.S. Central Intelligence Agency (CIA):

> Youthful dissidence, involving students and non-students alike, is a worldwide phenomenon. It is shaped in every instance by local conditions, but nonetheless there are striking similarities, especially in the more advanced countries. As the underdeveloped countries progress, these similarities are likely to become even more widespread. A truly radical concept of industrial society and its institutions prompts much of the dissidence—but it, alone, does not

explain the degree to which young agitators have won a wide following in such countries as France, the Federal Republic [of Germany] and the United States.[3]

Protesters at the time could not see it, but government leaders in nearly every nation became preoccupied, sometimes obsessed, with understanding the sources of social unrest and addressing its challenges to established authority. Policy makers frequently agreed with West German chancellor Kurt Georg Kiesinger when he privately lamented the "international sickness" that had allegedly overcome protest-prone citizens, but these words were hardly a dismissal of the problem.[4] Quite the contrary, by 1968 leaders entered a period of continual crisis decision making, fueled by a pressing need to clear the streets, reestablish authority, and formulate a positive political program to counteract public criticisms. The year marked a moment of "global revolutions" because the cumulative effect of worldwide protest activities undermined basic assumptions about who rules, even in the eyes of the rulers themselves.

Differences in political systems, ideologies, and cultures meant that leaders and citizens experienced 1968 in dissimilar ways. While students in the United States and Western Europe could openly condemn their leaders, dissidents in the Soviet Union had to circulate their ideas secretly. Red Guards in China dismantled governing institutions in the name of their titular leader, Mao Zedong. Protesters throughout Latin America and Africa took to the streets to overthrow their leaders and eradicate the influence of their foreign sponsors. Youthful rebellion was simultaneous and contagious, but its aims and expressions were not identical worldwide.

Every government sought to mix reform with repression. Of course, the balance between these two reactions varied markedly from one society to another. The Western democracies (including the United States) employed state-sanctioned violence—including

---

[3] "Restless Youth," CIA Report, September 1968, Lyndon Baines Johnson Presidential Library, National Security File, Files of Walt W. Rostow, Box 13, Folder: Youth and Student Movements, page i.

[4] Conversation between Chancellor Kiesinger and Iranian Ambassador Malek, 15 June 1967, in *Akten zur Auswärtigen Politik der Bundesrepublik Deutschland*, 1967 (Munich: R. Oldenbourg Verlag, 1998), 2:911–17, quotation on 916.

police beatings, temporary detentions, and infrequent shootings—to smother domestic challengers. This state violence, though harsh, never approached the brutality of Soviet "psychological hospitals," Chinese "reeducation camps," and "disappearances" throughout Latin America. 1968 marked a convergence of social disorder across societies, but differences in political systems shaped the nature of domestic responses. The most radical critic of Western democracy benefited from the limits on the repressive apparatus of the state he or she condemned. In contrast, the most moderate dissident under a communist or authoritarian regime lived with constant fear for his or her security. The global revolutions of 1968 transcended systems of rule, but Cold War divisions between liberal democracy and authoritarian communism still mattered enormously.

Many of the documents from policy makers in this volume will point to the continued relevance of the Cold War, and also to the ways in which the social unrest of the period changed foreign and domestic policies. For some citizens and leaders, the global revolutions of 1968 were an inspiration for broad reform. For others, the violence on the streets created a strong urge for enforced order at home and abroad. These two basic reactions characterized the Cold War in the 1970s and 1980s—a period of both increased human rights activism and extensive cooperation among the dominant states to maintain international stability. Future Soviet leader Mikhail Gorbachev's maturation during this period, as recounted on page 290, is an excellent example of this post-1968 duality. The attempts to build "socialism with a human face" in Czechoslovakia moved Gorbachev to embrace the ideal of a freer and more open communist system. At the same time, he sought to achieve this vision by strengthening the power of the Soviet government, not weakening it. Gorbachev was both a Cold Warrior and a Cold War reformer. He mirrored the simultaneous permanence and transformation of the international system in the two decades after 1968.[5]

The materials in this volume provide the grounding for a rigorous and broad analysis of this crucial global turning point. The

---

[5] For more on this general point, and the connections between the global revolutions of 1968 and the end of the Cold War, see Jeremi Suri, "Explaining the End of the Cold War: A New Historical Consensus?" *Journal of Cold War Studies* 4 (Fall 2002), 60–92.

arrangement of the volume offers a coherent narrative of social and political change ranging over more than forty years, but centered around 1968. This narrative asserts global connections but also encourages attention to the diverse ways that different peoples and cultures shaped the world around them. Most important, the materials in this volume give attention to a truly global range of voices and experiences. Many societies and peoples remain absent not because they are irrelevant, but because the editor could not locate appropriate materials. This volume is a multi-vocal global history, but like all histories, it remains incomplete.

The Origins of the Global Revolutions

The first section in this volume provides a variety of perspectives on the origins of the global revolutions. Each document highlights an event or text that contributed to a breakdown in established structures of authority and a search for new alternatives. Critics of politics and society at the time included government leaders, intellectuals, revolutionaries, civil rights advocates, anti-colonial fighters, and student activists, among many others. They included people of varied nationalities, cultures, races, and genders. Most significant, critics held a diverse range of ideological convictions. They identified as liberals, conservatives, social democrats, and communists, among others. Some of the most eloquent young critics identified with a self-proclaimed "New Left" or "New Right"— one attacking liberals for sacrificing their ideals of social justice, the other attacking conservatives for forsaking religion and morality.

These diverse groups disagreed on many key issues and they fought against one another. Nonetheless, they all believed that the social and political status quo could not hold. They all found it lacking in personal meaning. Students for a Democratic Society, which became the largest New Left group in the United States during the 1960s, captured this sentiment in its cogent "Port Huron Statement" of 1962:

> The conventional moral terms of the age, the politician moralities
> —"free world," "people's democracies"—reflect realities poorly,
> if at all, and seem to function more as ruling myths than as descriptive principles. . . . Theoretic chaos has replaced the idealistic

thinking of old—and, unable to reconstitute theoretic order, men have condemned idealism itself. Doubt has replaced hopefulness—and men act out a defeatism that is labeled realistic. The decline of utopia and hope is in fact one of the defining features of social life today.[6]

Contemporary society lacked personal meaning because it was boring. Large impersonal institutions and complex bureaucracies made citizens, particularly students, feel insignificant. Leaders also found that the inertia of their societies foiled promises for active reform. In addition, a militarized stalemate throughout Europe, Asia, and parts of Latin America and Africa, meant that foreign policy failed to offer hope for anything but a continuing Cold War. In the early 1960s no one foresaw an end to the arms races, the military threats, and the resulting domestic tensions. Similarly, people living under systems of oppression—including Algerian independence advocates like Frantz Fanon and civil rights activists like Martin Luther King Jr.—feared that a permanent Cold War would setback any hope for social improvement.

Energetic leaders and citizens across the globe rebelled against these stagnant conditions. The materials in this volume show how they not only identified similar Cold War grievances, but also worked to inspire new avenues of change. For some leaders, including both Soviet general secretary Nikita Khrushchev and American president John F. Kennedy, this meant instilling their citizens with a sense hope, a promise that renewed courage and creativity on a national scale would make life meaningful again. Others, including Frantz Fanon, Ernesto "Che" Guevara, and Herbert Marcuse, called for grassroots resistance to the status quo. They advocated popular revolution, often through violence, as a creative force for change.

Common dissatisfaction with the current situation, shared by influential members of different societies, elicited enormous pressures for radical change. Even conservative and New Right groups were radical in their demand to escape an allegedly morally vacuous contemporary social situation. The same could be said for forward-thinking leaders like Khrushchev and Kennedy, who were

[6] Students for a Democratic Society, "The Port Huron Statement" (New York: Students for a Democratic Society, 1962), 3–4.

indeed seen as radicals by many of their elder counterparts. Promises of slow reform gave way to expectations of rapid transformation in the early 1960s.

The diverse aims and tactics of those advocating radical change, however, promised disorder rather than consensus. The heated rhetoric of the period left little room for compromise. It also valorized acts of defiance against both the inherited forces of political authority and rival proponents of change. Most significant, the political language of the early 1960s manifested growing frustration with the hindrances to political openness, civil rights reform, nuclear disarmament, economic equality, and other programs. Frustration bred rage—an emotional call for the alleged cleansing power of violent retribution—that became more common in the years before 1968, especially among oppressed groups. Frantz Fanon famously advocated the redemptive role of violence on behalf of Algerians fighting against a brutal French colonial regime. The National Liberation Front for South Vietnam, the Red Army Faction in West Germany, the Black Panthers in the United States, and other groups soon adopted this argument as well.[7] In a context where activists encouraged violence, social upheaval on a wide scale became almost inevitable.

1968

The social explosions of 1968 were the culmination of increasing pressures for violent change. They began before this iconic year and extended a few years after it. What made 1968 special was the rapid succession of disorders, their intensity, and their geographic range. The CIA joined other observers in pronouncing 1968 a year of global revolutions from which many societies would not recover.

The materials in this section of the volume are designed to give readers a flavor for the violence, anger, and conflict that drove events, and popular perceptions of events, in 1968. Within communist China the events of 1968 began not with public violence,

[7] For a provocative study of how student activists, particularly in West Germany and the United States, came to view violence as a positive and redemptive force, see Jeremy Varon, *Bringing the War Home: The Weather Underground, the Red Army Faction, and Revolutionary Violence in the Sixties and Seventies* (Berkeley, CA: University of California Press, 2004).

but with Mao Zedong's official call for a "Cultural Revolution" against the established sources of authority that allegedly thwarted the Great Leader's promises of national achievement. The revolution would be "cultural" in its challenge not only to institutions, but to perceived "bourgeois" habits of mind that limited human capabilities. Mao provoked the formation of "Red Guard" groups throughout the country, largely comprised of young students who physically attacked parents, principals, and political figures. They quite literally brought chaos to China, and they eventually attacked Mao himself.[8]

Though only faintly understood outside of China, images of the Cultural Revolution inspired activists around the world. West German, Mexican, and American youth, among many others, called for similar popular mobilization against inherited habits of mind in their own countries. They also advocated, in some circumstances, the use of violence to defeat the alleged forces of repression. Mao Zedong, Che Guevara, and the image of the "urban guerilla" became commonplace among student activists. Violence, anti-authoritarianism, and "people power" emerged as slogans of global revolution—deeply believed by many, manipulated for self-interested purposes by many others.

Not everyone was inspired by the promise of revolution. Government leaders and perhaps a majority of citizens across societies feared that protests and domestic violence had spun out of control. Political figures like Soviet general secretary Leonid Brezhnev, French president Charles de Gaulle, and American president Lyndon Johnson did not relish the idea of deploying force against the young, idealistic citizens in the streets. As the materials in this volume show, government leaders resorted to police action and military retaliation out of panic and perceived necessity. In retrospect, they overreacted and employed excessive brutality, but these legitimate criticisms should not blind us to the pressures these heads of state faced at a time when it appeared their world was crumbling around them. Demands for "law and order" in the face of global

[8] The extraordinary chaos of the Chinese Cultural Revolution, and Mao Zedong's contradictory role, defy easy explanation. For more background, see Wang Shaoguan, *Failure of Charisma: The Cultural Revolution in Wuhan* (New York: Oxford University Press, 1995); Roderick MacFarquhar, *The Origins of the Cultural Revolution*, Volume 3 (New York: Columbia University Press, 1997).

revolution came from a broad cross-section of voices, not just threatened government elites.

The figures who emerge from 1968 with the most heroic historic image are the intellectual and student dissidents in the former Soviet bloc states, especially the Soviet Union and Czechoslovakia. Andrei Sakharov and Ludvík Vaculík, in particular, offered passionate arguments against established communist authority, emphasizing how it had become an oppressive, self-interested, and ineffective form of government. They called not for revolution per se, but for a reassertion of basic human freedoms and values including rights of free speech, conscience, and equality. Sakharov, Vaculík, and other dissidents were not anti-communist or pro-capitalist; they believed that the two systems were converging at a middle ground that would include greater human freedoms and more attention to social equality. The simultaneous protest activities in communist and capitalist societies provided evidence, for the dissidents, that this moment of change would come soon.

They were incorrect making this prediction, in part because of the willingness of communist leaders to employ military force against their own citizens and allies. The brutal Soviet invasion of Czechoslovakia in August 1968 offered disturbingly clear evidence of the deep resistance to internal change within Eastern Europe and other Cold War battlefields. The personal courage and deep humanity of Sakharov, Vaculík, and other Soviet bloc dissidents shines as a bright light through the dark moments of violence in 1968. Their aspirations continue to shape political thinking in the present post-communist world and beyond.

The same is true, to some extent, for the feminist activists of 1968. They had, by that time, become a powerful political and social force across societies, arguing for more attention to the inherited chauvinist attitudes that prolonged sex inequalities despite legislation to the contrary. Betty Friedan's book, *The Feminine Mystique*, was very influential among the early "second wave" of 1960s feminists.[9] By the end of the decade, as her contribution to this volume

---

[9] See Betty Friedan, *The Feminine Mystique* (New York: Dell Publishing, 1983, originally published in 1963). For an insightful analysis of the book, and its limitations, see Daniel Horowitz, *Betty Friedan and the Making of the Feminine Mystique* (Amherst: University of Massachusetts Press, 1998).

indicates, an emerging group of feminists criticized Friedan and others for failing to adopt more radical calls for women to reject traditional definitions of sex and womanhood.[10]

Debates among feminists notwithstanding, they joined civil rights activists, Soviet bloc dissidents, and other groups in challenging and fundamentally transforming public attitudes across the globe. Although old habits of mind remained evident in various institutions, chauvinism, racism, and authoritarianism were on the retreat. The 1960s movements delegitimized these long-standing belief systems. "Ordinary life" after 1968 changed not only because of the contention and violence, but also because of the positive examples provided by courageous women and men.

Reactions and Legacies

Reactions to the global revolutions of 1968 were as diverse as the sources of the revolutions themselves. The materials in this volume show that many prominent political figures sought to preserve basic order against perceived anarchy, almost at any cost. For Chinese, Soviet, and American leaders this meant a turn toward Cold War détente—forging new cooperative arrangements among former adversaries to counteract common disorders at home. The reader should note that, by the early 1970s, men like Mao Zedong, Leonid Brezhnev, and Richard Nixon were more comfortable working with one another than with their own citizens. Cold War leaders adopted a set of tacit rules to manage the spreading internal disorder they perceived after 1968. To a great extent, these rules were codified in the agreement on "Basic Principles of Relations Between the United States of America and the Union of Soviet Socialist Republics," signed in Moscow by Brezhnev and Nixon on May 29, 1972. Among other things, this extraordinary document codified "peaceful coexistence," "mutual accommodation," and the "special responsibility" of the United States and the Soviet Union to manage international tensions. At a moment when citizens in the most powerful states demanded a radical transformation of Cold

[10] For a discussion of "second wave" feminism, see Ruth Rosen, *The World Split Open: How the Modern Women's Movement Changed America* (New York: Viking, 2000). Historians generally refer to three "waves" of feminism—roughly corresponding to the late nineteenth century, the 1960s, and the late twentieth century.

War politics, leaders in Moscow, Washington, and other capitals worked to protect the status quo.[11]

Eliminating threatening sources of disorder often meant that the superpowers would scheme to overthrow distrusted foreign regimes. The Soviet Union acted in this way when it invaded Czechoslovakia and destroyed the popular "Prague Spring" government. The United States worked indirectly for the same end in Chile when it supported a military-led coup against the elected government of Salvador Allende Gossens. The Chilean leader frightened President Nixon and Secretary of State Henry Kissinger because of his socialist background and his ties to Fidel Castro's revolutionary activities in Latin America. Nixon and Kissinger also coupled negotiations for withdrawal from South Vietnam with increased bombing in the region, including the neutral country of Cambodia. As in Czechoslovakia and Chile, a superpower escalated its use of force on the Cold War "periphery" in pursuit of global order and an image of strength at home.[12]

The amazing fact about each of these Cold War escalations is that the superpowers generally refrained from criticizing one another. This was part of their agreement on "mutual accommodation." When the Soviet ambassador brought Lyndon Johnson news of the invasion of Czechoslovakia, the president did not condemn this infringement on sovereignty, but instead inquired about a planned summit meeting with Brezhnev. Despite his calls for communist support, Allende received little help from Moscow, and Soviet leaders did not condemn strongly the American-sponsored coup in Chile. The Soviet Union also continued to pursue détente with the United States as the Nixon administration increased its brutality in Vietnam. After 1968 the superpowers affirmed a joint commitment to "peaceful coexistence" in their bilateral relations, and the expansion of force to repress potential sources of domestic and international disorder.

[11] "Basic Principles of Relations Between the United States of America and the Union of Soviet Socialist Republics," 29 May 1972. *The U.S. Department of State Bulletin*, Volume 66 (26 June 1972), 898–899.

[12] For more on the Nixon administration's policies in Vietnam, and their connections to post-1968 domestic politics, see Jeffrey Kimball, *Nixon's Vietnam War* (Lawrence: University Press of Kansas, 1998); Larry Berman, *No Peace, No Honor: Nixon, Kissinger, and Betrayal in Vietnam* (New York: Free Press, 2001); Jeremi Suri, *Henry Kissinger and the American Century* (Cambridge, MA: Harvard University Press, 2007).

Not everyone accepted this Faustian bargain. One of the most enduring legacies of the 1960s is a lingering controversy over the legitimacy of policies that sacrificed revolutionary change for political order. Critics of the détente arrangements pursued by post-1968 government leaders are very diverse. They include human rights activists, such as the Soviet bloc dissidents who joined together to promulgate a public declaration of their rights known as "Charter 77." Ronald Reagan emerged as another prominent détente critic, claiming that the basic principles negotiated to stabilize the Cold War sacrificed America's anti-communist moral mission. Reagan sought to mobilize citizens at home and abroad around a restored faith in the United States' ability to defeat communist threats in Vietnam, Latin America, and the Soviet Union itself.

As mentioned earlier, Mikhail Gorbachev also came of age as a political leader in the shadow of 1968. He affirmed both the desire for global order that grew out of the period and the moral claims to change embodied by diverse voices. Gorbachev's mixed legacy—the end of communist oppression and the failure to build a legitimate government in the former Soviet Union—mirrors the mixed legacies of 1968. The global revolutions reformed personal attitudes, but they did not build new institutions to implement change.

Interpretations

This volume concludes with excerpts from three recent interpretations of the global revolutions of 1968. The period has inspired many other accounts, but these three authors have been most explicit in their attempts to examine the period as global history. Paul Berman points to an evolving utopianism from the pursuit of "direct democracy" and "revolutionary socialism" in 1968 to "liberal democracy" in 1989. For Berman, the activists of 1968 lost touch with political realities, but they inspired the more successful reform voices that brought down communist oppression two decades later.[13]

Arthur Marwick focuses more closely on the cultural side of 1968. He argues that the global revolutions liberated countless

---

[13] Paul Berman, *A Tale of Two Utopias: The Political Journey of the Generation of 1968* (New York: W. W. Norton, 1996), quotations on 14.

"ordinary people" from the "stuffy conservatism of previous decades." Personal freedoms expanded unevenly but significantly across societies. Activism was about lifestyle as much as politics, and in this sense the events of 1968 transformed the world for the better, according to Marwick. "[T]he consequences of what happened in the sixties were long-lasting: the sixties cultural revolution in effect established the enduring cultural values and social behaviour for the rest of the century."[14]

The excerpt from my own book, *Power and Protest*, draws a deep connection between Cold War conditions, the rise of global social unrest, and the conservative policies of détente. This interpretation criticizes leaders across societies for repressing progressive ideas and prolonging the Cold War. It also laments the ideological rigidity of many activists in the late 1960s, and their frequent adoption of an anti-political posture, refusing to work through existing political institutions. *Power and Protest* argues that the global revolutions of 1968 produced a wide chasm between popular aspirations and political institutions around the world.[15]

These historical interpretations differ from the perspectives of many who experienced these events. (One should note, however, that Berman and Marwick were both participants before they became historians.) The materials in this volume allow the reader to form his or her own interpretation that will not only reflect a global perspective on the period, but also a set of judgments based on the conditions of the contemporary world. New, creative, and useful histories of this tumultuous period remain to be written.

The history of 1968 is about much more than lived experience. It involves a dialogue between diverse actors and different time periods. It grows from a reading and re-reading of original documentary materials. The global revolutions of 1968 provide fertile soil for a continuing cross-generational discussion about politics and social change. This is a living global history.

[14] Arthur Marwick, *The Sixties: Cultural Revolution in Britain, France, Italy, and the United States, c. 1958–c. 1974* (Oxford: Oxford University Press, 1998), quotations on 802 and 806.

[15] Jeremi Suri, *Power and Protest: Global Revolution and the Rise of Détente* (Cambridge, MA: Harvard University Press, 2003).

Origins of the Global Revolutions

Nikita Sergeyevich Khrushchev

20th Party Congress Speech (24–25 February 1956)

The death of Soviet dictator Josef Stalin in 1953 marked a turning point in the Cold War and the history of the Soviet people. Stalin had built an empire of fear and terror. Within the Soviet Union he had initiated a series of violent purges, killing millions of "internal enemies." In February 1956 Stalin's successor, Nikita Khrushchev, denounced Stalin's crimes in a "secret speech" that quickly became public. Khrushchev's words opened a brief "thaw" in the Soviet empire, when citizens felt emboldened to criticize Stalin and some of his lieutenants for straying from the correct path of communism. Khrushchev sought to strengthen his authority by distancing himself from Stalin, but he inspired limited dissent and even some public protest, particularly in Eastern Europe.

* * *

As later events have proven, Lenin's anxiety was justified: in the first period after Lenin's death Stalin still paid attention to his [i.e., Lenin's] advice, but later he began to disregard the serious admonitions of Vladimir Ilyich.

When we analyze the practice of Stalin in regard to the direction of the Party and of the country, when we pause to consider everything which Stalin perpetrated, we must be convinced that Lenin's fears were justified. The negative characteristics of Stalin, which, in Lenin's time, were only incipient, transformed themselves during the last years into a grave abuse of power by Stalin, which caused untold harm to our Party.

1

We have to consider seriously and analyze correctly this matter in order that we may preclude any possibility of a repetition in any form whatever of what took place during the life of Stalin, who absolutely did not tolerate collegiality in leadership and in work, and who practiced brutal violence, not only toward everything which opposed him, but also toward that which seemed to his capricious and despotic character, contrary to his concepts. Stalin acted not through persuasion, explanation, and patient co-operation with people, but by imposing his concepts and demanding absolute submission to his opinion. Whoever opposed this concept or tried to prove his viewpoint, and the correctness of his position, was doomed to removal from the leading collective and to subsequent moral and physical annihilation. This was especially true during the period following the XVIIth Party Congress, when many prominent Party leaders and rank-and-file Party workers, honest and dedicated to the cause of Communism, fell victim to Stalin's despotism.

We must affirm that the Party had fought a serious fight against the Trotskyites, rightists and bourgeois nationalists, and that it disarmed ideologically all the enemies of Leninism. This ideological fight was carried on successfully, as a result of which the Party became strengthened and tempered. Here Stalin played a positive role.

The Party led a great political ideological struggle against those in its own ranks who proposed anti-Leninist theses, who represented a political line hostile to the Party and to the cause of socialism. This was a stubborn and a difficult fight but a necessary one, because the political line of both the Trotskyite-Zinovievite bloc and of the Bukharinites led actually toward the restoration of capitalism and capitulation to the world bourgeoisie. Let us consider for a moment what would have happened if in 1928–1929 the political line of right deviation had prevailed among us, or orientation toward "cotton-dress industrialization," or toward the kulak, etc. We would not now have a powerful heavy industry, we would not have the kolkhozes, we would find ourselves disarmed and weak in a capitalist encirclement.

It was for this reason that the Party led an inexorable ideological fight and explained to all Party members and to the non-Party masses the harm and the danger of the anti-Leninist proposals of the Trotskyite opposition and the rightist opportunists. And this great work of explaining the Party line bore fruit; both the Trotskyites and the rightist opportunists were politically isolated; the overwhelming Party majority supported the Leninist line and the Party was able to awaken and organize the working masses to apply the Leninist Party line and to build socialism.

Worth noting is the fact that even during the progress of the furious ideological fight against the Trotskyites, the Zinovievites, the Bukharinites and others, extreme repressive measures were not used against them. The fight was on ideological grounds. But some years later when socialism in our country was fundamentally constructed, when the exploiting classes were generally liquidated, when the Soviet social structure had radically changed, when the social basis for political movements and groups hostile to the Party had violently contracted, when the ideological opponents of the Party were long since defeated politically—then the repression directed against them began.

It was precisely during this period (1935–1937–1938) that the practice of mass repression through the government apparatus was born, first against the enemies of Leninism—Trotskyites, Zinovievites, Bukharinites, long since politically defeated by the Party, and subsequently also against many honest Communists, against those Party cadres who had borne the heavy load of the Civil War and the first and most difficult years of industrialization and collectivization, who actively fought against the Trotskyites and the rightists for the Leninist Party line.

Stalin originated the concept "enemy of the people." This term automatically rendered it unnecessary that the ideological errors of a man or men engaged in a controversy be proven; this term made possible the usage of the most cruel repression, violating all norms of revolutionary legality, against anyone who in any way disagreed with Stalin, against those who were only suspected of hostile intent, against those who had bad reputations. This concept, "enemy of the people," actually eliminated the possibility of any kind of ideological fight or the making of one's views known on this or that issue, even those of a practical character. In the main, and in actuality, the only proof of guilt used, against all norms of current legal science, was the "confession" of the accused himself; and, as subsequent probing proved, "confessions" were acquired through physical pressures against the accused.

This led to glaring violations of revolutionary legality, and to the fact that many entirely innocent persons, who in the past had defended the Party line, became victims.

We must assert that in regard to those persons who in their time had opposed the Party line, there were often no sufficiently serious reasons for their physical annihilation. The formula, "enemy of the people," was specifically introduced for the purpose of physically annihilating such individuals.

It is a fact that many persons, who were later annihilated as enemies of the Party and people, had worked with Lenin during his life. Some of these persons had made errors during Lenin's life, but, despite this, Lenin benefited by their work, he corrected them and he did everything possible to retain them in the ranks of the Party; he induced them to follow him.

In this connection the delegates to the Party Congress should familiarize themselves with an unpublished note by V. I. Lenin directed to the Central Committee's Political Bureau in October 1920. Outlining the duties of the Control Commission, Lenin wrote that the Commission should be transformed into a real "organ of Party and proletarian conscience."

> As a special duty of the Control Commission there is recommended a deep, individualized relationship with, and sometimes even a type of therapy for, the representatives of the so-called opposition— those who have experienced a psychological crisis because of failure in their Soviet or Party career. An effort should be made to quiet them, to explain the matter to them in a way used among comrades, to find for them (avoiding the method of issuing orders) a task for which they are psychologically fitted. Advice and rules relating to this matter are to be formulated by the Central Committee's Organizational Bureau, etc.

Everyone knows how irreconcilable Lenin was with the ideological enemies of Marxism, with those who deviated from the correct Party line. At the same time, however, Lenin, as is evident from the given document, in his practice of directing the Party demanded the most intimate Party contact with people who had shown indecision or temporary nonconformity with the Party line, but whom it was possible to return to the Party path. Lenin advised that such people should be patiently educated without the application of extreme methods.

Lenin's wisdom in dealing with people was evident in his work with cadres.

An entirely different relationship with people characterized Stalin. Lenin's traits—patient work with people; stubborn and painstaking education of them; the ability to induce people to follow him without using compulsion, but rather through the ideological influence on them of the whole collective—were entirely foreign to Stalin. He [Stalin] discarded the Leninist method of convincing and educating; he abandoned the method of ideological struggle for that of administrative violence, mass repressions, and terror. He acted on an increasingly larger scale and more stubbornly through punitive organs, at the same time often violating all existing norms of morality and of Soviet laws.

Arbitrary behavior by one person encouraged and permitted arbitrariness in others. Mass arrests and deportations of many thousands of people, execution without trial and without normal investigation created conditions of insecurity, fear and even desperation.

This, of course, did not contribute toward unity of the Party ranks and of all strata of working people, but on the contrary brought about annihilation and the expulsion from the Party of workers who were loyal but inconvenient to Stalin.

Our Party fought for the implementation of Lenin's plans for the construction of socialism. This was an ideological fight. Had Leninist principles been observed during the course of this fight, had the Party's devotion to principles been skillfully combined with a keen and solicitous concern for people, had they not been repelled and wasted but rather drawn to our side—we certainly would not have had such a brutal violation of revolutionary legality and many thousands of people would not have fallen victim of the method of terror. Extraordinary methods would then have been resorted to only against those people who had in fact committed criminal acts against the Soviet system.

Let us recall some historical facts.

In the days before the October Revolution two members of the Central Committee of the Bolshevik Party—Kamenev and

Zinoviev—declared themselves against Lenin's plan for an armed uprising. In addition, on October 18 they published in the Menshevik newspaper, *Novaya Zhizn*, a statement declaring that the Bolsheviks were making preparations for an uprising and that they considered it adventuristic. Kamenev and Zinoviev thus disclosed to the enemy the decision of the Central Committee to stage the uprising, and that the uprising had been organized to take place within the very near future.

This was treason against the Party and against the revolution. In this connection, V. I. Lenin wrote: "Kamenev and Zinoviev revealed the decision of the Central Committee of their Party on the armed uprising to Rodzyanko and Kerensky. . . ." He put before the Central Committee the question of Zinoviev's and Kamenev's expulsion from the Party.

However, after the Great Socialist October Revolution, as is known, Zinoviev and Kamenev were given leading positions. Lenin put them in positions in which they carried out most responsible Party tasks and participated actively in the work of the leading Party and Soviet organs. It is known that Zinoviev and Kamenev committed a number of other serious errors during Lenin's life. In his "testament" Lenin warned that "Zinoviev's and Kamenev's October episode was of course not an accident." But Lenin did not pose the question of their arrest and certainly not their shooting.

Or let us take the example of the Trotskyites. At present, after a sufficiently long historical period, we can speak about the fight with the Trotskyites with complete calm and can analyze this matter with sufficient objectivity. After all, around Trotsky were people whose origin cannot by any means be traced to bourgeois society. Part of them belonged to the Party intelligentsia and a certain part were recruited from among the workers. We can name many individuals who in their time joined the Trotskyites; however, these same individuals took an active part in the workers' movement before the revolution, during the Socialist October Revolution itself, and also in the consolidation of the victory of this greatest of revolutions. Many of them broke with Trotskyism and returned to Leninist positions. Was it necessary to annihilate such people? We are deeply convinced that had Lenin lived such an extreme method would not have been used against many of them.

Such are only a few historical facts. But can it be said that Lenin did not decide to use even the most severe means against enemies of the revolution when this was actually necessary? No, no one can say this. Vladimir Ilyich demanded uncompromising dealings with the enemies of the revolution and of the working class and when necessary resorted ruthlessly to such methods. You will recall only V. I. Lenin's fight with the Socialist Revolutionary organizers of the anti-Soviet uprising, with the counter-revolutionary kulaks in 1918 and with others, when Lenin without hesitation used the most extreme methods against the enemies. Lenin used such methods, however, only against actual class enemies and not against those who blunder, who err, and whom it was possible to lead through ideological influence, and even retain in the leadership.

Lenin used severe methods only in the most necessary cases, when the exploiting classes were still in existence and were vigorously opposing the revolution, when the struggle for survival was decidedly assuming the sharpest forms, even including a civil war. Stalin, on the other hand, used extreme methods and mass repressions at a time when the revolution was already victorious, when the Soviet state was strengthened, when the exploiting classes were already liquidated and Socialist relations were rooted solidly in all phases of national economy, when our Party was politically consolidated and had strengthened itself both numerically and ideologically. It is clear that here Stalin showed in a whole series of cases his intolerance, his brutality and his abuse of power. Instead of proving his political correctness and mobilizing the masses, he often chose the path of repression and physical annihilation, not only against actual enemies, but also against individuals who had not committed any crimes against the Party and the Soviet government. Here we see no wisdom but only a demonstration of the brutal force which had once so alarmed V. I. Lenin.

Lately, especially after the unmasking of the Beria gang, the Central Committee has looked into a series of matters fabricated by this gang. This revealed a very ugly picture of brutal willfulness connected with the incorrect behavior of Stalin. As facts prove, Stalin, using his unlimited power, allowed himself many abuses, acting in the name of the Central Committee, not asking for the opinion of the Committee members nor even of the members of the Central Committee's Political Bureau; often he did not inform them about his personal decisions concerning very important Party and government matters.

Considering the question of the cult of an individual we must first of all show everyone what harm this caused to the interests of our Party.

Vladimir Ilyich Lenin had always stressed the Party's role and significance in the direction of the socialist government of workers and peasants; he saw in this the chief precondition for a successful building of socialism in our country. Pointing to the great responsibility of the Bolshevik Party, as a ruling party in the Soviet state, Lenin called for the most meticulous observance of all norms of Party life; he called for the realization of the principles of collegiality in the direction of the Party and the state.

Collegiality of leadership flows from the very nature of our Party, a party built on the principles of democratic centralism. "This means," said Lenin, "that all Party matters are accomplished by all Party members—directly or through representatives—who without any exceptions are subject to the same rules; in addition, all administrative members, all directing collegia, all holders of Party positions are elective, they must account for their activities and are recallable."

It is known that Lenin himself offered an example of the most careful observance of these principles. There was no matter so important that Lenin himself decided it without asking for advice and approval of the majority of the Central Committee members or of the members of the Central Committee's Political Bureau.

In the most difficult period for our Party and our country, Lenin considered it necessary regularly to convoke congresses, Party conferences, and plenary sessions of the Central Committee at which all the most important questions were discussed and where resolutions, carefully worked out by the collective of leaders, were approved.

We can recall, for an example, the year 1918 when the country was threatened by the attack of the imperialistic interventionists. In this situation the VIIth Party Congress was convened in order to discuss a vitally important matter which could not be postponed—the matter of peace. In 1919, while the Civil War was raging, the VIIIth Party Congress convened which adopted a new Party program, decided such important matters as the relationship with the peasant masses, the organization of the Red Army, the leading role of the Party in the work of the Soviets, the correction of the social composition of the Party, and other matters. In 1920 the IXth Party Congress was convened which laid down guiding principles pertaining to the Party's work in the sphere of economic construction. In 1921, the Xth Party Congress accepted Lenin's New Economic Policy and the historical resolution called "About Party Unity."

During Lenin's life Party Congresses were convened regularly; always, when a radical turn in the development of the Party and the country took place, Lenin considered it absolutely necessary that the Party discuss at length all the basic matters pertaining to internal and foreign policy and to questions bearing on the development of Party and government.

It is very characteristic that Lenin addressed to the Party Congress as the highest Party organ his last articles, letters and remarks. During the period between congresses the Central Committee of the Party, acting as the most authoritative leading collective, meticulously observed the principles of the Party and carried out its policy.

So it was during Lenin's life.

Were our Party's holy Leninist principles observed after the death of Vladimir Ilyich?

Whereas during the first few years after Lenin's death Party Congresses and Central Committee plenums took place more or less regularly, later, when Stalin began increasingly to abuse his power, these principles were brutally violated. This was especially evident during the last 15 years of his life. Was it a normal situation when over 13 years elapsed between the XVIIIth and XIXth Party Congresses, years during which our Party and our country had experienced so many important events? These events demanded categorically that the Party should have passed resolutions pertaining to the country's defense during the Patriotic War and to peacetime construction after the war. Even after the end of the war a Congress was not convened for over 7 years.

In *Khrushchev Remembers*, trans. Strobe Talbott (Boston: Little, Brown, 1970), 564–571.

Martin Luther King Jr.

The Rising Tide of Racial Consciousness (1960)

By the early 1960s the U.S. civil rights movement had become a national phe-nomenon, with sit-ins, freedom rides, and public marches attracting widespread attention. The Reverend Dr. Martin Luther King Jr. emerged as a prominent spokesman for many activist groups. His eloquent words helped to articulate the purposes of the movement. King's 1960 speech on "The Rising Tide of Racial Consciousness" pointed to a new racial sensibility that gave African-Americans hope for dignity, integration, and freedom in a society where these had long been denied. King connected this hope to a worldwide struggle, that included anti-colonial movements in Asia and Africa.

What are the factors that have led to this new sense of dignity and self-respect on the part of the Negro? First, we must mention the population shift from rural to urban life. For many years the vast majority of Negroes were isolated on the rural plantation. They had very little contact with the world outside their geograph-ical boundaries. But gradually circumstances made it possible and necessary for them to migrate to new and larger centers—the spread of the automobile, the Great Depression, and the social up-heavals of the two world wars. These new contacts led to a broad-ened outlook. These new levels of communication brought new and different attitudes.

A second factor that has caused the Negroes' new self-consciousness has been rapid educational advance. Over the years there has been a steady decline of crippling illiteracy. At emancipation only five percent of the Negroes were literate; today more than ninety-five percent are literate. Constant streams of Negro students are finish-ing colleges and universities every year. More than sixteen hundred

Negroes have received the highest academic degree bestowed by an American university. These educational advances have naturally broadened his thinking. They have given the Negro not only a larger view of the world, but also a larger view of himself.

A third factor that produced the new sense of pride in the Negro was the gradual improvement of his economic status. While the Negro is still the victim of tragic economic exploitation, significant strides have been made. The annual collective income of the Negro is now approximately eighteen billion dollars, which is more than the national income of Canada and all of the exports of the United States. This augmented purchasing power has been reflected in more adequate housing, improved medical care, and greater educational opportunities. As these changes have taken place they have driven the Negro to change his image of himself.

A fourth factor that brought about the new sense of pride in the Negro was the Supreme Court's decision outlawing segregation in the public schools. For all men of good will May 17, 1954, came as a joyous daybreak to end the long night of enforced segregation. In simple, eloquent, and unequivocal language the court affirmed that "separate but equal" facilities are inherently unequal and that to segregate a child on the basis of his race is to deny that child equal protection of the law. This decision brought hope to millions of disinherited Negroes who had formerly dared only to dream of freedom. Like an exit sign that suddenly appeared to one who had walked through a long and desolate corridor, this decision came as a way out of the darkness of segregation. It served to transform the fatigue of despair into the buoyancy of hope. It further enhanced the Negro's sense of dignity.

A fifth factor that has accounted for the new sense of dignity on the part of the Negro has been the awareness that his struggle for freedom is a part of a worldwide struggle. He has watched developments in Asia and Africa with rapt attention. On these vast prodigious continents dwell two-thirds of the world's people. For years they were exploited economically, dominated politically, segregated and humiliated by foreign powers. Thirty years ago there were only three independent countries in the whole of Africa— Liberia, Ethiopia, and South Africa. By 1962, there may be as many as thirty independent nations in Africa. These rapid changes have naturally influenced the thinking of the American Negro. He knows that his struggle for human dignity is not an isolated event. It is a drama being played on the stage of the world with spectators and supporters from every continent.

Determination and Resistance

This growing self-respect has inspired the Negro with a new determination to struggle and sacrifice until first-class citizenship becomes a reality. This is at bottom the meaning of what is happening in the South today. Whether it is manifested in nine brave children of Little Rock walking through jeering and hostile mobs, or fifty thousand people of Montgomery, Alabama, substituting tired feet for tired souls and walking the streets of that city for 381 days, or thousands of courageous students electrifying the nation by quietly and nonviolently sitting at lunch counters that have been closed to them because of the color of their skin, the motivation is always the same—the Negro would rather suffer in dignity than accept segregation in humiliation.

This new determination on the part of the Negro has not been welcomed by some segments of the nation's population. In some instances it has collided with tenacious and determined resistance. This resistance has risen at times to ominous proportions. A few states have reacted in open defiance. The legislative halls of the South ring loud with such words as "interposition" and "nullification." Many public officials are going to the absurd and fanatical extreme of closing the schools rather than to comply with the law of the land. This resistance to the Negroes' aspirations expresses itself in the resurgence of the Ku Klux Klan and the birth of White Citizens Councils.

The resistance to the Negroes' aspirations expresses itself not only in obvious methods of defiance, but in the subtle and skillful method of truth distortion. In an attempt to influence the minds of northern and southern liberals, the segregationists will cleverly disseminate half-truths. Instead of arguing for the validity of segregation and racial inferiority on the basis of the Bible, they set their arguments on cultural and sociological grounds. The Negro is not ready for integration, they say; because of academic and cultural lags on the part of the Negro, the integration of schools will pull the white race down. They are never honest enough to admit that the academic and cultural lags in the Negro community are themselves the result of segregation and discrimination. The best way to solve any problem is to remove the cause. It is both rationally unsound and sociologically untenable to use the tragic effects of segregation as an argument for its continuation.

The great challenge facing the nation today is to solve this pressing problem and bring into full realization the ideals and dreams of our democracy. How we deal with this crucial situation will determine our political health as a nation and our prestige as a leader of the free world. The price that America must pay for the continued oppression of the Negro is the price of its own destruction. The hour is late; the clock of destiny is ticking out. We must act now! It is a trite yet urgently true observation that if America is to remain a first-class nation, it cannot have second-class citizens.

Our primary reason for bringing an end to racial discrimination in America must not be the Communist challenge. Nor must it be merely to appeal to Asian and African peoples. The primary reason for our uprooting racial discrimination from our society is that it is morally wrong. It is a cancerous disease that prevents us from realizing the sublime principles of our Judeo-Christian tradition. Racial discrimination substitutes an "I-it" relationship for the "I-thou" relationship. It relegates persons to the status of things. Whenever racial discrimination exists it is a tragic expression of man's spiritual degeneracy and moral bankruptcy. Therefore, it must be removed not merely because it is diplomatically expedient, but because it is morally compelling.

A National Problem

The racial issue that we confront in America is not a sectional but a national problem. Injustice anywhere is a threat to justice everywhere. Therefore, no American can afford to be apathetic about the problem of racial justice. It is a problem that meets every man at his front door.

There is need for strong and aggressive leadership from the federal government. There is a pressing need for a liberalism in the

North that is truly liberal, that firmly believes in integration in its own community as well as in the deep South. There is need for the type of liberal who not only rises up with righteous indignation when a Negro is lynched in Mississippi, but will be equally incensed when a Negro is denied the right to live in his neighborhood, or join his professional association, or secure a top position in his business. This is no day to pay mere lip service to integration; we must pay life service to it.

There are several other agencies and groups that have significant roles to play in this all-important period of our nation's history; the problem of racial injustice is so weighty in detail and broad in extent that it requires the concerted efforts of numerous individuals and institutions to bring about a solution.

The Primary Responsibility

In the final analysis if first-class citizenship is to become a reality for the Negro he must assume the primary responsibility for making it so. The Negro must not be victimized with the delusion of thinking that others should be more concerned than himself about his citizenship rights.

In this period of social change the Negro must work on two fronts. On the one hand we must continue to break down the barrier of segregation. We must resist all forms of racial injustice. This resistance must always be on the highest level of dignity and discipline. It must never degenerate to the crippling level of violence. There is another way—a way as old as the insights of Jesus of Nazareth and as modern as the methods of Mahatma Gandhi. It is a way not for the weak and cowardly but for the strong and courageous. It has been variously called passive resistance, nonviolent resistance, or simply Christian love. It is my great hope that, as the Negro plunges deeper into the quest for freedom, he will plunge deeper into the philosophy of nonviolence. As a race we must work passionately and unrelentingly for first-class citizenship, but we must never use second-class methods to gain it. Our aim must be not to defeat or humiliate the white man, but to win his friendship and understanding. We must never become bitter nor should we succumb to the temptation of using violence in the struggle, for if this happens, unborn generations will be the recipients of a long and desolate night of bitterness and our chief legacy to the future will be an endless reign of meaningless chaos.

I feel that this way of nonviolence is vital because it is the only way to reestablish the broken community. It is the method which seeks to implement the just law by appealing to the conscience of the great decent majority who through blindness, fear, pride, or irrationality have allowed their consciences to sleep.

The nonviolent resisters can summarize their message in the following simple terms: we will take direct action against injustice without waiting for other agencies to act. We will not obey unjust laws or submit to unjust practices. We will do this peacefully, openly, and cheerfully because our aim is to persuade. We adopt the means of nonviolence because our end is a community at peace with itself. We will try to persuade with our words, but, if our words fail, we will try to persuade with our acts. We will always be willing to talk and seek fair compromise, but we are ready to suffer when necessary and even risk our lives to become witnesses to the truth as we see it.

I realize that this approach will mean suffering and sacrifice. It may mean going to jail. If such is the case the resister must be willing to fill the jail houses of the South. It may even mean physical death. But if physical death is the price that a man must pay to free his children and his white brethren from a permanent death of the spirit, then nothing could be more redemptive. This is the type of soul force that I am convinced will triumph over the physical force of the oppressor.

This approach to the problem of oppression is not without successful precedent. We have the magnificent example of Gandhi who challenged the might of the British Empire and won independence for his people by using only the weapons of truth, noninjury, courage, and soul force. Today we have the example of thousands of Negro students in the South who have courageously challenged the principalities of segregation. These young students have taken the deep groans and the passionate yearnings of the Negro people and filtered them in their own souls and fashioned them in a creative protest which is an epic known all over our nation. For the last few months they have moved in a uniquely meaningful orbit imparting light and heat to distant satellites. Through their nonviolent direct action they have been able to open hundreds of formerly segregated lunch counters in almost eighty cities. It is no overstatement to characterize these events as historic. Never before in the United States has so large a body of students spread a struggle over so great an area in pursuit of a goal of human dignity and freedom. I am convinced that future historians will have to record this student movement as one of the greatest epics of our heritage.

Let me mention another front on which we must work that is equally significant. The Negro must make a vigorous effort to improve his personal standards. The only answer that we can give to those who through blindness and fear would question our readiness and capability is that our lagging standards exist because of the legacy of slavery and segregation, inferior schools, slums, and second-class citizenship, and not because of an inherent inferiority. The fact that so many Negroes have made lasting and significant contributions to the cultural life of America in spite of these crippling restrictions is sufficient to refute all of the myths and half-truths disseminated by the segregationist.

Yet we cannot ignore the fact that our standards do often fall short. One of the sure signs of maturity is the ability to rise to the point of self-criticism. We have been affected by our years of economic deprivation and social isolation. Some Negroes have become cynical and disillusioned. Some have so conditioned themselves to the system of segregation that they have lost that creative something called *initiative*. So many have used their oppression as an excuse for mediocrity. Many of us live above our means, spend money on nonessentials and frivolities, and fail to give to serious causes, organizations, and educational institutions that so desperately need funds. Our crime rate is far too high.

Constructive Action

Therefore there is a pressing need for the Negro to develop a positive program through which these standards can be improved. After we have analyzed the sociological and psychological causes of these problems, we must seek to develop a constructive program to solve them. We must constantly stimulate our youth to rise above the stagnant level of mediocrity and seek to achieve excellence in their various fields of endeavor. Doors are opening now that were not open in the past, and the great challenge facing minority groups is to be ready to enter these doors as they open. No greater tragedy could befall us at this hour but that of allowing new opportunities to emerge without the concomitant preparedness to meet them.

We must make it clear to our young people that this is an age in which they will be forced to compete with people of all races and nationalities. We cannot aim merely to be good Negro teachers, good Negro doctors, or good Negro skilled laborers. We must set out to do a good job irrespective of race. We must seek to do our life's work so well that nobody could do it better. The Negro who seeks to be merely a good Negro, whatever he is, has already flunked his matriculation examination for entrance into the university of integration.

This then must be our present program: nonviolent resistance to all forms of racial injustice, even when this means going to jail; and bold, constructive action to end the demoralization caused by the legacy of slavery and segregation. The nonviolent struggle, if conducted with the dignity and courage already shown by the sit-in students of the South, will in itself help end the demoralization; but a new frontal assault on the poverty, disease, and ignorance of a people too long deprived of the God-given rights of life, liberty, and the pursuit of happiness will make the victory more certain.

We must work assiduously and with determined boldness to remove from the body politic this cancerous disease of discrimination which is preventing our democratic and Christian health from being realized. Then and only then will we be able to bring into full realization the dream of our American democracy—a dream yet unfulfilled. A dream of equality of opportunity, of privilege and property widely distributed; a dream of a land where men will not take necessities from the many to give luxuries to the few; a dream of a land where men to [sic] not argue that the color of a man's skin determines the content of his character; a dream of a place where all our gifts and resources are held not for ourselves alone but as instruments of service for the rest of humanity; the dream of a country where every man will respect the dignity and worth of all human personality, and men will dare to live together as brothers—that is the dream. Whenever it is fulfilled we will emerge from the bleak and desolate midnight of man's inhumanity to man into the bright and glowing daybreak of freedom and justice for all of God's children.

In James Melvin Washington, ed., *A Testament of Hope: The Essential Writings and Speeches of Martin Luther King Jr.* (San Francisco: HarperCollins, 1986), 145–151.

Frantz Fanon

Concerning Violence

Frantz Fanon's diagnosis of the rising racial consciousness in the 1960s differed significantly from Martin Luther King's. Born in French-controlled Martinique, Fanon became a prominent exponent of violent decolonization, particularly in French Algeria. He argued that the world had been forcibly divided along racial lines, with white domination and black repression at all levels of society. To overcome this "Manichean" division, Fanon advocated revolutionary violence. Only through violence, he claimed, could oppressed peoples transform the racial and economic ordering of the world.

National liberation, national renaissance, the restoration of nationhood to the people, commonwealth: whatever may be the headings used or the new formulas introduced, decolonization is always a violent phenomenon. At whatever level we study it—relationships between individuals, new names for sports clubs, the human admixture at cocktail parties, in the police, on the directing boards of national or private banks—decolonization is quite simply the replacing of a certain "species" of men by another "species" of men. Without any period of transition, there is a total, complete, and absolute substitution. It is true that we could equally well stress the rise of a new nation, the setting up of a new state, its diplomatic relations, and its economic and political trends. But we have precisely chosen to speak of that kind of *tabula rasa* which characterizes at the outset all decolonization. Its unusual importance is that it constitutes, from the very first day, the minimum demands of the colonized. To tell the truth, the proof of success lies in a whole social structure being changed from the bottom up. The extraordinary importance of this change is that it is willed, called for, demanded. The need for this change exists in its crude state, impetuous and compelling, in the consciousness and in the lives of the men and women who are colonized. But the possibility of this change is equally experienced in the form of a terrifying future in the consciousness of another "species" of men and women: the colonizers.

Decolonization, which sets out to change the order of the world, is, obviously, a program of complete disorder. But it cannot come as a result of magical practices, nor of a natural shock, nor of a friendly understanding. Decolonization, as we know, is a historical process: that is to say that it cannot be understood, it cannot become intelligible nor clear to itself except in the exact measure that we can discern the movements which give it historical form and content. Decolonization is the meeting of two forces, opposed to each other by their very nature, which in fact owe their originality to that sort of substantification which results from and is nourished by the situation in the colonies. Their first encounter was marked by violence and their existence together—that is to say the exploitation of the native by the settler—was carried on by dint of a great array of bayonets and cannons. The settler and the native are old acquaintances. In fact, the settler is right when he speaks of knowing "them" well. For it is the settler who has brought the native into existence and who perpetuates his existence. The settler owes the fact of his very existence, that is to say, his property, to the colonial system.

Decolonization never takes place unnoticed, for it influences individuals and modifies them fundamentally. It transforms spectators crushed with their inessentiality into privileged actors, with the grandiose glare of history's floodlights upon them. It brings a natural rhythm into existence, introduced by new men, and with it a new language and a new humanity. Decolonization is the veritable creation of new men. But this creation owes nothing of its legitimacy to any supernatural power; the "thing" which has been colonized becomes man during the same process by which it frees itself.

In decolonization, there is therefore the need of a complete calling in question of the colonial situation. If we wish to describe it precisely, we might find it in the well-known words: "The last shall be first and the first last." Decolonization is the putting into practice of this sentence. That is why, if we try to describe it, all decolonization is successful.

The naked truth of decolonization evokes for us the searing bullets and bloodstained knives which emanate from it. For if the last shall be first, this will only come to pass after a murderous and decisive struggle between the two protagonists. That affirmed intention to place the last at the head of things, and to make them climb at a pace (too quickly, some say) the well-known steps which characterize an organized society, can only triumph if we use all means to turn the scale, including, of course, that of violence.

You do not turn any society, however primitive it may be, upside down with such a program if you have not decided from the very beginning, that is to say from the actual formulation of that program, to overcome all the obstacles that you will come across in so doing. The native who decides to put the program into practice, and to become its moving force, is ready for violence at all times. From birth it is clear to him that this narrow world, strewn with prohibitions, can only be called in question by absolute violence.

The colonial world is a world divided into compartments. It is probably unnecessary to recall the existence of native quarters and European quarters, of schools for natives and schools for Europeans; in the same way we need not recall apartheid in South Africa. Yet, if we examine closely this system of compartments, we will at least be able to reveal the lines of force it implies. This approach to the colonial world, its ordering and its geographical layout will allow us to mark out the lines on which a decolonized society will be reorganized.

The colonial world is a world cut in two. The dividing line, the frontiers are shown by barracks and police stations. In the colonies it is the policeman and the soldier who are the official, instituted go-betweens, the spokesmen of the settler and his rule of oppression. In capitalist societies the educational system, whether lay or clerical, the structure of moral reflexes handed down from father to son, the exemplary honesty of workers who are given a medal after fifty years of good and loyal service, and the affection which springs from harmonious relations and good behavior—all these aesthetic expressions of respect for the established order serve to create around the exploited person an atmosphere of submission and of inhibition which lightens the task of policing considerably. In the capitalist countries a multitude of moral teachers, counselors and "bewilderers" separate the exploited from those in power. In the colonial countries, on the contrary, the policeman and the soldier, by their immediate presence and their frequent and direct action maintain contact with the native and advise him by means of rifle butts and napalm not to budge. It is obvious here that the agents of government speak the language of pure force. The intermediary does not lighten the oppression, nor seek to hide the domination; he shows them up and puts them into practice with the clear conscience of an upholder of the peace; yet he is the bringer of violence into the home and into the mind of the native.

The zone where the natives live is not complementary to the zone inhabited by the settlers. The two zones are opposed, but not in the service of a higher unity. Obedient to the rules of pure Aristotelian logic, they both follow the principle of reciprocal exclusivity. No conciliation is possible, for of the two terms, one is superfluous. The settlers' town is a strongly built town, all made of stone and steel. It is a brightly lit town; the streets are covered with asphalt, and the garbage cans swallow all the leavings, unseen, unknown and hardly thought about. The settler's feet are never visible, except perhaps in the sea; but there you're never close enough to see them. His feet are protected by strong shoes although the streets of his town are clean and even, with no holes or stones. The settler's town is a well-fed town, an easygoing town; its belly is always full of good things. The settlers' town is a town of white people, of foreigners.

The town belonging to the colonized people, or at least the native town, the Negro village, the medina, the reservation, is a place of ill fame, peopled by men of evil repute. They are born there, it matters little where or how; they die there, it matters not where, nor how. It is a world without spaciousness; men live there on top of each other, and their huts are built one on top of the other. The native town is a hungry town, starved of bread, of meat, of shoes, of coal, of light. The native town is a crouching village, a town on its knees, a town wallowing in the mire. It is a town of niggers and dirty Arabs. The look that the native turns on the settler's town is a

look of lust, a look of envy; it expresses his dreams of possession—
all manner of possession: to sit at the settler's table, to sleep in the
settler's bed, with his wife if possible. The colonized man is an en-
vious man. And this the settler knows very well; when their glances
meet he ascertains bitterly, always on the defensive, "They want to
take our place." It is true, for there is no native who does not dream
at least once a day of setting himself up in the settler's place.

This world divided into compartments, this world cut in two is
inhabited by two different species. The originality of the colonial
context is that economic reality, inequality, and the immense difference of ways of life never come to mask the human realities. When
you examine at close quarters the colonial context, it is evident that
what parcels out the world is to begin with the fact of belonging to
or not belonging to a given race, a given species. In the colonies the
economic substructure is also a superstructure. The cause is the
consequence; you are rich because you are white, you are white because you are rich. This is why Marxist analysis should always
be slightly stretched every time we have to do with the colonial
problem.

Everything up to and including the very nature of precapitalist
society, so well explained by Marx, must here be thought out again.
The serf is in essence different from the knight, but a reference to
divine right is necessary to legitimize this statutory difference. In
the colonies, the foreigner coming from another country imposed
his rule by means of guns and machines. In defiance of his successful transplantation, in spite of his appropriation, the settler still
remains a foreigner. It is neither the act of owning factories, nor es-
tates, nor a bank balance which distinguishes the governing classes.
The governing race is first and foremost those who come from elsewhere, those who are unlike the original inhabitants, "the others."

The violence which has ruled over the ordering of the colonial
world, which has ceaselessly drummed the rhythm for the destruction of native social forms and broken up without reserve the systems of reference of the economy, the customs of dress and
external life, that same violence will be claimed and taken over by
the native at the moment when, deciding to embody history in his
own person, he surges into the forbidden quarters. To wreck the
colonial world is henceforward a mental picture of action which is

very clear, very easy to understand and which may be assumed by each one of the individuals which constitute the colonized people. To break up the colonial world does not mean that after the frontiers have been abolished lines of communication will be set up between the two zones. The destruction of the colonial world is no more and no less that [*sic*] the abolition of one zone, its burial in the depths of the earth or its expulsion from the country.

The natives' challenge to the colonial world is not a rational confrontation of points of view. It is not a treatise on the universal, but the untidy affirmation of an original idea propounded as an absolute. The colonial world is a Manichean world. It is not enough for the settler to delimit physically, that is to say with the help of the army and the police force, the place of the native. As if to show the totalitarian character of colonial exploitation the settler paints the native as a sort of quintessence of evil.* Native society is not simply described as a society lacking in values. It is not enough for the colonist to affirm that those values have disappeared from, or still better never existed in, the colonial world. The native is declared insensible to ethics; he represents not only the absence of values, but also the negation of values. He is, let us dare to admit, the enemy of values, and in this sense he is the absolute evil. He is the corrosive element, destroying all that comes near him; he is the deforming element, disfiguring all that has to do with beauty or morality; he is the depository of maleficent powers, the unconscious and irretrievable instrument of blind forces. Monsieur Meyer could thus state seriously in the French National Assembly that the Republic must not be prostituted by allowing the Algerian people to become part of it. All values, in fact, are irrevocably poisoned and diseased as soon as they are allowed in contact with the colonized race. The customs of the colonized people, their traditions, their myths—above all, their myths—are the very sign of that poverty of spirit and of their constitutional depravity. That is why we must put the DDT which destroys parasites, the bearers of disease, on the same level as the Christian religion which wages war on embryonic heresies and instincts, and on evil as yet unborn. The recession of yellow fever and the advance of evangelization form

*We have demonstrated the mechanism of this Manichean world in *Black Skin, White Masks* (New York: Grove Press, 1967).

part of the same balance sheet. But the triumphant *communiqués* from the missions are in fact a source of information concerning the implantation of foreign influences in the core of the colonized people. I speak of the Christian religion, and no one need be astonished. The Church in the colonies is the white people's Church, the foreigner's Church. She does not call the native to God's ways but to the ways of the white man, of the master, of the oppressor. And as we know, in this matter many are called but few chosen.

At times this Manicheism goes to its logical conclusion and dehumanizes the native, or to speak plainly, it turns him into an animal. In fact, the terms the settler uses when he mentions the native are zoological terms. He speaks of the yellow man's reptilian motions, of the stink of the native quarter, of breeding swarms, of foulness, of spawn, of gesticulations. When the settler seeks to describe the native fully in exact terms he constantly refers to the bestiary. The European rarely hits on a picturesque style; but the native, who knows what is in the mind of the settler, guesses at once what he is thinking of. Those hordes of vital statistics, those hysterical masses, those faces bereft of all humanity, those distended bodies which are like nothing on earth, that mob without beginning or end, those children who seem to belong to nobody, that laziness stretched out in the sun, that vegetative rhythm of life—all this forms part of the colonial vocabulary. General de Gaulle speaks of "the yellow multitudes" and François Mauriac of the black, brown, and yellow masses which soon will be unleashed. The native knows all this, and laughs to himself every time he spots an allusion to the animal world in the other's words. For he knows that he is not an animal; and it is precisely at the moment he realizes his humanity that he begins to sharpen the weapons with which he will secure its victory.

As soon as the native begins to pull on his moorings, and to cause anxiety to the settler, he is handed over to well-meaning souls who in cultural congresses point out to him the specificity and wealth of Western values. But every time Western values are mentioned they produce in the native a sort of stiffening or muscular lockjaw. During the period of decolonization, the native's reason is appealed to. He is offered definite values, he is told frequently that decolonization need not mean regression, and that he must put his trust in qualities which are well-tried, solid, and highly esteemed. But it so happens that when the native hears a speech about Western culture he pulls out his knife—or at least he makes sure it is within reach. The violence with which the supremacy of white values is affirmed and the aggressiveness which has permeated the victory of these values over the ways of life and of thought of the native mean that, in revenge, the native laughs in mockery when Western values are mentioned in front of him. In the colonial context the settler only ends his work of breaking in the native when the latter admits loudly and intelligibly the supremacy of the white man's values. In the period of decolonization, the colonized masses mock at these very values, insult them, and vomit them up.

In *The Wretched of the Earth*, trans. Constance Farrington (New York: Grove Press, 1963; originally published in 1961), 35–43.

John F. Kennedy

Address of the Honorable John F. Kennedy Accepting the Nomination for the Presidency of the United States (15 July 1960)

The presidency of John F. Kennedy marked an important transition in the image and aspirations of political leaders. In his campaign and in office, Kennedy called for Americans to embark on a "new frontier" that would include more energetic reform at home and more active engagement with the outside world. Kennedy promised to bring a new purpose and creativity to the Cold War. The rhetoric of the "new frontier" inspired young people around the world. Their political activism, however, soon went far beyond Kennedy's chosen initiatives.

Senator Kennedy: Governor Stevenson, Senator Johnson, Mr. Butler, Senator Symington, Senator Humphrey, Speaker Rayburn, Fellow Democrats, I want to express my thanks to Governor Stevenson for his generous and heart-warming introduction. (Applause)

It was my great honor to place his name in nomination at the 1956 Democratic Convention, and I am delighted to have his support and his counsel and his advice in the coming months ahead. (Applause)

With a deep sense of duty and high resolve, I accept your nomination. (Applause)

I accept it with a full and grateful heart—without reservation—and with only one obligation—the obligation to devote every effort of body, mind and spirit to lead our Party back to victory and our Nation back to greatness.

I am grateful, too, that you have provided me with such an eloquent statement of our Party's platform. Pledges which are made so eloquently are made to be kept. "The Rights of Man"—the civil and economic rights essential to the human dignity of all men—are indeed our goal and our first principles. This is a Platform on which I can run with enthusiasm and conviction. (Applause)

And I am grateful, finally, that I can rely in the coming months on so many others—on a distinguished running-mate who brings unity to our ticket and strength to our Platform, Lyndon Johnson (Applause)—on one of the most articulate statesmen of our time, Adlai Stevenson (Applause)—on a great spokesman for our needs as a Nation and a people, Stuart Symington (Applause)—and on that fighting campaigner whose support I welcome, President Harry S. Truman—on my traveling companion in Wisconsin and West Virginia, Senator Hubert Humphrey. (Applause) On Paul Butler, our devoted and courageous Chairman. (Applause)

I feel a lot safer now that they are on my side again. (Laughter) And I am proud of the contrast with our Republican competitors. For their ranks are apparently so thin that not one challenger has come forth with both the competence and the courage to make theirs an open convention. (Applause)

I am fully aware of the fact that the Democratic Party, by nominating someone of my faith, has taken on what many regard as a new and hazardous risk—new, at least, since 1928. But I look at it this way: the Democratic Party has once again placed its confidence in the American people, and in their ability to render a free, fair judgment. And you have, at the same time, placed your confidence in me, and in my ability to render a free, fair judgment (Applause)—to uphold the Constitution and my oath of office—and to reject any kind of religious pressure or obligation that might directly or indirectly interfere with my conduct of the Presidency in the national interest. (Applause) My record of fourteen years supporting public education—supporting complete separation of church and state—and resisting pressure from any source on any issue should be clear by now to everyone. (Applause)

I hope that no American, considering the really critical issues facing this country, will waste his franchise by voting either for me or against me solely on account of my religious affiliation. It is not relevant. (Applause) I want to stress, what some other political or religious leader may have said on this subject. It is not relevant what abuses may have existed in other countries or in other times. It is not relevant what pressures, if any, might conceivably be brought to bear on me. I am telling you now what you are entitled to know: that my decisions on every public policy will be my own—as an American, a Democrat and a free man. (Applause)

Under any circumstances, however, the victory we seek in November will not be easy. We all know that in our hearts. We recognize the power of the forces that will be aligned against us. We know they will invoke the name of Abraham Lincoln on behalf of their candidate—despite the fact that the political career of their candidate has often seemed to show charity toward none and malice for all. (Applause)

We know that it will not be easy to campaign against a man who has spoken or voted on every known side of every known issue. Mr. Nixon may feel it is his turn now, after the New Deal and the Fair Deal—but before he deals, someone had better cut the cards. (Laughter and applause)

That "someone" may be the millions of Americans who voted for President Eisenhower but balk at his would be, self-appointed successor. For just as historians tell us that Richard I was not fit to fill the shoes of bold Henry II—and that Richard Cromwell was not fit to wear the mantle of his uncle—they might add in future years that Richard Nixon did not measure to the footsteps of Dwight D. Eisenhower. (Applause)

Perhaps he could carry on the party policies—the policies of Nixon, Benson, Dirksen and Goldwater. But this Nation cannot afford such a luxury. Perhaps we could better afford a Coolidge following Harding. And perhaps we could afford a Pierce following Fillmore. But after Buchanan this nation needed a Lincoln—after Taft we needed a Wilson—after Hoover we needed Franklin

Roosevelt. . . . And after eight years of drugged and fitful sleep, this nation needs strong, creative Democratic leadership in the White House. (Applause)

But we are not merely running against Mr. Nixon. Our task is not merely one of itemizing Republican failures. Nor is that wholly necessary. For the families forced from the farm will know how to vote without our telling them. The unemployed miners and textile workers will know how to vote. The old people without medical care—the families without a decent home—the parents of children without adequate food or schools—they all know that it's time for a change. (Applause)

But I think the American people expect more from us than cries of indignation and attack. The times are too grave, the challenge too urgent, and the stakes too high—to permit the customary passions of political debate. We are not here to curse the darkness, but to light the candle that can guide us through that darkness to a safe and sane future. (Applause) As Winston Churchill said on taking office some twenty years ago: if we open a quarrel between the present and the past, we shall be in danger of losing the future.

Today our concern must be with that future. For the world is changing. The old era is ending. The old ways will not do.

Abroad, the balance of power is shifting. There are new and more terrible weapons—new and uncertain nations—new pressures of population and deprivation. One-third of the world, it has been said, may be free—but one-third is the victim of cruel repression—and the other one-third is rocked by the pangs of poverty, hunger and envy. More energy is released by the awakening of these new nations than by the fission of the atom itself.

Meanwhile, Communist influence has penetrated further into Asia, stood astride the Middle East and now festers some ninety miles off the coast of Florida. Friends have slipped into neutrality—and neutrals into hostility. As our keynoter reminded us, the President who began his career by going to Korea ends it by staying away from Japan. (Applause)

The world has been close to war before—but now man, who has survived all previous threats to his existence, has taken into his mortal hands the power to exterminate the entire species some seven times over.

Here at home, the changing face of the future is equally revolutionary. The New Deal and the Fair Deal were bold measures for their generations—but this is a new generation.

A technological revolution on the farm has led to an output explosion—but we have not yet learned to harness that explosion usefully, while protecting our farmers' right to full parity income.

An urban population revolution has overcrowded our schools, cluttered up our suburbs, and increased the squalor of our slums.

A peaceful revolution for human rights—demanding an end to racial discrimination in all parts of our community life—has strained at the leashes imposed by timid executive leadership. (Applause)

A medical revolution has extended the life of our elder citizens without providing the dignity and security those later years deserve. And a revolution of automation finds machines replacing men in the mines and mills of America, without replacing their incomes or their training or their needs to pay the family doctor, grocer and landlord.

There has also been a change—a slippage—in our intellectual and moral strength. Seven lean years of drouth and famine have withered a field of ideas. Blight has descended on our regulatory agencies—and a dry rot, beginning in Washington, is seeping into every corner of America—in the payola mentality, the expense account way of life, the confusion between what is legal and what is right. Too many Americans have lost their way, their will and their sense of historic purpose.

It is a time, in short, for a new generation of leadership—new men to cope with new problems and new opportunities.

All over the world, particularly in the newer nations, young men are coming to power—men who are not bound by the traditions of the past—men who are not blinded by the old fears and hates and rivalries—young men who can cast off the old slogans and delusions and suspicions.

The Republican nominee-to-be, of course, is also a young man. But his approach is as old as McKinley. (Laughter and applause) His party is the party of the past. His speeches are generalities from Poor Richard's Almanac. Their platform, made up of left-over Democratic planks, has the courage of our old convictions. Their pledge is a pledge to the status quo—and today there can be no status quo.

For I stand tonight facing west on what was once the last frontier. From the lands that stretch three thousand miles behind me, the pioneers of old gave up their safety, their comfort and sometimes their lives to build a new world here in the West. They were not the captives of their own doubts, the prisoners of their own price tags. Their motto was not "every man for himself"—but "all for the common cause." They were determined to make that new world strong and free, to overcome its hazards and its hardships, to conquer the enemies that threatened from without and within.

Today some would say that those struggles are all over—that all the horizons have been explored—that all the battles have been won—that there is no longer an American frontier.

But I trust that no one in this vast assemblage will agree with those sentiments. For the problems are not all solved and the battles are not all won—and we stand today on the edge of a New Frontier—the frontier of the 1960's—a frontier of unknown opportunities and perils—a frontier of unfulfilled hopes and threats.

Woodrow Wilson's New Freedom promised our nation a new political and economic framework. Franklin Roosevelt's New Deal promised security and succor to those in need. But the New Frontier of which I speak is not a set of promises—it is a set of challenges. It sums up not what I intend to *offer* the American people, but what I intend to *ask* of them. It appeals to their pride, not to their pocketbook—it holds out the promise of more sacrifice instead of more security.

But I tell you the New Frontier is here, whether we seek it or not. Beyond that frontier are the uncharted areas of science and space, unsolved problems of peace and war, unconquered pockets of ignorance and prejudice, unanswered questions of poverty and surplus. It would be easier to shrink back from that frontier, to look to the safe mediocrity of the past, to be lulled by good intentions and high rhetoric—and those who prefer that course should not cast their votes for me, regardless of Party.

But I believe the times demand invention, innovation, imagination, decision. I am asking each of you to be new pioneers on that New Frontier. My call is to the young in heart, regardless of age— to the stout in spirit, regardless of Party—to all who respond to the

Scriptural call: "Be strong and of a good courage; be not afraid, neither be thou dismayed."

For courage—not complacency—is our need today—leadership—not salesmanship. And the only valid test of leadership is the ability to lead, and lead vigorously. (Applause) A tired nation, said David Lloyd George, is a Tory nation—and the United States today cannot afford to be either tired or Tory. (Applause)

There may be those who wish to hear more—more promises to this group or that—more harsh rhetoric about the men in the Kremlin—more assurances of a golden future, where taxes are always low and subsidies ever high. But my promises are in the platform you have adopted—our ends will not be won by rhetoric and we can have faith in the future only if we have faith in ourselves.

For the harsh facts of the matter are that we stand on this frontier at a turning-point in history. We must prove all over again whether this nation—or any nation so conceived—can long endure—whether our society—with its freedom of choice, its breadth of opportunity, its range of alternatives—can compete with the single-minded advance of the Communist system.

Can a nation organized and governed such as ours endure? That is the real question. Have we the nerve and the will? Can we carry through in an age where we will witness not only new breakthroughs in weapons of destruction—but also a race for mastery of the sky and the rain, the ocean and the tides, the far side of space and the inside of men's minds?

Are we up to the task—are we equal to the challenge? Are we willing to match the Russian sacrifice of the present for the future—or must we sacrifice our future in order to enjoy the present?

That is the question of the New Frontier. That is the choice our nation must make—a choice that lies not merely between two men or two parties, but between the public interest and private comfort—between national greatness and national decline—between the fresh air of progress and the stale, dank atmosphere of "normalcy"—between determined dedication and creeping mediocrity.

All mankind waits upon our decision. A whole world looks to see what we will do. We cannot fail their trust, we cannot fail to try.

It has been a long road from that first snowy day in New Hampshire to this crowded convention city. Now begins another long journey, taking me into your cities and homes all over America. Give me your help, your hand, your voice, your vote. (Applause) Recall with me the words of Isaiah: "They that wait upon the Lord shall renew their strength; they shall mount up with wings as eagles; they shall run, and not be weary."

As we face the coming challenge, we too, shall wait upon the Lord, and ask that He renew our strength. Then shall we be equal to the test. Then we shall not be weary. And then we shall prevail. Thank you. (Standing applause)

In Paul A. Smith, ed., *Official Reports of the Proceedings of the Democratic National Convention and Committee* (Washington, D.C.: National Document Publishers, 1964), 239–245.

Young Americans for Freedom

The Sharon Statement (11 September 1960)

Young political activists in the 1960s formed many diverse groups. Some took their cue from ideas of Marxism and social democracy (the political Left.) Others looked to a set of conservative and religious principles (the political Right.) Initially formed by about ninety university students meeting on the Connecticut estate of William F. Buckley Jr., Young Americans for Freedom (YAF) became one of the most influential "New Right" groups in the United States. The founding members of YAF articulated their basic principles of liberty, morality, and anti-communism in their "Sharon Statement."

Adopted by the Young Americans for Freedom
in conference at Sharon, Conn., September 9–11, 1960

In this time of moral and political crisis, it is the responsibility of the youth of America to affirm certain eternal truths.

We, as young conservatives, believe:

That foremost among the transcendent values is the individual's use of his God-given free will, whence derives his right to be free from the restrictions of arbitrary force;

That liberty is indivisible, and that political freedom cannot long exist without economic freedom;

That the purposes of government are to protect these freedoms through the preservation of internal order, the provision of national defense, and the administration of justice;

That when government ventures beyond these rightful functions, it accumulates power which tends to diminish order and liberty;

That the Constitution of the United States is the best arrangement yet devised for empowering government to fulfill its proper role, while restraining it from the concentration and abuse of power;

That the genius of the Constitution—the division of powers—is summed up in the clause which reserves primacy to the several states, or to the people, in those spheres not specifically delegated to the Federal Government;

That the market economy, allocating resources by the free play of supply and demand, is the single economic system compatible with the requirements of personal freedom and constitutional government, and that it is at the same time the most productive supplier of human needs;

That when government interferes with the work of the market economy, it tends to reduce the moral and physical strength of the nation; that when it takes from one man to bestow on another, it diminishes the incentive of the first, the integrity of the second, and the moral autonomy of both;

That we will be free only so long as the national sovereignty of the United States is secure: that history shows periods of freedom are rare, and can exist only when free citizens concertedly defend their rights against all enemies;

That the forces of international Communism are, at present, the greatest single threat to these liberties;

That the United States should stress victory over, rather than coexistence with, this menace; and

That American foreign policy must be judged by this criterion: does it serve the just interests of the United States?

In John A. Andrew III, *The Other Side of the Sixties: Young Americans for Freedom and the Rise of Conservative Politics* (New Brunswick, N.J.: Rutgers University Press, 1997), 221–222.

National Liberation Front for South Vietnam

Ten-Point Manifesto (December 1960)

In late 1960 the government of North Vietnam worked with insurgent forces in South Vietnam to create the National Liberation Front for South Vietnam (NLF). The NLF attacked the authority of the South Vietnamese government and its American sponsors. It also created international representation to promote the cause of revolution in South Vietnam. The NLF used its "Ten-Point Manifesto" to promote an image of itself as a democratic collection of peasants fighting for freedom from colonization. This image attracted wide support among foreign observers, many of whom did not recognize the complex relationship between the NLF and North Vietnam.

1. To overthrow the disguised colonial regime of the U.S. imperialists and the dictatorial Ngo Dinh Diem administration-lackey of the United States and to form a national democratic coalition administration.

2. To bring into being a broad and progressive democracy and to promulgate freedom of expression, of the press, of belief, of assembly, of association, and of movement and other democratic freedoms; to grant general amnesty to all political detainees, dissolve all concentration camps ("prosperity zones") and "resettlement centers," and abolish the fascist law 10–59 and other antidemocratic laws.

3. To abolish the economic monopoly of the United States and its henchmen, protect homemade products, encourage home industry and trade, expand agriculture, and build an independent and sovereign economy; to provide jobs for the unemployed and increase wages for workers, army personnel, and office employees; to abolish arbitrary fines and apply an equitable and rational tax system; to help displaced persons return home if that is their wish, and to provide jobs for those among them who want to remain in the South.

4. To reduce land rents, guarantee the peasants' right to till the plots of land they currently hold, redistribute communal land, and advance toward land reform.

5. To eliminate the enslaving and depraved U.S.-style culture, construct a national and progressive culture and educational system; to eliminate illiteracy, open more schools, carry out reform in the educational and examination systems.

6. To abolish the system of American military advisers, eliminate foreign military bases in Viet Nam, and build a national army for defense of the Fatherland and the people.

7. To guarantee equality between men and women and among nationalities and the autonomy of national minorities; to protect the legitimate interests of foreign residents in Viet Nam; to protect the interests of Vietnamese living abroad.

8. To carry out a foreign policy of peace and neutrality, and to establish diplomatic relations with all countries that respect the independence and sovereignty of Viet Nam.

9. To establish normal relations between the two zones and to work toward the peaceful reunification of the Fatherland.

10. To oppose aggressive war and actively to defend world peace.

In Robert K. Brigham, *Guerrilla Diplomacy: The NLF's Foreign Relations and the Viet Nam War* (Ithaca, N.Y.: Cornell University Press, 1996), 153–154.

Deng Tuo

The Kingly Way and the Tyrannical Way
(25 February 1962)

During the late 1950s the People's Republic of China embarked on a disastrous "Great Leap Forward," designed to strengthen communist control of the countryside and mobilize peasants for industrial production. Imposed on the nation by Chairman Mao Zedong, the Great Leap Forward undermined Chinese agriculture. More than 20 million people died of starvation. In the aftermath of this tragedy, many former supporters of Mao Zedong and the Chinese Communist Party began to criticize, at least indirectly, the political leadership. Deng Tuo, the editor of the People's Daily *(the official Chinese government newspaper) used historical allegory to condemn Mao. He contrasted the good "Kingly*

Way" from the bad "Tyrannical Way." A few years later, Chinese officials arrested Deng. He was never seen again.

In reading ancient history we can discover everywhere people and methods following the Kingly Way and the Tyrannical Way. Historians of the past, too, have written numerous commentaries on the Kingly Way and the Tyrannical Way. Yet, from our present perspective how should we view the Kingly Way and the Tyrannical Way?

There was a great scholar in the Han period called Liu Xiang. An erudite and accomplished man, he discussed with some originality the political successes and failures of past dynasties and syn-

The Cultural Revolution in China swept up young boys and girls into Red Guard factions that violently uprooted established authority, including parents and school teachers, throughout the country.

thesized the theories of astronomy, geography, the Three Doctrines [Confucianism, Daoism, and Legalism], and the Nine Schools. Emperor Yuandi of the Han [r. 48–33 B.C.] placed him in charge of the library of Heavenly Emoluments, where he both read and wrote. In his "New Preface" to *A Collection of Good Plans* he wrote: "The Kingly Way is like a whetstone. It originates from human feeling and emerges through rites and justice." In another part of the same chapter he wrote: "The Three Dynasties all had different Ways, yet all were Kingly; the Five Hegemons all had different laws, yet all were Tyrannical." We can see that Liu Xiang praises the Kingly Way and not the Tyrannical Way. He regarded the Kingly Way as the result of combining human sympathy and legal morality. This is reasonable, since the *Book of Rites* much earlier had said, "When Rites, Music, Punishments, and Administration are thoroughly understood and not confused, then the Kingly Way is complete."

In other words, what is called the Kingly Way is actually the various attitudes and actions people take when solving problems under specific historical circumstances, according to the common human sentiments and criteria of social morality of their time and under the premise of not violating the political and legal systems of their day. Conversely, if regardless of all else one relies on force, is arbitrary, flaunts power, orders others around with a wave of the hand, and snatches their goods by force or trickery, then that is what is called the Tyrannical Way.

However, this interpretation is quite insufficient and most certainly is not our view today. From our current perspective, we can see that what the ancients called the Kingly and the Tyrannical Way essentially were not very different. In the slave and feudal societies of the ancient period, the effects of carrying out the Kingly Way or the Tyrannical Way could be identical. Even though they sometimes divided into two camps and even attacked each other without respite, those who praised the Kingly Way and those who praised the Tyrannical Way still at times could be one and the same group, or individual, now championing the Kingly Way and now again championing the Tyrannical Way. This is especially true for the "School of Diplomatists" in the Spring and Autumn Period, who were always adapting themselves to changing circumstances—supporting Qin in the morning, Chu in the evening. They could propagandize the Kingly Way or the Tyrannical Way, but their sole object was political opportunism.

The most striking example of this is Shang Yang. According to "The Biography of Lord Shang" in Sima Qian's *Records of the Grand Historian*:

> . . . [Shang Yang] went west and entered Qin. Through the offices of Duke Xiao's favorite Eunuch, Jing, he sought an audience with the Duke. Duke Xiao met with Wei Yang [i.e., Shang Yang], who spoke on affairs a long while. The Duke dozed and did not listen. Afterwards the Duke with indignation said to the Eunuch Jing, "Your hanger-on is absurd. How could I possibly use him?" Jing then reproached Wei Yang. Wei Yang said, "I counselled the Duke on the Emperors' Way, but his ambitions were not awakened." After five days [the Duke] sought out Yang again. When Yang met the Duke again, though better, it still did not suit [the Duke's] wishes. Afterwards the Duke reproached Jing, and Jing in turn reproached Yang. Yang said, "I told the Duke of the Kingly Way, but it was not acceptable." Once again Yang was invited to an audience. When Yang met the Duke again, the Duke thought he was good but did not employ him. [Yang] departed. Duke Xiao said to Jing, "Your hanger-on is good; I could talk to him." Yang said, "Since I counselled the Duke on the Tyrannical Way he means to use me. If he will see me again, I know what to say." Wei Yang met with Duke Xiao again. As they talked the Duke unconsciously moved closer to [Yang].

Each time it was the same Shang Yang. In all he visited Duke Xiao of Qin four times, changing what he said each time. The first time, he expounded on the so-called Way of the Emperors. His purpose was to sound out the situation, and he felt something was amiss. The second time, he changed his tune and spoke on the theories of the so-called Kingly Way. But the results were still no good. The third time, he again changed his tune and set out the so-called Tyrannical Way. The result was far better than the previous two efforts. Still, he wasn't satisfied. Thus, when they met the fourth time, Shang Yang proceeded to elaborate fully his ideas on implementing the "Tyrannical Way," and so he achieved his goal. This clearly demonstrates that whether the ancients sometimes discussed the Kingly Way or the Tyrannical Way or even some other Way, they were always using these methods to promote their political opportunism. Just like an itinerant quack they talked nonsense, and nothing more.

But since ancient times the practical results of the Kingly Way and the Tyrannical Way have differed considerably. It is only the interpretation of the Kingly Way and the Tyrannical Way by the ancients that, from our present perspective, cannot avoid imprecision.

Thus, from our current standpoint and using our own language, what in the last analysis is the Kingly Way and what is the Tyrannical Way? That which is called the Kingly Way can be interpreted as the honest ideological workstyle of a mass line based on practical reality. And that which is called the Tyrannical Way can be interpreted as the blustering ideological workstyle of willful acts based on subjective and arbitrary decisions. This interpretation, however, cannot be imposed upon the ancients, whom it would be unrealistic to judge from such a standpoint.

Nevertheless, it is easy to find lessons from ancient history that illustrate that even in ancient times the Kingly Way was much better than the Tyrannical Way. Ban Gu, the author of *The Standard History of the Han*, in his account of the struggle for hegemony among the princes before the Qin-Han period, ridicules the Tyrannical Way in a number of places. For example, he says, "Duke Wen of [the state of] Jin carried out the Tyrannical Way and invaded [the state of] Wei. He seized the Earl of Cao, defeated Chu at Chengpu, and finally called a conference of the Princes." At a single glance people can see how those who wanted to rule as tyrants at that time made enemies everywhere and became very unpopular.

A few people in history have tried with a so-called balanced attitude to find a middle path between the Kingly Way and the Tyrannical Way. For instance, *Han's Unofficial Commentary on the Book of Odes* by Han Ying records: "Those who cherish its Constant Way, and take advantage of its changing force, are worthies." The thought here is to find a compromise "Constant Way" between the Kingly Way and the Tyrannical Way, add a few expedient and flexible methods, and then praise yourself for a "government of worthies." In fact, such a compromise road can only serve to deceive oneself as well as others, because in reality it does not exist!

---

*In *Chinese Law and Government*, trans. Timothy Cheek (Winter 1983–1984), Vol. 16, No. 4, 64–68.†
†"Wangdao he badao," Beijing wanbao, February 25, 1962 [YSYH/79:319–22]. The translator thanks James Feinerman for his helpful suggestions on translating this particularly turgid essay.

Students for a Democratic Society

The Port Huron Statement (1962)

In the middle 1960s Students for a Democratic Society (SDS) became the largest "New Left" student group in the United States. The influence of SDS grew, in part, from the eloquent and inspirational "agenda for a generation" that fifty-nine members of the group formulated in June 1962, at a retreat in Port Huron, Michigan. The "Port Huron Statement" called for a return to idealism in American policy at home and abroad. It emphasized democratic participatory values and a leading role for students in changing the world.

Introduction: Agenda for a Generation

We are people of this generation, bred in at least modest comfort, housed now in universities, looking uncomfortably to the world we inherit.

When we were kids the United States was the wealthiest and strongest country in the world: the only one with the atom bomb, the least scarred by modern war, an initiator of the United Nations that we thought would distribute Western influence throughout the world. Freedom and equality for each individual, government of, by, and for the people—these American values we found good, principles by which we could live as men. Many of us began maturing in complacency.

As we grew, however, our comfort was penetrated by events too troubling to dismiss. First, the permeating and victimizing fact of human degradation, symbolized by the Southern struggle against racial bigotry, compelled most of us from silence to activism. Second, the enclosing fact of the Cold War, symbolized by the presence of the Bomb, brought awareness that we ourselves, and our friends, and millions of abstract "others" we knew more directly because of our common peril, might die at any time. We might deliberately ignore, or avoid, or fail to feel all other human problems, but not these two, for these were too immediate and crushing in their impact, too challenging in the demand that we as individuals take the responsibility for encounter and resolution.

While these and other problems either directly oppressed us or rankled our consciences and became our own subjective concerns, we began to see complicated and disturbing paradoxes in our surrounding America. The declaration "all men are created equal . . ." rang hollow before the facts of Negro life in the South and the big cities of the North. The proclaimed peaceful intentions of the United States contradicted its economic and military investments in the Cold War status quo.

We witnessed, and continue to witness, other paradoxes. With nuclear energy whole cities can easily be powered, yet the dominant nation-states seem more likely to unleash destruction greater than that incurred in all wars of human history. Although our own technology is destroying old and creating new forms of social organization, men still tolerate meaningless work and idleness. While two-thirds of mankind suffers undernourishment, our own upper classes revel amidst superfluous abundance. Although world population is expected to double in forty years, the nations still tolerate anarchy as a major principle of international conduct and uncontrolled exploitation governs the sapping of the earth's physical resources. Although mankind desperately needs revolutionary leadership, America rests in national stalemate, its goals ambiguous and tradition-bound instead of informed and clear, its democratic system apathetic and manipulated rather than "of, by, and for the people."

Not only did tarnish appear on our image of American virtue, not only did disillusion occur when the hypocrisy of American ideals was discovered, but we began to sense that what we had originally seen as the American Golden Age was actually the decline of an era. The worldwide outbreak of revolution against colonialism and imperialism, the entrenchment of totalitarian states, the menace of war, overpopulation, international disorder, supertechnology— these trends were testing the tenacity of our own commitment to democracy and freedom and our abilities to visualize their application to a world in upheaval.

Our work is guided by the sense that we may be the last generation in the experiment with living. But we are a minority—the vast majority of our people regard the temporary equilibriums of our society and world as eternally-functional parts. In this is perhaps the outstanding paradox: we ourselves are imbued with urgency, yet the message of our society is that there is no viable alternative to the present. Beneath the reassuring tones of the politicians, beneath the common opinion that America will "muddle through," beneath the stagnation of those who have closed their minds to the future, is the pervading feeling that there simply are no alternatives, that our times have witnessed the exhaustion not only of Utopias, but of any new departures as well. Feeling the press of complexity upon the emptiness of life, people are fearful of the thought that at any moment things might thrust out of control. They fear change itself, since change might smash whatever invisible framework seems to hold back chaos for them now. For most Americans, all crusades are suspect, threatening. The fact that each individual sees apathy in his fellows perpetuates the common reluctance to organize for change. The dominant institutions are complex enough to blunt the minds of their potential critics, and entrenched enough to swiftly dissipate or entirely repel the energies of protest and reform, thus limiting human expectancies. Then, too, we are a materially improved society, and by our own improvements we seem to have weakened the case for further change.

Some would have us believe that Americans feel contentment amidst prosperity—but might it not better be called a glaze above deeply-felt anxieties about their role in the new world? And if these anxieties produce a developed indifference to human affairs, do they not as well produce a yearning to believe there *is* an alternative to the present, that something *can* be done to change circumstances in the school, the workplaces, the bureaucracies, the government? It is to this latter yearning, at once the spark and engine of change, that we direct our present appeal. The search for truly democratic alternatives to the present, and a commitment to social experimentation with them, is a worthy and fulfilling human enterprise, one which moves us and, we hope, others today. On such a basis do we offer this document of our convictions and analysis: as an effort in understanding and changing the conditions of humanity in the late twentieth century, an effort rooted in the ancient, still unfulfilled conception of man attaining determining influence over his circumstances of life.

Values

Making values explicit—an initial task in establishing alternatives—is an activity that has been devalued and corrupted. The conventional moral terms of the age, the politician moralities—"free world," "people's democracies"—reflect realities poorly, if at all, and seem to function more as ruling myths than as descriptive principles. But neither has our experience in the universities brought us moral enlightenment. Our professors and administrators sacrifice controversy to public relations; their curriculums change more slowly than the living events of the world; their skills and silence are purchased by investors in the arms race; passion is called unscholastic. The questions we might want raised—what is really important? can we live in a different and better way? if we wanted to change society, how would we do it?—are not thought to be questions of a "fruitful, empirical nature," and thus are brushed aside.

Unlike youth in other countries we are used to moral leadership being exercised and moral dimensions being clarified by our elders. But today, for us, not even the liberal and socialist preachments of the past seem adequate to the forms of the present. Consider the old slogans: Capitalism Cannot Reform Itself, United Front Against Fascism, General Strike, All Out on May Day. Or, more recently, No Cooperation with Commies and Fellow Travellers, Ideologies Are Exhausted, Bipartisanship, No Utopias. These are incomplete, and there are few new prophets. It has been said that our liberal and socialist predecessors were plagued by vision without program, while our own generation is plagued by program without vision. All around us there is astute grasp of method, technique—the committee, the ad hoc group, the lobbyist, the hard and soft sell, the make, the projected image—but, if pressed critically, such expertise is incompetent to explain its implicit ideals. It is highly fashionable to identify oneself by old categories, or by naming a respected political figure, or by explaining "how we would vote" on various issues.

Theoretic chaos has replaced the idealistic thinking of old—and, unable to reconstitute theoretic order, men have condemned idealism itself. Doubt has replaced hopefulness—and men act out a defeatism that is labelled realistic. The decline of utopia and hope is in fact one of the defining features of social life today. The reasons are various: the dreams of the older left were perverted by Stalinism and never recreated; the congressional stalemate makes men narrow their view of the possible; the specialization of human activity leaves little room for sweeping thought; the horrors of the twentieth century, symbolized in the gas-ovens and concentration camps and atom bombs, have blasted hopefulness. To be idealistic is to be considered apocalyptic, deluded. To have no serious aspirations, on the contrary, is to be "tough-minded."

In suggesting social goals and values, therefore, we are aware of entering a sphere of some disrepute. Perhaps matured by the past, we have no sure formulas, no closed theories—but that does not mean values are beyond discussion and tentative determination. A first task of any social movement is to convince people that the search for orienting theories and the creation of human values is complex but worthwhile. We are aware that to avoid platitudes we must analyze the concrete conditions of social order. But to direct such an analysis we must use the guideposts of basic principles. Our own social values involve conceptions of human beings, human relationships, and social systems.

We regard *men* as infinitely precious and possessed of unfulfilled capacities for reason, freedom, and love. In affirming these principles we are aware of countering perhaps the dominant conceptions of man in the twentieth century: that he is a thing to be manipulated, and that he is inherently incapable of directing his own affairs. We oppose the depersonalization that reduces human beings to the status of things—if anything, the brutalities of the twentieth century teach that means and ends are intimately related, that vague appeals to "posterity" cannot justify the mutilations of the present. We oppose, too, the doctrine of human incompetence because it rests essentially on the modern fact that men have been "competently" manipulated into incompetence—we see little reason why men cannot meet with increasing skill the complexities and responsibilities of their situation, if society is organized not for minority, but for majority, participation in decision-making.

Men have unrealized potential for self-cultivation, self-direction, self-understanding, and creativity. It is this potential that we regard as crucial and to which we appeal, not to the human potentiality for violence, unreason, and submission to authority. The goal of man and society should be human independence: a concern not with image of popularity but with finding a meaning in life that is personally authentic; a quality of mind not compulsively driven by a sense of powerlessness, nor one which unthinkingly adopts status values, nor one which represses all threats to its habits, but one which has full, spontaneous access to present and past experiences, one which easily unites the fragmented parts of personal history, one which openly faces problems which are troubling and unresolved; one with an intuitive awareness of possibilities, an active sense of curiosity, an ability and willingness to learn.

This kind of independence does not mean egoistic individualism—the object is not to have one's way so much as it is to have a way that is one's own. Nor do we deify man—we merely have faith in his potential.

Human relationships should involve fraternity and honesty. Human interdependence is contemporary fact; human brotherhood must be willed however, as a condition of future survival and as the most appropriate form of social relations. Personal links between man and man are needed, especially to go beyond the partial and fragmentary bonds of function that bind men only as worker to worker, employer to employee, teacher to student, American to Russian.

Loneliness, estrangement, isolation describe the vast distance between man and man today. These dominant tendencies cannot be overcome by better personnel management, nor by improved gadgets, but only when a love of man overcomes the idolatrous worship of things by man.

As the individualism we affirm is not egoism, the selflessness we affirm is not self-elimination. On the contrary, we believe in generosity of a kind that imprints one's unique individual qualities in the relation to other men, and to all human activity. Further, to dislike isolation is not to favor the abolition of privacy; the latter differs from isolation in that it occurs or is abolished according to individual will. Finally, we would replace power and personal uniqueness rooted in possession, privilege, or circumstance by power and uniqueness rooted in love, reflectiveness, reason, and creativity.

As a *social system* we seek the establishment of a democracy of individual participation, governed by two central aims: that the individual share in those social decisions determining the quality and direction of his life; that society be organized to encourage independence in men and provide the media for their common participation.

In a participatory democracy, the political life would be based in several root principles:

—that decision-making of basic social consequence be carried on by public groupings;

—that politics be seen positively, as the art of collectively creating an acceptable pattern of social relations;

—that politics has the function of bringing people out of isolation and into community, thus being a necessary, though not sufficient, means of finding meaning in personal life;

—that the political order should serve to clarify problems in a way instrumental to their solution; it should provide outlets for the expression of personal grievance and aspiration; opposing views should be organized so as to illuminate choices and facilitate the attainment of goals; channels should be commonly available to relate men to knowledge and to power so that private problems—from bad recreation facilities to personal alienation—are formulated as general issues.

The economic sphere would have as its basis the principles:

—that work should involve incentives worthier than money or survival. It should be educative, not stultifying; creative, not mechanical; self-direct, not manipulated, encouraging independence, a respect for others, a sense of dignity and a willingness to accept social responsibility, since it is this experience that has crucial influence on habits, perceptions and individual ethics;

—that the economic experience is so personally decisive that the individual must share in its full determination;

—that the economy itself is of such social importance that its major resources and means of production should be open to democratic participation and subject to democratic social regulation.

Like the political and economic ones, major social institutions— cultural, education, rehabilitative, and others—should be generally organized with the well-being and dignity of man as the essential measure of success.

In social change or interchange, we find violence to be abhorrent because it requires generally the transformation of the target, be it a human being or a community of people, into a depersonalized object of hate. It is imperative that the means of violence be abolished and the institutions—local, national, international—that encourage nonviolence as a condition of conflict be developed.

These are our central values, in skeletal form. It remains vital to understand their denial or attainment in the context of the modern world.

The Students

In the last few years, thousands of American students demonstrated that they at least felt the urgency of the times. They moved actively and directly against racial injustices, the threat of war, violations of individual rights of conscience and, less frequently, against economic manipulation. They succeeded in restoring a small measure of controversy to the campuses after the stillness of the McCarthy period. They succeeded, too, in gaining some concessions from the people and institutions they opposed, especially in the fight against racial bigotry.

The significance of these scattered movements lies not in their success or failure in gaining objectives—at least not yet. Nor does the significance lie in the intellectual "competence" or "maturity" of the students involved—as some pedantic elders allege. The significance is in the fact the students are breaking the crust of apathy and overcoming the inner alienation that remain the defining characteristics of American college life.

If student movements for change are rareties still on the campus scene, what is commonplace there? The real campus, the familiar campus, is a place of private people, engaged in their notorious "inner emigration." It is a place of commitment to business-as-usual, getting ahead, playing it cool. It is a place of mass affirmation of the Twist, but mass reluctance toward the controversial public stance. Rules are accepted as "inevitable," bureaucracy as "just circumstances," irrelevance as "scholarship," selflessness as "martyrdom," politics as "just another way to make people, and an unprofitable one, too."

Almost no students value activity as a citizen. Passive in public, they are hardly more idealistic in arranging their private lives: Gallup concludes they will settle for "low success, and won't risk high failure." There is not much willingness to take risks (not even in business), no setting of dangerous goals, no real conception of personal identity except one manufactured in the image of others, no real urge for personal fulfillment except to be almost as successful as the very successful people. Attention is being paid to social status (the quality of shirt collars, meeting people, getting wives or husbands, making solid contacts for later on); much too, is paid to academic status (grades, honors, the med school rat-race). But neglected generally is real intellectual status, the personal cultivation of the mind.

"Students don't even give a damn about the apathy," one has said. Apathy toward apathy begets a privately-constructed universe, a place of systematic study schedules, two nights each week for beer, a girl or two, and early marriage; a framework infused with personality, warmth, and under control, no matter how unsatisfying otherwise.

Under these conditions university life loses all relevance to some. Four hundred thousand of our classmates leave college every year.

But apathy is not simply an attitude; it is a product of social institutions, and of the structure and organization of higher education itself. The extracurricular life is ordered according to *in loco parentis* theory, which ratifies the Administration as the moral guardian of the young. The accompanying "let's pretend" theory of student extracurricular affairs validates student government as a training center for those who want to spend their lives in political pretense, and discourages initiative from more articulate, honest, and sensitive students. The bounds and style of controversy are delimited before controversy begins. The university "prepares" the student for "citizenship" through perpetual rehearsals and, usually, through emasculation of what creative spirit there is in the individual.

The academic life contains reinforcing counterparts to the way in which extracurricular life is organized. The academic world is founded in a teacher-student relation analogous to the parent-child relation which characterizes *in loco parentis*. Further, academia includes a radical separation of student from the material of study. That which is studied, the social reality, is "objectified" to sterility, dividing the student from life—just as he is restrained in active involvement by the deans controlling student government. The specialization of function and knowledge, admittedly necessary to our complex technological and social structure, has produced an exaggerated compartmentalization of study and understanding. This has contributed to: an overly parochial view, by faculty, of the role of its research and scholarship; a discontinuous and truncated understanding, by students, of the surrounding social order; a loss of personal attachment, by nearly all, to the worth of study as a humanistic enterprise.

There is, finally, the cumbersome academic bureaucracy extending throughout the academic as well as extracurricular structures, contributing to the sense of outer complexity and inner powerlessness that transforms so many students from honest searching to ratification of convention and, worse, to a numbness of present and future catastrophes. The size and financing systems of the university enhance the permanent trusteeship of the administrative bureaucracy, their power leading to a shift to the value standards of business and administrative mentality within the university. Huge foundations and other private financial interests shape the underfinanced colleges and universities, not only making them more commercial, but less disposed to diagnose society critically, less open to dissent. Many social and physical scientists, neglecting the liberating heritage of higher learning, develop "human relations" or "morale-producing" techniques for the corporate economy, while others exercise their intellectual skills to accelerate the arms race.

Tragically, the university could serve as a significant source of social criticism and an initiator of new modes and molders of attitudes. But the actual intellectual effect of the college experience is hardly distinguishable from that of any other communications channel—say, a television set—passing on the stock truths of the day. Students leave college somewhat more "tolerant" than when they arrived, but basically unchallenged in their values and political orientations. With administrators ordering the institution, and faculty the curriculum, the student learns by his isolation to accept elite rule within the university, which prepares him to accept later forms of minority control. The real function of the educational system—as opposed to its more rhetorical function of "searching for truth"—is to impart the key information and styles that will help the student get by, modestly but comfortably, in the big society beyond.

* * *

New York: Students for a Democratic Society, 1962), 1–9.

Lyndon B. Johnson

Special Message to the Congress: The American Promise (15 March 1965)

On 7 March 1965 Alabama police viciously attacked a peaceful civil rights march outside the city of Selma. President Lyndon Johnson was personally appalled by this event, and he worked over the course of the next week to push civil rights legislation farther than most people expected at the time. On 15 March 1965 he gave a stirring address to Congress, condemning racist violence, advocating full equality for African-Americans, and proposing a Voting Rights Act that would guarantee the right to vote against interference. He also elaborated on his vision of a "great society," first articulated less than a year before. Johnson's words inspired many civil rights activists, but they were insufficient for those who began to look outside government for broader solutions.

Mr. Speaker, Mr. President, Members of the Congress:

I speak tonight for the dignity of man and the destiny of democracy.

I urge every member of both parties, Americans of all religions and of all colors, from every section of this country, to join me in that cause.

At times history and fate meet at a single time in a single place to shape a turning point in man's unending search for freedom. So it was at Lexington and Concord. So it was a century ago at Appomattox. So it was last week in Selma, Alabama.

There, long-suffering men and women peacefully protested the denial of their rights as Americans. Many were brutally assaulted. One good man, a man of God, was killed.

There is no cause for pride in what has happened in Selma. There is no cause for self-satisfaction in the long denial of equal rights of millions of Americans. But there is cause for hope and for faith in our democracy in what is happening here tonight.

For the cries of pain and the hymns and protests of oppressed people have summoned into convocation all the majesty of this great Government—the Government of the greatest Nation on earth.

Our mission is at once the oldest and the most basic of this country: to right wrong, to do justice, to serve man.

In our time we have come to live with moments of great crisis. Our lives have been marked with debate about great issues; issues of war and peace, issues of prosperity and depression. But rarely in any time does an issue lay bare the secret heart of America itself. Rarely are we met with a challenge, not to our growth or abundance, our welfare or our security, but rather to the values and the purposes and the meaning of our beloved Nation.

The issue of equal rights for American Negroes is such an issue. And should we defeat every enemy, should we double our wealth and conquer the stars, and still be unequal to this issue, then we will have failed as a people and as a nation.

For with a country as with a person, "What is a man profited, if he shall gain the whole world, and lose his own soul?"

There is no Negro problem. There is no Southern problem. There is no Northern problem. There is only an American problem.

And we are met here tonight as Americans—not as Democrats or Republicans—we are met here as Americans to solve that problem.

This was the first nation in the history of the world to be founded with a purpose. The great phrases of that purpose still sound in every American heart, North and South: "All men are created equal"—"government by consent of the governed"—"give me liberty or give me death." Well, those are not just clever words, or those are not just empty theories. In their name Americans have fought and died for two centuries, and tonight around the world they stand there as guardians of our liberty, risking their lives.

Those words are a promise to every citizen that he shall share in the dignity of man. This dignity cannot be found in a man's possessions; it cannot be found in his power, or in his position. It really rests on his right to be treated as a man equal in opportunity to all others. It says that he shall share in freedom, he shall choose his leaders, educate his children, and provide for his family according to his ability and his merits as a human being.

To apply any other test—to deny a man his hopes because of his color or race, his religion or the place of his birth—is not only to do injustice, it is to deny America and to dishonor the dead who gave their lives for American freedom.

The Right to Vote

Our fathers believed that if this noble view of the rights of man was to flourish, it must be rooted in democracy. The most basic right of all was the right to choose your own leaders. The history of this country, in large measure, is the history of the expansion of that right to all of our people.

Many of the issues of civil rights are very complex and most difficult. But about this there can and should be no argument. Every American citizen must have an equal right to vote. There is no reason which can excuse the denial of that right. There is no duty which weighs more heavily on us than the duty we have to ensure that right.

Yet the harsh fact is that in many places in this country men and women are kept from voting simply because they are Negroes.

Every device of which human ingenuity is capable has been used to deny this right. The Negro citizen may go to register only to be told that the day is wrong, or the hour is late, or the official in charge is absent. And if he persists, and if he manages to present himself to the registrar, he may be disqualified because he did not spell out his middle name or because he abbreviated a word on the application.

And if he manages to fill out an application he is given a test. The registrar is the sole judge of whether he passes this test. He may be asked to recite the entire Constitution, or explain the most complex provisions of State law. And even a college degree cannot be used to prove that he can read and write.

For the fact is that the only way to pass these barriers is to show a white skin.

Experience has clearly shown that the existing process of law cannot overcome systematic and ingenious discrimination. No law that we now have on the books—and I have helped to put three of them there—can ensure the right to vote when local officials are determined to deny it.

In such a case our duty must be clear to all of us. The Constitution says that no person shall be kept from voting because of his race or his color. We have all sworn an oath before God to support and to defend that Constitution. We must now act in obedience to that oath.

Guaranteeing the Right to Vote

Wednesday I will send to Congress a law designed to eliminate illegal barriers to the right to vote.

The broad principles of that bill will be in the hands of the Democratic and Republican leaders tomorrow. After they have reviewed it, it will come here formally as a bill. I am grateful for this opportunity to come here tonight at the invitation of the leadership to reason with my friends, to give them my views, and to visit with my former colleagues.

I have had prepared a more comprehensive analysis of the legislation which I had intended to transmit to the clerk tomorrow but which I will submit to the clerks tonight. But I want to really discuss with you now briefly the main proposals of this legislation.

This bill will strike down restrictions to voting in all elections—Federal, State, and local—which have been used to deny Negroes the right to vote.

This bill will establish a simple, uniform standard which cannot be used, however ingenious the effort, to flout our Constitution.

It will provide for citizens to be registered by officials of the United States Government if the State officials refuse to register them.

It will eliminate tedious, unnecessary lawsuits which delay the right to vote.

Finally, this legislation will ensure that properly registered individuals are not prohibited from voting.

I will welcome the suggestions from all of the Members of Congress—I have no doubt that I will get some—on ways and means to strengthen this law and to make it effective. But experience has plainly shown that this is the only path to carry out the command of the Constitution.

To those who seek to avoid action by their National Government in their own communities; who want to and who seek to maintain purely local control over elections, the answer is simple:

Open your polling places to all your people.

Allow men and women to register and vote whatever the color of their skin.

Extend the rights of citizenship to every citizen of this land.

The Need for Action

There is no constitutional issue here. The command of the Constitution is plain.

There is no moral issue. It is wrong—deadly wrong—to deny any of your fellow Americans the right to vote in this country.

There is no issue of States rights or national rights. There is only the struggle for human rights.

I have not the slightest doubt what will be your answer.

The last time a President sent a civil rights bill to the Congress it contained a provision to protect voting rights in Federal elections. That civil rights bill was passed after 8 long months of debate. And when that bill came to my desk from the Congress for my signature, the heart of the voting provision had been eliminated.

This time, on this issue, there must be no delay, no hesitation and no compromise with our purpose.

We cannot, we must not, refuse to protect the right of every American to vote in every election that he may desire to participate in. And we ought not and we cannot and we must not wait another 8 months before we get a bill. We have already waited a hundred years and more, and the time for waiting is gone.

So I ask you to join me in working long hours—nights and weekends, if necessary—to pass this bill. And I don't make that request lightly. For from the window where I sit with the problems of our country I recognize that outside this chamber is the outraged conscience of a nation, the grave concern of many nations, and the harsh judgment of history on our acts.

We Shall Overcome

But even if we pass this bill, the battle will not be over. What happened in Selma is part of a far larger movement which reaches into every section and State of America. It is the effort of American Negroes to secure for themselves the full blessings of American life.

Their cause must be our cause too. Because it is not just Negroes, but really it is all of us, who must overcome the crippling legacy of bigotry and injustice.

And we shall overcome.

As a man whose roots go deeply into Southern soil I know how agonizing racial feelings are. I know how difficult it is to reshape the attitudes and the structure of our society.

But a century has passed, more than a hundred years, since the Negro was freed. And he is not fully free tonight.

It was more than a hundred years ago that Abraham Lincoln, a great President of another party, signed the Emancipation Proclamation, but emancipation is a proclamation and not a fact.

A century has passed, more than a hundred years, since equality was promised. And yet the Negro is not equal.

A century has passed since the day of promise. And the promise is unkept.

The time of justice has now come. I tell you that I believe sincerely that no force can hold it back. It is right in the eyes of man and God that it should come. And when it does, I think that day will brighten the lives of every American.

For Negroes are not the only victims. How many white children have gone uneducated, how many white families have lived in stark poverty, how many white lives have been scarred by fear, because we have wasted our energy and our substance to maintain the barriers of hatred and terror?

So I say to all of you here, and to all in the Nation tonight, that those who appeal to you to hold on to the past do so at the cost of denying you your future.

This great, rich, restless country can offer opportunity and education and hope to all: black and white, North and South, sharecropper and city dweller. These are the enemies: poverty, ignorance, disease. They are the enemies and not our fellow man, not our neighbor. And these enemies too, poverty, disease and ignorance, we shall overcome.

An American Problem

Now let none of us in any sections look with prideful righteousness on the troubles in another section, or on the problems of our neighbors. There is really no part of America where the promise of equality has been fully kept. In Buffalo as well as in Birmingham, in Philadelphia as well as in Selma, Americans are struggling for the fruits of freedom.

This is one Nation. What happens in Selma or in Cincinnati is a matter of legitimate concern to every American. But let each of us look within our own hearts and our own communities, and let each of us put our shoulder to the wheel to root out injustice wherever it exists.

As we meet here in this peaceful, historic chamber tonight, men from the South, some of whom were at Iwo Jima, men from the North who have carried Old Glory to far corners of the world and brought it back without a stain on it, men from the East and from the West, are all fighting together without regard to religion, or color, or region, in Viet-Nam. Men from every region fought for us across the world 20 years ago.

And in these common dangers and these common sacrifices the South made its contribution of honor and gallantry no less than any other region of the great Republic—and in some instances, a great many of them, more.

And I have not the slightest doubt that good men from everywhere in this country, from the Great Lakes to the Gulf of Mexico, from the Golden Gate to the harbors along the Atlantic, will rally together now in this cause to vindicate the freedom of all Americans. For all of us owe this duty; and I believe that all of us will respond to it.

Your President makes that request of every American.

Progress Through the Democratic Process

The real hero of this struggle is the American Negro. His actions and protests, his courage to risk safety and even to risk his life, have awakened the conscience of this Nation. His demonstrations have been designed to call attention to injustice, designed to provoke change, designed to stir reform.

He has called upon us to make good the promise of America. And who among us can say that we would have made the same progress were it not for his persistent bravery, and his faith in American democracy.

For at the real heart of battle for equality is a deep-seated belief in the democratic process. Equality depends not on the force of arms or tear gas but upon the force of moral right; not on recourse to violence but on respect for law and order.

There have been many pressures upon your President and there will be others as the days come and go. But I pledge you tonight that we intend to fight this battle where it should be fought: in the courts, and in the Congress, and in the hearts of men.

We must preserve the right of free speech and the right of free assembly. But the right of free speech does not carry with it, as has been said, the right to holler fire in a crowded theater. We must preserve the right to free assembly, but free assembly does not carry with it the right to block public thoroughfares to traffic.

We do have a right to protest, and a right to march under conditions that do not infringe the constitutional rights of our neighbors. And I intend to protect all those rights as long as I am permitted to serve in this office.

We will guard against violence, knowing it strikes from our hands the very weapons which we seek—progress, obedience to law, and belief in American values.

In Selma as elsewhere we seek and pray for peace. We seek order. We seek unity. But we will not accept the peace of stifled rights, or the order imposed by fear, or the unity that stifles protest. For peace cannot be purchased at the cost of liberty.

In Selma tonight, as in every—and we had a good day there—as in every city, we are working for just and peaceful settlement. We must all remember that after this speech I am making tonight, after the police and the FBI and the Marshals have all gone, and after you have promptly passed this bill, the people of Selma and the other cities of the Nation must still live and work together. And when the attention of the Nation has gone elsewhere they must try to heal the wounds and to build a new community.

This cannot be easily done on a battleground of violence, as the history of the South itself shows. It is in recognition of this that men of both races have shown such an outstandingly impressive responsibility in recent days—last Tuesday, again today.

Rights Must Be Opportunities

The bill that I am presenting to you will be known as a civil rights bill. But, in a larger sense, most of the program I am recommending is a civil rights program. Its object is to open the city of hope to all people of all races.

Because all Americans just must have the right to vote. And we are going to give them that right.

All Americans must have the privileges of citizenship regardless of race. And they are going to have those privileges of citizenship regardless of race.

But I would like to caution you and remind you that to exercise these privileges takes much more than just legal right. It requires a trained mind and a healthy body. It requires a decent home, and the chance to find a job, and the opportunity to escape from the clutches of poverty.

Of course, people cannot contribute to the Nation if they are never taught to read or write, if their bodies are stunted from hunger, if their sickness goes untended, if their life is spent in hopeless poverty just drawing a welfare check.

So we want to open the gates to opportunity. But we are also going to give all our people, black and white, the help that they need to walk through those gates.

The Purpose of This Government

My first job after college was as a teacher in Cotulla, Tex., in a small Mexican-American school. Few of them could speak English, and I couldn't speak much Spanish. My students were poor and they often came to class without breakfast, hungry. They knew even in their youth the pain of prejudice. They never seemed to know why people disliked them. But they knew it was so, because I saw it in their eyes. I often walked home late in the afternoon, after the classes were finished, wishing there was more that I could do. But all I knew was to teach them the little that I knew, hoping that it might help them against the hardships that lay ahead.

Somehow you never forget what poverty and hatred can do when you see its scars on the hopeful face of a young child.

I never thought then, in 1928, that I would be standing here in 1965. It never even occurred to me in my fondest dreams that I might have the chance to help the sons and daughters of those students and to help people like them all over this country.

But now I do have that chance—and I'll let you in on a secret— I mean to use it. And I hope that you will use it with me.

This is the richest and most powerful country which ever occupied the globe. The might of past empires is little compared to ours. But I do not want to be the President who built empires, or sought grandeur, or extended dominion.

I want to be the President who educated young children to the wonders of their world. I want to be the President who helped to feed the hungry and to prepare them to be taxpayers instead of taxeaters.

I want to be the President who helped the poor to find their own way and who protected the right of every citizen to vote in every election.

I want to be the President who helped to end hatred among his fellow men and who promoted love among the people of all races and all regions and all parties.

I want to be the President who helped to end war among the brothers of this earth.

And so at the request of your beloved Speaker and the Senator from Montana; the majority leader, the Senator from Illinois; the minority leader, Mr. McCulloch, and other Members of both parties, I came here tonight—not as President Roosevelt came down one time in person to veto a bonus bill, not as President Truman came down one time to urge the passage of a railroad bill—but I came down here to ask you to share this task with me and to share it with the people that we both work for. I want this to be the Congress, Republicans and Democrats alike, which did all these things for all these people.

Beyond this great chamber, out yonder in 50 States, are the people that we serve. Who can tell what deep and unspoken hopes are in their hearts tonight as they sit there and listen. We all can guess, from our own lives, how difficult they often find their own pursuit of happiness, how many problems each little family has. They look most of all to themselves for their futures. But I think that they also look to each of us.

Above the pyramid on the great seal of the United States it says—in Latin—"God has favored our undertaking."

God will not favor everything that we do. It is rather our duty to divine His will. But I cannot help believing that He truly understands and that He really favors the undertaking that we begin here tonight.

In *Public Papers of the Presidents of the United States: Lyndon Johnson, Containing the Public Messages, Speeches, and Statements of the President* (Washington, D.C.: U.S. Government Printing Office, 1966), 281–287.

Ernesto Guevara

Excerpt from **The African Dream: The Diaries of the Revolutionary War in the Congo**

In the middle 1960s the Cuban government, under Fidel Castro, sought to spread its model of guerilla revolution to other parts of the world. Cubans looked to Africa because of their own ethnic ties to the continent, and also because decolonization made Africa appear ripe for radical change. One of the charismatic heroes of the Cuban Revolution, Ernesto "Che" Guevara, led approximately 200 Cuban soldiers to the Congo in 1965, hoping to make this region a staging ground for insurgency throughout the continent. Che's mission failed terribly—the revolutionaries did not fight effectively, they did not inspire outpourings of popular support, and they had trouble coordinating with local allies. Cuban racial condescension to the Africans also became a problem. In his diary, Che reflects on these failures and attempts to prepare for more effective revolutionary action elsewhere.

Preface

This is the history of a failure. It descends into anecdotal detail, as one would expect in episodes from a war, but this is blended with reflections and critical analysis. For in my view, any importance the story might have lies in the fact that it allows the experiences to be extracted for the use of other revolutionary movements. Victory is a great source of positive experiences, but so is defeat, especially if the unusual circumstances surrounding the incident are taken into account: the actors and informants are foreigners who went to risk their lives in an unknown land where people spoke a different language and were linked to them only by ties of proletarian internationalism, so that a method not practised in modern wars of liberation was thereby inaugurated.

The narrative closes with an epilogue which poses some questions about the struggle in Africa and, more generally, the national liberation struggle against the neo-colonialism that is the most redoubtable form of imperialism—most redoubtable because of the disguises and deceits that it involves, and the long experience that the imperialist powers have in this type of exploitation.

These notes will be published some time after they were dictated, and it may be that the author will no longer be able to take responsibility for what is said in them. Time will have smoothed many rough edges and, if its publication has any importance, the editors will be able to make the corrections they deem necessary (with appropriate indications) to explain the events or people's views in the light of the passage of time.

More correctly, this is the history of a decomposition. When we arrived on Congolese soil, the revolution was in a period of reflux; then a number of incidents occurred which brought about its final regression, at this time and place at least, in the immense field of struggle that is the Congo. The most interesting aspect here is not the story of the decomposition of the Congolese revolution, whose causes and key features are too profound to be all encompassed from my particular vantage point, but rather the decomposition of our own fighting morale, since the experience we inaugurated should not go to waste and the initiative of the International Proletarian Army should not die at the first failure. It is essential to analyse in depth the problems that are posed, and to find a solution to them. A good battlefield instructor does more for the revolution than one who teaches a large number of raw recruits in a context of peace, but the characteristics of this instructor who fires the training of the future technical cadres of the revolution should be carefully studied.

The idea that guided us was to ensure that men experienced in liberation battles (and subsequently in the struggle with reactionary forces) fought alongside men without experience, and thereby to bring about what we called the "Cubanization" of the Congolese. It will be seen that the effect was the exact opposite, in that a "Congolization" of the Cubans took place over a period of time. In speaking of Congolization, we had in mind the series of habits and attitudes to the revolution that characterized the Congolese soldier at those moments of the struggle. This does not imply any derogatory view about the Congolese people, but it does about the soldiers at that time. In the course of the story, an attempt will be made to explain why those fighters had such negative traits.

As a general norm, one that I have always followed, nothing but the truth will be told in these pages—or at least my interpretation of the facts—although this may be confronted with other subjective evaluations or with factual corrections, should any errors have crept into my account.

At some moments when the truth would be indiscreet or inadvisable to relate, a particular reference has been omitted. For there are certain things that the enemy should not know, and some of the problems posed may be of help to friends in a possible reorganization of the struggle in the Congo (or in a launching of the struggle in another country in Africa or elsewhere whose problems are similar). Among the omitted references are our ways and means of reaching Tanzania, our springboard into the setting of this story.

The names given for the Congolese are their real ones, but nearly all men of our own contingent are mentioned by the names given to them in Swahili when they first arrived in the Congo; the true names of the comrades who took part will feature in an appendix, if the editors consider this useful. Lastly, it should be said that, in keeping to the strict truth and the importance it may have for future liberation movements, we have emphasized various cases of weakness on the part of individuals or groups of men, as well as the general demoralization that eventually came over us. But this does not in any way detract from the heroism of the gestures, while the heroic nature of the Cuban involvement derives from the general attitude of our government and the people of Cuba. Our country, the only socialist bastion at the gates of Yankee imperialism, sends its soldiers to fight and die in a foreign land, on a distant continent, and assumes full public responsibility for its actions. This challenge, this clear position with regard to the great contemporary issue of relentless struggle against Yankee imperialism, defines the heroic significance of our participation in the struggle of the Congo.

In this can be seen the readiness of a people and its leaders not only to defend themselves, but to attack. For, in relation to Yankee imperialism, it is not enough to be resolute in defence. It has to be attacked in its bases of support, in the colonial and neo-colonial lands that serve as the underpinning of its world domination.

First Act

In a story of this kind, it is difficult to locate the first act. For narrative convenience, I shall take this to be a trip I made in Africa which gave me the opportunity to rub shoulders with many leaders of the various Liberation Movements. Particularly instructive was my visit to Dar es Salaam, where a considerable number of Freedom Fighters had taken up residence. Most of them lived comfortably in hotels and had made a veritable profession out of their situation, sometimes lucrative and nearly always agreeable. This was the setting for the interviews, in which they generally asked for military training in Cuba and financial assistance. It was nearly everyone's leitmotif.

I also got to know the Congolese fighters. From our first meeting with them, we could clearly see the large number of tendencies and opinions that introduced some variety into this group of revolutionary leaders. I made contact with Kabila and his staff; he made an excellent impression on me. He said he had come from the interior of the country. It appears he had come only from Kigoma, a small Tanzanian town on Lake Tanganyika and one of the main scenes in this story, which served as a point of embarkation for the Congo and also as a pleasant place for the revolutionaries to take shelter when they tired of life's trials in the mountains across the strip of water.

Kabila's presentation was clear, specific and resolute; he gave some signs of his opposition to Gbenye and Kanza and his broad lack of agreement with Soumaliot. Kabila's argument was that there could be no talk of a Congolese government because Mulele, the initiator of the struggle, had not been consulted, and so the president could claim to be head of government only of North-East Congo. This also meant that Kabila's own zone in the South-East, which he led as vice-chairman of the Party, lay outside Gbenye's sphere of influence.

Kabila realized perfectly well that the main enemy was North American imperialism, and he declared his readiness to carry the fight against it through to the end. As I said, his statements and his note of confidence made a very good impression on me.

Another day, we spoke with Soumaliot. He is a different kind of man, much less developed politically and much older. He hardly had the basic instinct to keep quiet or to speak very little using vague phrases, so that he seemed to express great subtlety of thought but, however much he tried, he was unable to give the impression of a real popular leader. He explained what he has since made public: his involvement as defence minister in the Gbenye government, how Gbenye's action took them by surprise, and so on. He also clearly stated his opposition to Gbenye and, above all, Kanza. I did not personally meet these last two, except for a quick handshake with Kanza when we met at an airport.

We talked at length with Kabila about what our government considered a strategic flaw on the part of some African friends: namely, that, in the face of open aggression by the imperialist powers, they thought the right slogan must be: "The Congo problem is an African problem," and acted accordingly. Our view was that the Congo problem was a world problem, and Kabila agreed. On behalf of the government, I offered him some 30 instructors and whatever weapons we might have, and he was delighted to accept. He recommended that both should be delivered urgently, as did Soumaliot in another conversation—the latter pointing out that it would be a good idea if the instructors were blacks.

I decided to sound out the other Freedom Fighters, thinking that I could do this by having a friendly chat with them at separate meetings. But because of a mistake by the embassy staff, there was a "tumultuous" meeting attended by 50 or more people, representing Movements from ten or more countries, each divided into two or more tendencies. I gave them a speech of encouragement and analysed the requests they had nearly all made for financial assistance and personnel training. I explained the cost of training a man in Cuba, the investment of money and time that it required, and the uncertainty that it would result in useful fighters for the Movement.

I gave an account of our experience in the Sierra Maestra, where we obtained roughly one soldier for every five recruits, and a single good one for every five soldiers. I put the case as forcefully as I could to the exasperated Freedom Fighters that most of the money invested in training would not be well spent; that a soldier, especially a revolutionary soldier, cannot be formed in an academy but only in warfare. He may be able to get a diploma from some college or other, but his real graduation—as is the case with any professional—takes place in the practice of his profession, in the way he reacts to enemy fire, to suffering, defeat, relentless pursuit, unfavourable situations. You can never predict from what someone says, or from his previous history, how he will react when faced with all these ups and downs of struggle in the people's war. I therefore suggested that training should take place not in our faraway Cuba but in the nearby Congo, where the struggle was not against some puppet like Tshombe but against North American imperialism, which, in its neo-colonial form, was threatening the newly acquired independence of nearly every African people or helping to keep the colonies in subjection. I spoke to them of the fundamental importance which the Congo liberation struggle had in our eyes. Victory would be continental in its reach and its consequences, and so would defeat.

The reaction was worse than cool. Although most refrained from any kind of comment, some asked to speak and took me violently to task for the advice I had given. They argued that their respective peoples, who had been abused and degraded by imperialism, would protest if any casualties were suffered not as a result of oppression in their own land, but from a war to liberate another country. I tried to show them that we were talking not of a struggle within fixed frontiers, but of a war against the common enemy, present as much in Mozambique as in Malawi, Rhodesia or South Africa, the Congo or Angola. No one saw it like that.

The farewells were cool and polite, and we were left with the clear sense that Africa has a long way to go before it reaches real revolutionary maturity. But we had also had the joy of meeting people prepared to carry the struggle through to the end. From that moment, we set ourselves the task of selecting a group of black Cubans and sending them, naturally as volunteers, to reinforce the struggle in the Congo.

Second Act

The second act opens in the Congo and includes a number of episodes which, for the time being, still cannot be described in detail: my appointment at the head of the Cuban forces, even though I am white; the selection of future combatants; the organization of my secret departure, the limited possibility for leave-taking, the explanatory letters, the whole series of concealed manoeuvres that it would be dangerous even today to put on paper, and which can anyway be clarified at a later date.

After the hectic round of bittersweet farewells, which in the best of scenarios would be for a long time, the last step was the clandestine journey itself. That, too, it would be unwise to relate.

I was leaving behind nearly eleven years of work alongside Fidel for the Cuban Revolution, and a happy home, if that is the right word for the abode of a dedicated revolutionary and a lot of children who scarcely knew of my love for them. The cycle was beginning again.

One fine day I appeared in Dar es Salaam. No one recognized me; not even the ambassador, an old comrade-in-arms who had been with us in the initial landing and become a captain in the Rebel Army, was able to identify me.

We settled into a small farm, rented as temporary accommodation as we awaited the group of 30 men who were to accompany us. At that point there were three of us: Comandante Moja, a black man, who was the official head of our force; Mbili, a white comrade with great experience in these struggles; and Tatu—myself, pretending to be a doctor—who explained my colour by the fact that I spoke French and had guerrilla experience. Our names meant: one, two, three, in that order. To save ourselves headaches, we had decided to number ourselves by order of arrival, and to use the corresponding Swahili word as our pseudonym.

I had not informed any Congolese of my decision to fight in their country, nor did I now of my presence there. I had not mentioned it in my first conversation with Kabila, because I had not yet made up my mind; and once the plan had been approved, it would have been dangerous to reveal it until my journey through a lot of hostile territory had been completed. I therefore decided to present my arrival as a *fait accompli* and to go on from there according to how they reacted. I was not unaware that a negative response would put me in a tricky position (since I could no longer turn back), but I also reckoned that it would be difficult for them to refuse me. I was operating a kind of blackmail with my physical presence. An unexpected problem arose, however. Kabila was in Cairo with all the members of the Revolutionary Government, discussing aspects of combat unity and the new constitution of the revolutionary organization. His deputies, Masengo and Mitoudidi, were there with him. The only man left to whom authority had been delegated was Chamaleso, later to acquire the Cuban nickname "Tremendo Punto." Chamaleso accepted on his own responsibility the 30 instructors whom we initially offered, but when we told him that we had some 130 men, all black, ready to begin the struggle, he accepted this too on his own responsibility. This slightly changed the first part of our strategy, because we had thought we would be operating on the basis of 30 Cubans accepted as instructors.

A delegation set off for Cairo to tell Kabila and his comrades that the Cubans had arrived (but not that I was there), while we waited for the first of our contingents.

Our most pressing task was to find a speedboat with good engines, so that we would be able to cross in relative safety the 70 kilometres that was the width of Lake Tanganyika at that point. One of our fine experts had arrived in advance, to take charge both of buying launches and of exploring the way across the lake.

After a wait of several days in Dar es Salaam—a wait which, though short, made me anxious because I wanted to be inside the Congo as soon as possible—the first group of Cubans arrived at night on 20 April. Fourteen of us then set off, leaving behind four new arrivals for whom equipment had not yet been purchased. We were accompanied by two drivers, the Congolese Representative (Chamaleso), and someone from the Tanzanian police to clear up any problems en route.

Right from the start, we came face to face with a reality that would pursue us through the struggle: the lack of organization. This worried me because our passage must have been detected by Imperialism (which has power over all the airline companies and airports in the region), apart from the fact that the purchase of unusual quantities of backpacks, nylon sheeting, knives, blankets, etc. must have attracted attention in Dar es Salaam.

Not only was the Congolese organization bad; ours was too. We had not thoroughly prepared for the task of equipping a company, and had obtained only rifles and ammunition for the soldiers (all armed with Belgian FALs).

Kabila was expected to be two more weeks in Cairo, so that, unable to discuss with him my own involvement, I had to press on incognito and even to refrain from announcing myself to the Tanzanian government and requesting its acquiescence. To be honest, these problems did not bother me all that much, because I was eager to play a role in the Congo struggle and I feared that my offer might arouse excessively sharp reactions, that the Congolese— or the friendly government itself—might ask me not to enter the fray.

On the night of 22 April we reached Kigoma after a tiring journey, but the launches were not ready and we had to wait there all the next day for a crossing. The regional commissioner, who received us and put us up, immediately told me of the Congolese complaints. Unfortunately, everything indicated that many of his judgements were correct: the commanders in the area, who had received our first exploratory delegation, were now in Kigoma; and we could tell that they were granting passes for men to go there from the front. That little town was a haven where the luckiest ones could go and live away from the hazards of the struggle. The nefarious influence of Kigoma—its brothels, its alcohol, and especially its assurance of refuge—would never be sufficiently understood by the Revolutionary Command.

Eventually, on 24 April at dawn, we landed on Congolese soil and met a surprised group of well-armed infantry, who solemnly formed up into a little guard of honour. We were shown into a hut that had been specially vacated for us.

Our original information, obtained (I know not how) by our inspection agents, had been that on the Congolese side a plain stretched 16 kilometres inland to the mountains. In reality, however, the lake is a kind of ravine and the mountains, both at Kigoma and on the other side, begin right at the water's edge. At the headquarters location known as Kibamba, a difficult climb began ten paces or so from our point of disembarkation, all the more difficult given our lack of previous training.

An analysis should now be made of our own contingent. The great majority of the men were blacks. This could have added a sympathetic note of unity with the Congolese, but things did not work out like that. We did not see that it made much difference to our relations whether we were black or white; the Congolese knew how to identify each man's personal traits, and only in my own case did I sometimes suspect that my being white influenced matters. What is true is that our own comrades had a very poor cultural basis, as well as a relatively low level of political development. As often happens in such cases, they arrived brimming with optimism and good intentions, thinking that they would march triumphantly through the Congo. At one meeting before hostilities commenced, some men remarked that Tatu was too remote from military matters, that his timid concern for the relationship of forces would not stop them breaking in at one end and coming out at the other; then the country would be liberated and they could go back to Havana.

I always warned that the war would last three to five years, but no one believed it. They were all inclined to dream of a triumphal march, a departure with big speeches and great honours, then medals and Havana. The reality came as a shock: food was short, often consisting of plain manioc without even salt, or *bukali*, which is the same; there was not enough medicine, nor sometimes clothing or shoes; my dream of a fusion between our experienced men with army discipline and the Congolese never came true.

There was never the necessary integration, and it cannot be blamed on the colour of people's skin. Some Cubans were so black that they could not be told apart from the Congolese comrades; yet I heard one of them say: "Send me two of those blacks over there"—two Congolese, that is.

Our men were foreigners, superior beings, and they made it felt rather too frequently. The Congolese, ultra-sensitive because of past insults at the hands of the settlers, felt it in the core of their being when a Cuban displayed gestures of disdain towards them. I could never manage to obtain totally fair distribution of the food, and although it must be said that Cubans more often than not carried the heaviest burdens, they would rather insensitively load up a Congolese whenever the opportunity presented itself. It is not easy to explain this contradiction, which involved various subjective interpretations and subtle nuances, but one simple fact may throw some light on the subject: namely, my inability to get the

Cubans to use the term "Congolese." Instead, they referred to "the Congos"—apparently simpler and more intimate, but carrying a hefty dose of venom. Language was another real barrier, as it was difficult for a force such as ours—submerged in the mass of Congolese—to work without having their language. Some of those who from the start lived amicably alongside the Congolese very soon learnt to rattle things off in basic Swahili, a halfway language, but they were not many and they always ran the risk of a misunderstanding that might sour relations or lead us into error.

I have tried to paint the collapse of our force in the way in which it happened. It was a gradual but not steadily incremental process, which gathered explosive material and then burst out on occasions of defeat. Culminating moments were: the fiasco at Front de Force; the series of Congolese desertions at the Katenga ambushes, where the men suffered a lot from illness; my personal disaster in the procession carrying the wounded man, when we got very little help from the Congolese; and the desertion of our allies in the final stages. Each of these moments signalled a sharpening of the demoralization and loss of heart among our force.

By the end it had suffered contagion from the spirit of the lake. The men dreamt of returning home and, generally speaking, showed themselves incapable of laying down their lives so that the group would be safe, or so that the revolution as a whole could march on. All wanted to reach safety on the other shore. To such an extent did discipline break down that a number of really grotesque episodes took place, which would merit very severe penalties against some of the fighters.

* * *

Trans. Patrick Camiller (New York: Grove Press, 1999), 1–12, 230–231.

Herbert Marcuse

Political Preface 1966

By the second half of the 1960s Herbert Marcuse had become an international celebrity among student activists. The German émigré philosopher formulated an intellectual language of protest that synthesized many of the feelings and phrases circulating among young men and women. Marcuse condemned the United States and its West European allies for "overdevelopment" and repression of human instinct. He argued that human happiness required a dismantling of the destructive modernity on display in Vietnam and other Cold War conflicts. Marcuse looked to "backward" peoples, at home and abroad, who resisted the dominant powers and sought true liberation by "turning the wheel of progress to another direction." Marcuse called on his readers and listeners to refuse any further participation in modern society. Many of his followers also used his arguments to legitimize violence.

Eros and Civilization: the title expressed an optimistic, euphemistic, even positive thought, namely, that the achievements of advanced industrial society would enable man to reverse the direction of progress, to break the fatal union of productivity and destruction, liberty and repression—in other words, to learn the gay science (*gaya sciencia*) of how to use the social wealth for shaping man's world in accordance with his Life Instincts, in the concerted struggle against the purveyors of Death. This optimism was based on the assumption that the rationale for the continued acceptance of domination no longer prevailed, that scarcity and the need for toil were only "artificially" perpetuated—in the interest of preserving the system of domination. I neglected or minimized the fact that this "obsolescent" rationale had been vastly strengthened (if not replaced) by even more efficient forms of social control. The very forces which rendered society capable of pacifying the struggle for existence served to repress in the individuals the need for such a liberation. Where the high standard of living does not suffice for reconciling the people with their life and their rulers, the "social engineering" of the soul and the "science of human relations" provide the necessary libidinal cathexis. In the affluent society, the authorities are hardly forced to justify their dominion. They deliver the goods; they satisfy the sexual and the aggressive energy of their subjects. Like the unconscious, the destructive power of which they so successfully represent, they are this side of good and evil, and the principle of contradiction has no place in their logic.

As the affluence of society depends increasingly on the uninterrupted production and consumption of waste, gadgets, planned obsolescence, and means of destruction, the individuals have to be adapted to these requirements in more than the traditional ways. The "economic whip," even in its most refined forms, seems no longer adequate to insure the continuation of the struggle for existence in today's outdated organization, nor do the laws and patriotism seem adequate to insure active popular support for the ever more dangerous expansion of the system. Scientific management of instinctual needs has long since become a vital factor in the reproduction of the system: merchandise which has to be bought and used is made into objects of the libido; and the national Enemy who has to be fought and hated is distorted and inflated to such an extent that he can activate and satisfy aggressiveness in the depth dimension of the unconscious. Mass democracy provides the political paraphernalia for effectuating this introjection of the Reality Principle; it not only permits the people (up to a point) to chose their own masters and to participate (up to a point) in the government which governs them—it also allows the masters to disappear behind the technological veil of the productive and destructive apparatus which they control, and it conceals the human (and material) costs of the benefits and comforts which it bestows upon those who collaborate. The people, efficiently manipulated and organized, are free; ignorance and impotence, introjected heteronomy is the price of their freedom.

It makes no sense to talk about liberation to free men—and we are free if we do not belong to the oppressed minority. And it makes no sense to talk about surplus repression when men and women enjoy more sexual liberty than ever before. But the truth is that this freedom and satisfaction are transforming the earth into hell. The inferno is still concentrated in certain far away places: Vietnam, the Congo, South Africa, and in the ghettos of the "affluent society": in Mississippi and Alabama, in Harlem. These infernal places illuminate the whole. It is easy and sensible to see in them only pockets of poverty and misery in a growing society capable of eliminating them gradually and without a catastrophe. This interpretation may even be realistic and correct. The question is: eliminated at what cost—not in dollars and cents, but in human lives and in human freedom?

I hesitate to use the word—freedom—because it is precisely in the name of freedom that crimes against humanity are being perpetrated. This situation is certainly not new in history: poverty and exploitation were products of economic freedom; time and again, people were liberated all over the globe by their lords and masters, and their new liberty turned out to be submission, not to the rule of law but to the rule of the law of the others. What started as subjection by force soon became "voluntary servitude," collaboration in reproducing a society which made servitude increasingly rewarding and palatable. The reproduction, bigger and better, of the same ways of life came to mean, ever more clearly and consciously, the closing of those other possible ways of life which could do away with the serfs and the masters, with the productivity of repression.

Today, this union of freedom and servitude has become "natural" and a vehicle of progress. Prosperity appears more and more as the prerequisite and by-product of a self-propelling productivity ever seeking new outlets for consumption and for destruction, in outer and inner space, while being restrained from "overflowing" into the areas of misery—at home and abroad. As against this amalgam of liberty and aggression, production and destruction, the image of human freedom is dislocated: it becomes the project of the *subversion of this sort of progress*. Liberation of the instinctual needs for peace and quiet, of the "asocial" autonomous Eros presupposes liberation from repressive affluence: a reversal in the direction of progress.

It was the thesis of *Eros and Civilization*, more fully developed in my *One-Dimensional Man*, that man could avoid the fate of a Welfare-Through-Warfare State only by achieving a new starting point where he could reconstruct the productive apparatus without that "innerworldly asceticism" which provided the mental basis for domination and exploration. This image of man was the determinate negation of Nietzsche's superman: man intelligent enough and healthy enough to dispense with all heros and heroic virtues, man without the impulse to live dangerously, to meet the challenge; man with the good conscience to make life an end-in-itself, to live in joy a life without fear. "Polymorphous sexuality" was the term which I used to indicate that the new direction of progress would depend completely on the opportunity to activate repressed or arrested *organic*, biological needs: to make the human body an instrument of pleasure rather than labor. The old formula, the development of prevailing needs and faculties, seemed to be inadequate; the emergence of new, qualitatively different needs and faculties seemed to be the prerequisite, the content of liberation.

The idea of such a new Reality Principle was based on the assumption that the material (technical) preconditions for its development were either established, or could be established in the advanced industrial societies of our time. It was self-understood that the translation of technical capabilities into reality would mean a revolution. But the very scope and effectiveness of the democratic introjection have suppressed the historical subject, the agent of revolution: free people are not in need of liberation, and the oppressed are not strong enough to liberate themselves. These conditions redefine the concept of Utopia: liberation is the most realistic, the most concrete of all historical possibilities and at the same time the most rationally and effectively repressed—the most abstract and remote possibility. No philosophy, no theory can undo the democratic introjection of the masters into their subjects. When, in the more or less affluent societies, productivity has reached a level at which the masses participate in its benefits, and at which the opposition is effectively and democratically "contained," then the conflict between master and slave is also effectively contained. Or rather it has changed its social location. It exists, and explodes, in the revolt of the backward countries against the intolerable heritage of colonialism and its prolongation by neo-colonialism. The Marxian concept stipulated that only those who were free from the blessings of capitalism could possibly change it into a free society: those whose existence was the very negation of capitalist property could become the historical agents of liberation. In the international arena, the Marxian concept regains its full validity. To the degree to which the exploitative societies have become global powers, to the degree to which the new independent nations have become the battlefield of their interests, the "external" forces of rebellion have ceased to be extraneous forces: they are the enemy within the system. This does not make these rebels the messengers of humanity. By themselves, they are not (as little as the Marxian proletariat was) the representatives of freedom. Here too, the Marxian concept applies according to which the international proletariat would get its intellectual armor from outside: the "lightning of thought" would strike the "*naiven Volksboden.*" Grandiose ideas about the union of theory and practice do injustice to the feeble beginnings of such a union. Yet the revolt in the backward countries has found a response in the advanced countries where youth is in protest against repression in affluence and war abroad.

Revolt against the false fathers, teachers, and heroes—solidarity with the wretched of the earth: is there any "organic" connection between the two facets of the protest? There seems to be an all but instinctual solidarity. The revolt at home against home seems largely impulsive, its targets hard to define: nausea caused by "the way of life," revolt as a matter of physical and mental hygiene. The body against "the machine"—not against the mechanism constructed to make life safer and milder, to attenuate the cruelty of nature, but against the machine which has taken over the mechanism: the political machine, the corporate machine, the cultural and educational machine which has welded blessing and curse into one rational whole. The whole has become too big, its cohesion too strong, its functioning too efficient—does the power of the negative concentrate in still partly unconquered, primitive, elemental forces? The body against the machine: men, women, and children fighting, with the most primitive tools, the most brutal and destructive machine of all times and keeping it in check—does guerilla warfare define the revolution of our time?

Historical backwardness may again become the historical chance of turning the wheel of progress to another direction. Technical and scientific overdevelopment stands refuted when the radar-equipped bombers, the chemicals, and the "special forces" of the affluent society are let loose on the poorest of the earth, on their shacks, hospitals, and rice fields. The "accidents" reveal the substance: they tear the technological veil behind which the real powers are hiding. The capability to overkill and to overburn, and the mental behavior that goes with it are by-products of the development of the productive forces within a system of exploitation and repression; they seem to become more productive the more comfortable the system becomes to its privileged subjects. The affluent society has now demonstrated that it is a society at war; if its citizens have not noticed it, its victims certainly have.

The historical advantage of the late-comer, of technical backwardness, may be that of skipping the stage of the affluent society. Backward peoples by their poverty and weakness may be forced to forego the aggressive and wasteful use of science and technology, to keep the productive apparatus *à la mesure de l'homme*, under his control, for the satisfaction and development of vital individual and collective needs.

For the overdeveloped countries, this chance would be tantamount to the abolition of the conditions under which man's labor perpetuates, as self-propelling power, his subordination to the productive apparatus, and, with it, the obsolete forms of the struggle for existence. The abolition of these forms is, just as it has always been, the task of political action, but there is a decisive difference in the present situation. Whereas previous revolutions brought about a larger and more rational development of the productive forces, in the overdeveloped societies of today, revolution would mean reversal of this trend: elimination of overdevelopment, and of its repressive rationality. The rejection of affluent productivity, far from being a commitment to purity, simplicity, and "nature," might be the token (and weapon) of a higher stage of human development, based on the achievements of the technological society. As the production of wasteful and destructive goods is discontinued (a stage which would mean the end of capitalism in all its forms)— the somatic and mental mutilations inflicted on man by this production may be undone. In other words, the shaping of the environment, the transformation of nature, may be propelled by the liberated rather than the repressed Life Instincts, and aggression would be subjected to their demands.

The historical chance of the backward countries is in the absence of conditions which make for repressive exploitative technology and industrialization for aggressive productivity. The very fact that the affluent warfare state unleashes its annihilating power on the backward countries illuminates the magnitude of the threat. In the revolt of the backward peoples, the rich societies meet, in an elemental and brutal form, not only a social revolt in the traditional sense, but also an instinctual revolt—biological hatred. The spread of guerilla warfare at the height of the technological century is a symbolic event: the energy of the human body rebels against intolerable repression and throws itself against the engines of repression. Perhaps the rebels know nothing about the ways of organizing a society, of constructing a socialist society; perhaps they are terrorized by their own leaders who know something about it, but the rebels' frightful existence is in total need of liberation, and their freedom is the contradiction to the overdeveloped societies.

Western civilization has always glorified the hero, the sacrifice of life for the city, the state, the nation; it has rarely asked the question of whether the established city, state, nation were worth the sacrifice. The taboo on the unquestionable prerogative of the whole has always been maintained and enforced, and it has been maintained and enforced the more brutally the more the whole was supposed to consist of free individuals. The question is now being asked—asked from without—and it is taken up by those who refuse to play the game of the affluents—the question of whether the abolition of this whole is not the precondition for the emergence of a truly human city, state, nation.

The odds are overwhelmingly on the side of the powers that be. What is romantic is not the positive evaluation of the liberation movements in the backward countries, but the positive evaluation of their prospects. There is no reason why science, technology, and money should not again do the job of destruction, and then the job of reconstruction in their own image. The price of progress is frightfully high, but we shall overcome. Not only the deceived victims but also their chief of state have said so. And yet there are photographs that show a row of half naked corpses laid out for the victors in Vietnam: they resemble in all details the pictures of the starved, emasculated corpses of Auschwitz and Buchenwald. Nothing and nobody can ever overcome these deeds, nor the sense of guilt which reacts in further aggression. But aggression can be turned against the aggressor. The strange myth according to which the unhealing wound can only be healed by the weapon that afflicted the wound has not yet been validated in history: the violence which breaks the chain of violence may start a new chain. And yet, in and against this continuum, the fight will continue. It is not the struggle of Eros against Thanatos, because the established society too has its Eros: it protects, perpetuates, and enlarges life. And it is not a bad life for those who comply and repress. But in the balance, the general presumption is that aggressiveness in defense of life is less detrimental to the Life Instincts than aggressiveness in aggression.

In defense of life: the phrase has explosive meaning in the affluent society. It involves not only the protest against neo-colonial war and slaughter, the burning of draft cards at the risk of prison, the fight for civil rights, but also the refusal to speak the dead language of affluence, to wear the clean clothes, to enjoy the gadgets of affluence, to go through the education for affluence. The new bohème, the beatniks and hipsters, the peace creeps— all these "decadents" now have become what decadence probably always was: poor refuge of defamed humanity.

Can we speak of a juncture between the erotic and political dimension?

In and against the deadly efficient organization of the affluent society, not only radical protest, but even the attempt to formulate, to articulate, to give word to protest assume a childlike, ridiculous immaturity. Thus it is ridiculous and perhaps "logical" that the Free Speech Movement at Berkeley terminated in the row caused by the appearance of a sign with the four-letter word. It is perhaps equally ridiculous and right to see deeper significance in the buttons worn by some of the demonstrators (among them infants) against the slaughter in Vietnam: MAKE LOVE, NOT WAR. On the other side, against the new youth who refuse and rebel, are the representatives of the old order who can no longer protect its life without sacrificing it in the work of destruction and waste and pollution. They now include the representatives of organized labor—correctly so to the extent to which employment within the capitalist prosperity depends on the continued defense of the established social system.

Can the outcome, for the near future, be in doubt? The people, the majority of the people in the affluent society, are on the side of that which is—not that which can and ought to be. And the established order is strong enough and efficient enough to justify this adherence and to assure its continuation. However, the very strength and efficiency of this order may become factors of disintegration. Perpetuation of the obsolescent need for full-time labor (even in a very reduced form) will require the increasing waste of resources, the creation of ever more unnecessary jobs and services, and the growth of the military or destructive sector. Escalated wars, permanent preparation for war, and total administration may well suffice to keep the people under control, but at the cost of altering the morality on which the society still depends. Technical progress, itself a necessity for the maintenance of the established society, fosters needs and faculties which are antagonistic to the social organization of labor on which the system is built. In the course of automation, the value of the social product is to an increasingly smaller degree determined by the labor time necessary for its production. Consequently, the real social need for productive labor declines, and the vacuum must be filled with unproductive activities. An ever larger amount of the work actually performed becomes superfluous, expendable, meaningless. Although these activities can be sustained and even multiplied under total administration, there seems to exist an upper limit to their augmentation. This limit would be reached when the surplus value created by productive labor no longer suffices to pay for non-production work. A progressive reduction of labor seems to be inevitable, and for this eventuality, the system has to provide for occupation without work; it has to develop needs which transcend the market economy and may even be incompatible with it.

The affluent society is in its own way preparing for this eventuality by organizing "the desire for beauty and the hunger for community," the renewal of the "contact with nature," the enrichment of the mind, and honors for "creation for its own sake." The false ring of such proclamations is indicative of the fact that, within the established system, these aspirations are translated into administered cultural activities, sponsored by the government and the big corporations—an extension of their executive arm into the soul of the masses. It is all but impossible to recognize in the aspirations thus defined those of Eros and its autonomous transformation of a repressive environment and a repressive existence. If these goals are to be satisfied without an irreconcilable conflict with the requirements of the market economy, they must be satisfied within the framework of commerce and profit. But this sort of satisfaction would be tantamount to denial, for the erotic energy of the Life Instincts cannot be freed under the dehumanizing conditions of profitable affluence. To be sure, the conflict between the necessary development of noneconomic needs which would validate the idea of the abolition of labor (life as an end in itself) on the one hand, and the necessity for maintaining the need for earning a living on the other is quite manageable (especially as long as the Enemy within and without can serve as propelling force behind the defense of the status quo). However, the conflict may become explosive if it is accompanied and aggravated by the prospective changes at the very base of advanced industrial society, namely, the gradual undermining of capitalist enterprise in the course of automation.

In the meantime, there are things to be done. The system has its weakest point where it shows its most brutal strength: in the escalation of its military potential (which seems to press for periodic actualization with ever shorter interruptions of peace and preparedness). This tendency seems reversible only under strongest pressure, and its reversal would open the danger spots in the social structure: its conversion into a "normal" capitalist system is hardly imaginable without a serious crisis and sweeping economic and political changes. Today, the opposition to war and military intervention strikes at the roots: it rebels against those whose economic and political dominion depends on the continued (and enlarged) reproduction of the military establishment, its "multipliers," and the policies which necessitate this reproduction. These interests are not hard to identify, and the war against them does not require missiles, bombs, and napalm. But it does require something that is much harder to produce—the spread of uncensored and unmanipulated knowledge, consciousness, and above all, the organized refusal to continue work on the material and *intellectual* instruments which are now being used against man—for the defense of the liberty and prosperity of those who dominate the rest.

To the degree to which organized labor operates in defense of the status quo, and to the degree to which the share of labor in the material process of production declines, *intellectual* skills and capabilities become social and political factors. Today, the organized refusal to cooperate of the scientists, mathematicians, technicians, industrial psychologists and public opinion pollsters may well accomplish what a strike, even a large-scale strike, can no longer accomplish but once accomplished, namely, the beginning of the reversal, the preparation of the ground for political action. That the idea appears utterly unrealistic does not reduce the political responsibility involved in the position and function of the intellectual in contemporary industrial society. The intellectual refusal may find support in another catalyst, the instinctual refusal among the youth in protest. It is their lives which are at stake, and if not their lives, their mental health and their capacity to function as unmutilated humans. Their protest will continue because it is a biological necessity. "By nature," the young are in the forefront of those who live and fight for Eros against Death, and against a civilization which strives to shorten the "detour to death" while controlling the means for lengthening the detour. But in the administered society, the biological necessity does not immediately issue in action; organization demands counter-organization. Today the fight for life, the fight for Eros, is the *political* fight.

In *Eros and Civilization* (Boston: Beacon Press, 1966), xi–xxv.

1968

Mao Zedong

Talk to Leaders of the Centre (21 July 1966)

In 1966 Mao Zedong called upon young men and women in China to destroy their society. Formed into "Red Guard" groups, boys and girls attacked their teachers, government officials, and even parents for insufficient revolutionary zeal. Mao used these attacks to discredit his rivals. He also, paradoxically, strengthened his personal authority by undermining the very institutions he had built. Mao made himself into a deity for Chinese youth. He actively encouraged a "Great Proletarian Cultural Revolution" in the late 1960s, turning against it only when the chaos threatened his own safety. Although few observers understood the nature of events in China, the Cultural Revolution became an inspiration for young protesters in other parts of the world, especially in 1968.

Chairman Mao said that the 'May Twenty-fifth' big-character poster of Nieh Yüan-tzu is a manifesto of the Chinese Paris Commune of the sixties of the twentieth century, the significance of which surpasses the Paris Commune. This kind of big-character poster we are incapable of writing.

(Several Young Pioneers wrote big-character posters about their fathers saying that their fathers had forgotten their past, did not talk to them about Mao Tse-tung thought, but did ask them about the marks they got at school and rewarded them when they got good marks.)

Chairman Mao asked Comrade Ch'en Po-ta to pass on a message to these little friends: 'Your big-character posters are very well-written.' [He continued:]

83

I say to you all: youth is the great army of the Great Cultural Revolution! It must be mobilized to the full.

After my return to Peking I felt very unhappy and desolate. Some colleges even had their gates shut. There were even some which suppressed the student movement. Who is it who suppressed the student movement? Only the Pei-yang Warlords. It is anti-Marxist for communists to fear the student movement. Some people talk daily about the mass line and serving the people, but instead they follow the bourgeois line and serve the bourgeoisie. The Central Committee of the Youth League should stand on the side of the student movement. But instead it stands on the side of suppression of the student movement. Who opposes the great Cultural Revolution? The American imperialists, the Soviet revisionists, the Japanese revisionists and the reactionaries.

To use the excuse of distinguishing between 'inner' and 'outer' is to fear revolution. To cover over big-character posters which have been put up, such things cannot be allowed. This is a basic error of orientation. They must immediately change direction, and smash all the old conventions.

We believe in the masses. To become teachers of the masses we must first be the students of the masses. The present great Cultural Revolution is a heaven-and-earth-shaking event. Can we, dare we, cross the pass into socialism? This pass leads to the final destruction of classes, and the reduction of the three great differences.

To oppose, especially to oppose 'authoritative' bourgeois ideology, is to destroy. Without this destruction, socialism cannot be established nor can we carry out first struggle, second criticism, third transformation. Sitting in offices listening to reports is no good. The only way is to rely on the masses, trust the masses, struggle to the end. We must be prepared for the revolution to be turned against us. The Party and government leadership and responsible Party comrades should be prepared for this. If you now want to carry the revolution through to the end, you must discipline yourself, reform yourself in order to keep up with it. Otherwise you can only keep out of it.

There are some comrades who struggle fiercely against others, but cannot struggle with themselves. In this way, they will never be able to cross the pass.

It is up to you to lead the fire towards your own bodies, to fan the flames to make them burn. Do you dare to do this? Because it will burn your own heads.

The comrades replied thus: 'We are prepared. If we're not up to it, we will resign our jobs. We live as Communist Party members and shall die as Communist Party members. It doesn't do to live a life of sofas and electric fans.' [*Chairman Mao said:*]

It will not do to set rigid standards for the masses. When Peking University saw that the students were rising up, they tried to set standards. They euphemistically called it 'returning to the right track.' In fact it was 'diverting to the wrong track.'

There were some schools which labelled the students as counter-revolutionaries. (*Liaison officer Chang Yen went out and labelled twenty-nine people as counter-revolutionary.*) [*Chairman Mao said:*]

In this way you put the masses on the side of the opposition. You should not fear bad people. How many of them are there after all? The great majority of the student masses are good.

Someone raised the question of disturbances. What do we do in such cases about taking legal action? [*Chairman Mao said:*]

What are you afraid of? When bad people are involved you prove that they are bad. What do you fear about good people? You should replace the word 'fear' by the word 'dare.' You must demonstrate once and for all whether or not the pass into socialism has been crossed. You must put politics in command, go among the masses and be at one with them, and carry on the Great Proletarian Cultural Revolution even better.

In Stuart Schram, ed., *Chairman Mao Talks to the People: Talks and Letters, 1956–1971*, trans. John Chinnery and Tieyun (New York: Pantheon Books, 1974), 253–255.

Andrei Sakharov

Excerpt from **Memoirs**

---

*Andrei Sakharov emerged in 1968 as the most prominent and respected dissi-
dent in the Soviet Union. He was one of the foremost nuclear physicists of his
generation—the creator of the Soviet hydrogen bomb. Sakharov spoke out in
1968 against the militarism of Soviet policy and the repression within society.
He argued for a more cooperative policy with the United States and Western
Europe, foreseeing a time when the two Cold War systems—communism and
liberal capitalism—would converge into a common and peace-loving hybrid.
Sakharov's journey from Soviet hero to dissident inspired young people in his
home country and abroad. His decades of confinement by Soviet authorities
after 1968 made him a symbol for the cause of far-reaching political reform.*

---

19. The Turning Point

The years 1965–1967 were a turning point in my life. I was heavily involved in demanding scientific work, even as I was approaching a decisive break with the establishment.

I still spent most of my time at the Installation, where attention
was shifting from the development of nuclear devices to new ventures such as underground "breeder explosions" (which produce radioactive substances when uranium and thorium atoms capture
free neutrons and then split) and a nuclear propulsion system for
space flight. We spent much of our time developing specialized nuclear charges for nonmilitary applications, including copper mining
in Udokan and other strip mining projects, building dams and
canals, releasing underground oil reserves from shale, and capping
accidental blowoffs of oil and gas wells. The first and second Installations vied with each other in theoretical and experimental research into peaceful uses of nuclear explosions, but the serious risk
of contaminating the soil, groundwater, and atmosphere continually thwarted the practical application of our ideas.

Both Installations began to concentrate on problems requiring
an "operations research" approach. The first problem of this kind

we tackled was an investigation of antiballistic missile (ABM) systems and ways to counter them. In the course of many heated discussions, I, along with the majority of my colleagues, reached two conclusions which, in my view, remain valid today:

1) An effective ABM defense is not possible if the potential adversary can mobilize comparable technical and economic resources for military purposes. A way can always be found to neutralize an ABM defense system—and at considerably less expense than the cost of deploying it.

2) Over and above the burdensome cost, deployment of an ABM system is dangerous since it can upset the strategic balance. If both sides were to possess powerful ABM defenses, the main result would be to raise the threshold of strategic stability, or in somewhat simplified terms, increase the minimum number of nuclear weapons needed for mutual assured destruction.

These findings, which were apparently shared by American experts, probably helped pave the way for the 1972 Treaty on the Limitation of Antiballistic Missile Systems. I have continued to refine my ideas on ABM systems, and the evolution of my views can be traced in my written comments on the topic, especially *My Country and the World* (1975), my 1983 letter to Sidney Drell ("The Danger of Thermonuclear War"), and my talk on SDI [the Strategic Defense Initiative] delivered at the 1987 Forum for a Nuclear-Free World.

During the second half of the 1960s, I became involved in discussions of a still broader range of problems. I read economic and technical studies concerning the production of radioactive substances, nuclear weapons, and delivery systems, visited several secret military facilities (or "mailboxes" as we called them), and attended one or two conferences on military strategy. Inadvertently, I picked up quite a bit of information (I am thankful that I was not told everything, despite my high-level security clearance). What I learned was more than sufficient to impress upon me the horror, the real danger, and the utter insanity of thermonuclear warfare, which threatens everyone on earth. Our reports, and the conferences where we discussed a strategic thermonuclear strike on a potential enemy, transformed the unthinkable and monstrous into a subject for detailed investigation and calculation. It became a *fact of life*—still hypothetical, but already seen as something possible. I could not stop thinking about this, and I came to realize that the technical, military, and economic problems are secondary; the fundamental issues are political and ethical. Gradually, subconsciously, I was approaching an irrevocable step—a wide-ranging public statement on war and peace and other global issues. I took that step in 1968.

Adding my signature to a collective letter opposing the rehabilitation of Stalin was one of the significant harbingers of my 1968 essay.

In January 1966, Boris Geilikman, a neighbor formerly associated with FIAN and now at the Institute of Atomic Energy, escorted a short, energetic man to my apartment. He introduced himself as Ernst Henri, a journalist. (I later learned that Geilikman made this introduction at the request of Academician Vitaly Ginzburg.)

After Geilikman left, Henri came straight to the point. There was a real danger, he said, that the forthcoming Twenty-third Party Congress might adopt a resolution rehabilitating Stalin. Influential military and party circles—alarmed by the decay of ideology, the breakdown of values, and the loss of confidence following the failure of Alexei Kosygin's economic reforms—were pushing that idea. But many other Party members understood that Stalin's rehabilitation would have devastating consequences, and prominent representatives of the Soviet intelligentsia should support these "healthy forces."

Henri said he was aware of my stand on genetics, my major role in defense, and my authority. I read his draft letter, found nothing objectionable in it, and added my signature. Pyotr Kapitsa, Mikhail Leontovich, and five or six others had signed before me, but Henri's own name did not appear, because he wanted to limit the list to "celebrities." In total, twenty-five people eventually signed the letter, including the famous ballerina Maya Plisetskaya.

Rereading the letter now, I still agree with its assessment of Stalin's crimes, but I find the line of argument overly influenced by tactical considerations and the tone too deferential. At the time, however, my discussion of the letter with Henri and others greatly advanced my understanding of social issues.

Henri mentioned that foreign correspondents in Moscow would be briefed on the letter, and I made no objection. He asked me to pay a visit to Academician Andrei Kolmogorov, whose authority reached beyond mathematicians to Party and military circles.

Kolmogorov was then engaged in reorganizing the teaching of mathematics, but, in my opinion, his innovations were not constructive. Set theory and mathematical logic are too sophisticated for young students; they complicate the learning of practical mathematical techniques without inculcating a deeper understanding of mathematical principles. I prefer the traditional approach (after all, Euclid served many generations well before the advent of Bourbaki), and would add to it only the study of differential equations and other useful mathematical tools.

Kolmogorov agreed to see me, but made it clear that he was in a hurry. Although he was no longer young and his hair was streaked with gray, he appeared fit, suntanned, and vigorous. He was gentle in manner and speech, pronouncing his "r's" in the old, aristocratic way, and holding himself somewhat aloof. He read the letter, but refused to sign it, because, he said, the soldiers with whom he dealt all idolized Stalin for his wartime leadership. I replied that Stalin's role had been determined by his government post and not the other way around, and that he had committed numerous crimes and had made costly mistakes. Kolmogorov didn't disagree—but he still wouldn't sign. (A few weeks later, however, after foreign broadcasts reported our appeal, Kolmogorov did sign a similar collective letter opposing Stalin's rehabilitation.)

In retrospect, I now realize that Henri's letter was probably inspired by his influential friends in the Party machine or the KGB. Henri became a frequent visitor to my apartment and told me something of his past, leaving (I suspect) much unsaid. His real name is Semyon Rostovsky. In the 1920s he was a Comintern agent working underground in Germany, and he saw at first hand the absurdity of the Comintern's (that is, Stalin's) policy, which held Hitler's fascism to be a lesser evil than Social Democracy since the popularity of the latter's pluralist philosophy threatened the

Communists' monopoly of the working class. Stalin believed he could come to terms with Hitler on spheres of influence (or, if need be, destroy Hitler), but he feared the liberal center: it seemed dangerously beyond his control. Rostovsky wrote a number of articles warning against fascism, and his book *Hitler Over Europe?*[1] brought him fame under the pseudonym Ernst Henri, which he has maintained ever since.

Henri showed me a samizdat article he'd written on Stalin, and some correspondence with Ilya Ehrenburg on the subject. But Henri was never a "dissident."

In the fall of 1966, two men (one of whom, I think, was Geilikman; I don't recall the other) asked me to sign an appeal. Typed out on onionskin paper and addressed to the Supreme Soviet of the Russian Republic (the RSFSR), it opposed the impending enactment of Article 190-1 of the RSFSR Criminal Code [Circulation of Fabrications Known to Be False Which Defame the Soviet State or Social System; maximum sentence: three years labor camp] which would open the way for the prosecution of many more dissidents. Articles 70 [Anti-Soviet Propaganda; adopted in 1960; maximum sentence: ten years labor camp plus five years internal exile] and 190-1 subsequently served as the principal juridical weapons for the suppression of dissent [until they effectively were revoked in 1989].[2]

A prosecution under Article 70 required proof, at least in theory, of the defendant's anti-Soviet intent; Article 190-1 did not. On the other hand, the 1971 *Commentary on the Criminal Code* asserts that "the circulation of fabrications which are not known to be false by the party responsible, as well as the expression of mistaken opinions or suppositions do not constitute crimes under Article 190-1." In practice, however, no attention was paid to this commendable declaration. The courts regularly convicted dissidents for their beliefs, for expressing their opinions, and for reporting information they sincerely believed to be accurate. The statements at issue in such

[1][Simon and Schuster, 1934.]

[2][Harold Berman's *Soviet Criminal Law and Procedure*, 2nd edition (Harvard University Press, 1972), contains English translations of Article 70 (pp. 153–154) and Article 190-1 (pp. 180–181). The translation reflects the imprecise language of the Russian original.]

proceedings were based on actual fact (with the exception of a few accidental misunderstandings), and usually exposed human rights abuses such as dissident trials, conditions in labor camps, and the deportation of Crimean Tatars; or—even more telling—the secret additional protocol to the 1939 Soviet-German Non-aggression Pact, the mass executions of Polish officers at Katyn, and so on.[3]

Courts rarely bothered to try to demonstrate that a defendant's allegedly defamatory statements were false; it was enough to show that they were "anti-Soviet." Moreover, no attempt was made to prove that the defendant *deliberately* distorted facts.

Although the above comments are based on my subsequent experience in defending human rights, even in 1966 I realized that the alarm triggered by Article 190-1 was justified, and I signed the letter. In this case, it was clear that its authors were acting on their own initiative and accepted the responsibility for any repercussions. I not only signed the joint letter but, a couple of days later, sent a personal telegram to Mikhail Yasnov, chairman of the RSFSR Supreme Soviet, expressing my concern. There was no reply. (When I told the physicist Boris Ioffe what I had done, he said: "Andrei Dmitrievich, you really are a brave man!")

Since then, I have sent many other letters and telegrams to officials. With a few insignificant exceptions, I have never received a reply, and these efforts have produced little in the way of immediate results. Some people therefore regard them as a form of naïveté, while others condemn them as a dangerous and provocative "game." But I believe that statements on public issues are a useful means of promoting discussion, proposing alternatives to official policy, and focusing attention on specific problems. They educate the public at large, and just might stimulate significant changes, however belated, in the policy and practice of top government officials. Appeals on behalf of specific individuals and groups also attract attention to their cases, occasionally benefit a particular

[3][The Crimean Tatars are a Turkic people who since the early fifteenth century have considered themselves a national entity distinct from other descendants of the Mongols, a fact recognized by the Soviet authorities in 1921, when they created the Crimean Autonomous SSR. It was formally dissolved in 1945. See Alan Fisher, *Crimean Tatars* (Hoover Institution Press, 1978). For the Secret Protocol of the Molotov-Ribbentrop Pact, see *Nazi-Soviet Relations 1939–1941*, Department of State, 1948.]

individual, and inhibit future human rights violations through the threat of *glasnost* [public disclosure].

In dealing with civic issues and individual cases, it is most important that appeals be open. Private interventions are sometimes useful as a supplement—not a replacement—for public actions.

In this same year, 1966, I made an important new acquaintance—Zhores Medvedev's identical twin, Roy—who helped broaden my understanding of social problems. Roy, a historian by profession, visited me in my Moscow apartment, and told me about the book on Stalin he'd been working on since the Twentieth Party Congress in 1956.[4]

Roy's father, Alexander, a professor of philosophy, had been a member of a Communist opposition group in the early 1920s. He was arrested during the purges of the 1930s, and died in a labor camp. Roy told me he maintained close relations with many Old Bolsheviks, and their eyewitness accounts and unpublished memoirs provided a wealth of previously unknown details for *Let History Judge*.

Roy left several chapters of his manuscript with me. He was to come back many times, bringing me new chapters in return for the old. He loaned me other samizdat manuscripts, including Eugenia Ginzburg's *Journey into the Whirlwind*,[5] one of the better-known memoirs of Stalin's camps. He also brought me news about dissidents and events of social significance. Some of his reports may have been biased or slanted, but when all is said and done, they did help me escape from my hermetic world. One story he told me (I believe during our first meeting; I can't vouch for its reliability) was about Pyotr Yakir visiting Zeldovich to get his signature on the collective letter protesting Article 190-1. When asked whether he himself had signed, Yakir admitted he hadn't. "After you," he was told. Yakir signed, and Zeldovich followed suit. I'm not at all sure he would have done so later on.

I was fascinated by Medvedev's book on Stalin. I hadn't yet read Robert Conquest's *The Great Terror*, or any other works on the sub-

---

[4][Published in a slightly abridged English translation as: *Let History Judge* (Knopf, 1971) and reissued in a revised version by Columbia University Press in 1989.]

[5][Eugenia Ginzburg, *Journey into the Whirlwind* (Harcourt Brace & World, 1967). A second volume was published posthumously by Harcourt Brace Jovanovich in 1981.]

ject, and was largely ignorant of the crimes of the Stalin era. An example of the kind of material Medvedev succeeded in uncovering was the report of the special commission established by Khrushchev to investigate the 1934 murder of Sergei Kirov—a detailed description of the assassination of Stalin's rival and of the subsequent elimination of all eyewitnesses to the crime and to the cover-up.[6] The information contained in *Let History Judge* stimulated the evolution of my views at a crucial time in my life.

Even in 1966, however, I couldn't accept Medvedev's tendency to attribute all the tragic events of the 1920s to the 1950s to the idiosyncrasies of Stalin's personality. Although Medvedev agreed in principle that more fundamental causes were at work, his book failed to explore them. We must still look to the future for a satisfactory analysis of our history, one free from dogmatism, political prejudice, and other forms of bias.

Roy Medvedev and I continued to meet for some years, but then our paths, both public and private, diverged, until we broke off relations after 1973.

On December 3 or 4, 1966, I found an envelope in my mailbox containing two sheets of onionskin paper. The first sheet was an anonymous report on the arrest and confinement in a psychiatric hospital of Viktor Kuznetsov, an artist who had helped draft a model constitution for our country—Constitution II—which the authors hoped would spark discussion about the introduction of democracy.

The second sheet announced a silent demonstration on December 5, Constitution Day. It proposed that interested persons arrive at Pushkin Square a few minutes before six P.M., assemble near the monument, and then at the stroke of the hour remove their hats and observe a minute of silence as a sign of respect for the Constitution and support for political prisoners, including Kuznetsov. (I learned much later that Alexander Esenin-Volpin was the author of this Constitution Day appeal, and of several other original and effective ideas to promote respect for human rights.)

---

[6][*Let History Judge* (pp. 157–166) suggests Stalin's complicity in Kirov's murder, the act which triggered the bloody purges of the 1930s.]

I decided to attend. Klava didn't object, though she did say it was an odd thing to do. I took a taxi to Pushkin Square and found a few dozen people standing around the statue. Some were talking quietly; I didn't recognize anyone. At six o'clock, half of those present, myself included, removed our hats and stood in silence. (The other half, I later realized, were KGB.) After a minute or so we put our hats back on, but we did not disperse immediately. I walked over to the monument and read the inscription aloud:

> I shall be loved, and the people will long remember
> that my lyre was tuned to goodness,
> that in this cruel age I celebrated freedom
> and asked mercy for the fallen.[7]

After that, I left the Square with the others.

Sometime later, Yuri Zhivlyuk—another new acquaintance of 1966—told me that my "escapade" had been filmed by the KGB using infrared film (it had been dusk on the Square) and then shown to high officials. I have never completely understood Zhivlyuk. He was working at FIAN when I met him, and people there told me that in the mid-1960s he had been Komsomol secretary in one of the laboratories. A samizdat document, Valery Skurlatov's "A Code of Morals,"[8] was circulating among Komsomol members at the time; I don't know whether this fascist program represented Skurlatov's own views or was a trial balloon launched by some faction using him as a stalking-horse. In any event, Zhivlyuk wrote a bitter complaint to the Komsomol Central Committee, which proceeded to punish both parties—Skurlatov for his essay, and Zhivlyuk for "washing dirty linen in public."

Despite this rebuke, Zhivlyuk maintained some sort of relations with the Komsomol Central Committee, and was sent on a fact-finding mission to Bratsk and the far north in 1969. He told me about the economic and ecological problems of the region and described the deliberate corruption of Siberian trappers. A govern-

---

[7][Alexander Pushkin, "Unto myself I reared a monument," 1836.]

[8][English translation of Skurlatov's "A Code of Morals," in Stephen F. Cohen, ed., *An End to Silence* (Norton, 1982), pp. 171–174. Skurlatov worked in the propaganda department of the Moscow Komsomol.]

ment procurement official would fly into a settlement in a helicopter loaded with vodka. After a few days the trappers and their parents, wives, and children would all be drunk, and the helicopter would fly off with furs for export.

Zhivlyuk was of Ukrainian descent and had ties to dissidents in the Ukraine. He introduced me to Ivan Svetlichny, a poet and Ukrainian activist. Zhivlyuk also had contacts among Moscow dissidents, Andrei Tverdokhlebov in particular. I suspect Zhivlyuk may have had some sort of link with the KGB (perhaps with its "progressive circles"). In the 1970s he apparently became ensnared in this tangled skein of relationships, and he disappeared from my field of vision.

Early in 1967, Zhivlyuk told me about the case involving Alexander Ginzburg, Yuri Galanskov, Alexei Dobrovolsky, and Vera Lashkova, and the demonstration organized in their defense by Vladimir Bukovsky and Viktor Khaustov. These events, like the February 1966 trial of the writers Andrei Sinyavsky and Yuli Daniel, played a critical role in shaping public consciousness and in forging the human rights movement in our country.[9]

When I heard of the case of Ginzburg and the others, I recalled that in mid-1966 Ernst Henri had shown me Ginzburg's letter of recantation which had appeared in the newspaper *Vechernaya Moskva* [on June 3, 1965]. I still don't know who was behind Henri's attempt to scare me away from Ginzburg, but in February 1967, I decided to ignore his warning. I used Zhivlyuk's information to write Leonid Brezhnev in defense of Ginzburg, Galanskov, Lashkova, and Dobrovolsky. Although I neither circulated my letter in samizdat nor publicized it in any way, it was a milestone for me in that it was my first intervention on behalf of specific dissidents. (During the Sinyavsky-Daniel trial I was still "out of things," and I paid little attention to Mikhail Sholokhov's speech at the Twenty-third Party Congress recalling that "in the memorable twenties . . . scoundrels and turncoats" like Sinyavsky and Daniel were shot.)

---

[9][For information on the Sinyavsky-Daniel trial see: Max Hayward, editor, *On Trial* (2nd edition, Harper & Row, 1967); on the Ginzburg-Galanskov trial: Pavel Litvinov, ed., *The Trial of the Four* (Viking, 1972); and on the trials resulting from the Bukovsky-Khaustov demonstration: Pavel Litvinov, editor, *The Demonstration in Pushkin Square*, (Harvill Press, 1969). For a general history of the diverse dissident movements, see Ludmilla Alexeyeva, *Soviet Dissent* (Wesleyan University Press, 1985).]

The Ministry learned of my letter. Friends reported that Efim Slavsky had told participants in a Party conference held at the second Installation in March: "Sakharov is a good scientist. He's accomplished a great deal and we've rewarded him well. But as a politician he's muddleheaded, and we'll be taking measures."

Measures were indeed taken. I lost my post as department head, even though I remained deputy scientific director of the Installation. My salary was reduced from 1,000 to 550 rubles a month. (This wasn't the first reduction.) The Chief of Administration, Tsirkov (who had switched from experimental work on magnetic cumulation to administrative work) reportedly said that he didn't understand how anyone could live on so little, even though by ordinary Soviet standards I still enjoyed a high salary.

In April or May of 1967, Academician Vladimir Kirillin, then chairman of the Committee on Science and Technology and a deputy of Premier Kosygin, invited me to his office. At the appointed time, a dozen or so prominent scientists and engineers, including Vitaly Ginzburg, Yakov Zeldovich, and Ilya Lifshitz, sat down to a table set for tea. Kirillin told us that futurological studies were enjoying a vogue in the United States. Although some of the articles being published were trivial, sophisticated futurology could provide a long-range perspective useful for planning. Kirillin asked us to set down our thoughts on the development of science and technology in the coming decades. We should write without constraint, concentrating on the scientific fields we knew best, but touching on more general questions if we so desired.

I carried out Kirillin's assignment with enthusiasm and managed to include quite a few flights of fancy in a relatively short article. On the plane en route from the Installation to Moscow, I exchanged manuscripts with Zeldovich, and he complimented me on my essay. It was published in 1967 in *The Future of Science*, edited by Kirillin and distributed on a restricted basis.

The work I did on this article had a profound psychological effect on me, and turned my thoughts once again to global issues. Some of my propositions resurfaced later in *Reflections on Progress, Peaceful Coexistence, and Intellectual Freedom* and in the article "The World after Fifty Years."

* * *

That same year, I tried my hand at writing once more. Henri suggested that he and I collaborate on an article about the present-day role and responsibility of the intelligentsia: he would ask questions and I would respond. I agreed and we set to work, but my answers were more radical than he had anticipated—I was by now approaching the ideas which were to find expression in *Reflections*.

I took the manuscript to a typist who lived near the Sokol metro station, three bus stops from my Moscow apartment—a woman I had been employing for several years to type up scientific reports. When she handed back the last section of this new article, she was visibly upset. There had been a change in her family situation, she told me, and she could no longer work for me. It was obvious she was hiding something—a visit from the KGB, I suspect. After this experience, I had *Reflections* typed at the Installation.

The editors of *Literaturnaya gazeta* told Henri they needed permission from above to publish the article. Apparently, I'd gone further than they'd expected when they agreed in principle to the project. At Henri's request, I sent the manuscript to Mikhail Suslov via the Ministry. Two or three weeks later I received a letter from his secretary stating that Suslov found the manuscript interesting, but unsuitable for immediate publication since its ideas might be interpreted incorrectly. I returned the manuscript to Henri, visiting his apartment for the first time. It was spacious, evidently a bachelor's establishment, crammed with books and mementos of his years abroad. At that point, I promptly forgot the whole affair.

But that was not the end of the story. Some time later I discovered that the article had been included in a typescript periodical, *Political Diary*, rumored to be a KGB publication, or samizdat for officials. Several years after that, Roy Medvedev announced that he had been its editor. To this day, I wonder how my article ended up in his hands.[10]

---

[10][The Sakharov-Henri article, "Scientists and the Danger of Nuclear War," appears in *An End to Silence*, pp. 228–234. Roy Medvedev claims in his foreword (p. 20) that Sakharov was a regular reader of his monthly bulletin which circulated among a few dozen intellectuals from 1964 to 1971; but he did not recognize the name *Political Diary*, which was used only for foreign consumption.]

In June or July 1967, at Leontovich's suggestion, I was given Larisa Bogoraz's letter describing the desperate situation of her husband, Yuli Daniel, and an account of her visit to the Mordovian labor camp where he was serving his sentence. I was about to fly back to the Installation and took the letter with me.

I called Yuri Andropov on the high-frequency telephone from my office at the Installation. Andropov told me he'd already received eighteen requests to look into the Daniel case (even back then, I had some difficulty in believing his statement), and that he would do so. He urged me to send him the original of the letter, and when I asked why, he answered, "For my collection." I pretended I had misunderstood, and mailed him a retyped copy.

Six weeks later, Deputy Procurator General Mikhail Malyarov (the same man who in 1973 would warn me about my conduct) phoned my Moscow apartment. He said that he'd checked on Daniel at Comrade Andropov's request and that both Daniel and Sinyavsky would be released under an amnesty slated for the fiftieth anniversary of the October revolution. I thanked him for this information, which, however, turned out to be false. As usual, the amnesty did not apply to political prisoners. (Roy Medvedev later assured me that the decision to exclude political prisoners had been made at the last moment, but, as always with Medvedev, I don't know where he got his information, and I have some doubts about its accuracy.)

In 1967, I became involved in the effort to save Lake Baikal. The deepest lake in the world, it is an immense reservoir of fresh water. Even more important, the Baikal region is a unique phenomenon of nature, an area of surpassing beauty which has become for many a symbol of our nation. For several years, *Komsomolskaya pravda*, *Literaturnaya gazeta*, and other newspapers had been publishing alarming—and convincing—reports on threats to Baikal from industrial construction along its shores, the felling and rafting of timber, and the discharge of chemical wastes into its waters. Though our efforts to protect Baikal were unsuccessful, I did gain valuable insight into environmental problems, both in general and in the particular context of Soviet society. (Later on, in Gorky, I read Boris Komarov's *The Destruction of Nature*,[11] a comprehensive discussion of environmental problems in the USSR, including Baikal, and a work I recommend highly.)

Let me describe my part in the Baikal campaign. Early in 1967, a student at the Moscow Institute of Energy visited me on behalf of the Komsomol's Committee to Save Baikal. He invited me to attend the committee's meetings, to study the issue, and to join in the defense of Baikal. I took the matter seriously, and a few days later I visited the Komsomol building on Serov Passage where the meetings were held.

Among the committee's members, I recall Academician Igor Petryanov-Sokolov (the inventor of the Petryanov dust filter); the aircraft designer Oleg Antonov; the journalist Oleg Volkov, a former inmate of Stalin's camps; a member of the RSFSR State Construction Board whose name I have forgotten (he and Volkov were the two best informed and most active members); the limnologist Nikolai Nikolsky; and finally the student who had invited me and who represented the Komsomol on the committee. I was shown a number of startling documents on Baikal and on other ecological problems. Petryanov spoke about his specialty, industrial air pollution, which in some localities was catastrophic. Data on air pollution was classified and, as far as I know, remains so. I also learned about the long-term harm done by the flooding of arable land behind hydroelectric dams built in relatively flat regions.

I conducted some research on my own, meeting with Professor Rogozin, a specialist in the cellulose industry. I learned that in the late 1950s, Orlov, the minister in charge of the paper industry, had ordered construction of a large cellulose complex on the shores of Lake Baikal. This facility was designed to produce a particularly durable viscose rayon cord for airplane tires. It was assumed that polymerization would be facilitated by the pure Baikal water, and the resulting fibers would be stronger, but the plant's actual output showed that this hypothesis was unfounded. More important, the aviation industry switched from rayon cord to metallic cord. Thus,

[11][*The Destruction of Nature in the Soviet Union* (M. E. Sharpe, 1980). Boris Komarov is the pseudonym of Zev Wolfson, an ecologist educated at Moscow University who emigrated to Israel in 1981.]

whatever rationale the Baikal complex may once have had—and it never, in any case, offset the potential harm to the lake—vanished. Construction nevertheless went ahead, and whole armies of officials, defending their unfortunate decision and their "regimental honor," continued to insist on the importance of the complex for the defense of the country, the usual clinching argument.

The story goes that Orlov had chosen the site by simply pointing to a place on the shoreline while cruising in a motorboat with his cronies. Building was already under way when Baikal's defenders discovered that this was the precise spot where the famous Verninsky earthquake had caused the lake to swallow up thirty-five acres of shoreline in the last century; it was a seismically active region. Telegrams were duly dispatched to Moscow, but instead of canceling the project, the only reasonable course of action, the authorities transferred responsibility to a new contractor—the Ministry of Medium Machine Building. (Petryanov taunted me: "Do you know who's in charge of the murder of Baikal? Your own Slavsky!") New plans were drawn up for earthquake-resistant multistory aluminum and glass buildings supported by steel piles. It was an engineering miracle, but construction costs had multiplied, and the buildings are still vulnerable to the major earthquakes that have occurred there once or twice a century. As its reward, the Ministry of Medium Machine Building was permitted to cut timber in the Baikal preserve!

The big problem now was treatment of toxic waste. The appropriate institutes worked out a scheme for biological purification, after which the effluents were to flow through a canal into the Angara River, bypassing Baikal. The scientists defending the lake pointed to flaws in the proposal, and their fears proved more than justified when the complex began operating. The Academy of Sciences appointed a commission of experts chaired by Academician Nikolai Zhavoronkov, a chemist with little competence in this particular field but responsive to the wishes of the Academy's president and the State Planning Committee.

Our committee had assembled extensive documentation on the damage to the lake and its surrounding area which could come about through human activity. The pollution caused by floating logs down the rivers which empty into the lake kills the spawn of most fish, including the Baikal *omul*, which a century ago rivaled beef as a source of food for all Russia. The accidental discharge of effluents, deforestation, and fire are other hazards threatening the fragile ecological balance of the Baikal region. We proposed that the lake shores be closed to new industry and that existing enterprises be moved. We calculated the expense of such relocation and showed that it was not excessive—far less than had already been spent on the Baikal project. Our report, signed by us and also by a secretary of the Komsomol Central Committee, was sent to the Party Central Committee together with a sampling of the seven thousand letters on Baikal received by *Literaturnaya gazeta* and *Komsomolskaya pravda*.

For good measure, I decided to telephone Brezhnev personally; it was the last conversation we ever had. He was friendly and courteous, but complained of overwork and suggested that I talk to Kosygin, who was handling the Baikal matter. Unfortunately, I failed to follow up. I had never dealt with Kosygin, did not know him personally, and feared that without preliminary spadework, a call would be useless. I knew nothing about the relations between Brezhnev and Kosygin and didn't realize that Brezhnev was in fact shifting responsibility for an unpleasant task onto someone else. My call to the head of state, I thought, was all that was needed: if Brezhnev and Kosygin were interested (I made no distinction between them), they would take appropriate action. I was wrong.

I soon learned that a final decision had been made at a meeting of the Council of Ministers attended by Mstislav Keldysh, President of the Academy of Sciences, and, I think, Zhavoronkov. Kosygin asked Keldysh: "What does the Academy recommend? If the safeguards aren't reliable, we'll stop construction."

Keldysh reported the Zhavoronkov commission's conclusion: the water purification system and the other safeguards for Baikal were completely reliable. He may, of course, have been acting in good faith. Possibly he felt that he was choosing "the lesser evil"; the ecological peril most likely seemed less threatening to him than it did to our committee. Still, my feeling is that his stand and his general outlook were greatly influenced by the Academy's administrative dependence on the bureaucratic machine headed by the Central Committee, the State Planning Committee, the ministries, etc.

Keldysh and the Academy's presidium were predisposed to respect the wishes of this machine and to ignore the warnings of whistle-blowers, dismissing their arguments *a priori* as demagogic, exaggerated, impractical, and generally nonsensical.

Only a couple of years after these events, a Komsomol expedition brought back photographs showing the massive destruction of Baikal's fish and plankton caused by toxic wastes. But in accordance with standing instructions, no accidental discharges had been logged. As always, everything was fine on paper.

20. 1968

The Prague Spring.
*Reflections on Progress, Peaceful
Coexistence, and Intellectual Freedom.*

By the beginning of 1968, I felt a growing compulsion to speak out on the fundamental issues of our age. I was influenced by my life experience and a feeling of personal responsibility, reinforced by the part I'd played in the development of the hydrogen bomb, the special knowledge I'd gained about thermonuclear warfare, my bitter struggle to ban nuclear testing, and my familiarity with the Soviet system. My reading and my discussions with Tamm (and others) had acquainted me with the notions of an open society, convergence, and world government (Tamm was skeptical about the last two points). I shared the hopes of Einstein, Bohr, Russell, Szilard, and other Western intellectuals that these notions, which had gained currency after World War II, might ease the tragic crisis of our age. In 1968, I took my decisive step by publishing *Reflections on Progress, Peaceful Coexistence, and Intellectual Freedom.*

My work on *Reflections* happened to coincide with the Prague Spring. A year earlier, I'd finally bought a short-wave receiver, and I listened once in a while to the BBC and Voice of America, especially to programs on the Six Day War. In 1968, I began tuning in regularly to the news from Czechoslovakia, and heard Ludvík Vaculík's stirring manifesto, "2,000 Words"—and much more besides. Zhivlyuk and Roy Medvedev supplied additional details during their increasingly frequent visits.

What so many of us in the socialist countries had been dreaming of seemed to be finally coming to pass in Czechoslovakia: democracy, including freedom of expression and abolition of censorship; reform of the economic and social systems; curbs on the power of the security forces, limiting them to defense against external threats; and full disclosure of the crimes of the Stalin era (the "Gottwald era" in Czechoslovakia). Even from afar, we were caught up in all the excitement and hopes and enthusiasm of the catchwords: "Prague Spring" and "socialism with a human face."

Events in the Soviet Union echoed those in Prague, but on a much reduced scale. In the campaign in defense of Ginzburg, Galanskov, and Lashkova [who were tried in January 1968], more than a thousand signatures—an extraordinary number under Soviet conditions—were collected, mainly from the intelligentsia. A few years earlier, no one would have dreamed of publicly defending such "hostile elements." Later, after 1968, when everyone understood the consequences for himself and his family, even sympathetic people refused to lend their names to such initiatives. The signature campaign and other similar efforts were harbingers of the human rights movement, a sort of Prague Spring in miniature. They frightened the KGB into taking tough countermeasures: firing, blacklisting, public reprimand, expulsion from the Party.

To my shame, I must admit that the signature campaign simply passed me by at the time, just as had the 1964 banishment of Joseph Brodsky from Leningrad and the 1965 arrests of Sinyavsky and Daniel. For some reason, Roy Medvedev and Zhivlyuk delayed telling me about the campaign until it was over.

Sometime around the end of January 1968, Zhivlyuk suggested that I write an article on the role of the intelligentsia in today's world. The idea appealed to me, and I soon set to work. I did most of my writing at the Installation after working hours, from seven to midnight, and brought the draft home with me when I visited Moscow. Klava's attitude toward my project was ambivalent: she knew full well what I was doing and the potential consequences for our family, but she allowed me complete freedom of action. By this time her health was beginning to deteriorate, draining more and more of her physical and emotional energy.

The title I gave my essay, *Reflections on Progress, Peaceful Coexistence, and Intellectual Freedom,* seemed appropriate in tone for a non-specialist inviting his readers to join him in a discussion of public issues. Its scope far exceeded Zhivlyuk's original suggestion, encompassing virtually the entire range of my future public activities and laying a theoretical foundation for them. I wanted to alert my readers to the grave perils threatening the human race—thermonuclear extinction, ecological catastrophe, famine, an uncontrolled population explosion, alienation, and dogmatic distortion of our conception of reality. I argued for *convergence,* for a rapprochement of the socialist and capitalist systems that could eliminate or substantially reduce these dangers, which had been increased many times over by the division of the world into opposing camps. Economic, social, and ideological convergence should bring about a scientifically governed, democratic, pluralistic society free of intolerance and dogmatism, a humanitarian society which would care for the Earth and its future, and would embody the positive features of both systems.

I went into some detail on the threat posed by thermonuclear missiles—their enormous destructive power, their relatively low cost, the difficulty of defending against them. I wrote about the crimes of Stalinism and the need to expose them fully (unlike the Soviet press, I pulled no punches), and about the vital importance of freedom of opinion and democracy. I stressed the value of progress, but warned that it must be scientifically managed and not left to chance. I discussed the need for substantive changes in foreign policy. My essay outlined a positive, global program for mankind's future; I freely acknowledged that my vision was somewhat utopian, but I remain convinced that the exercise was worthwhile.

Later on, life (and Lusia) would teach me to pay more attention to the defense of individual victims of injustice, and a further step followed: recognition that human rights and an *open society* are fundamental to international confidence, security, and progress.

I prefaced *Reflections* with an epigraph taken from Goethe's *Faust*:

> He alone is worthy of life and freedom
> Who each day does battle for them anew!

The heroic romanticism of these lines echoes my own sense of life as both wonderful and tragic, and I still consider them a fitting choice for my essay. Years later I learned that Lusia, who then knew nothing about me, was captivated by the youthful and romantic spirit of this verse, and it established a spiritual bond between us before we ever met.

Another aspect of the truth that I prize and that complements Goethe's metaphor is contained in the following lines by Alexander Mezhirov:

> I lie in a trench under fire.
> A man enters his home, from the cold.

Mezhirov understands that struggle, suffering, and heroic exploits are not ends in themselves, but are worthwhile only insofar as they enable other people to lead normal, peaceful lives. Not everyone need spend time in the trenches. The meaning of life is life itself: that daily routine which demands its own form of unobtrusive heroism. Goethe's lines are often read as an imperative call to revolutionary struggle, but that seems to me unjustified; there is nothing peremptory or fanatical in them once they are stripped of their poetic imagery. *Reflections* rejected all extremes, the intransigence shared by revolutionaries and reactionaries alike. It called for compromise and for progress moderated by enlightened conservatism and caution. Marx notwithstanding, evolution is a better "locomotive of history" than revolution: the "battle" I had in mind was nonviolent.

I rewrote *Reflections* several times, and did, I feel, finally achieve a logical and coherent presentation of my thoughts. But the essay's literary quality leaves a lot to be desired; it suffered from my inexperience and lack of editorial counsel and, in some sections, from a lack of literary taste.

By mid-April, the essay was almost completed. Zhores Medvedev has written that I tried to keep its contents a secret by having several different secretaries type *Reflections*, and Solzhenitsyn has unfortunately repeated this fiction as evidence of my supposed naïveté.[1] The manuscript was in fact typed by a single secretary who had secret clearance. I realized that a copy might well end up in the KGB's ideological department, but I had no wish to lay myself open to allegations of engaging in covert activities. In my situation,

---

[1] [*The Oak and the Calf*, pp. 368–369.]

any attempts along these lines were bound to be uncovered, and I have always shunned clandestine behavior as a matter of principle.

As far as I know, the KGB did not intervene until *Reflections* began to circulate in Moscow. Before that, it's probable that only the counterintelligence department knew of the manuscript's existence, and they didn't care. At the end of May, however, the KGB was alerted at the Installation, and customs control was reinforced in Moscow. I've been told that two KGB divisions (this may well be an exaggeration) were involved in "Operation Sakharov," the fruitless attempt to prevent the circulation of *Reflections*. But I'm getting ahead of my story.

On the last Friday in April, I flew to Moscow for the holidays, bringing a typed copy of the essay in my briefcase. Roy Medvedev came to see me that evening, and I exchanged *Reflections* for the final chapters of his book on Stalin.

Medvedev claimed that Sergei Trapeznikov, head of the Central Committee's science department, was exerting a negative influence on Brezhnev and through him on domestic and foreign policy in general. I was persuaded to include a reference to Trapeznikov in *Reflections*; I now regret this personal attack, which was entirely out of character for me and alien to the style and spirit of an essay calling for reason, tolerance, and compromise. Moreover, my comments were based on uncorroborated hearsay; ever since meeting Trapeznikov in 1970, I have found it difficult to believe that he could have played a significant political role.

Medvedev came back a few days later. He had shown my essay to friends (which I had given him permission to do); they considered it a historic document, and he passed on some of their written comments. (These were unsigned, but the authors probably included Evgeny Gnedin, Yuri Zhivlyuk, and Eugenia Ginzburg, plus a few Old Bolsheviks and writers.) After adding the new paragraphs on Trapeznikov, and making a few other changes and corrections, I gave the manuscript back to Medvedev. He was going to produce a dozen or more carbon copies. Some of these, he warned me, might end up abroad. I replied that I had taken that into account. (We were communicating in writing to foil eavesdroppers.)

On May 18, I paid a call on Khariton at his dacha. In the course of our conversation, I mentioned that I was writing an essay on war and peace, ecology, and freedom of expression. Khariton asked what I intended to do with it. "I'll give it to samizdat," I answered. He became excited and said: "For God's sake, don't do that." "It's too late to stop it now," I confessed. Khariton became even more agitated and changed the subject. Later he pretended that this conversation never took place, which was fine from my point of view.

Early in June (probably on the 6th), I traveled with Khariton to the Installation in his personal railroad car, which contained a spacious compartment for him, a compartment for guests, the conductor's compartment, a kitchenette, and a lounge which could sleep several persons on folding cots (I often slept there myself). After the waitress had cleared the supper dishes and left the lounge, Khariton broached a subject that was plainly difficult for him: "Andropov called me in. His agents have been finding [in the course of clandestine searches] copies of your essay all over the place—it's circulating illegally, and it will cause a lot of harm if it gets abroad. Andropov opened his safe and showed me a copy. [From the way Khariton said this, it was obvious that he hadn't been allowed to examine the copy—hardly the way to treat a three-time Hero of Socialist Labor.] Andropov asked me to talk to you. You ought to withdraw your manuscript from circulation."

"Why don't you take a look at the copy I've got with me?" I suggested.

Khariton retired to his compartment, where he had a desk and a table lamp. I fell right to sleep in the guest compartment, despite the stuffiness of that prerevolutionary railroad car.

In the morning we met again.

"Well, what do you think?" I inquired.

"It's awful."

"The style?"

Khariton grimaced. "No, not the style. It's the *content* that's awful!"

"The contents reflect my beliefs. I accept full responsibility for circulating my essay. It's too late to withdraw it."

For the rest of June, I continued to tinker with the essay, but succeeded only in making it longer, not better. I sent a copy of the slightly revised version to Brezhnev, and showed another copy to Boris Efimov, who preferred the first version. I was unaware that an attempt had already been made to send my essay abroad through a

New York Times correspondent; he had refused, fearing a provocation.

In mid-June, Andrei Amalrik gave a copy of *Reflections* to Karel van het Reve, a Dutch correspondent.

On July 10, a few days after returning to the Installation and exactly seven years after my clash with Khrushchev, I tuned in the BBC (or VOA?) evening broadcast and heard my name. The announcer reported that on July 6, the Dutch newspaper *Het Parool* had published an article by A. D. Sakharov, a member of the Soviet Academy of Sciences who, according to Western experts, had worked on the Soviet hydrogen bomb. Sakharov called for rapprochement between the USSR and the West, and for disarmament; warned of the dangers of the thermonuclear war, ecological catastrophe, and world famine; condemned dogmatism, terror, and Stalin's crimes; and urged democratization, freedom of conscience, and convergence as the way to escape universal destruction. (I don't now recall the broadcast's exact words, but this is the gist of what I hope I heard, and in any case did read later in a number of well-informed reviews of my essay.)

The die was cast. That evening I had the most profound feeling of satisfaction. The following day I was due to fly to Moscow, but stopped at my office at nine in the morning and noticed Khariton at his desk.

"Foreign stations announced yesterday that my article's been published abroad."

"I knew it would happen" was all Khariton could say. He looked crushed.

Two hours later, I left for the airfield. I was never to set foot in my office again.

Toward the end of July, Slavsky summoned me to the Ministry. A translation of *Reflections* from the Dutch newspaper lay on his desk. "Your article?" he asked. I glanced through it and answered in the affirmative.

"Is it the same one you sent to the Central Committee?"

"Not quite, I revised it a bit."

"Give me the new text. Will you protest publication abroad of a preliminary draft without your permission?"

"No, I won't do that. I take full responsibility for the article as published, since it faithfully reflects my opinions."

Slavsky obviously wanted me to make some protest, if only about minor editorial details, but I didn't fall into that trap.

Clearly disappointed, Slavsky made no effort to hide his displeasure: "We won't discuss your opinions today. Party secretaries have been calling from all over the country, demanding firm measures to put a stop to counterrevolutionary propaganda in my ministry. I want you to think about what you've done to us and to yourself. You've got to disown this anti-Soviet publication. I'll read your revised version. Come back three days from now at the same time."

Three days later, Slavsky continued the lecture:

"I've taken a look, and the two versions are practically the same. It's a dangerous muddle. You write about the mistakes of the personality cult as though the Party had never condemned them. You criticize the leaders' privileges—you've enjoyed the same privileges yourself. Individuals who bear immense responsibilities, difficult burdens, deserve *some* advantages. It's all for the good of the cause. You pit the intelligentsia against the leadership, but aren't we, who manage the country, the real intelligentsia of the nation?

"What you wrote about convergence is utopian nonsense. Capitalism can't be made humane. Their social programs and employee stock plans aren't steps toward socialism. And there's no trace of state capitalism in the USSR. We'll never give up the advantages of our system, and capitalists aren't interested in your convergence either.

"The Party has condemned the cult of personality, but without a strong hand, we could never have rebuilt our economy after the war or broken the American atomic monopoly—you yourself helped do that. You have no moral right to judge our generation—Stalin's generation—for its mistakes, for its brutality; you're now enjoying the fruits of our labor and our sacrifices.

"Convergence is a dream. We've got to be strong, stronger than the capitalists—then there'll be peace. If war breaks out and the imperialists use nuclear weapons, we'll retaliate at once with everything we've got and destroy their launch sites and every target necessary to ensure victory."

My understanding then and my recollection now is that Slavsky was speaking only about a *retaliatory* strike, but our response would be an immediate, all-out nuclear attack on enemy cities and industry as well as on military targets. The most alarming thing was that he completely ignored the question of what, other than military force, might prevent war. In a world where contradictions, conflicts, and mistrust are rife, and where each side has an arsenal of awesome weapons at its disposal, brute force alone cannot be relied upon to guarantee the peace. As for my suggestions for an open society and for replacing confrontation with rapprochement, Slavsky evidently considered them too foolish to discuss, and simply skipped over them.

I pointed out to him that *Reflections* warned against exactly the kind of approach he was taking, in which life-and-death decisions are made behind the scenes by people who have usurped power (and privilege) without accepting the checks of free opinion and open debate. Then I raised the issue of Czechoslovakia: was there any guarantee against Soviet intervention there? For that would be a tragedy.

Slavsky said the matter was under discussion in the Central Committee, and that armed intervention had been ruled out, provided there was no overt counterrevolutionary violence such as occurred in Hungary. Words alone would not bother us, he added. (On August 21, this turned out to be untrue, but the decision to invade may have been made after our meeting; in any case, it's unlikely that Slavsky would have been privy to discussions at the very top.)

I've reproduced this conversation in some detail because it's virtually the only serious discussion I've ever had with anyone in authority about *Reflections* or any other statement of mine on public issues.

A couple of weeks after this, Khariton asked me to stop by his home. Slavsky, he told me, opposed my return to the Installation. I asked why.

"Efim Pavlovich [Slavsky] is afraid there might be a provocation against you."

"That's absurd—who would organize it?"

"Those are Efim Pavlovich's orders. You're to remain in Moscow for the time being."

This was tantamount to being fired, and there was nothing I could do about it. I stayed in Moscow, which had been our family's permanent home since 1962. Klava and the children normally joined me at the Installation for the summer, but they were still in Moscow when I was suspended.

On July 22, *Reflections* was published in the *New York Times*. After it was reprinted in August at several American universities, a flood of publications and reactions burst forth. (To my regret, I managed to collect and save only a small fraction of them.) The International Publishers Association released statistics showing that in 1968–1969 more than eighteen million copies of my essay were published around the world, in third place after Mao Zedong and Lenin, and ahead of Georges Simenon and Agatha Christie.

Reflections was well received by liberal intellectuals abroad. The views I had expressed—the threat of thermonuclear war, the value of democracy and intellectual freedom, the need to provide economic assistance to developing countries, the recognition of merit in socialism *and* capitalism, etc.—coincided in large part with theirs. More important, I represented a vindication of their hopes: a kindred voice had reached them from behind the Iron Curtain and, moreover, from a member of a profession which in America was dominated by "hawks." There were even some—mainly journalists—who saw my essay as a trial balloon launched by a Soviet government eager to reduce the risk of war; in this scenario, I was being used as a quasi-official spokesman. On the other hand, my criticism of Soviet society appealed to conservative circles, and everyone seemed pleased by my comments on the environment, my humanitarian concerns, and my scenarios for the future. For all the essay's shortcomings, the publication of *Reflections* was an event, and it had a considerable impact on public opinion in the West.

It circulated widely in the USSR as well—samizdat was flourishing—and the response was enthusiastic. Pyotr Grigorenko's letter has stuck in my mind: he praised my essay as "handy as a spoon at dinnertime." Solzhenitsyn sent me a lengthy critique, anticipating the comments he was to make when we met in person for the first time (see below). I deeply regret that many people were punished for circulating *Reflections*. I know the names of a few: Vladlen Pavlenkov, Sergei Ponomarev, Anatoly Nazarov.[2]

I was particularly gratified by a letter I received from the eminent theoretical physicist Max Born, which was accompanied by a very handsomely inscribed copy of his memoirs in German. Born wrote that he admired my courage and shared most of my ideas, but felt I overrated socialism, which he had always considered a creed for idiots. Nonetheless, he admitted that he had voted Labour while living in England. When Born's memoirs were published posthumously in the USSR, the chapter on his social, ethical, and philosophical views was left out, without any caveat to the Russian reader. Born was criticized for returning to Germany in 1953, but he'd missed the linden trees of his native Rhineland.

I also recall a letter from Georges Pire, the Belgian Dominican priest who won the 1958 Nobel Peace Prize. Vladimir Poremsky sent an interesting letter and Western press clippings about my essay, including his own article.[3]

During the first months following publication of my essay, I received quite a few letters by ordinary mail, although they were probably only a fraction of those that had been sent.

On August 21 I went out to buy a newspaper. According to a front-page article, Warsaw Pact troops had entered Czechoslovakia at the request of Party and government officials (unnamed, of course) and were "fulfilling their international duty." The invasion had begun. The hopes inspired by the Prague Spring collapsed. And "real socialism" displayed its true colors, its stagnation, its inability to tolerate pluralistic or democratic tendencies, not just in the Soviet Union but even in neighboring countries. Two natural and rational reforms—the abolition of censorship and free elections to a Party Congress—were regarded as too risky and contagious.

---

[2][Vladlen Pavlenkov, a teacher born in 1929, was sentenced in Gorky to seven years in labor camp for circulating anti-Soviet works and planning to found an anti-Soviet organization. Ponomarev, a writer born in 1945, was sentenced as Pavlenkov's codefendant to five years labor camp. Nazarov, a Dushanbe driver born in 1946, was sentenced to three years labor camp in 1972 for slandering the Soviet system (he mailed Sakharov's essay to a friend).]

[3][Poremsky's article appeared in *Posev*, Frankfurt, no. 8, August 1968.]

The international repercussions of the invasion were enormous. For millions of former supporters, it destroyed their faith in the Soviet system and its potential for reform.

By coincidence, Anatoly Marchenko's trial opened the day Czechoslovakia was invaded.

Marchenko had been a young worker in Kazakhstan in 1958 when he was first sentenced to labor camp for a barracks brawl with some Chechens. He wasn't guilty of any crime, but judges aren't overly scrupulous in such cases and ethnic politics may have influenced the verdict. Marchenko escaped from his labor camp and in 1960 was caught trying to cross the Iranian frontier. This time he was sent to a Mordovian camp for political prisoners to serve a six-year sentence. His whole life changed after Yuli Daniel arrived in the camp in 1966; influenced by him, Marchenko chose a new tack of rigorous self-examination, nonconformity, social activism, and struggle, which led to his eventual martyrdom. His distinguishing feature was his absolute honesty, a determination to stick to principle that was often mistaken for sheer obstinacy.

Following his release in November 1966, Marchenko drew on his considerable experience of prison and camp life to write *My Testimony*, a powerful and graphic description of the barbaric penal system that replaced Stalin's Gulag.[4]

He was arrested again in July 1968 and tried for a technical violation of passport regulations: spending more than three days in Moscow without permission. This law was enforced only selectively, but the KGB hated Marchenko's independent attitude and his book, which was popular with human rights activists in the USSR and had been published abroad in many languages. Marchenko received a one-year camp sentence, but that didn't satisfy the KGB. He was tried again while in confinement and sentenced to two additional years for slander; when another prisoner asked him why he was so thin, he allegedly answered: "Because the Communists have drunk my blood."

[4][*My Testimony* (Dutton, 1969).]

On the morning of August 21, Marchenko's friends were greeted at the courthouse by Pavel Litvinov, who announced: "Our tanks are in Prague!"[5]

Four days later, at noon on Sunday, August 25, Litvinov and Larisa Bogoraz, along with Konstantin Babitsky, Vadim Delone, Vladimir Dremlyuga, Viktor Fainberg, and Natasha Gorbanevskaya, went out onto Red Square to protest the Soviet invasion of Czechoslovakia. With this bold action—many people were punished just for refusing to attend the innumerable official meetings held in support of the intervention—Litvinov, Bogoraz, and their comrades restored our country's honor. They managed to sit for a minute by Lobnoe Mesto, a traditional place of execution in pre-revolutionary Russia, and then KGB agents began beating them and tore up their signs reading "Hands Off Czechoslovakia." All seven were arrested, but their protest had broken a shameful silence. Minutes later, cars carrying Dubček, Smrkovsky, and the other Czechoslovak leaders brought to Moscow by force, shot out of the Kremlin's Spassky Gate and raced across Red Square.

I had no advance notice of the demonstration. One of the participants came to see me on the 24th, but I was out and he didn't tell Klava the reason for his visit. It is possible that my absence was arranged. Zhivlyuk had arrived half an hour earlier and urged: "Andrei Dmitrievich, we have to go see Vuchetich right away. He's waiting for you. He's got access to 'himself' [Brezhnev]; who knows whose idea this meeting is. It could help a lot of people."

I had nothing to lose, so I went. I knew little about artistic circles, and had no clear idea what to expect. (Evgeny Vuchetich had unquestioned talent as a sculptor, but politically he was far to the right.)

On the way, Zhivlyuk told me: "You'll meet Fyodor Shakhmagonov, I gave you his manuscript."

Zhivlyuk had in fact brought me the typescript of a short story by Shakhmagonov about a retired KGB officer, praising it as more courageous and profound than Solzhenitsyn's work, a gross exaggeration.

[5]Pavel is the grandson of Maxim Litvinov, an Old Bolshevik who served for many years as Commissar of Foreign Affairs, until he was replaced by Molotov in 1939 to clear the way for rapprochement with Nazi Germany.

Vuchetich *was* waiting for us. A man of average height with a loud voice and aggressive manner, he was still suffering from the aftereffects of a recent stroke. Shakhmagonov arrived a few minutes later; he embraced Vuchetich, kissing him three times in Russian fashion.

Vuchetich showed me around his studio, pointing out works he'd done "for the money" and others done "for my soul." An enormous female figure symbolizing the Motherland had been commissioned for the Stalingrad memorial.

"The bosses ask me why her mouth is open; it doesn't look pretty. I tell them: She's shouting 'For the Motherland, you mother-f—ers!' That shuts them up."

The memorial for the Battle of the Kursk Salient captured the charm of youth and, at the same time, the horror of war and death, in the bent head of a dying tank soldier.

"For the soul" Vuchetich had portrayed Lenin in his last years, lost in deep and painful thought.

I never saw Vuchetich again. I've since heard that he carved a bust of me using photographs and his memory of our meeting.

Of Shakhmagonov I was told that he had served as Mikhail Sholokhov's secretary and had written Sholokhov's horrifying address to the Twenty-third Party Congress. Shakhmagonov is rumored to be a KGB general. In 1969, he suggested that I write an essay along the same lines as *Reflections* for the Sovetskaya Rossiya publishing house. The article would have to be "publishable"—i.e., acceptable to the Soviet censors. This may have been an attempt to "tame" me. I left an outline of my proposed article at the publisher's office, and Shakhmagonov phoned a few days later to say that there was no sense in going any further: even the essay's title, which included the word "democratization," seemed "provocative." To whom? To the KGB?

The day after visiting Vuchetich, I had my first meeting with Alexander Solzhenitsyn. Tamara Khachaturova, a widow who worked in FIAN's library and was a friend of Solzhenitsyn's first wife, had passed on his suggestion that we meet. Our rendezvous was postponed several times, but finally took place at the apartment of a friend of mine on August 26. (Solzhenitsyn was the first person to tell me about the demonstration the day before on Red Square.)

In *The Oak and the Calf,* Solzhenitsyn writes about the vivid impression I made on him.[6] I can easily return the compliment. With his lively blue eyes and ruddy beard, his tongue-twistingly fast speech delivered in an unexpected treble, and his deliberate, precise gestures, he seemed an animated concentration of purposeful energy.

Before I arrived, Solzhenitsyn had drawn the curtains. He later wrote that our meeting escaped the notice of the KGB. In this I believe he was mistaken, although I don't pretend to be an expert in detecting surveillance. Since I have nothing to hide, I simply ignore our army of highly paid shadows. On this occasion, however, I noted that the taxi driver who picked me up after the meeting made provocative remarks and seemed unusually intent on engaging me in conversation.

I had read almost everything Solzhenitsyn had written and felt enormous respect for him, which has since been reinforced by publication of his epic work, *The Gulag Archipelago.* Real life is never simple, however, and our relations are now difficult—perhaps unavoidably so, since we are not at all alike and differ markedly on questions of principle.

At our first meeting, I listened attentively as he talked away in his usual manner—passionately and with absolute conviction. He began by complimenting me on breaking the conspiracy of silence at the top of the pyramid. Then he voiced his disagreements with me in incisive fashion: Any kind of convergence is out of the question. (Here he repeated Slavsky almost word for word.) The West has no interest in our becoming democratic. The West is caught up in materialism and permissiveness. Socialism may turn out to be its final ruin. Our leaders are soulless robots who have latched onto power and the good life, and won't let go until forced to do so.

Solzhenitsyn claimed that I had understated Stalin's crimes. Furthermore, I was wrong to differentiate him from Lenin: corruption and destruction began the day the Bolsheviks seized power, and have continued ever since. Changes in scale or method are not

[6][*The Oak and the Calf,* pp. 369–371.]

changes in principle. According to Professor Kurganov, sixty million people had perished as a result of terror, famine, and associated disease. My figure of ten million deaths in labor camps was too low.

It's a mistake, he continued, to seek a multiparty system; what we need is a nonparty system. Every political party betrays its members in order to serve the interests of the party bosses. Scientists and engineers have a major role to play, but in the absence of an underlying spiritual goal any hope that we can use the tools of science to regulate progress is a delusion that will end in our being suffocated by the smoke and cinders of our cities.

Despite the passage of time, I believe I have faithfully reproduced the gist of Solzhenitsyn's critique.[7]

In response, I acknowledged that there was much truth in his comments. Still, my own opinions were expressed in *Reflections* although in an attempt to make constructive recommendations, I had introduced some simplifications into my argument. My primary aim was to point out the dangers we faced and a possible course of action to avert them. I was counting on people's good will. I didn't expect an immediate response to my essay, but I hoped to influence public thinking over the long term. I might revise it at some future date, but first wanted to think things through.

We went on to discuss the punishment facing the demonstrators who had been arrested in Red Square. A few days later, I phoned Andropov on their behalf. Kurchatov had left instructions that I was to be allowed into the Atomic Energy Institute without a pass or other formalities. I went to the office of Anatoly Alexandrov, then the Institute's director, and used his special telephone to call Andropov. I told him:

"I'm concerned about the people arrested on August 25 on Red Square. Czechoslovakia has become the center of world attention: Communist Parties in the West are following developments, and it will make matters worse if the demonstrators are tried and sentenced."

[7]Solzhenitsyn later sent me a written memorandum, entitled "The Agony of Free Speech," repeating and expanding upon his remarks. He published it, with minor revisions and a new title ("As Breathing and Consciousness Return"), in *From Under the Rubble* [Little, Brown, 1975].

Andropov said he was preoccupied with Czechoslovakia and had hardly slept all week. The Procurator's Office, not the KGB, was investigating the demonstration. Andropov added, however, that he didn't think the sentences would be severe.[8]

That was my second and last conversation with Andropov.

Trans. Richard Lourie (New York: Alfred A. Knopf, 1990), 267–294.

Rudi Dutschke

The Students and the Revolution (7 March 1968)

An immigrant to West Berlin from the communist-controlled Eastern half of the city, Rudi Dutschke emerged by 1968 as a fiery spokesman for student revolution in West Germany, and throughout much of Europe. Combining the philosophical ideas of Herbert Marcuse with the guerrilla ethos of Che Guevara, he called on students to lead an insurgency against the weakest links in the chain of capitalist "neo-fascism." The dominant powers needed a growing cohort of technically proficient citizens, and Dutschke called upon these young men and women to rebel. He connected the fight against domestic authorities with a struggle against foreign imperialism, most particularly in Vietnam. He helped organize an "International Vietnam Congress" at the Free University in West Berlin during February 1968, and he carried his anti-war message to other countries, including Sweden, after that. On 11 April 1968 Dutschke became a martyr for the student movement. An unemployed West German worker, Josef Bachmann, shot him three times at close range. Dutschke survived, but never fully recovered.

Rational and irrational authorities, ladies, gentlemen, students, comrades! I am glad that the tradition which says that only German fascists appear in Sweden has been broken and that German anti-fascists are allowed to speak. This is also something new, as German fascism has lost its definite historical form. I am going to

---

[8][Dremlyuga was sentenced to three years labor camp; Delone to thirty months labor camp; Litvinov to five years exile; Bogoraz to four years exile; Babitsky to three years exile. Fainberg was sent to a prison psychiatric hospital.]

speak about the new form of fascism in our and in other countries as I consider that it is important that at some point you hear from Germany another message than the message about the growth of neo-fascism.

University and Society

The subject for this evening is "Students and Politics." In this is contained something both true and false. It is true that today students are looked upon as being connected with politics in many parts of the world. It is false if the real problem behind this is not seen i.e. "university and society." This question is important because the traditional division of university and society (in the spirit we are taught at the university "You are something special, you are the nation's elite, its pets and you will soon be very well paid") is nothing but the expression of a normal repressive capitalistic division of labour in both intellectual and material production. Intellectual and material production has been divided simply because of the wish to better organise the maximum returns and profits for capitalism. Those who produce society's wealth and those who make use of this for themselves are differentiated. This is always an expression of the main conflict in the bourgeois capitalist society— the gap between wage earning and capital, between producers and the means of production, the division of those who produce the riches of the society but do not have power over the conditions and instruments of production. Historically speaking this fundament conflict constantly assumes new forms. Today it takes a very subtle form. That wages are paid, concessions are given, TVs produced en masse, that cars can be bought cheaply does not mean that the basic conflict—the division between labour and capital—between producers and means of production—has been eliminated, but only that it has found its highest and most subtle form. An illusory freedom has been attained by the producers, who in reality are entirely unfree because the private individual in the bourgeois capitalist society is not allowed to develop his creative capacities. There is an ideology which says that all have the same chances, but this is not true, because individual development is very varied and the difference between material and intellectual output continues to exist.

The students account for only a small percentage of the whole population. To study is still a privilege which is used to give us an

image of independence and superiority, which nevertheless in practice means only that we have capitulated and sold ourselves so that
capital can show returns and can rule. We devote ourselves to a
knowledge of capitalism rather than a knowledge of the people.
This is true from philology to mathematics! We must not ask questions but accept the structure as it is, and thus as students and scientists we become more or less useful idiots within the system of
maximisation of profits. In this way the following happens to us.
We are only given the task and the chance to sell ourselves, to get a
good or bad job, later to yield to cynicism and be unable to develop
any real creative abilities. Where in this society is science not an instrument of oppression, an instrument of capitalism? Or do you
believe that there are protected areas where one can be creative and
say "My home is my castle"? None of us should have this illusion.

I consider, however, that the students and the professors have a
wonderful opportunity, a chance to understand what is happening
to them. To be able to think systematically is a privilege that we
possess and which the masses do not, and in this respect we hold a
sociological middle-position. On the one hand we can educate ourselves, on the other hand we always run the risk of educating ourselves for interests which are not our own, the interest of the rulers.
We know the history of the American universities where this has
become very clear and is now the pattern for science, which has become an instrument of American imperialism's direct machinery of
destruction.

The existing institutions make use of science. Scientists carry out
an illusory objective-science but what is implied in this concept of
objectivity? Objectivity which is often defined as freedom from
evaluations, neutrality, something apart from the frontlines of politics is, in my opinion, entirely a political position, as it identifies
with and yields to the interests of the rulers. By pretending to be
uncommitted they make themselves an instrument of the system.
Every critical view of science must mean that one asks oneself what
is the direction of science in advanced capitalist society, what function does it have, who should make use of it?

Originally science was a productive force for the liberation of
mankind from uncontrolled mechanisms in both nature and society, for social and political freedom. The concept of science quickly

became used by capital for its own ends, it became an instrument of rule. Today it is more than ever a direct productive force in the process of exploitation in our society, an increasingly important part of the stabilising of the present power structure. Scientists, students and academics now have the job of winning back science's basic origins, as the productive force for the liberation of the people, and of putting to use this productive force against all the mechanisms, and of organising themselves against the utilisation of science in the ruler's interests. This has been vital as the starting point of our movement in West Germany, about which I will now speak.

Neo-Fascism

I will begin with a new definition of fascism. Traditional fascism was distinguished by an ideology, it was organised, had a party and a leader—there was a militarily organised terrorist fascism. In the 1920s and 30s the function of fascism was to stop the proletarian revolution and also, because the bourgeois society was in difficulties, to carry through the trick of integrating the anti-capitalist elements which existed in fascism in a pro-capitalist pro-imperialist movement. This was fascism's historical function and its task was to carry it through until it was defeated by the Allies.

After the Second World War a new form of fascism was taught in all of the west so-called free world. This is characterised by the fact that fascism is no longer structured and organised in one party or one person. The new fascism reveals itself through the organised authoritarian institutions in all parts of the advanced capitalist society. I am now primarily talking about the advanced capitalist society of West Germany. This society is characterised by the system of authoritarian institutions. In these institutions (whether they are concerned with the economy, the university or the church) people are every day being educated in an authoritarian-personality structure, a structure geared to adaptation, passivity, paralysis, fear—people who only wait for the signal from the rulers, the signal from manipulation and production. When they send out the signal "Crisis!" people do not question this but react with passivity and experience suffering. They are afraid—begin to work quicker for fear of losing their jobs. By this, I mean a basic structure of authoritarian-fascism. People are not being moulded into anti-authoritarianism, filled with a sense of their own power, able to understand history as being their own, but every day they are moulded into being useless, frightened. They are being made into 'functions' made afraid of society, afraid of the bosses, afraid of losing their jobs, afraid of examinations. Every day they experience frustrations which become aggressions—the authoritarian personality is produced! This is the new form of fascism. When there is alarming news from West Germany of 8–10% NPD voters the outside world should not imagine or believe that this will not increase, nor that, if NPD is banned, fascism will be eliminated. It lies deeper than this! It lies in the fact that every day people are being moulded to organise their lives not with independence but as useful objects.

Against this form of fascism we have begun our struggle in the weakest spot in the authoritarian system of imperialism of West Germany, which is secondary to (and often assumes the functions of) American imperialism. We have begun with the weakest link—West Berlin—and in West Berlin, again with the weakest link—the university. West Berlin is the weakest link because economically it is entirely dependent on the West German Republic. Every seventh West-Berliner is employed by the senate. We have a fantastically developed bureaucracy and immense costs for this. I would now like to say a few words about the premises of our anti-authoritarian struggle at the University of West Berlin.

The Requirements of Capital for Increased Education

In the fifties the Left in West Germany believed that capitalism no longer contained any contradictions. The period of affluence was immense and the Left could not understand why capital was so stable. All Marxist theories seemed to have broken down and all the signs implied that an organised stabilised capitalism had found the solution of all its inherent contradictions. No-one within the Left understood that after 25 years work had been destroyed by the war (the war which was probably the greatest excess of consumption in history) they now had 35 years at their disposal to rebuild all that had been destroyed, and that this rebuilding followed a normal pattern of developed capitalism. It took a long time before we understood this! Now until 1964–65 when the growth of industry suddenly sank from 6–8% per annum to 2.5–4% per annum did we begin to realise that capitalism had not eliminated its inherent contradictions. That it hadn't succeeded in mastering the economic forces, that although it had found new means of handling the economy, these means were contradictory. We realised that the so-called economic wonder of West Germany was in reality a period of economic reconstruction which had to stop at the point when the important productive forces behind this growth—labour and the structure of the labour force—had been emptied and a new step in the use of technology became necessary, a step which could no longer be taken by automation of the existing labour force structure.

Suddenly the problem of the university, which had been neglected for decades, came to the attention of the rulers. They needed a larger output of technological and economic intelligence in industry to make possible the new step in the use of capital. The university became of interest because technical and economic intelligence in advanced capitalism is more and more important for the reproduction of capital. Thus the whole problem of technocrats within automised industry! Therefore the rulers suddenly initiated university reforms and suggested to us "Now we are going to rationalise a bit. You spend too much time studying. It must be possible to do this quicker and more effectively. We suggest a better system of education—a quicker one—that makes it possible for you to reach the flesh-pots, the well paid jobs, sooner. You have to agree to this!"

More Effect for Whom?

We within the Left-oriented student organisations could then explain to the rest of the students that these suggestions of rationalisation, these so-called 'reforms' can not be seen apart from the difficulties experienced by capital in finding new forms of returns. We could make it clear to the students that science and politics, science and economy, science and capital is an inseparable union.

They talk of recruitment restrictions and a shortened period of study, so that studies can be more effective. But more effective for whom? Effective for you, for your individual development, your emancipation? For the emancipation and liberation of society? Or effective for the social emancipation of capital? This alternative was clear to a large number of the students. They realised that they were going to be exploited and made use of for the requirements of capital, and not their own requirements. The day of settlement was at hand!

The Anti-Authoritarian Struggle—Politics in a New Sense

We began to organise anti-authoritarian movements in the universities. This was made possible by a prevalent tendency which you too must have felt, towards on the one hand a bureaucratised student representation, and on the other hand non-political student unions, dependent on each other, and also by the fact that the Left was not split into sectarian groups. We began to organise meetings at which university reform was discussed. We invited professors and politicians, who did not come or who, when they did come, showed themselves to be idiots outside their own political area, who no longer knew what the requirements of the students were. They showed themselves to be the agents of capitalism. By this unmasking of the activities of agents amongst the university personnel and in the social bureaucracy we could begin to mobilise, create political awareness and organise anti-authoritarian activities within the union.

I consider this to be politics in a new sense. It has nothing to do with the ruling party politics. In reality, we take the party of the under-privileged, the party for our own interests and needs, for that which we have realised is right and human. We do not allow ourselves to be made into functions any longer! When we began this struggle it was very clear that we would meet with total resistance from the authoritarian and irrational authorities, which could no longer be seen as rational, but as irrational, in insisting, "We need reforms—you must not ask who this will profit, or why. You must not demand the emancipation of society but the stabilising of the rulers."

Science and Vietnam

The immediate interests of the students can be co-ordinated and combined with the situation between science and politics, science and humanism. The starting point of science (which is described as the starting point in the struggle for human freedom) is another level of which Vietnam, for example, can be explained to the students. In Vietnam there is a clear relationship between science and politics, science and liberation, science and capital. There, we are openly confronted with science used for the systematic slaughter of a people, for the systematic suppression of a social revolution. This tendency is found in the whole of the Third World.

In Vietnam we learned what happened to science and began to understand what could also happen to us, and also, tendentially, through us!

New Alternative

We must not pretend that Vietnam is something which has nothing to do with us. The international process of settlement must no longer be seen as the false alternative in the East-West conflict, which is the cold-war ideology in the world after the war. East-West is a mistaken alternative, precisely as the alternative North-South is mistaken. Now the world-wide alternative is very clear: anti-authoritarianism, world-wide revolution, and authoritarian imperialistic counter-revolution. This also concerns scientists and students. When we accept the idea of using science as a productive force for liberation and also use it as such, we must organise ourselves so that science cannot be mis-used. This is precisely what is being done in practice in West Berlin, with the creation of the critical university, where science is used for anti-authoritarian struggle and liberation. We see ourselves as scientists who, when our studies are over, shall no longer work in institutions as their "objects" but will work as subversive elements in the liberation process. This means for example that a technician must ask himself what is the product of his scientific labour. He must organise himself, together with other technicians so that he can bring about an anti-authoritarian, anti-fascist struggle together with the political powers outside the institution in which he works, outside the whole apparatus. Yet again, I aim at the concept "politics." The concept of party-name in the new sense. This is not the politics of the establishment, of the rulers and the parties. This is not a party-name for a definite party, but for the individual and the social and individual emancipation of all, a party-name for the underprivileged everywhere. It is a new form of politics, science and organisation!

The Traditional Parties

The traditional parties were distinguished by the fact that they used people as objects. Parties were formed where an apparatus, a party oligarchy, superficially represented the interests of the members. But what happened? The whole time the parties used the members as objects for the party's rule, and not as subjects for social emancipation. Thus, one can say that the parties now, just as earlier, have been the instruments of repression of the people's spontaneity and will always be so. I do not want to make a binding historical law of this, but I consider that we need a new form of organisation for individual needs and interests. These must no longer be repressed and made into functions by a bureaucracy, a clique, whether it calls itself Left or Right.

The Role of Education

We must organise ourselves so that we can lead our anti-authoritarian, anti-fascist struggle and this means also anti-sectarianism. That is, we must educate ourselves "all-around" and not become knowledgeable idiots within a special area. However, this is the function of the university. I have heard that your university system in Sweden is noted for a short study period, just like in the schools, with a definite teaching syllabus and quick examinations and student loans right from the start. But if this means that it is non-political (in the sense that I have earlier defined politics) you should see in this a subtle form of rule and not progress. And it is not only progress to go through non-political "idiotic" studies, and afterwards give oneself up to the apparatus, then to be forced to yield to others' need for profit.

Studying can only mean the following: individual specialised education within an area—what I have been talking about when I made my own reflections on the emancipation of the individual. How can I become a person? However, we are not people only because at one time or another we were born. It is also possible to be an idiot, an object, and one can also clearly seem to be a person, and yet still be an object of the rulers. What we need is a society which is typified by the fact that the individual can develop his capacities, that he can fully develop his individual physical and mental abilities. In such a society the individual will not be frustrated and stunted in his development, not be a non-person, an object for the use of parties and institutions, but as 'subject' in a society which he can accept. Where he would not be alienated, where he can work and recognise himself in his work, and not need to be afraid of world wide catastrophes. He shall not need to mourn because of war, as now in Vietnam or soon in Greece, not need to be afraid of a NATO-system which bears the seeds of a new war. All these are things that the individual student and the individual professor must consider in their own education. Finally, he must understand that he must educate himself as a person, that is, the specialised education must be included in a unified social education. It must not dominate, rather, the collective social education must form the framework of the specialised training. When specialised training dominates, people will always be objects for use in the rulers' interests. If general education dominates, society is seen as something which must be further developed, something which, whether it is capitalist or authoritarian socialist, must be reformed.

Swedish Society

As students we are privileged. Most people in society have not had the opportunities to be educated that we have. Up to now, we have used our education in the capacity of the nation's elite. Our task has been to manipulate the people and not to emancipate them. I maintain that in order to counteract this oppression of the people by the elite, who allow themselves to be used in the interests of the establishment, we must organise ourselves so that our struggle and our science becomes political.

I believe that as we in West Berlin have begun this anti-authoritarian struggle in the weakest place in society, there is perhaps something for you to learn from us. Even if Swedish capitalism and its methods seem ever so nice and superficially without conflict, it must be seen as a system which despite all is characterised by the basic conflict—namely, the gap between producer and the means of production. It is a social structure with a ruling minority, a steady functionalising of science, pressure on the masses by the elite and parties used as instruments for the functionalising and making into 'objects' of the people. Therefore, I would say that your situation in principle does not differ from our situation! The difference is only that we in West Berlin have already begun a struggle which has very quickly shown us that a democratic university (or a university which is attempting to make itself democratic) is a logical impossibility in the authoritarian society. No gap exists between the university and society, between politics and science. There is only one possible chance i.e. to begin the anti-authoritarian struggle in the weakest link of society, the university. When this weak link begins the struggle by involving itself in politics, it is immediately met by opposition from the state, because advanced capitalism is specifically characterised by the fact that the state is above all, that everywhere it has its agents and bureaucrats, that the university bureaucracy works hand in hand with the social bureaucracy. And this has taught us that we are not objects in history, but as people we constantly make our own history.

The Bourgeois View of History

It has always been said that history is a result of the personalities of world history—historians, politicians, those who call themselves this, lawyers and others are supposed to have made history. In fact, individual leaders have made all revolutions, not the masses. Bourgeois thinking can only understand the conflict in society, which means the conflict of the masses, many people's conflict, as a result of outstanding individuals. As a result, they can only understand a student movement, or apprentices' movement, or workers' movement, anti-authoritarian struggle, in terms of rabble leaders. It is Dutschke, or Mario Savio, or some other who is responsible. Behind this hides the so-called 'puppet-theatre thinking.' This thinking can not understand that people are beginning to work for their own needs and interests in order to live like people, to undertake the science of humanity, work politically as people. It is not understood that this is work that is interesting, that develops the individual skills, a work that emancipates and that does not need leaders as chief ideologists, manipulators. Certainly the anti-authoritarian movements have a temporary provisional representative leadership, but this leadership stands or falls by criticism and self-criticism, by dialogue with the conscious anti-authoritarian forces. Our political work has always been a work whereby the individual temporarily dominated by politics, must allow himself to be controlled and criticised by the assembly of students, the conscious students.

And the central point of our organisation work is always—and to this extent we are revolutionary Marxists—the third paragraph in Feuerbach—"The educator must be educated." This means that the new politicians must be characterised by the fact that they take part in a steady critical dialogue (with criticism and self-criticism) with the conscious, anti-authoritarians and that any personal powers they have can be removed at any time.

The Problem of the Revolution

When we think about the possibilities which exist in the world today, and what exists really in the form of hunger, suffering, subtle and open exploitation, subtle and open mechanisms for rule, we consider that a new world is being denied to us. In this, is concerned the problems of revolution today. The authoritarian society can no longer bring about reforms within itself, in the radical meaning of real change. Reforms are only the refuse of the rulers who are concerned with stabilising their positions. Just as reform in Vietnam is only a part of the military extinction, so also is reform within higher education in West Germany only a side product in the process of capital returns.

The revolution is not an event that takes two or three days, in which there is shooting and hanging. It is a long drawn out process in which new people are created, capable of renovating society so that the revolution does not replace one elite with another, but so that the revolution creates a new anti-authoritarian structure with anti-authoritarian people who in their turn re-organise the society so that it becomes a non-alienated human society, free from war, hunger and exploitation. Here in the university we have begun this struggle.

As students, we have opportunities for anti-authoritarianism, but very soon after our studies have ended we must go through authoritarian experiences. We become the best paid intellectual workers. We get a job, perhaps with the illusion of emancipation, so that we can travel a bit and perhaps not have such long working hours. But in terms of what we really want to achieve, it is nothing. It will probably satisfy fewer and fewer professors and students to work in institutions which one knows co-operate with huge corporations or oligopolies. When this is understood and one's own function in the power structure is analysed one becomes less ready to bow to these requirements. One may become cynical and accept the situation, or may be satisfied with an illusory emancipation, for example "O well, I'll work now, but after work I'll be a person."

This is a traditional contradiction in every science, that one believes that whilst working one can accept all kinds of compromises, whilst outside work one is a person. This must produce schizophrenic character structures with cynical or masochistic features. This contradiction is the basis for us and our future.

The Situation Today

In West Germany we can only achieve a revolutionary situation when we succeed in destroying the national and international isolation of the students. We must make more of the wage-earning masses politically aware. Our struggle must be anti-esoteric. In West Berlin and West Germany we are working within the Left, together with other leftist groups. We have no sectarian tradition in the meaning that we in the Left should fight each other, but we have a tradition where the problems of emancipation and anti-imperialism are the focal point and the ideological pseudo-differences are secondary. We concentrate on the struggle against the authoritarian structure, on the widening of anti-authoritarianism. We are not stuck in any allegiance to the church or the communist party. Fidel Castro was quite right when he once said "There are today parts of the Catholic church which are revolutionary, and Communist Parties which have been transformed into old churches!" In this lies something which is structurally new. The programme of the revolution is no longer administered by one party, the revolution's identity with the Communist Party is something long passed. The question of the identity of the revolution with a certain country, whether it is the USSR or China, has also passed. I say 'yes' to the Cuban revolution, to the cultural revolution in China. I say 'no' to certain Soviet international positions. The theory of peaceful coexistence is a mystery—an ideology that accepts that imperialism should be peaceful!

Our political line for the near future is clearly anti-NATO. This struggle will be carried out in two ways. First in the form of politically clarifying mass-actions, but also subversive actions. This means that the revolutionary terrorism in big cities today does not take the form of terrorism against people, but against inhuman machinery. In the third world, for example Haiti (Duvalier), Vietnam (Ky, Thieu) or in Persia (the Shah), the leaders are not character-masks for capital which can be changed at any time, but they are individual representatives. To terrorise them, to destroy by a revolutionary attentat is politically right and necessary in a social revolutionary strategy. But I can't agree to the liquidation of character-masks like Kiesinger, Brandt, Strauss, co-operative-fascists like Thadden or others. In this way, one liquidates nothing, one liquidates no structure, all that happens is that persons are done away with who in every instance are inter-changeable.

The revolutionary terror is rather used against inhuman machines, e.g. Springer concern in West Berlin. This concern dominates and rules politics by its manipulations. We have consequently begun a broad anti-manipulation campaign with the final aim of directly attacking Springer—not Springer the person but the institution—in order to destroy this machinery. The aim is that today we terrorise the machinery in order to regain it and make it human and controlled.

When we struggle against NATO I can very well believe that action groups in Sweden during the coming year will take part in definite action in Norway and Denmark. By means of anti-NATO campaigns the contradictions in Sweden could be sharpened. Because there seems to be a contradiction in that there are

five universities in Sweden, but at the same time a very strong defence. What, and against whom, are we really defending ourselves?
Who speaks about limited local conflicts in middle Europe? Even
Adenauer (amongst others) spoke just before he died about the
peaceful Soviet. And would not a big war give us enough to think
about anyway? Why should we not create a hundred Swedish universities from the defence budget? In which an elite is no longer
educated but instead people, who educate themselves in an anti-
authoritarian way and who have the capacity to create an anti-
authoritarian society. There, people would work in a human
manner, and not allow themselves to be used, but instead, as "subjects," rather than "objects," would decide their own destinies and
no longer strive after the maximisation of profit, but the maximisation of individual happiness within society.

Speech in Uppsala, trans. Patricia Howard, *London Bulletin*, No. 6 (Autumn 1968),
4–14.

Daniel Cohn-Bendit

Interview by Jean-Paul Sartre (20 May 1968)

*In May 1968 protests throughout Paris turned the city into a virtual war zone.
Student barricades created an atmosphere of impending revolution. Violent
clashes between students and police produced chaos along the city's famous
streets. The protesters appealed to French workers, especially the General Con-
federation of Labor (CGT), for solidarity with their attacks on the government.
This call for student-worker unity contributed to some initial successes, including a general strike on 13 May 1968. Within days, however, student and
worker priorities diverged, as unions representing the latter entered negotiations
with the government. In this conversation between one of the leading postwar
French intellectuals, Jean-Paul Sartre, and one of the most recognized student
protesters, Daniel Cohn-Bendit, the two men discuss the hopes of the students.
In particular, they emphasize a vision of popular student-worker revolution
based on "spontaneity," rather than the dominance of established political
parties.*

*Our action has proved that popular
spontaneity has kept
its place in the social movement.*

JEAN-PAUL SARTRE: Within a few days, although no one called for a general strike, France has been practically paralyzed by work stoppages and factory occupations. And all because the students took control of the streets in the Latin Quarter. What is your analysis of the movement you have unleashed? How far might it go?

DANIEL COHN-BENDIT: It has grown much larger than we could have foreseen at the start. The aim is now the overthrow of the regime. But it is not up to us whether or not this is achieved. If the Communist Party, the CGT, and the other union headquarters shared it there would be no problem; the regime would fall within a fortnight, as it has no counterthrust against a trial of strength supported by all working-class forces.

J-P. S.: For the moment there is an obvious disproportion between the massive nature of the strike movement, which does, indeed, make possible a direct confrontation with the regime, and the demands the trade unions have presented, which are still limited ones: for wages, work organization, pensions, etc.

D. C-B.: There has always been a disjunction in workers' struggles between the strength of the action and the initial demands. But it might be that the success of the action, the dynamism of the movement, could alter the nature of the demands *en route*. A strike launched for a partial victory may change into a movement for insurrection.

Even so, some of the demands put forward by the workers today are very far-reaching: a real 40-hour week, for example, and, at Renault's, a minimum wage of 1,000 francs per month. The Gaullist regime cannot accept them without a total loss of face and, if it holds out, then there will be a confrontation. Suppose the workers hold out, too, and the regime falls. What will happen then? The left will come to power. Everything will then depend on what it does. If it really changes the system—I must admit I doubt if it will—it will have an audience, and all will be well. But if we have a Wilson-style government, with or without the Communists, which only proposes minor reforms and adjustments, then the extreme left will regain its strength and we shall have to go on posing the real problems of social control, workers' power, and so on.

But we have not reached that stage yet, and it is not at all certain even that the regime will fall.

J-P. S.:   When the situation is a revolutionary one, a movement like your own may not be stopped, but it may be that its impetus will fade. In that case you will have to try to go as far as possible before you come to a halt. What irreversible results do you think the present movement will achieve, supposing that it soon stops?

D. C-B.:   The workers will obtain the satisfaction of a number of material demands, and the moderates in the student movement and the teachers will put through important university reforms. These will not be the radical reforms we should like to see, but we shall still be able to bring some pressure to bear: we will make particular proposals, and no doubt a few of them will be accepted because they won't dare refuse us everything. That will be some progress, of course, but nothing basic will have changed and we shall continue to challenge the system as a whole.

Besides, I don't believe the revolution is possible overnight like that. I believe that all we can get are successive adjustments of more or less importance, but these adjustments can only be imposed by revolutionary action. That is how the student movement, which, even if it does temporarily lose its energy, will still have achieved an important university reform, can act as an example to many young workers. By using the traditional means of action of the workers' movement—strikes, occupations of the streets and workplaces—we have destroyed the first barrier: the myth that "nothing can be done about the regime." We have proved that this is not true. And the workers rushed into the breach. Perhaps this time they won't go right to the end. But there will be other explosions later on. What matters is that the effectiveness of revolutionary methods has been proved.

The union of workers and students can only be achieved in the dynamics of action if the student's movement and the workers' movement each sustain their own impetus and converge on one aim. At the moment, naturally and understandably enough, the workers distrust the students.

J-P. S.: This distrust is not natural, it has been acquired. It did not exist at the beginning of the nineteenth century, and did not appear until after the massacres of June 1848. Before that, republicans—who were intellectuals and petty bourgeois—and workers marched together. This unity has been out of the question ever since, even in the Communist Party, which has always carefully separated workers and intellectuals.

D. C-B.: But something did happen during the crisis. At Billancourt, the workers would not let the students into the factories. But even the fact that students went to Billancourt was new and important. In fact, there were three stages. First, open mistrust, not only in the working-class press, but among the workers themselves. They said, "Who are all these father's boys who have come here to annoy us?" Then, after the street battles, the students' struggle with the police, this feeling disappeared and solidarity was effectively achieved.

Now we are in a third stage: the workers and peasants have entered the struggle in their turn, but they tell us, "Wait a little, we want to fight our own battles for ourselves!" That is to be expected. Union can only take place later on if the two movements, the students' movement and the workers' movement, maintain their impetus. After fifty years of distrust, I don't think what is called "dialogue" is possible. It is not just a matter of talk. We should not expect the workers to welcome us with open arms. Contact will only be made when we are fighting side by side. We might for example set up common revolutionary action groups in which workers and students raise problems and act together. There are places where that will work, and others where it won't.

J-P. S.: The problem remains the same: adjustments or revolution. As you have said, everything you do by force is recovered positively by the reformists. Thanks to your action, the university will be readjusted, but only within the framework of a bourgeois society.

D. C-B.: Obviously, but I believe that is the only way to advance. Take the examinations, for example. There can be no doubt that they will take place. But certainly not in the way they used to. A new formula will be found. And once they take place in an unusual way, an irreversible process of reforms will have been set moving. I don't know how far it will go, and I know it will be a slow process, but it is the only possible strategy.

I am not interested in metaphysics, in looking for ways to "make the revolution." As I have said, I think that we are moving toward a perpetual change of society, produced by revolutionary actions at each stage. A radical change in the structure of our society would only be possible if, for example, a serious economic crisis, the action of a powerful workers' movement and vigorous student activity suddenly converged. These conditions have not all been realized today. At best we can hope to bring down the government. We must not dream of destroying bourgeois society. That does not mean that there is nothing to be done; on the contrary, we must struggle step by step, on the basis of a global challenge.

I am not really interested in whether there can still be revolutions in advanced capitalist societies, and what we should do to induce them. Everyone has his own theory. Some say: the revolutions of the third world will bring about a collapse of the capitalist world. Others: only thanks to revolution in the capitalist world can the third world advance. All these analyses are more or less correct, but, to my mind, of little importance.

Look at what has just happened. Many people spent a long time searching for the best way to set off an explosion among the students. Finally, no one found it, an *objective situation* produced the explosion. There was the authorities' heavy-handedness, of course—the police occupation of the Sorbonne—but it is clear that that absurd mistake was not the sole source of the movement. The police had already entered Nanterre several months earlier without setting off a chain reaction. This time there was a chain reaction that could not be stopped—which allows us to analyse the role an active minority can play.

What has happened in the last fortnight is to my mind a refutation of the famous theory of the "revolutionary vanguard" as the force leading a popular movement. At Nanterre and Paris there was simply an objective situation, arising from what is vaguely called "student unrest" and from a desire for action on the part of some young people disgusted by the inaction of the ruling classes. Because it was more conscious theoretically and better prepared, the active minority was able to light the fuse and make the breach. But that is all. The others could follow or not. They happen to have followed. But from then on no vanguard, neither of the UEC [Union of Communist Students], the JCR [Revolutionary Communist Youth], nor the Marxist-Leninists have been able to seize control of the movement. Their militants can participate decisively in the actions, but they have been drowned in the movement. They are to be found on the co-ordination committees, where their role is important, but there has never been any question of one of these vanguards taking a leading position.

This is the essential point. It shows that we must abandon the theory of the "leading vanguard" and replace it by a much simpler and more honest one of the active minority functioning as a permanent leaven, pushing for action without ever leading it. In fact, though no one will admit it, the Bolshevik Party did not "lead" the Russian Revolution. It was borne along by the masses. It might have elaborated its theory *en route*, and pushed the movement in one direction or another, but it did not by itself launch the movement; that was largely spontaneous. In certain objective situations—with the help of an active minority—spontaneity can find its old place in the social movement. Spontaneity makes possible the forward drive, not the orders of a leading group.

J-P. S.: What many people cannot understand is the fact that you have not tried to work out a program or to give your movement a structure. They attack you for trying to "smash everything" without knowing—or at any rate saying—what you would like to put in place of what you demolish.

D. C-B.: Naturally! Everyone would be reassured, particularly Pompidou, if we set up a Party and announced: "All these people here are ours now. Here are our aims and this is how we are going to attain them." They would know who they were dealing with and how to counter them. They would no longer have to face "anarchy," "disorder," "uncontrollable effervescence."

Our movement's strength is precisely that it is based on an "uncontrollable" spontaneity, that it gives an impetus without trying to canalize it or use the action it has unleashed to its own profit. There are clearly two solutions open to us today. The first

would be to bring together half-a-dozen people with political experience, ask them to formulate some convincing immediate demands, and say, "Here is the student movement's position, do
what you like with it!" That is the bad solution. The second is to
try to give an understanding of the situation not to the totality of
the students nor even to the totality of demonstrators, but to a
large number of them. To do so we must avoid building an
organization immediately, or defining a program; that would inevitably paralyze us. The movement's only chance is the disorder that lets men speak freely, and which can result in a form of
self-organization. For example, we should now give up mass-
spectacular meetings and turn to the formation of work and
action groups. That is what we are trying to do at Nanterre.

But now that speech has been suddenly freed in Paris, it is essential first of all that people should express themselves. They
say confused, vague things and they are often uninteresting
things, too, for they have been said a hundred times before, but
when they have finished, this allows them to ask "So what?" This
is what matters, that the largest possible number of students say
"So what?" Only then can a program and a structure be discussed. To ask us today, "What are you going to do about the
examinations?" is to wish to drown the fish, to sabotage the
movement, and interrupt its dynamics. The examinations will
take place and we shall make proposals, but give us time. First we
must discuss, reflect, seek new formulae. We shall find them. But
not today.

J-P. S.:   You have said that the student movement is now on the
crest of a wave. But the vacation is coming, and with it a de-
celeration, probably a retreat. The government will take the
opportunity to put through reforms. It will invite students to
participate and many will accept, saying either, "Reformism is all
we want," or, "It is only reformism, but it is better than nothing,
and we have obtained it by force." So you will have a transformed university, but the changes may be merely superficial
ones, dealing particularly with the development of material facilities, lodgings, university restaurants. These things would
make no basic changes in the system. They are demands that the
authorities could satisfy without bringing the regime into ques-

tion. Do you think that you could obtain any "adjustments" that would really introduce revolutionary elements into the bourgeois university—for example, that would make the education given at the university contradictory to the basic function of the university in the present regime: the training of cadres who are well integrated into the system?

D. C-B.:   First, purely material demands may have a revolutionary content. On university restaurants we have a demand which is basic. We demand their abolition as university restaurants. They must become youth restaurants in which all young people, whether students or not, can eat for 1.40 francs. No one can reject this demand: if young workers are working during the day, there seems no reason why they should not dine for 1.40 francs in the evening. Similarly with the university cities. There are many young workers and apprentices who would rather live away from their parents but who cannot take a room because that would cost them 30,000 francs per month; let us welcome them to the cities, where the rent is from 9,000 to 10,000 francs per month. And let the well-to-do students in law and postgraduate students in political science go elsewhere.

Basically, I don't think that any reforms the government might make would be enough to demobilize the students. There obviously will be a retreat during the vacation, but they will not "break" the movement. Some will say: "We have lost our chance," without any attempt to explain what has happened. Others will say: "The situation is not yet ripe." But many militants will realize that we must capitalize on what has just taken place, analyze it theoretically and prepare to resume our action next term. For there will be an explosion then, whatever the government's reforms. And the experience of disorderly, unintentional, authority-provoked action we have just been through will enable us to make any action launched in the autumn more effective. The vacation will enable students to come to terms with the disarray they showed during the fortnight's crisis, and to think about what they want to and can do.

As to the possibility of making the education given at the university a "counter-education" manufacturing not well-integrated cadres but revolutionaries, I am afraid that seems to

me a somewhat idealist hope. Even a reformed bourgeois education will still manufacture bourgeois cadres. People will be
caught in the wheels of the system. At best they will become
members of a right-thinking left, but objectively they will remain
cogs ensuring the functioning of society.

Our aim is to pursue successfully a "parallel education" which
will be technical and ideological. We must launch a university
ourselves, on a completely new basis, even if it only lasts a few
weeks. We shall call on left and extreme left teachers who are
prepared to work with us in seminars and assist us with their
knowledge—renouncing their "professional" status—in the in-
vestigations we shall undertake.

In all faculties we shall open seminars—not lecture courses,
obviously—on the problems of the workers' movement, on the
use of technology in the interests of man, on the possibilities
opened up by automation. And all this not from a theoretical
viewpoint (every sociological study today opens with the words:
"Technology must be made to serve man's interests"), but by
posing concrete problems. Obviously, this education will go in
the opposite direction to the education provided by the system
and the experiment could not last long; the system would quickly
react and the movement give way. But what matters is not working out a reform of capitalist society, but launching an experiment that completely breaks with that society, an experiment
that will not last, but which allows a glimpse of a possibility:
something which is revealed for a moment and then vanishes.
But that is enough to prove that that something could exist.

We do not hope to make some kind of socialist university in
our society, for we know that the function of the university will
stay the same so long as the system is unchanged as a whole. But
we believe that there can be moments of rupture in the system's
cohesion and that it is possible to profit by them to open
breaches in it.

J-P. S.:   That presupposes the permanent existence of an "anti-
institutional" movement preventing the student forces from
structuring themselves. In fact, you could attack the UNEF for
being a trade union, that is, a necessarily sclerosed institution.

D. C-B.:   We attack it primarily for its inability to make any demands because of its forms of organization. Besides, the defense

of the students' interests is something very problematic. What are their "interests"? They do not constitute a class. Workers and peasants form social classes and have objective interests. Their demands are clear and they are addressed to the management and to the government of the bourgeoisie. But the students? Who are their "oppressors," if not the system as a whole?

J-P. S.: Indeed, students are not a class. They are defined by an age and a relation to knowledge. By definition, a student is someone who must one day cease to be a student in any society, even the society of our dreams.

D. C-B.: That is precisely what we must change. In the present system, they say: there are those who work and those who study. And we are stuck with a social division of labor, however intelligent. But we can imagine another system where everyone will work at the tasks of production—reduced to a minimum, thanks to technical progress—and everyone will still be able to pursue his studies at the same time: the system of simultaneous productive work and study.

Obviously, there would be special cases: very advanced mathematics or medicine cannot be taken up while exercising another activity at the same time. Uniform rules cannot be laid down. But the basic principle must be changed. To start with we must reject the distinction between student and worker.

Of course, all this is not immediately foreseeable, but something has begun and must necessarily keep going.

In Hervé Bourges, ed., *The French Student Revolt: The Leaders Speak*, trans. B. R. Brewster (New York: Hill and Wang, 1968), 73–83.

Betty Friedan

The Politics of Sex (Fall 1968)

Betty Friedan's 1963 book, The Feminine Mystique, *broadened the popular base for a feminist movement that long preceded the 1960s. By the end of the decade, women had become more visible political actors than ever before. In the United States, Western Europe, the Soviet bloc, and other parts of the world feminist movements pushed for an end to sexual discrimination. They attacked not only institutions and laws, but also cultural assumptions that reinforced in-equality. Though many feminists found Betty Friedan insufficiently radical in the late 1960s, she remained deeply connected to diverse groups within the United States and abroad. During 1968 she pushed for a more powerful femi-nist voice in the American presidential election. She also warned that continued repression of women's voices would motivate increasing radicalism, and perhaps even an "Armageddon between the sexes," on the scale of racial violence at the time.*

Considering that women of voting age outnumber men by more than 7½ million in the U.S. today, politicians of both parties this election year have given remarkably little attention to the interests of women themselves. The women's vote has been left to the can-didate's wife, with some attention in this television era to the candi-date's sex appeal. At both Miami Beach and Chicago there was virtually a separate women's agenda of brunches, luncheons, style shows and teas, for women delegates and wives alike, to keep them out of the way while the men were in the smoke-filled rooms. In the serious business of both conventions, the wheeling and dealing in those smoke-filled rooms, the gut-level decisions that forge political power—from the fight over party platform and challenge of dele-gates' credentials to the manoeuverings [*sic*] for the presidential nomination—the 10% of the U.S. population who are black seemed somehow more visible, in 1968, than the 51% who are women. The Negroes, of course, are no longer "invisible men" in the U.S. today—hated, feared, not asking to be loved, they are, at least, *seen* finally as people whose generations of exploitation must be undone. Sex discrimination is the only kind of discrimination still considered moral, even fashionable, in the U.S.—or a joke. In both political parties, up until now, women have been flattered and fon-dled absentmindedly—in feminine mystique cliches—and have done the political housework, the envelope-addressing, stamp-licking,door-bell ringing, telephone chores—but they haven't been in on the pol-icy decisions in those smoke-filled rooms; they haven't had a real voice in the naming of candidates or run for major office themselves, or received the political appointments or the rewards of political service in even token representation of their half of the vote. With only one woman in the Senate—one out of 100, for 51% of the vote—and no woman governor or Supreme Court judge or big-city mayor or political boss, women are still invisible in the power structure of American politics. It seems to me that women, and the women's vote, has not been taken seriously because it hasn't had to be. But part of the unpredictability of this whole incredible election year is that the invisible 51%—the women's vote—is not being manipulated, delivered, the way possibly it used to be—any more than the ethnic vote or the Negro vote. Perhaps even more important than the students and the Negroes in the new politics is the emergence, for the first time, of an independent woman's vote; and it's beginning to make the political pros a bit uneasy. Could woman power emerge, in 1968, as formidably as black power, without riots in the streets?

Not, I think, until and unless we climb down from the sexual pedestal—which somehow invites contempt—and break out of the sexual ghetto, which perpetuates the denigration of women by patronizing male-only political bosses—and get over our own self-denigration of women which won't let us run for Senate or vote for other women, and get down to the real nitty gritty of American power politics.

* * *

This year I decided to practice what I preach and get into mainstream politics. Not the woman's committee, not hostess fundraising affairs, not just my name and a token role, but the smoke-filled rooms: I'd run for convention delegate myself.

In 1964, I'd been invited to the White House by Lyndon Johnson, with a dozen other "prominent" ladies, to head a national nonpartisan committee of women for Johnson against Goldwater. We were actually allowed to sit around the Cabinet table (I think I sat in the Secretary of Defense's chair)—Ethel Merman, Betty Furness, the Nobel prize winner in physics from California, and such —and LBJ talked to us for nearly an hour about peace and sabre-rattling, and the importance of women, and we had our pictures taken on television, and went upstairs for tea and cookies with

Ladybird. It was all very flattering. I could hardly wait until we were called again to offer our views and suggestions on matters of national policy or campaign strategy. But we were never asked to *do* anything. (I did get invited to the Inaugural Ball, and to various White House receptions where "prominent women" are needed for a "Good Housekeeping Seal of approval"—until I joined other writers in protest against the war in Viet Nam and began also to demand, in public, that the administration give more than lip service, and token appointments, to equal opportunity for women in the United States.) I had lived to regret my token role in electing LBJ to the White House. I swore to myself never again to take a token role in politics.

At the national conference of NOW, in Washington this past November, I had proposed that we draw up a Bill of Rights for Women in 1968, as a touchstone for the evaluation of all major candidates for national office, that we organize a voting power bloc (I did not want to call it "woman power" for it included men; we needed a synonym for "sexual equality power") and "cross party lines to elect candidates who give more than lip service to equality for women, and to defeat its enemies." I had called for the abolition of the separate-but-not-equal ladies' auxiliaries in the political parties, and urged women to refuse to do the traditional menial work of sealing envelopes, ringing doorbells, raising pin-money and holding kaffee clatches, unless they are also admitted to the policy-making mainstream of the political parties. I said:

> We must make it understood that there are many issues facing our nation today of as great or even greater importance to us than equality for women, but it is the very nature of our own commitment to that equality that we wish to speak out and act on those issues in the decision-making mainstream rather than as members of women's ghettos, whether these be Democratid [*sic*] or Republican Women's Divisions, the League of Women Voters, or Women Strike for Peace. My own revulsion toward the war in Viet Nam does not stem from the milk that once flowed from my breast, nor even from the fact of my draft-age sons, but from my moral conscience as a human being and as an American. And it is to that conscience which most Americans share—our common commitment to human

freedom, equality, individual dignity—that we must address our Bill of Rights for Women in 1968.

A few weeks later I got a telegram from Senator McCarthy inviting me to meet with him and other Democratic leaders at a conference in Chicago at which he would announce his candidacy for president. I went for the same reason everyone else was there; because Senator McCarthy had the courage to buck the machine and say "No" to the immoral war and run against the President responsible for it. I also went because, though nobody there but me seemed to know it, Eugene McCarthy is the chief sponsor in the Senate of the Equal Rights Amendment to the Constitution (it would provide that "equality of rights under the law shall not be denied or abridged by the United States or by any State on account of sex") which had been pigeonholed in Congress for over 40 years. He had also introduced legislation eliminating discrimination against women in income taxes. I told my district leader I'd like to run for delegate and, meanwhile, noting in the early days of the McCarthy campaign a lack of literature, got together some fellow writers and editors to do, for free, what we usually get well paid for doing. We finally got an assignment, to put out the Sunday supplement used in New Hampshire, Wisconsin, etc. We got the major thrust from the Senator and a staff man and got down to the center spread, record and program, and specific assignments. Viet Nam, the crisis in the cities, Civil Rights, labor, veterans, business, senior citizens, Negroes, Mexican Americans—"Well, I suppose you want me to do the one on women." I said: "I'd just as soon do something else for a change, but it would save someone else research." "Women?" My colleagues and the new political pros from McCarthy headquarters gave me that blank stare. "Not *here*." As if to say, "Well, we all know that's your hang up, but this is *serious politics*." I apologized: "Well, it *is* 51% of the vote, and his record is really different from all the others on women." They all averted their eyes, as one would say in a Victorian novel; I was *embarrassing* them. "We have a picture of the Senator with Mrs. McCarthy and the girls—that takes care of women and the family." Just before it went to the printers I sat down at the typewriter and added *one* sentence, after Veterans, I think. (*Women*: Senator McCarthy is committed to full equality between the sexes. He is the chief sponsor in the Senate of the Equal Rights Amendment. . . .) It was deleted; a political decision, no doubt.

Then I was summoned by the caucus of Democratic leaders in the 17th Congressional district to be interviewed for the slate of convention delegates. How would I campaign? Well, after talking about the issue of war and peace, I said I might mention Senator McCarthy's approach to the question of real equality for women; it was one issue which set him apart from all other candidates. "That's really very interesting," one man said, "it's the first I heard of it. But you can't seriously suggest it's an *issue*, like the crisis in the cities." "But women are the crux of the crisis in the cities." I said. Didn't they know that 80% of the welfare load in New York City was women—women and their children—considered unemployable because they had no job-training, and no child care centers to help take of [*sic*] their children—and yet the poverty program offered neither serious job-training nor child care centers to women, and welfare laws denied them sexual privacy, self-respect, bare human dignity. As for our own silk stocking district, all the widows, divorcees, bachelor girls, educated young housewives, were suffering one kind of sex discrimination or another.

They didn't put me on the delegate slate. As the discussion leaked back to me, I was too hipped on the woman question. Besides, they already had one woman, Eleanor Clark French, the vice chairlady of the State Democratic Party. And one woman out of six delegates and alternates was enough!

Then somebody called and asked if I wanted to head Women for McCarthy in the State. "Not unless I have a real voice in campaign policy," I said. Big pause—they'd call me back. The next day somebody apologized for bothering me about that; they'd found somebody not so "busy" to head the women's committee. Well, I was still useful from time to time, as a "celebrity." A young person took over the Speaker's Bureau, and discovered I could even make a good campaign speech; I was asked to substitute once for Robert Lowell. And once, when they were quite desperate, they even asked me to debate Arthur Schlesinger. Only, by then I was out in California campaigning in the primary for Senator McCarthy—Abigail sent me a message to come. I didn't go to the Democratic convention as a delegate; back to the press badge this time. But I'm beginning to have the feel of what "woman power" really is, and can be, in the New Politics—and what it isn't.

In the old politics, being played out at Miami and Chicago, you could see that the traditional power of a woman, based on sex, doesn't count politically, and that the traditional political approach to women, in sexual terms, was obsolete for 1968. There was only the faintest glimmer of real political power in female clothes.

In Miami both Reagan and Nixon had official hostesses who were a cross between old-time chorus girls or high school cheer leaders and Playboy bunnies. They wore micromini skirts and were urged to show more leg there." There was even a group of former Goldwater Girls, calling themselves GOP girls, who were willing to display their sexual charms for *any* candidate. In the Wallace campaign, such "girls" went around selling their kisses, or whatever, for $20 for the campaign. None of these "hostesses" could ever explain why she was for this candidate or that. Women for Reagan wore huge buttons that simply said "I believe."

According to political custom, the token woman vice chairman—or chairman of the women's division—of the Republican or Democratic Party is last on the agenda, her "remarks" (as women's speeches are listed on the convention program) sandwiched in between the "addresses" of the men. If there's time to get around to her at all, nobody is expected to listen, so she doesn't say anything much. Both parties have a rule that each state must have a woman vice chairman, and a national committee-woman as well as a committee-man. But the woman vice chairman is simply the head of the ladies' auxiliary. Her job is to keep the women quiet, and deliver that 51% of the vote, which until now the real pros didn't have to think about—it simply went along with the husbands' vote. "We're not supposed to deal with the issues," Mary Brooks, head of the Republican women's division, told me. "I'm so sick of fashion shows." Margaret Price, who held the same token post in the Democratic national committee until her recent death, was never even consulted about political appointments of women. Segregated in those separate sexual ghettos, in both political parties, no matter how much political housework they do, women just aren't taken seriously.

But for the first time, this year, there was a Republican woman state chairman—not just a lady vice chairman—Elly Peterson of Michigan, a big wheeler-dealer in the Rockefeller campaign. "When you're the lady vice chairman you're expected to deal just with the women," she told me. "You aren't included in party councils. But you can't advance in the political world and get the men to take you seriously just by using your femininity. I got elected because I went into the organizational work on the same level as the men."

There were only 224 women among the 1,333 delegates to the Republican convention—fewer than in '64—and some states had no women delegates at all. There were a few younger women among these delegates—Tina Harrower of Connecticut, Congressman Margaret Heckler of Massachusetts, and others, mainly Rockefeller liberals—who fought on the platform committee to have the GOP face up to the fact that "there is a crisis in our cities," and to match the crusade for law and order with a crusade for social justice to eliminate the causes of violence. But there was no woman who could even begin to talk back to Everett Dirksen.

No woman gave a major speech to the convention. Women were permitted to sing the national anthem, present an orangewood gavel to the temporary chairman (male) of the convention, hand a bouquet of flowers to Mrs. Ray Bliss, wife of the chairman of the Republican national convention; keep the minutes; run the luncheons; and call the roll of the states when the balloting began—the apex of token glory. (The Miami Herald ran a cartoon, the last day of the convention, with a Republican official handing a woman a broom, and saying: "After the keynote address, the lady delegates can sweep up behind the speaker's podium.")

The word "women" hardly appears in the Republican platform. Nixon, with Reagan and Wallace, didn't even bother to answer our request for commitment to a Bill of Rights for Women in 1968. The younger women on the Republican platform committee, at the very end, managed to add to the vaguep [sic] plank of "concern for the unique problems of citizens long disadvantaged in our total society by race and color" the word "sex"—with a titter from the men.

But the Republican campaign is counting very strongly on women's traditional sexual fears to elect Richard Nixon president. Nixon's "militant crusade against crime" aims specifically at "the millions of women who refuse to walk in their neighborhoods or visit their parks after dark out of fear."

The assumption of a special sexual timidity in women may be a bit old hat for 1968. There aren't many women still around who see rapists behind every tree. American women these days aren't repressing their own sexual desires that much. But Nixon—less openly then Reagan and Wallace—appeals to another repressed emotion in women, a venting of pent-up frustration and hate, when he speaks of using force to put down Negro rioters and the dissident college students. Some of the older women at the Republican convention were more extreme than the men, on using violence against looters (they even wanted to be able to order guns through the mail). It's interesting that the first woman to *nominate* a majoy [*sic*] presidential candidate—and not just second the nomination, women's usual role—was Ivy Baker Priest, former Treasurer of the United States, who took the rostrum, white-haired and smiling in a blue lace dress, to nominate Ronald Reagan, "a man who will confront the radicals on our campuses and the looters on our streets and say: 'The laws will be abeyed . . .' . . . and (in Viet Nam) make it clear that if we must fight for freedom, we will fight to win." And one old GOP pro told me: "The women are going to vote us in this year; they're all worked up, can't walk in the streets, prisoners in their own homes—hysterical."

The alienation and futility which breeds violence is, in fact, suffered by millions of women in this country, in inner city poverty, meek office anonymity, and even affluent suburban isolation. Like other oppressed people, women for generations have been taking their own violence out on themselves (see them crowd the doctors' offices) and inadvertently on their husbands and children (see the psychiatric case histories, the marriage counselling columns, the battered child syndrome) instead of taking action against the conditions which oppress them. But the new woman emerging from the sexual ghettos of the old politics to confront, in the new politics, the real problems that are tearing our nation apart—and the violence we are inflicting on the world—is not suffering from that suppressed female violence that can be stampeded into a crusade to suppress other people's acts.

* * *

The old pros in the Democratic party—and even certain old-fashioned feminine mystique types in the New Politics—are playing to "woman power" in different but equally specious terms. Hubert Humphrey is a big "woman power" man, in the lip service sense in which President Johnson announced he was going to purify the government by appointing women in great numbers to "high office." The offices, of course, were only token ones, outside the power structure—Special Assistant to the Deputy Assistant Secretary of State, in charge of flower arranging at embassies. (Several of LBJ's "top jobs" for ladies actually were specially created jobs to arrange fashion shows, and select paintings, for embassies). And Ladybird had all kinds of "women doers" and women's clubs presidents to the White House, just before Congressional appropriations were to be passed, whom LBJ would bless as the heart and only possible saviors of the war on poverty.

Some of that same note has even been sounded by Coretta King, who said, in the Poor People's March, "Women, if the soul of the nation is to be saved, I believe that you must become its soul." (A ladies' magazine wrote:—McCalls, in the June issue—intoning: "The women of this country have heard enough about black power, white power, student power, senior citizen power. The greatest power of all for good is theirs—woman power. No force on earth can stand against it.") Even at a Women for McCarthy conference, former White House resident intellectual Charles Frankel told women that by staying outside dirty old American politics—which they couldn't "domesticate" themselves to—they could transform it with love and pure, uncorrupted hearts.

Such politicians kid themselves, women kid themselves, with all this flattery about "woman power"—that mystical, natural, inborn, moral purity and superiority of women which will clean up the world—by miracle, evidently—without women having a decision-making voice in any political party, a seat in the power structure of right, center, or left—the military-industrial complex, the labor unions, the universities, or the churches, and in fact without such a voice or seat in the anti-establishment power structure either, including the student movement. Women, quite simply, have not had any real political power in America until now, because they were "outside." As columnist Clayton Fritchey put it (Newsday, June 26):

"The sad truth is that, politically, women have been one of the great disappointments of the 20th Century. The disappointment has been magnified because such great expectations attended the passage 50 years ago of the 19th Amendment, giving women the right to vote. The suffragette leaders had argued passionataly [*sic*] and persuasively that the enfrachisement [*sic*] of women would end wars, and promote humane, social-minded society. Considering the stake women have in a peaceful, stabilized, civilised culture, it seemed a logical conclusion. Except—

"The first thing the women of America did after getting the vote was to help elect Warren G. Harding as President in 1920, thereby killing the last hopes for the League of Nations and the World Court, and slamming the brakes on the liberal social programs initiated by Woodrow Wilson, under whose administration suffrage was finally achieved.

"Now, five decades later, there is little evidence that suffrage has changed the U.S. much one way or the other. By and large, women have voted like their husbands. The politicians long ago came to the conclusion that there is no such thing as a 'woman's vote.'"

Well, if women only voted as sexual appendages of men—wives, mothers—that was the only role they could play—the only role their actual power warranted—in the old politics. The woman's vote was appealed to sexually, and not even a very adult sex at that. Women were thought to vote for Eisenhower because his image gave them a fatherly sense of security. Jack Kennedy was supposed to have had so much more sex appeal than Nixon. Women, who now outnumber male voters in France, were held responsible for De Gaulle's recent victory—out of similar "feminine" need for a strong man to lean on. If women did have that innately superior "power for good," moral sensitivity and humane tenderness the feminine mystique oracles of the right, or left, proclaim—for Woemn [*sic*] Strike for Peace and the Jeanette Rankin Brigade share an image of women that is similar to a reactionary Southern Congressman's pedestal—then French women should have voted De Gaulle out, for his brutality to their children, at least. The sad truth is, women don't have any special claim to human conscience, compassion, love, tenderness, or even an instinct for peace. Think of Shirley Temple Black and Louise Day Hicks, the vicious Southern white "sisters" who stoned Negro children entering school, and the women who form the John Birch shock troops, the pornography book-burners, taking out their own pent-up venom and frustrations by stamping out even *language* that frankly celebrates sex or any other *free* expression of human beings. Those mystical qualities of love, intuition, sensitivity, purity, are read into women—even exalting them on a pedestal—by *default*, hiding, even making a virtue of the fact that they must specialize exclusively in love, children, home, serving others' simplest human needs—because they are barred from taking part in more complex affairs requiring education, training, self-confidence, and broad independent vision. All that natural purity mystique was in fact a perversion of the early feminism (which was simply a matter of human right) that kept women from progressing further, after they won the vote nearly 50 years ago. Men had so inflated women's "natural moral superiority"—to justify their own guilt at keeping them out of the really important business of society—and women had to so inflate it, to justify their own feelings of inferiority, excluded as they were from any real say in the big decisions of their cities and country—that just giving them the vote was expected to magically purify society.

But for women, as for Negroes, the vote is not power—unless they have the economic mobility, the jobs and education, that give them a decision-making voice in the power structure, or the revolutionary consciousness and skills—born of education and/or action—to make a counter power structure. The Negroes couldn't do it either until they got off the plantations, until the Negro kids had enough education, in school, on television, to spell their own names instead of letting Whitey spell it—and could get together in the cities, in counter-action, if they couldn't get in on the real thing.

Women in the isolation of their separate homes, denied education or jobs beyond the most menial, completely dependent on their husbands for support and for status, can be more easily manipulated than any minority group because they are too isolated—and too self-denigrating—to get together and demand power, as the discriminated-against minorities have done.

But the new woman emerging in the politics of 1968 is not the same as the old housewife to be kept happily quiet in the ladies' auxiliary, with her teas and fashion shows, appealed to in politics by the candidate's sex appeal or the homely virtues of the candidate's wife, and voting finally as her husband does—or even the college graduate, using her liberal education to study the issues, pure and simple, out of the politician's way. The big difference is, quite simply, that half of all women over 18 now work outside the isolated home, and growing millions have education beyond high school. The two-income family is now more common than the one-income family. Of younger women recently out of college 90% either work or expect to work in society after their children go to school. They are not, and do not expect to be, completely dependent on their husbands. True, three out of four women who work are in the least rewarding sales, service and clerical jobs, doing the housework still in home, hospital, or industry. It is not surprising that women hold only one seat out of 100 in the Senate, when only 2% of the lawyers in the U.S. are women, and even fewer women executives or leaders of labor, civil rights or student movements—the new avenues to political leadership.

The New Women—28 million women now working, almost a million a year coming out of the colleges, all those housewives with kids off to school, going back to school themselves, or to work—and the welfare mothers marching—these women are becoming visible to themselves finally, as people first and not just somebody else's wife, mother, housewife, secretary, Girl Friday or welfare mother. That's surely why that invisible 51%—the woman's vote—can not be passively manipulated, delivered along with the husbands' vote. It is indeed a new vote, of conscience and choice and hunger for participation in the big decisions—perhaps all the more so because women, with all their new independence, are still—as both a price and a privilege of something less than equality—not tied into the power structure as much as thier [sic] men. And perhaps women, not burdened by the masculine mystique, can look at questions of war and peace without feeling they have to prove their virility, as men do, for fear of being chicken.

The columnist quoted above remarked: "In the 1966 election there were 60,055,000 females of voting age versus only 52,849,000 males, but 58 per cent of the men actually voted, as against 53 per cent for women. There are faint intimations of a change. Until a few months ago women, as usual, appeared to take their cue from men on Viet Nam, but recent polls indicate that a clear "woman's vote" is emerging on this issue, with 49% of women now classed as "doves," as compared with only 33% of men in that category. The results so apparent in the primary victories of Senator Eugene McCarthy and Senator Robert Kennedy have just begun to sink in on the politicians."

In the ~~most recent~~ Gallup Poll, just before the Republican convention, though men favored Nixon over Rockefeller, 48 to 41%, women favored Rockefeller over Nixon, in almost opposite degree. The Harris Poll showed a similar woman's vote in terms of Democratic candidates, the women favoring McCarthy over Humphrey in virtually equal and opposite percentages from the men. The Gallup Poll just before the Democratic convention showed only 28% of women for Humphrey against Nixon—where 40% would be for McCarthy versus Nixon.

* * *

In the New Politics, women, like the former ethnic blocs, are breaking out of that passive dependency so easily manipulated, and voting from conscience and from choice. They are also beginning to show a hunger for the participation and voice in the political process that they have been barred from in the job market. (And in this they also resemble the ethnic blocs and Negro minority.) I was struck, in McCarthy's campaign in California, with the numbers of women in the crowds, in the rallies and at airport stops, in small new cities and large ones. Young, intelligent looking women, often carrying children, or with husbands—often not—listening intently to what he was saying.

No woman I ever questioned at a McCarthy rally talked about the way he looked, his sex appeal. I think they were quite clearly re-

sponding to the questions and issues he was raising—and to the total quality of the man, which is not the usual American definition
of sex appeal. And if some women showed greater courage, independence, conscience, than their husbands, by so doing, I don't
think it's because women are born with more soul, or even because
they love their sons more—but because they are still so removed
from the power structure, on the periphery, as to be relatively free
from the corrupting, compromising, influence of political "realism"
and "careerism." One of the illusory advantages of women's inequality is that they are not expected to share equal responsibility
for the mortgage, bank-loan and the grocer.

In the campaign command that came out of the student movement, the young men in the key jobs were almost always teamed
with a young woman co-director. "All our top men have strong
women behind them," is the way one girl put it to me. But it
seemed to me more significant than that, for young women like
Jessie Tuchman in California and Sarah Koones in New York
seemed to be doing the same work as their male co-directors. They
were not assistants, secretaries or girl fridays or token women in any
sense. Their voices carried full weight in strategy conclaves. Sarah
Koones dreamed up and organized the final M-day rally by which
McCarthy in Madison Square Garden was linked by closed circuit
television to people in 22 other cities—a new departure in participation politics. The politicos who ran the petition campaigns were
often women. One woman organized the simultaneous petition
parties all over California on the first night filing was legal, so that
the thousands of petitions could be signed and filled out instanta-
neously and get the McCarthy slate first on the ballot. There were
also women who had joined the campaign as volunteers in New
Hampshire and were then taken on the student staff's very minimum per diem, and had risen to very responsible jobs by the time
of the California campaign, running speakers' bureaus, press, research, headquarters and field operations, though they'd never
taken part in party politics before. They'd had education, they'd
had the usual trouble trying to use it, in volunteer work, in part-
time employment, while raising kids. This chance to take a real,
essential, even decision-making part in a political process that was
obviously changing the course of history, was changing their lives.

Cal Rossiter, a soft-spoken woman from New England, had left [*sic*] her children and her husband to "make do" temporarily without her after New Hampshire as she worked on through California. "I never thought women counted before, I never thought we could be important," she said. "Now, by golly, I know how important women can be. In this campaign I count." And another one, in her twenties, doing research, even briefing the Senator when need be, while her doctor husband waited back home, called me at my hotel: "Some of us have been thinking the Senator should give a major speech on the woman question. The women in the campaign—well, we worry about it. You can't go back from being part of what's happening after you've helped make it happen—and stay home with the kids the way women are expected to do. And yet sooner or later we all want to have kids."

* * *

It would be a shame if the New Politics continues to cast women in the same old role as the old politics, the establishment, the far right; looks at them through the same stereotypes, and misses the boat—still not seeing the formerly invisible 51% for the power it really could be. In the New Politics the urgent questions of the unfinished business of equality for women shouldn't be the domain of the candidate's wife; they should be of urgent concern to the candidate himself.

When we put our Bill of Rights for Women in 1968 to all of the presidential candidates this spring, only Senators Kennedy and McCarthy bothered to answer at first. Rockefeller and Humphrey got around to answering in July. Nixon didn't take women seriously enough to answer at all. For the historic record, there was a big difference in the others' answers. Kennedy didn't think the Equal Rights Amendment to the Constitution was necessary, and Humphrey weaseled on that too. It is essential, in the politics of sex, to understand that the Labor Establishment, the old-time leaders of the AFL-CIO who comprise Humphrey's machine, are as much, or even more, reactionary about "protecting" women from equal job opportunity than corporate managers. They are violently opposed to the Equal Rights Amendment because it would make unconstitutional the so-called state protective laws which are the only way employers and unions can get away with barring women from recall, promotion or training for jobs "for men only," now that sex discrimination in employment is barred by the Federal Civil Rights Act, Title 7.

For the record, the Johnson Administration and specifically Hubert Humphrey, whi [*sic*] was in charge of the strategy for getting the Civil Rights Act of 1964 through Congress, most emphatically opposed barring sex discrimination in employment along with race discrimination. Administration "Aunt Toms" Esther Peterson and Mary Keyserling of the Women's Bureau told Congress women didn't need such protection. When an unexpected revolt of women in Congress got sex added to the law, the Johnson Administration made it clear that this provision would not be seriously enforced. Officials of the Equal Employment Opportunity Commission made Playboy bunny jokes about sex discrimination at their press conferences and the Attorney General has not yet used his power under the law to intervene in a single court case of sex discrimination.

In my testimony to the Republican and Democratic Platform Committees, I said that sex discrimination "has been too often treated as a joke by politicians, executives, newspapers and even the government administrators entrusted with enforcement of laws "against discrimination."

I asked that a Bill of Rights for Women in 1968 include: Immediate passage by Congress of the Equal Rights Amendment to the Constitution; action requiring the Equal Employment Opportunity Commission to enforce prohibitions against sex discrimination "as vigorously as it enforces prohibitions against racial discrimination" under the Civil Rights Act of 1964; legal protection ensuring women's rights to return to their jobs within a reasonable time after childbirth without loss of seniority or other accrued benefits; immediate revision of tax laws to permit deduction of home and child care expenses for working parents; child care facilities "established by law on the same basis as parks, libraries and public schools, adequate to the needs of children from the pre-school years through adolescence, as a community resource to be used by citizens from all income levels;" laws abolishing discrimination against women at all levels of education, including not only universities and professional schools but also Federal and State training programs such as the Job Corps; "revision of welfare legislation and poverty programs which deny women dignity, privacy and self-respect;" and abolition of penal code laws limiting access to contraceptive information and devices, and laws governing abortion.

"We believe the time has come to move beyond the abstract argument, discussion and symposia over the status and special nature of women which has raged in America in recent years; the time has come to confront, with concrete action, the conditions that now prevent women from enjoying the equality of opportunity and freedom of choice which is their right, as individual Americans, and as human beings," I said. "Men are not the enemies of women's unfinished revolution, but fellow victims, along with children, of the suppressed violence bred by sexual inequality. But if the real problems dividing the sexes are not faced, if the urgent demand for some real voice and power for women in the mainstream of our society is not met, this presently suppressed violence could also burst into an Armageddon between the sexes that could make the riots in Newark and Detroit, and the torn up paving stones of Paris, seem like child's play."

(more to come)

Arthur and Elizabeth Schlesinger Library on the History of Women in America, Radcliffe Institute, Harvard University, Betty Friedan Papers, Box 26, Folder 925.

Ludvík Vaculík

Two Thousand Words for Workers, Farmers, Scientists, Artists, and Everyone (27 June 1968)

In early 1968 a reform-minded communist government lifted some of the restrictions on personal freedom in Czechoslovakia. Young writers and students began to criticize Soviet influence, calling for their state to pursue its own separate path to socialism—"socialism with a human face." This period of relative freedom and experimentation became known as the "Prague Spring." In June 1968

Czechoslovak writer Ludvík Vaculík pushed reform in a radical direction. He condemned the corruption and brutality of the communist party, judging it incapable of reform. In its place he called for new political parties and the creation of pluralist democracy. Vaculík's "Two Thousand Words" were communist heresy, but they inspired thousands of young citizens in Czechoslovakia and other countries.

The life of this nation was first of all threatened by the war. Then still more bad times followed, together with events which threatened the spiritual health and character of the nation. Most of the people of Czechoslovakia optimistically accepted the socialist program, but its direction got into the wrong people's hands. It would not have mattered so much that they did not possess enough experience as statesmen, have enough practical knowledge or intellectual training, if they had at least had more common sense and humanity, if they had been able to listen to other people's opinions, and if they had allowed themselves to be replaced as time passed by more capable people.

After the war people had great confidence in the Communist party, but it gradually preferred to have official positions instead of the people's trust, until it had only official positions and nothing else. This has to be said: Communists among us know that it's true, and their disappointment about the results is just as great as that of others. The incorrect line of the leadership turned the party from a political party and ideological grouping into a power organization which became very attractive to power-hungry egotists, reproachful cowards, and people with bad consciences. When they came into the party, its character and behavior began to be affected. Its internal organization was such that good people, who might have maintained its development for it to have fitted into the modern world, could not wield any influence at all without shameful incidents occurring. Many communists opposed this decline, but not in one single case did they have any success in preventing what happened.

The conditions in the Communist party were the model for and the cause of an identical situation in the state. Because the party became linked with the state it lost the advantage of being able to keep its distance from the executive power. There was no criticism of the activity of the state and economic organizations. Parliament forgot how to debate: The government forgot how to govern and the directors how to direct. Elections had no significance, and the laws lost their weight. We could not trust representatives on any committee, and even if we did, we could not ask them to do anything, because they could accomplish nothing. What was still worse was that we could hardly trust each other anymore. There was a decline of individual and communal honor. You didn't get anywhere by being honest, and it was useless expecting ability to be appreciated. Most people, therefore, lost interest in public affairs; they worried only about themselves and about their money. Moreover, as a result of these bad conditions, now one cannot even rely on money. Relationships between people were harmed, and they didn't enjoy working any more. To sum up, the country reached a point where its spiritual health and character were both threatened.

We are all of us together responsible for the present state of affairs, and the communists among us are more responsible than others. But the main responsibility rests with those who were part of, or the agents of, uncontrolled power. The power of a determined group was conveyed, with the help of the party apparatus, from Prague to every district and community. This apparatus decided what one might or might not do: It directed the cooperatives for the cooperative workers, the factories for the workers, and the National Committees for the citizens. No organizations actually belonged to their members, not even the communist ones.

These rulers' greatest guilt, and the worst deception they perpetrated, was to make out that their arbitrary rule was the will of the workers. If we were to continue to believe this deception, we would have now to blame the workers for the decline of our economy, for the crimes committed against innocent people, for the introduction of the censorship which made it impossible for all this to be written about. The workers would now have to be blamed for the wrong investments, for the losses in trade, for the shortage of flats. Of course, no sensible person believes in such guilt on the part of the workers. We all know, and especially every worker knows, that in actual fact the workers made no decisions about anything. Someone else controlled the voting of the workers' representatives. While many workers had the impression that they were in control, a specially educated group of party officials and officials of the state apparatus ruled. In fact, they took the place of the overthrown class and themselves became the new aristocracy.

In all fairness, we should say that some of them were aware of what was going on a long time ago. We can recognize these people now by the fact that they are redressing wrongs, correcting mistakes, returning the power of making decisions to the party members and the citizens, and limiting the authority and the number of the apparatchiks. They are with us in opposing the backward, obsolete views among the party membership. But many officials are still defending themselves against changes, and they still carry a lot of weight. They still have means of power in their hands, especially in the districts and in the small communities, where they may use these instruments secretly and without any risk to themselves.

Since the beginning of the year, we have been taking part in the revival process of democratization. It began in the Communist party. Even noncommunists, who until recently expected no good to come from it, recognize this fact. We should add, however, that the process could not have begun anywhere else. After all, only the communists could for twenty years lead anything like a full political life; only the communists were in a position to know what was happening and where; only the opposition within the Communist party were privileged enough to be in contact with the enemy. The initiative and efforts of democratic communists are therefore only a part of the debt which the party as a whole owes to noncommunists, whom it has kept in a position of inequality. No thanks, therefore, is due to the Communist party, although it should probably be acknowledged that it is honestly trying to use this last opportunity to save its own and the nation's honor.

The revival process hasn't come up with anything very new. It is producing ideas and suggestions, many of which are older than the errors of our socialism and others which came up to the surface after being in existence underground for a long time. They should have come out into the open a long time ago, but they were suppressed. Don't let's kid ourselves that these ideas are now winning the day because truth has a force and strength. The fact that they are now winning is much more because of the weakness of the old leadership, which apparently had to be weakened beforehand by twenty years of unopposed rule during which no one interrupted it. Obviously, all the faults hidden in the very foundations and ideology of this system had to mature before they could be seen properly developed.

Let us not, therefore, underestimate the significance of criticism from the ranks of writers and students. The source of social changes lies in the economy. The right word carries significance only if it is said in conditions which have already been duly prepared. And by duly prepared conditions in our country we have to understand our general poverty and the complete disintegration of the old system of rule, in which politicians of a certain type quite calmly compromised themselves, but at our expense. So you can see that truth is not victorious here, truth is what remains when everything else has gone to pot. We have no reason to be patting ourselves on the back, but there is reason to be a little more optimistic.

We turn to you in this optimistic moment because it is still being threatened. It took several months for many of us to believe that we really could speak out, and many people still do not believe it. But nevertheless, we have spoken out, and such a huge number of things have come out into the open that somehow we must complete our aim of humanizing this regime. If we don't, the revenge of the old forces would be cruel. So we are turning now mainly to those who have been waiting. This moment will be a decisive one for many years to come.

The summer is approaching, with its holidays, when, as is our habit, we shall want to drop everything and relax. We can be quite sure however that our dear adversaries will not indulge in any summer recreations, that they will mobilize all their people, and that even now they are trying to arrange for a calm Christmas! So let us be careful about what happens, let's try to understand it and respond to it. Let's give up this impossible demand that someone above us must always provide us with the only possible interpretation of things, one simple conclusion. Every single one of us will have to be responsible for arriving at his own conclusions. Commonly accepted conclusions can only be arrived at by discussions, and this requires the freedom of expression which is actually our only democratic achievement of the last year.

In the future, we shall have to display personal initiative and determination of our own.

Above all, we shall have to oppose the view, should it arise, that it is possible to conduct some sort of a democratic revival without the communists or possibly against them. This would be both unjust and unreasonable. The communists have well-constructed organizations, and we should support the progressive wing within them. They have experienced officials, and last but not least, they also have in their hands the decisive levers and buttons. Their Action Program has been presented to the public. It is a program for the initial adjustment of the greatest inequalities, and no one else has any similarly concrete program. We must demand that local Action Programs be submitted to the public in each district and each community. By doing so, we shall have suddenly taken very ordinary and long-expected steps in the right direction. The Czechoslovak Communist party is preparing for the Congress which will elect a new Central Committee. Let us demand that it should be better than the present one. If the Communist party now says that in the future it wants to base its leading position on the confidence of the citizens and not on force, then we should believe what it says as long as we can believe in the people it is sending as delegates to the district and regional conferences.

Fears have recently been expressed that the democratization process has come to a halt. This feeling is partly caused by the fatigue brought on by the worrying times and partly because the times of surprising revelations, resignations from high places, and intoxicating speeches of a quite unprecedented bravery are now past. The conflict of forces, however, has merely become hidden to a certain extent. The fight is now being waged about the content and form of laws, over the kind of practical steps that can be taken. And we must also give the new people, the ministers, prosecutors, chairmen and secretaries, time to work. They have the right to this time so that they can either prove their worth or their worthlessness. One cannot expect any more of the central political organs than this. They have, after all, shown that they are responsible enough.

The practical quality of the future democracy depends on what becomes of the enterprises and what will happen in them. In spite of all our discussions, it is the economists who control things. We have to find good managers and back them up. It is true that, in comparison with the developed countries, we are all badly paid, and some are worse off than others.

We can demand more money—but although it can be printed, it will be worth less. We should instead demand that directors and chairmen explain to us the nature and extent of the capital they want for production, to whom they want to sell their products and for how much, what profit they can expect to make, and the percentage of this profit that is to be invested in the modernization of production and the percentage to be shared out.

Under quite superficially boring headlines, a very fierce struggle is going on in the press about democracy and who leads the country. Workers can intervene in this struggle by means of the people they elect to enterprise administrations and councils. As employees, they can do what is best for themselves by electing as their representatives on trade union organs their natural leaders, capable and honest people, no matter what their party affiliation is.

If at the moment we cannot expect any more from the central political organs, we must achieve more in the districts and smaller communities. We should demand the resignation of people who have misused their power, who have damaged public property, or who have acted in a dishonest or brutal way. We have to find ways and means to persuade them to resign, through public criticism, for instance, through resolutions, demonstrations, demonstration work brigades, collections for retirement gifts for them, strikes, and picketing their houses. We must however, reject improper or illegal methods, since these might be used as weapons against Alexander Dubček.

We must so strongly condemn the writing of insulting letters that if some official still receives one, then we shall know that he has written it to himself. Let us revive the activity of the National Front. Let us demand that the meetings of the National Committees should be held in public. And let us set up special citizens' committees and commissions to deal with subjects that nobody is yet interested in. It's quite simple, a few people get together, elect a chairman, keep regular minutes, publish their findings, demand a solution, and do not allow themselves to be intimidated.

We must turn the district and local press, which has degenerated into a mouthpiece for official views, into a platform for all the positive political forces. Let us demand that editorial councils composed of members from the National Front be set up, and let us found other newspapers. Let us establish committees for the defence of the freedom of the press. Let us organize our own monitoring services at meetings. If we hear strange news, let's check on it ourselves, and let's send delegations to the people concerned and, if need be, publish their replies. Let us support the security organs when they prosecute real criminal activity. We do not mean to cause anarchy and a state of general instability. Let's not quarrel amongst ourselves; let's give up spiteful politics. And let's show up informers.

The recent apprehension is the result of the possibility that foreign forces may intervene in our internal development. Face to face with these superior forces, the only thing we can do is to hold our own and not indulge in any provocation. We can assure our government—with weapons if need be—as long as it does what we give it a mandate to do, and we must assure our allies that we will observe our alliance, friendship, and trade agreements. But excited accusations and ungrounded suspicions will make our government's position much more difficult and cannot be of any help to us. After all, we can ensure equal relations only by improving our internal situation and by carrying the process of revival so far that one day at elections we will be able to elect statesmen who will have enough courage, honor, and political talent to establish and maintain such relations. This, of course, is the problem of the government of every small country in the world.

This spring, as after the war, we have been given a great chance. We have once again the opportunity to take a firm grip on a common cause, which has the working title of socialism, and to give it a form which will much better suit the once good reputation that we had and the relatively good opinion that we once had of ourselves. The spring has now come to an end, and it will never return. By winter we will know everything.

And so we come to the end of our statement to workers, farmers, officials, artists, scholars, scientists, technicians, everybody. It was written at the suggestion of the scientists.

In Gale Stokes, ed., *From Stalinism to Pluralism* (New York: Oxford University Press, 1991), 126–130.

Memorandum of Conversation between Leonid Brezhnev and Alexander Dubček (13 August 1968)

Soviet leader Leonid Brezhnev initially supported reform in Czechoslovakia. He hoped it would increase communist authority and economic productivity in the country. Pursuing a series of cooperative agreements with the United States, West Germany, and other Western countries, Brezhnev did not want to intervene militarily in Czechoslovakia. It would jeopardize his hopes for internal reform and inspire hostility from the Western states. The growing anti-Soviet rhetoric of the "Prague Spring," however, forced Brezhnev's hand. In extended discussions with Czechoslovak leader Alexander Dubček, Brezhnev called on "Sasha" to rein in the young activists who pushed for too much independence. Dubček could not do this; the "Prague Spring" had become a broad-based national movement. Frustrated with Dubček and fearful of the young activists in Czechoslovakia, Brezhnev ordered a Soviet bloc invasion of the country on the night of 20 August 1968. Soviet tanks easily repressed public activism, but they could not counteract the growth of anti-Soviet sentiment in Czechoslovakia.

Comrade L. I. Brezhnev's conversation with Comrade A. S. Dubček

13 August 1968

Start of the conversation: 5:35 P.M.
End of the conversation: 6:55 P.M.

BREZHNEV: Aleksandr Stepanovich, I felt the need to speak with you today. I called you early in the morning and then later in the day, but you were away the whole time in Karlovy Vary, and then you called me back, but at that point I had gone to have a talk with the comrades. Now that I've returned, they told me that you have a presidium meeting going on, and so I hope I'm not greatly disturbing you by having this conversation.

DUBČEK: No, not at all, the comrades already told me that you wanted to speak with me. I just now got back from Karlovy Vary. I had a meeting there with Cde. Ulbricht.

BREZHNEV: How did the meeting go?

DUBČEK: I think it went well. Cde. Ulbricht and the comrades accompanying him returned today to the GDR, and I just finished seeing them off.

BREZHNEV: We have little time, and so let me get straight to the point. I'm again turning to you with anxiety about the fact that the mass media in your country are not only incorrectly depicting our conferences in Čierna nad Tisou and Bratislava, but are also stepping up their attacks against the healthy forces and continuing to purvey anti-Sovietism and anti-socialist ideas. What I'm referring to here are not some isolated instances but an organized campaign; and judging by the content of the materials, these press organs have come to serve as a mouthpiece for the right-wing, anti-socialist forces. We in the Politburo exchanged views about this matter and unanimously concluded that there is every basis for regarding the unfolding situation as a violation of the agreement reached in Čierna nad Tisou. I have in mind the agreement you and I reached during our one-on-one discussions, as well as the agreement we thrashed out during the four-on-four meetings and the agreement that emerged between the Politburo of our party and the Presidium of the Central Committee of your party.

DUBČEK: I have already told you what sorts of measures we are taking to put an end to the anti-Soviet and anti-socialist manifestations in the mass media. I have already told you what sorts of measures we are preparing and in what sequence we will carry them out. But I also told you at the time that it's impossible to do all this in a single day. We need time to take care of it. We're not able to restore order in the operations of the mass media in just two to three days.

BREZHNEV: Sasha, that's true, and we warned you at the time that the rightist forces will not easily give up their positions and that it would of course be impossible to do everything in just two to three days. But a lot more time than two to three days has already passed, and the success of your work in this regard depends on your willingness to take decisive measures to restore order in the mass media. Of course if the CPCz leadership and the ČSSR government continue to pursue a policy of non-interference in this matter in the future, these processes will continue unabated. It's simply impossible to halt them through a policy of non-interference. You *must* resort to concrete measures. This is precisely the point on which we reached concrete agreement in connection with the role of Pelikán, and we said that it was essential to dismiss Pelikán. This would be the first step needed to restore order in the mass media.

DUBČEK: Leonid Ilyich, we studied these questions and are continuing to study them. I told Cde. Černík what sorts of measures we'd have to take, and I gave Cde. Lenárt the task of carrying out the necessary measures. As far as I know, no sorts of attacks have been appearing recently against the CPSU or the Soviet Union or against the socialist order.

BREZHNEV: How can you say such a thing when literally all the newspapers—*Literární listy, Mladá fronta, Reportér, Práce*—every day are publishing anti-Soviet and anti-party articles?

DUBČEK: That was going on *before* Bratislava. Since Bratislava that hasn't been happening.

BREZHNEV: What do you mean it was only "before Bratislava"? On 8 August *Literární listy* featured an article entitled "From Warsaw to Bratislava," which was a full-blown, vicious attack against the CPSU and the USSR and against all the fraternal socialist countries. The 8th of August, needless to say, was after Bratislava.

DUBČEK: That's an isolated case. I don't know of any others. All the rest appeared before Bratislava. We're opposed to this article and are now taking appropriate measures.

BREZHNEV: Sasha, I can't agree with this. Over the past two to three days, the newspapers I mentioned have been doggedly continuing to occupy themselves with the publication of defamatory ravings about the Soviet Union and the other fraternal countries. My comrades on the Politburo insist that we make an urgent request to you on this matter and that we send you a diplomatic note to this effect, and I'm not able to restrain the comrades from sending such a note. But I only wanted to make sure that before a note is sent to you about this matter, I got a chance to speak with you personally.

DUBČEK: We had a meeting with members of the press. The session condemned the reporters at the newspapers you were speaking about for their incorrect actions; and a decision was reached there to put an end to all polemical expressions.

BREZHNEV: Sasha, that's not the point—whether you had a meeting with members of the press or not. What we agreed about was not just to hold some meeting. We agreed that all the mass media—the press, the radio, and the television—would be brought under the control of the CPCz Central Committee and the government, and that you would put an end to anti-Soviet and anti-socialist publications after Bratislava. For our part, we in the Soviet Union are strictly abiding by this agreement and are not engaging in any sorts of polemics. As far as the Czechoslovak organs of mass media are concerned, they're keeping up their relentless attacks against the CPSU and the Soviet Union and have even reached the point where they've been attacking the leaders of our party. They've already been branding us as "Stalinists" and other such things. And what, I might ask, do you say about this?

DUBČEK: [Falls silent.]

BREZHNEV: I think I'm correct in telling you that so far we haven't witnessed any actions on the part of the CPCz CC Presidium that would fulfill the obligations taken on in this sphere. I must candidly say to you, Sasha, that by dragging your feet in the fulfillment of these obligations, you're committing outright deceit and are blatantly sabotaging the decisions we jointly reached. This posture toward the obligations you undertook is creating a new situation and is prompting us to reevaluate your statement. For this same reason we are considering new, independent decisions that would defend both the CPCz and the cause of socialism in Czechoslovakia.

DUBČEK: I only want to say to you, Cde. Brezhnev, that we are working in this direction. If you were able to be here with us, you'd see what great efforts we're expending in this direction. But this is a difficult matter and we're not able to resolve it in just two to three days, as I already told you. We need time for this.

BREZHNEV: Aleksandr Stepanovich, I'm also obliged to say that we're not able to wait much longer and that you shouldn't force us to open new polemics with your mass media and to respond to all the articles and activities that are being permitted now in Czechoslovakia against our country, against our party, and against all the socialist parties.

During the negotiations we didn't force you to agree to anything. You yourselves took on the obligation to restore order in the mass media. And once you promised it, you should have been willing to carry it out. Well, fine, I perhaps can even agree with you that the restoration of order in this sphere requires time. But how are you coming along in carrying out the agreement on personnel questions? One must say that on this matter, too, we had a fully concrete agreement, and we also settled on a fully concrete timeframe for carrying it out.

DUBČEK: I would only like to say to you, Cde. Brezhnev, that these are very complex matters, which can't be resolved as easily as you might think.

BREZHNEV: I understand how complicated these matters are. I'm only asking you to resolve them along the lines we agreed on at Čierna nad Tisou. Was it not already clear to you and Černík and Smrkovský and Svoboda, when we met in our four-on-four sessions, how complex it would be to resolve these matters? Yet at the time you yourselves very easily and very independently, without any sort of coercion from us, raised these matters and promised to resolve them as soon as possible.

DUBČEK: I already told you, Cde. Brezhnev, that this is a complex question, the resolution of which requires that we convene a plenum. And in order to examine and resolve these questions, there must be due preparation. I must consult with the comrades about how best to resolve this question.

BREZHNEV: But back in Čierna nad Tisou all your comrades were present, and I don't think you took on all these obligations then without having consulted among yourselves. We adopted the obligations, shook hands, and said that the question was decided and that you would take care of it as soon as possible.

DUBČEK: I didn't promise to resolve this matter in two to three days. We need ample preparation in order to resolve the question properly.

BREZHNEV: But it's impossible to keep on resolving these questions *ad infinitum*, Sasha. When you were preparing for the last presidium meeting, you and I had a conversation. In particular, a conversation about personnel matters. I'm referring to my conversation with you on 9 August. At that time you said to me that you weren't yet ready to handle things at that presidium meeting, but that you would definitely prepare these matters and resolve them at the next presidium meeting. And now you say that you have a presidium meeting under way. So, will you be considering these matters today at this presidium meeting, or will you not?

DUBČEK: These matters can be taken up only by a plenum of the Central Committee.

BREZHNEV: Fine. You also told me that you were preparing to convene a plenum within the next ten days.

DUBČEK: Yes, we're thinking about holding a plenum by the end of the month. But it may be that it won't occur until the beginning of September.

BREZHNEV: But will you be considering personnel questions at this plenum? Will you resolve them positively, as we agreed at Čierna nad Tisou?

DUBČEK: [Gives an evasive answer to this question, in the sense that what happens will be whatever the plenum decides.]

BREZHNEV: This is where the problem lies. Both our problem and your problem. I'll tell you honestly that when you and I were speaking in Čierna nad Tisou, I thought that I was dealing with the leader of the chief party organ, the organ that has complete power. And everything that you promised us we accepted in good faith; and like friends, we believed you in all you said. Personally, Sasha, I can't understand at all why and to what end you've deferred the resolution of these matters until a new plenum, that is, an extraordinary plenum. We believe that today, at this presidium meeting, you could resolve personnel questions; and believe me, you could resolve them without any great loss. If you place these matters before the presidium today, it would still be possible—this would be the last chance—to salvage matters without great detriment or great loss. It will be worse if these losses are very large.

DUBČEK: [Again insists that these matters can be resolved only by a plenum.]

BREZHNEV: If I understood you correctly, you don't intend to consider these matters today. I want to ask you directly, Sasha, what you mean by this, and what I'm getting at here is that you're deceiving us! I'm not able to regard it as anything other than deceit.

DUBČEK: Leonid Ilyich, if you could see how these matters are being prepared now in the presidium, you wouldn't talk this way. We promised to resolve these matters, and we are taking all the measures needed to resolve them correctly.

BREZHNEV: Sasha, I'm not just speaking here personally for myself. The entire Politburo has instructed me to speak with you and to ask you concretely: Will you be resolving the personnel questions or not?

DUBČEK: [Evades a direct answer, explaining that it is impossible to resolve all the personnel questions at once, that these questions are very complex and imposing, and that, as he already said, these questions must be considered by a plenum.]

BREZHNEV: My comrades are interested in finding out, and I would ask you to let me know so that I can transmit your answer to the members of our Politburo, what sorts of questions you are thinking of considering today at the CC Presidium meeting?

DUBČEK: [Enumerates the questions and says that among them the bifurcation of the Interior Ministry will be considered, as was agreed at Čierna nad Tisou.]

BREZHNEV: And how is this question to be resolved? Will it be as we decided? I want to remind you, as you no doubt remember, that when this question was put to you, you turned to Černík. Černík said to you that the question had already been decided and that a candidate for the second post had already been designated, and within five days they would transmit orders about this to Smrkovský. You then turned to Smrkovský, and he said that as soon as Černík issued this document, your council would resolve the matter within five days.

DUBČEK: Yes, he said that back in Čierna, but now the situation has fundamentally changed. We now have a process of federalization under way. There will be a federation of Slovakia with the Czech lands. And this question simply cannot be decided now by a central order for the country as a whole until Slovakia and the Czech Republic separately have adopted the corresponding decisions. For that reason, we at today's presidium meeting are able to resolve this question only as an instruction to the government and minister to prepare the requisite ideas for the final resolution of this matter somewhat later.

BREZHNEV: How much later?

DUBČEK: In the month of October, toward the end of October.

BREZHNEV: Well, what can I say to you about this, Sasha, except that it seems to be yet another manifestation of deceit. This is just one more sign that you're deceiving us, and I can't regard it as anything other than that, let me say to you in all honesty. If you're not even able to resolve this matter now, then it seems to me that your presidium in general has lost all its power.

DUBČEK: I don't see any deceit in this. We're trying to carry out the obligations we undertook. But we're carrying them out as best we can in a fundamentally changing situation.

BREZHNEV: But surely you understand that this arrangement, this way of fulfilling the obligations undertaken at Čierna nad Tisou, will create a completely new situation which we, too, hadn't reckoned with, and that this obviously will compel us to reevaluate the whole situation and resort to new, independent measures.

DUBČEK: Cde. Brezhnev, you should resort to all the measures that your CC Politburo believes are appropriate.

BREZHNEV: But if that's how you're going to answer me, I must say to you, Sasha, that this is a flippant statement.

DUBČEK: I'm not able to answer in any other way. We're working very hard to carry out the agreement. But in these conditions over the last week to ten days we haven't yet fully coped with it. We're not able to do more than what we've been doing. This is a large matter to deal with, and we're not able to complete all our work in just 10–15 days. How could it all be done in such a short time? I'm not able to take responsibility upon myself for doing everything in just five to seven days; this is a complex process, which has encompassed the whole party, the whole country, and the whole nation. And the party must keep control of this process, bringing the nation along with it in the construction of socialism. We see this as our duty and our obligation, but it's impossible to do this in as short a time as you are suggesting, Cde. Brezhnev. I tell you that if you don't believe me, if you believe we are deceiving you, then you should take the measures that your Politburo believes are necessary.

BREZHNEV: Sasha, I understand that you're nervous, I understand that this situation is very complex for you. But don't you see that I'm talking with you as a friend, and that I wish only the best for you? If you recall the conversation you and I had one-on-one, as well as the conversation during our four-on-four sessions, and when you proposed your measures for restoring order in the mass media, it was we, not you, who pointed out that this would not be an easy task and that it would take time to bring the mass media back under control because the rightists had planted their agents everywhere, literally everywhere. In all the outlets of the mass media and information organs the rightists are firmly implanted, and the whole arrangement is being masterminded by Pelikán, Císař, Kriegel, and other scoundrels. But you at that time, in Čierna nad Tisou, said you could handle this work and that you didn't need any sort of help from us. We firmly agreed then that after Bratislava we would put an end to all polemics. I can understand that you're having difficulty, but the one thing I don't understand is why you've done nothing to overcome these difficulties. For example, let's turn back to the personnel questions. Again one can say that during the Čierna talks you also, without any pressure from us and completely of your own free will, said to us that you would be resolving all these questions literally as soon as possible.

DUBČEK: I can't just resolve these matters myself. It's not so simple, Cde. Brezhnev, to resolve such matters.

BREZHNEV: Yet, how simple it was back in Čierna nad Tisou to have a conversation, are you now really implying that those were just irresponsible conversations at the level of the two highest organs of the leadership of the party? If it's clear that some question or other is difficult to resolve, then we shouldn't have had completely irresponsible discussions about it. That's how I understand this matter. It's impossible to overstate, Sasha, how irritated I am by what you're doing now. You and I spoke about very important and very far-reaching matters, which will decide the fate not only of the Communist Party of Czechoslovakia, but also of the whole socialist camp. I'm not demanding anything new, and I haven't raised a single new issue for you. I only want to get from you a firm indication of when you're thinking of fulfilling the obligations on which we agreed at the meeting in Čierna nad Tisou. You have to understand that this isn't the way things are done—to have two fraternal parties meet and adopt a decision, and then just 10 days later have one side change its tune.

DUBČEK: We aren't changing our tune, it's just that the situation is complex and it requires a prolonged amount of time to carry out the agreement that was adopted.

BREZHNEV: Well, fine, Sasha, then permit me to ask you openly and directly one additional question. Do you personally support the notion of fulfilling the obligations which you undertook at Čierna nad Tisou, or not?

DUBČEK: There will be a plenum, Leonid Ilyich, the plenum will decide everything.

BREZHNEV: When will the plenum be?

DUBČEK: This question, I believe, will be resolved by us today in the presidium meeting. I think we'll convene a plenum before the end of the month. But I can't give you a precise date because if I don't get it right and the presidium schedules the plenum at a time different from the one I tell you, you'll again accuse me of having given you an insincere answer. This is difficult for me, Cde. Brezhnev, I still have a party congress ahead and I am completely unprepared for this congress.

BREZHNEV: That's an entirely different matter. But by the way, since you've raised it, let me convey to you my personal view on this matter. I have participated in many congresses, and I've already conducted one congress independently as the first secretary of our party. I personally can't imagine how it is possible to prepare a congress in such a short time. After all, the congress resolves weighty questions in the life of the party, and you must seriously prepare for such things, without any slip-ups. I'm surprised that you would even think a congress could be prepared in such a short time. But this, as they say, is your own affair. I've digressed from our conversation.

DUBČEK: Yes. That's right, but since we have to deal with the situation as it exists, we are working night and day to prepare for the congress. We have an Action Program, draft party statutes, and personnel questions. In general, I think, we will succeed in preparing for the congress.

BREZHNEV: Let's return to the thrust of our conversation. I don't know whether you'll be able to let your comrades on the presidium know about our conversation and tell them about the anxiety I've expressed to you at the way the situation is unfolding.

DUBČEK: Absolutely, without delay, I will tell Cdes. Černík and Smrkovský about this.

BREZHNEV: Yes, that's good, you should tell Černík and Smrkovský, but I think, Sasha, that the other comrades are also full-fledged members of the presidium, and that you're obliged to say something to them about my phone call. I must tell you, Sasha, that they are very fond of you and can help you a great deal. I can assure you that these are your real friends both in their past work—before the January plenum—and in carrying out the January plenum, and if you'd really like to know, I think they can help you more than Černík and Smrkovský can.

DUBČEK: Right now we already have a different agenda for the presidium meeting, but I'll try to find the opportunity to tell all the comrades about this conversation.

BREZHNEV: Sasha, if I've understood you correctly, you're saying that at today's presidium meeting you won't be considering a single one of the questions we agreed on at Čierna nad Tisou.

DUBČEK: Only the question of the Interior Ministry.

BREZHNEV: But as I understood you, you won't be deciding even this question the way we agreed—or at least not completely the way we agreed—in Čierna nad Tisou.

DUBČEK: [Very irritably repeats everything he said earlier about the difficulties attending the resolution of such matters.]

BREZHNEV: Aleksandr Stepanovich, I regret that you're talking with me in such an irritable manner. On such momentous issues, emotions won't do anyone any good. What is needed here are common sense, reason, and will. Emotions here are of no help at all.

DUBČEK: I would be content to toss everything aside and go back to working at my old place. Why am I irritated? Because we're taking action here, we're working, we're doing everything we can to fulfill the agreement reached at Čierna nad Tisou, and yet the whole time you're accusing us. This is already the second conversation in which you've accused me of doing nothing, of deceiving you, and of not wanting to resolve the matters on which we agreed.

BREZHNEV: Sasha, I'd like to believe you, but you must understand me. What troubles me most of all is that you haven't dismissed the three whom we agreed to dismiss, and this leaves a very big question. If you're sincerely convinced that you must release Císař, Kriegel, and Pelikán, and that this must be done, then I'm deeply convinced that a sincere effort on your part would allow you to do this very easily and simply.

DUBČEK: What reasons do you have for suggesting that this can be done quickly?

BREZHNEV: We explained these things to you in Čierna nad Tisou. I'm not even referring here to the things that were not in the protocol—that is, the things we discussed in our one-on-one or four-on-four meetings. What I'm referring to are what was discussed in our plenary sessions, when we were all together. Go take a look at the stenographic report of my speech at the plenary session. You'll find there all our views. We told Kriegel directly that he is who he is. We openly said this at the plenary session. What further basis can you possibly want, Sasha? Fine, you say that you're not able to resolve these questions in the presidium, and that it's necessary to convene a regular plenum. But from your answers, if you'll forgive me, I didn't understand whether even at the plenum you'll actually resolve these matters or not.

DUBČEK: At the regular plenum another CPCz CC first secretary will be chosen.

BREZHNEV: Sasha, don't go to such extremes, this sort of talk is completely unnecessary. I don't know what would prompt you to speak with me this way; perhaps you feel uncomfortable about

speaking with me more openly, or perhaps someone there is acting as a constraint on you. Well, then, let's agree that after the
presidium meeting, Cde. Chervonenko will come to your office
and you can tell him in greater detail when and how you
are thinking about resolving the matters on which we agreed at
the Čierna meeting.

DUBČEK: I can say nothing more. I already said everything there
is to say, Cde. Brezhnev, and I can say nothing more to Cde.
Chervonenko.

BREZHNEV: Then let me ask you to tell me whether you'll be resolving these matters at the plenum or not.

DUBČEK: And who said that I won't?

BREZHNEV: Again you're evading a direct response. You don't
want to say whether you will or you won't.

DUBČEK: The last time I told you everything, and now I'm only
able to repeat what I said earlier: that we're going to convene a
plenum, that we must prepare for the plenum, and that we need
time for this. If you believe that we're deceiving you, then take
the measures you regard as appropriate. That's your affair.

BREZHNEV: Don't you see, Sasha, that we undoubtedly *will* be
adopting the measures we believe are appropriate? You're absolutely correct in saying that this is our affair. But as far as this
affair is not only ours but a matter of common concern, the
measures would be easier for us to adopt if you and your comrades would more openly say that these are the measures you are
expecting of us.

DUBČEK: We're able to resolve all these matters on our own, but
if you believe it's necessary for you to adopt certain measures,
then by all means go ahead.

BREZHNEV: I'm not asking you why you didn't resolve any particular matter or another. I'm asking you something else, Sasha:
namely, when you plan to resolve the things we agreed on.

DUBČEK: You're not asking me, you're rebuking me.

BREZHNEV: I'm not rebuking you; I'm simply saying that in the
wake of our meetings nothing has changed, and that we don't
detect any sort of concrete actions aimed at fulfilling the agreement that exists between us. And insofar as that is the case, we
are naturally alarmed. It seems to us that you're simply deceiv-

ing us and are completely unwilling to fulfill what we agreed on so firmly face to face, as well as during our four-on-four meetings. But if you're saying that at the regular plenum you'll resolve all the matters we agreed on at Čierna nad Tisou, then this of course will considerably alleviate our doubts. I'm not saying that our doubts will be eliminated altogether, but at least they'll be alleviated. After all, we're accustomed to believing you, and we see in you the leader of a fraternal party whom we can treat with great confidence.

DUBČEK: I'd just as soon go where it would be pleasant to work. I don't set great store by this post. Let whoever wants to occupy it, take it. Let whoever wants to be CPCz CC first secretary, take up the post. I can't work without enjoying support and in a situation of constant attacks.

BREZHNEV: Sasha, I want to tell you openly that you yourself have created all the difficulties you're referring to. You saw how, before your very eyes, Císař and Kriegel installed their people in the press, radio, and television. These are people who have nothing in common with the Communist Party of Czechoslovakia. You yourself have created the personnel problem. You yourself have created all the problems you were mentioning. We didn't create these problems for you. It's precisely because of you that everything has gotten out of hand, and that you've lost power. And yet now you're bemoaning it. And I very much regret that you regard our conversation as an attack against you rather than a gesture of support. For it is precisely as a gesture of support that you should regard everything I've been talking about with you now. This hasn't been an attack against you.

DUBČEK: Leonid Ilyich, I ask you to tell me how this can be.

BREZHNEV: It's hard for me to give you any suggestions. But I want to tell you that if you continue to operate alone and if you continue to fluctuate between the leftists and rightists, you won't end up doing anything. Without the party *aktiv* you won't do anything. All around you are so many of your close comrades; they're good people and good communists. If you seek out the support of the party *aktiv* and rally them around you, there will no longer be any Císařs and Kriegels. In Čierna nad Tisou we were not inhibited about saying everything directly to Kriegel's face, without holding back. And yet you for some reason are still coddling him and sucking up to him.

You, Sasha, should take a close look around. I don't want to name names for you, but you know the people it would be worthwhile for you to rely on. By relying on them, you could resolve all your problems. I again say to you that by telling you this, by having this conversation, I am simply doing all I can to help you.

Right now we all are waiting: our party as well as the other fraternal parties from the Bratislava meeting and the documents of the Bratislava conference. I'm conveying all our doubts to you as frankly and openly and directly as I can. Let's just fulfill what we agreed on, and not an ounce more. As for your question of what will become of you, I can't give you an answer. If you want us to avoid a falling-out, let's just fulfill what we agreed on. Let's give an appropriate communist rebuff to the rightist forces. You'll have to strike a blow against them before the congress. It will have to be a blow from which they won't recover. Only in that case will the Communist Party of Czechoslovakia be able to show its best face at the congress.

DUBČEK: And you think that I don't want this?

BREZHNEV: No, I don't think so. I believe you, Sasha. I believe that everything we wish for you is for the best, and that you will see what you will as your duty, while we for our part are ready to give you any help you need. But I ask you to understand that if you don't fulfill everything we agreed on—and I emphasize once again that these were things we agreed on; I'm not raising any new issues of any sort—then that will be an end to our trust in you. The whole point of our meeting in Čierna nad Tisou was to maintain the greatest trust in one another. All of our decisions were adopted in a spirit of enormous trust, and this is precisely what obliges us, in the most conscientious manner, to fulfill everything we agreed on. For a very long time you've been speaking in detail about the difficulties you've encountered while trying to carry out the decisions we reached and the agreement we arrived at. But I want to tell you that any question can always be made more complicated than it should be.

DUBČEK: We're not complicating anything; we're simply trying to deal with the situation that actually exists in our country.

BREZHNEV: Why do you say this? Take this simple matter of dividing the Interior Ministry. Just as we agreed and as you yourselves said, this is a simple matter, one that you could resolve within the next five to ten days. And yet what has happened? You've done nothing.

DUBČEK: That's because the situation has changed. I told you that neither Černík nor I had foreseen that the situation would change. But our underlying view that such a step should be taken has not changed. We still firmly adhere to the view that this step should be taken. Only the situation has changed. But this means that the whole question must be approached differently. The outcome no longer depends on us alone.

BREZHNEV: Sasha, let me ask you a question: What, if anything, *does* depend on your CC Presidium?

DUBČEK: Cde. Brezhnev, I once again ask you not to insist that I carry out this decision, considering that the situation has changed.

BREZHNEV: Indeed I'm not insisting on it. I'm just saying that you on the CC Presidium are not in control of anything, and that it's a great pity we weren't aware of that during the meeting in Čierna nad Tisou. It now turns out that we were discussing things with an organ that is not in control of anything. It turns out that our conversation wasn't serious at all.

DUBČEK: The reasons for holding up the resolution of the matter are simply that Slovakia is now a federal territory while the ministry is a union-republic organ, and it's now necessary to follow a whole series of procedures if we are to settle this question once and for all.

BREZHNEV: I believe you, but you must also understand me. I'm not able to decide new matters behind the backs of the other members of my Politburo. I'm not able to give consent to any of your arguments. From what you've said it turns out that new circumstances have arisen for you, and so it's now totally unclear whether, or when at all, you'll be fulfilling our agreement about the division of the Interior Ministry. Doesn't it follow, then, that we have to reassess our whole agreement? You're aware that we agreed to these things at the very highest level. You and I spoke one on one. This is high level. We also spoke in four-on-four sessions. This was at the level of first secretaries, the level of chairmen of Councils of Ministers, and the level of chairmen of Supreme Soviets (or, as you have, a National Assembly). That is, our talks involved people who should be able to decide any matter. And it now turns out that these people can't decide anything. And now you're saying to me: "Take whatever measures the CPSU CC Politburo believes are necessary." Of course, one must obviously agree with you that we'll have to take whatever measures we believe are necessary. And by the way, I wanted to ask you something about the decisions we adopted during the four-on-four sessions. Did you convey the results to Cde. Bil'ak and the other comrades who are close to you?

DUBČEK: Yes, I informed Cde. Bil'ak about the things we decided during the four-on-four meetings.

BREZHNEV: It's good that you did so, Sasha. These are your most dependable and closest friends. I would only urge you to rely on them. By relying on them, you can emerge triumphant. And you won't even need to wait for a plenum; with their help, you'll be able to resolve all these matters within the presidium.

DUBČEK: Please wait, nonetheless, Leonid Ilyich, until the plenum.

BREZHNEV: Well, if this plenum is held soon, then of course I'll wait, and we all will wait.

DUBČEK: Leonid Ilyich, I well understand your benevolent intentions, and I only ask that you take into account the difficulties we are facing.

BREZHNEV: I very clearly see your difficulties, Sasha, but you must put up a struggle against these difficulties. The struggle against them will be successful only on one condition, namely, that you yourself take direct charge of this struggle. You must surround yourself with reliable members of the party *aktiv*, and by depending on these comrades, you'll be able to overcome your difficulties.

DUBČEK: I'm running out of steam; it wasn't by chance that I told you that the new plenum would choose a new secretary. I'm thinking of giving up this work. Dear Leonid Ilyich, I ask that you forgive me for perhaps having spoken somewhat irritably today, I very much hope that you'll forgive me.

BREZHNEV: I understand, Sasha, it's your problems and your nerves: I want you to understand that in the context of what we agreed on at Čierna nad Tisou, you have to adopt measures and fulfill your obligations.

DUBČEK: Our desire is no less than yours, Cde. Brezhnev, to have these matters successfully resolved.

BREZHNEV: Sasha, I take heart at your statement because the whole point of our conversation has been to help you fulfill these obligations. But you must also understand what it's like for us; for us, too, things aren't so easy. We reported back on that agreement to the plenum and to the Central Committee, and now we find it isn't being fulfilled. And so the party is asking us, as the leaders, why this is so. I want you to understand that good relations between our parties can be preserved only on the condition that there is mutual, honest fulfillment of the obligations by both sides. I think that you have no complaints about our party and our Politburo with regard to our fulfillment of the agreement achieved in Čierna nad Tisou.

DUBČEK: Leonid Ilyich, once again I affirm that we are *not* refusing to fulfill the agreement we reached in Čierna nad Tisou. The whole question is how much time we will be given to fulfill it, since there was no concrete timeframe specified in the agreement, and we still need more time to fulfill everything.

BREZHNEV: You shouldn't pose the question that way, since on every issue a concrete timeframe was stipulated. If we said that this was all to be decided as soon as possible and before the congress, this establishes a well-defined deadline. That's not to imply it all had to be done in two to three days, but if we say "before the congress," then it's clear that everything should be resolved, say, in August.

DUBČEK: I promise you, Cde. Brezhnev, that I'll do everything necessary to fulfill our agreement.

BREZHNEV: Good, we'll closely follow the course of events. I again earnestly request that you pass on my regards to all your working comrades and that you tell them about the alarm I've expressed to you. And now, Sasha, I would like to reach agreement with you on the desirability of continuing our conversations. If you don't want to meet Cde. Chervonenko, then let's agree that we'll continue our conversation after you're done with the CC Presidium meeting. I understand that it's awkward to have all your comrades sitting there while you've gone off to have a conversation with me.

DUBČEK: I agree. So let's definitely say that we'll speak again after the Presidium meeting.

In Jaromír Navrátil, ed., *The Prague Spring 1968: A National Security Archive Document Reader*, trans. Mark Kramer et al. (Prague: Central European University Press, 1998), 345–356.

Strike Committee of the Faculty of Philosophy and Letters of the University of Mexico

The Mexican Student Movement: Its Meaning and Perspectives

During the summer of 1968 clashes between student activists and police forces in Mexico City grew in frequency and violence. Inspired in part by similar movements in France and other countries, Mexican students condemned the ruling single-party state that had long repressed their freedoms. The policies pursued by the governing Institutional Revolutionary Party (PRI) emphasized economic growth and social stability, neglecting student concerns for economic equality and social justice. The PRI used brutal force to repress critics. The students reached out to trade unions and peasant groups for solidarity against the might of the PRI. Violent clashes continued through the early fall of 1968, culminating in the army and police massacre of hundreds of protesters on 2 October in La Plaza de las Tres Culturas at Tlatelolco. The government took this drastic action because of growing frustration with the student activists, and the coming of the Olympic Games to Mexico City less than two weeks later. President Gustavo Díaz Ordaz did not want the sight of the demonstrators to tarnish his image of international power. The "Tlatelolco Massacre," however, elicited public outrage across the globe, and especially in Latin America.

Until recently Mexico was looked upon as a model of economic progress and political harmony. For almost a decade there had been

Students in Mexico City protested against the repressive nature of their government, on the eve of the 1968 International Olympic Games. They were inspired by revolutionary figures and protest movements around the world. The Mexican government brutally broke up these protests in what became known as the Tlatelolco Massacre, named for the site of the protests and the crackdown.

no large-scale political or social disturbances; the economy was expanding at the rate of six percent annually; industry, commerce, and transport were flourishing in Mexico City and other urban centers. Mexico's great capital city of seven million inhabitants was beginning to follow the consumption-oriented patterns of today's world metropolitan centers.

Such were the facts, among others, that led most politicians and observers of the Mexican scene to conclude that Mexico's progress had brought it to a stage beyond the political violence which had characterized it and many other Latin American countries for long years. However, what happened on July 26 and later demonstrated that these assumptions would have to be revised and corrected.

It all began with a clash between students of a private school on one side and two vocational schools affiliated with the National Polytechnical Institute on the other. On July 24 the municipal authorities decided to squash the scuffle by sending in the "glorious" *granaderos*, an unconstitutional, anti-riot squad organized for the purpose of repression. The *granaderos* acted with their customary brutality, using excessive, disproportionate force not only against the students but also against the teachers of Trade School No. 5, which the police had broken into.

This invasion of the premises of the Polytechnical Institute and the accompanying repressions aroused the indignation of the students of this institution, second in national importance only to the National University (UNAM). On July 25 assemblies were held in all the affiliated schools of the Polytech and it was decided to organize a protest demonstration in the streets on the following day.

The National Federation of Technical Students (FNET), a government-controlled and financed group, managed to capture the leadership of the movement, and took it upon itself to ask the authorities' permission to hold the demonstration; it also attempted to limit the scope of the protest. The march, it was decided, would proceed toward Casco de Santo Tomás, by way of the Monument of the Revolution—though many students wanted to head for the National Palace in order to express their protest to President Díaz Ordaz himself.

On the 26th of July some 30,000 people took part in the march. On reaching the Monument of the Revolution, a column of about 15,000 students continued marching toward the National Palace. At Avenida San Juan de Letrán the column encountered several hundred students who had been attending a celebration in honor of the Cuban Revolution. These students wanted to join the march but were not permitted to do so, because they were allegedly communists. The Polytech students continued their march and the other students went back to their own meeting.

When the Polytech column neared the National Palace, battalions of *granaderos* emerged from the sidestreets, Motolinia and Isabel la Católica, charging the students and hemming them in. Such an attack had not been anticipated even remotely by the defenseless students. Those who were naive enough to obey the *granaderos'* orders to lie down were beaten mercilessly. Fleeing students were pursued and attacked; hundreds were wounded and five students were killed. All the streets in the vicinity of the National Palace were the scenes of similar brutality, of which both student demonstrators and passers-by were victims.

Then, students began to resist, aided by residents of the area who hurled flowerpots, dishes, bottles, and stones at the police. Some groups began to take reprisals against business establishments; display windows of jewelry stores, other shops and banks were destroyed. When the chief of police himself, thinking he was dealing with a terrorized mass of people, attempted to address the crowds, he was met with a rain of stones that sent him running, along with some twenty of his henchmen.

In the face of this development, the police received orders to attack any group of young people in sight, thus turning the midtown area of the city into a battleground. This led to the police attack on Preparatory School No. 3, a few blocks from the National Palace.

It happened that on the 26th this school was holding a public-speaking contest. At its conclusion, the homeward-bound student audience was fiercely set upon by the *granaderos*. The students' reaction was immediate: they fought back, improvising a barricade of two commandeered buses which they set afire, blocking the street. Then they accumulated stones, bottles, bricks, building materials and holed up inside their building. Such was the first round between the students and the government forces.

The next day the newspaper headlines in the commercial press revealed another "Communist plot discovered by the police"; since Díaz Ordaz took power such "plots" have been "discovered" every six months. Among those arrested much publicity was given to five members of the Mexican Communist Youth, who were accused of being the fomenters of the events, a Chilean, a Puerto Rican and a U.S. citizen (Nika Satter Seeger, daughter of Pete Seeger). Offered as clear proof of the "plot" was the fact that half a ton of propaganda was found in Mexican Communist Party headquarters—pamphlets, books and magazines which are on sale in bookshops all over Mexico.

The police, attempting to arrest the greatest possible number of left militants, succeeded in jailing 76. Meanwhile, in all the branches of the Polytechnic and all the faculties of the National University, meetings were held to discuss the events of the previous day. Other students took possession of buses, defying the police and moving through the city to inform the people of what had really been happening, since the newspapers were not only distorting the facts but resorting to outright invention.

Sunday was a day of much activity on both sides, especially by the police, who arraigned 45 of those arrested, and announced that there were warrants out for the arrest of 50 others, among them five French citizens who, it was alleged, had come to Mexico to foment the disorders.

On Monday the 29th, students of the Polytech and the University began to coordinate their activities; by this time they had spontaneously moved to commandeer such a large number of buses that the city had been virtually paralyzed since early morning. Clashes with the police multiplied and the number of arrested and wounded reached the hundreds. Student brigades operated in all parts of the city; as they talked to the people, many who had disapproved of the students' actions began to change their minds and fraternize. The number of buses set afire continued to grow. Petitions were circulated, calling for the removal of the *granaderos* and the dismissal of the chief of police and his aides. That evening the police made their last (and unsuccessful) attempt to defeat the students, especially those in Preparatory #3.

At dawn on the 30th the Army went into action. With bayonets drawn, they took most of the Polytechnic-affiliated schools and the Preparatory schools. But "Prepa" #3, scene of the most violent clashes and a concentration point for all university students, was taken only after its doors were blown open by a bazooka, leaving a toll of nearly twenty students dead and dozens wounded. There were no less than 1,000 students inside who, in the face of the bazooka attack, resisted heroically. "Every student got what was coming to him," said one of the *granaderos* who took part in the attack; "the soldiers used their bayonets on at least 500 of them. They had to because the students were drugged and you never saw such resistance and courage . . . they must have been drugged . . ." The bodies of the dead were removed in Army trucks, to an unknown destination. The survivors were arrested and later taken to the Attorney General's headquarters, where they were kicked and beaten as they ran the gauntlet between two rows of secret-service men.

That same day the morning papers carried the story of the Army's attack on the schools, and announced the indefinite closing of the University and the Polytech on orders from the Rector of the University and the Minister of Education. Nonetheless, the students returned to the school buildings and attempted, unsuccessfully, to retake them. They then went into the streets; in spite of the atmosphere of intimidation created by the continuous movement through the city's main streets of tanks, cannon, and troops, they proceeded to hold demonstrations. Whenever two or three hundred students would appear openly on a street, their numbers were likely to grow within the space of a few blocks to five or six thousand.

University City, which had not been occupied by the Army, saw the largest agglomeration of students. Signs at the entrance to University buildings announced: "UNIVERSITY AUTONOMY HAS BEEN VIOLATED. ASSEMBLY TODAY." That day the Rector ordered the flag flown at half-mast, in mourning for the students who had fallen in the struggle. The newspapers announced that the flags were flown at half mast to commemorate the anniversary of the death of Father Hidalgo (Mexico's most illustrious fighter in the war for independence from Spain).

The next day the Rector, Javier Barros Sierra, announced to an audience of some 20,000 students that he would lead a demonstration in protest against the violation of university autonomy and against military occupation of educational institutions. Governmental in-fighting reached fever-pitch when the Ministry of the Interior announced that it would not authorize the protest. But the authorities later announced that the protest would be permitted, with the proviso that it not move toward the mid-town area. Permission was granted when it was learned that not only University students but also those from the Polytechnic, the Agricultural School at Chapingo, the Teacher Training College, the Colegio de México, and other schools were determined to hold a demonstration, with or without permission.

The success of this dramatic demonstration of 120,000 people was all the more impressive in contrast with the spectacle presented by the government, which flooded the city with soldiers. It is calculated that no less than 20,000 soldiers were mobilized for duty in the city on Thursday, August first; they were transported in trucks, tanks, and jeeps, and threatened a contemptuous populace with machine-guns, bazookas, mortars, and heavy artillery.

The demonstration took place in sections of town inhabited primarily by members of the upper-middle class, normally characterized by conservatism. But when the demonstrators were caught in a downpour the response of the residents was forthright: newspapers and large plastic bags were dropped from the windows for use as makeshift raincoats and umbrellas. Sympathy for the students was even more enthusiastically expressed in working-class districts.

At the end of the protest the Rector spoke again; his remarks, like those of the other speakers, contained subtle allusions to "provocateurs," remarks which could be interpreted as referring either to the politicians who ordered the crackdown or to those whom the police had labelled "provocateurs"—Communists, Trotskyists, and others. Naturally the commercial press attempted to play down the size and importance of the demonstration, characterizing it as "another instance of repudiation of the extremist left agitators."

Friday brought new surprises. Early that morning the engineering students, who had formerly been considered highly conservative, mounted a new protest, this time against the labelling of some protesters as "provocateurs"; they proposed that *all* Mexican students proclaim themselves "provocateurs," just as French students, in solidarity with Daniel Cohn-Bendit, had proclaimed themselves "undesirables."

It appeared that the movement was declining, though no one dismissed the possibility that it might regain strength during the following week. The commercial press began to concentrate on the earthquake that had occurred and gave little space to Friday's student activities, limiting such news to small items concerning clashes between students and police in the vicinity of the Polytechnic, and the attack by a few thousand students on an outdoor market in the northern part of the city, near Villa Guadalupe.

In order to understand the twists and turns of Mexican governmental policy, which are both cause and effect of the present crisis, we must consider the basic factors that determine national policy: the imminence of the Olympics; the beginnings of factional struggles within the official party (Partido Revolucionario Institucional, better known as PRI) among prospective candidates for the presidency; and the prospect of an end to the economic boom. The interaction of these factors is bound to give rise to contradictory lines of action. On the one hand, the success of the approaching Olympics requires that tranquility reign, so that Mexico may preserve the confidence of international capital; on the other hand, the unleashing of the inner-party struggle adds to the existing social unrest and threatens tranquility. Furthermore, looming economic uncertainties lead to the emergence of contradictory positions within the bourgeoisie and polarize the political attitudes of the ruling class.

The Alignment of Forces

Permission for the Polytechnic students' demonstration on July 26 was in part a political maneuver, the goal of which was to discredit one of the strongest candidates for the presidency: the Mayor of Mexico City (Alfonso Corona del Rosal). This maneuver was the work of another equally strong candidate: the Minister of the Interior (Luis Echeverría).

For many years Mexico has suffered a *de facto* prohibition of public protest against any government action whatsoever; demonstrations in support of Cuba or Vietnam were barely tolerated. For the Minister of the Interior to authorize a demonstration against the *granaderos* was to make a direct attack on the Mayor. Furthermore, it was known that the demonstration would be repressed, a fact which made the attack all the stronger.

However, what was not taken into account or correctly anticipated was the student response. The combativeness of the students caused the maneuver to boomerang against both the rival candidates, whose only remaining alternative was for each to convert his campaign into a desperate crusade against "the Communist menace."

The introduction of anti-communism into the battle for the presidential succession—a development clearly motivated by the desire to curry favor with the President of the United States—led to the emergence of new political forces: The military made its entrance, making known through the language of the bazooka that if an iron fist were needed they were ready and willing; and the liberal group, which had lost so much ground since Díaz Ordaz took power, took on new life. At this point we must clarify certain political changes that have taken place in recent years.

1958 saw a change in the relationship of forces within the PRI, changes which were simply responses to the new economic era. After 1958, the repercussions in Mexico of the recession in the U.S. made continued expansion possible only through a drastic increase in state expenditures and investments. To make this possible, aid from private national and international capital was essential. The response from these sectors was graphically expressed in the growth of the public debt, which rose from 13,500 million pesos in 1958 to 67,200 million in 1967 (one peso = .08 U.S.). The importance of big business in maintaining the economy was bound to be reflected in the political sphere. Encouraged by the openly reactionary course taken by the U.S.—e.g., Cuba and the war in Vietnam—this sector brought to power the only candidate that the liberals and traditional left sectors had rejected: Díaz Ordaz.

The policies of the López Mateos regime—policies of political repression and of forcing the workers to bear the brunt of the country's growing economic difficulties—were expanded and perfected by Díaz Ordaz. Repression was no longer *ex post facto*; it was now preventive as well. Left radical groups were especially victimized but they were not the only ones. Within the PRI repression took the form of forced resignations by those cabinet members and state governors who were not partisans of the administration.

For quite a long period, there used to be serious discussion concerning the nature of the Mexican state. Time and again, it was pointed out that Mexico had traits which distinguished it from a liberal bourgeois state, which in the limited imagination of the traditional left is construed to be the typical state of Capitalist society. But with Díaz Ordaz's rise to power, it became generally accepted that Mexico was a bourgeois state. However absurd these discussions may appear, now that the intervention of the bourgeois state in the economy is total, they do reflect a certain reality. The post-revolutionary Mexican state has always served the bourgeoisie, but it is true that a change has taken place: the state, no longer an *indi-*

rect instrument of the bourgeoisie, has become a *direct* agent of big business. With Díaz Ordaz at the helm, finance capital has at last succeeded in playing the same primary role in politics as it plays in the economic sphere. Only those who have not recognized this new development will be puzzled by the increasing number of business tycoons who now occupy the governors' seats in many states.

The Present Political Situation

The Mexican bourgeoisie has a reputation for astuteness and flexibility, and the ineptness that it has shown during the present crisis is merely the result of recent changes and the contradictions arising from them, superimposed on earlier existing contradictions. The rise to power of a regime directly linked with big business was bound to effect changes in economic policy, and in the PRI itself.

One area of conflict centers on the utilization of government revenues. As we all know, the public treasury was the generative force of an important sector of the Mexican bourgeoisie. A struggle is taking place between a sector that wants this relationship to continue and a sector that struggles to divert this social surplus value to swell the profits of big business. The drift toward technocracy and Díaz Ordaz's fruitless attempts to introduce morality into the public sector must be analyzed within this context. Besides, the discredit into which traditional politicians have fallen, precisely because of their corruption, acts to strengthen the new dominant tendency in the government.

However, this circumstance, far from stabilizing the government or the new sector which is clamoring for power, is merely an indication that a point of no return is being approached, which threatens not only a group but the system itself. For there is a determining factor in the present crisis of the official party which is hinted at in the recent defeats. The common denominator of the rival groups within the party is their divorce from the working class and the people at large; no possibility exists of their gaining the lasting confidence of the people without threatening the system which sustains them.

It is the evolution of the official party that throws the most light on this situation. A multi-class party that was able to gain strength only in the struggle against the big landowners and certain sectors of the bourgeoisie, it succeeded in welding an alliance of workers, peasants, middle class and other sectors of the bourgeoisie; once this struggle ended, it was bound to become an anachronism. The obsolescence of the official party began to reveal itself in 1940 when the rightist, Manuel Avila Camacho, "inherited" the presidency from Lázaro Cárdenas. There were two reasons why the official party did not crumble at that time: on the one hand, the absence of a revolutionary alternative—the Communist Party followed the national-front line and had rejected any revolutionary solution—and, on the other, the possibilities open to capitalism in Mexico due to domestic reforms and the new economic opportunities that arose during and after the war. The official party's policy of controlling the masses was carried out through the corruption of their leaders who continued for a period to enjoy a certain prestige.

The accelerated expansion of the economy in the period between 1940–1956 and the government's policy of avoiding open clashes with the populace made it possible for workers at least to maintain wage levels, even though their relative share of the national income dropped steadily. This permitted the trade-union bureaucracy to maintain its control. However, by the second half of the 1950's it was precisely this control that prevented workers from bettering their conditions. It was in these circumstances that a popular working-class movement arose and grew, culminating in the railroad workers' movement of 1958–1959.

The defeat of these movements opened a new stage in Mexico's political and social life. Bourgeois economists and sociologists have focused exclusively on the economy's expansion, taking care not to point out the many distortions that accompany it. Even more important has been the growth of social unrest and the development of a crisis in the PRI which threatens its very existence.

Union leaders who, in spite of their corruption, still enjoyed certain support by more backward sectors of workers—to say nothing of honest leaders like Demetrio Vallejo (of the Railroad Workers Union) whose honesty is costing him 14 years in prison—were replaced by underworld gangs, who maintained themselves in power with bayonets. This has led to a further lowering of the masses' standard of living and has forced a definitive rupture between the working masses on the one hand and the government and the PRI on the other. The role of these gangsters is to coerce workers, peasants, government workers, and others to vote for the official party candidates; this is precisely why the party is currently so feeble.

The more or less liberal sectors of the PRI think that they still have influence among the masses and that if they can regain their former positions in the party they will be able to salvage it. They are attempting at present to play a dual role: they pretend to defend the interests of the masses while offering security to the bourgeoisie which is threatened by revolution. How far they will go in this game can be seen in the position taken in the current crisis by the Rector of the National University who, on the one hand, ordered the flag flown at half-mast in honor of the fallen students and, on the other, added his voice to the reactionary chorus of those who claimed that the conflict was the work of "provocateurs." They wish to regain their old positions in the party not in order to resolve social problems but to enrich themselves through access to public funds, government contracts, contacts with foreign capital, bribery, and so forth.

In the present crisis the ultra-rightists (Díaz Ordaz, Alfonso Corona del Rosal, Luis Echeverría, among others) have lost ground to the liberals, but this is not definitive or important; had it not been for the cowardice and ineptness of the liberals Díaz would never have come to power. The important fact is the political advance made by the students and their awareness that energetic action by the masses can neutralize repression.

Perspectives and Tasks of the Revolutionary Students

Whatever the results of the present crisis, the political advances achieved are important: high school and university students have become a political force capable of going into action at any moment; vast sectors of the population are beginning to realize that the student movement has interests in common with their own and can serve as support for their own struggles.

However, there are elements that not only can frustrate such an advance but can even force a retreat in the politicization that has grown out of the movement: there is a lack of organization and cohesion of the revolutionary and progressive forces, whereas the opportunist and reactionary elements are well organized and cohesive. We have already witnessed maneuvers by conservative elements in the *Comites de Lucha* (Struggle Committees), and manifestations of opportunism; before long, we shall witness divisions within the committees. No less important is the action of the government authorities who concentrate their attention on corrupt organizations like the FNET, granting it a role it has not earned, while attempting to bribe the leaders of the Struggle Committees. Then, there are the ultra-rightist gangs who, taking advantage of lack of organization in the movement, send in small organized groups who, by the use of violence and demagogy, attempt to take over the leadership of the movement.

Revolutionary sectors must preserve and extend the political gains won by the present movement. If it is difficult, at this stage, to overcome the lack of a cohesive, revolutionary organization, it is nonetheless possible to lay down some tactical and strategic guidelines, indicating forms of action and goals. It is of primary importance to point out clearly that student action, however important, is not socially definitive and that future action will be determined in the last analysis by the position adopted by the working masses. The present movement has succeeded in changing the attitudes of various social sectors toward the students but it has not succeeded in activating them. For this to have happened it would have been necessary for these sectors to be convinced that they were directly involved in a struggle of this kind.

The students have mobilized around a specific grievance, one which exists on a national scale: against repression as a means of freezing or lowering the standard of living of working people. Political activity among workers cannot be limited to mere denunciations, but must include a call to the masses to struggle in defense of their violated rights. This is the best way to support the students' struggle.

The students must concentrate their efforts in the near future on winning support by increasing the workers' political understanding and by utilizing the fissures in the power structure to undertake struggles that will not lead to repression.

It is equally important that the most advanced elements should seek out forms of action for the future. Study circles must be organized, lectures, contacts with workers, and all other activities that could broaden the political horizons of the new generation of potentially militant students. At the same time, it is necessary to initiative activities which all students can support; for example, the erection of monuments to the students who have fallen in the struggle, the placing of commemorative plaques at the spots where military and police attacks occurred, and above all the mobilization of students against police spies and agents, "scabs," and ultra-rightist student groups such as MURO.

There is need right now for a newspaper or magazine which would provide a forum for information and analysis, in which all aspects of the struggle would be examined with the utmost clarity and frankness. Such an organ would be an irreplaceable complement to organizational action and political effectiveness.

It is probable that a national student organization is in the offing. Most likely, opportunist elements will capture its leadership. But this does not mean that we should not participate. On the contrary, only the participation of the organized revolutionary left can guarantee that this organization will play an important role. Our participation in a national student organization should include two fundamental objectives: to encourage it to move leftward and to recruit the most advanced elements. The urgency of these tasks cannot be minimized. In the short run the Mexican economy will have to confront a multitude of problems arising from the contradictions of capitalism, and the bourgeoisie will once again attempt to let the burden of these difficulties fall on the shoulders of the workers. The masses, whose patience has been worn thin, will in all likelihood begin to express their opposition; if such opposition is not organized it risks being drowned in blood. We have seen that the bourgeoisie loses its head after a mere three days of student resistance; what will it not be willing to do when faced with a mass movement which directly threatens its economic interests?

An organized mass movement cannot be repressed; we must achieve the organization of such a movement as an immediate step toward victory. August 3, 1968

In *Mexico '68: The Students Speak*, trans. Richard Garza et al. (New York: United States Committee for Justice to Latin American Political Prisoners, 1968), 6–12.

Mexican Student Poems

Cueto

'Twas the year of the Olympics
this tale I have to tell.
They broke into the schoolrooms
and our rights and freedom fell.

The bought-off press as usual
the people misinformed.
Against those loafing students
they railed and raged and stormed.

But listen to what happened;
the truth to you I'll tell
of the terrible misfortune
that on Mexico befell.

The grenadiers of Cueto
arrived to pacify;
they beat up all the students
but couldn't make them cry.

They came into the classrooms,
as they themselves explained,
on government orders
to do as they were trained.

The Constitution gives us
the rights that we demand.
It was our Revolution
that brought them to our land.

That Cueto has no mother
is the medical students' claim,
and if perchance he had one
Agrippina would be her name.†

---

†Agrippina was Nero's mother.

That Cueto is a bastard
is what every student knows
and they do not cease to shout it
while they suffer from his blows.

With this I'll end my story
and bid you all goodnight.
Let every single Mexican
know in his heart, we're right.

Prayer
(to a gorilla)

Gustavo
who art in "Los Pinos"*
hallowed
be thy name,
thy government come,
thy will be done
from Sonora to Yucatán.
Lead us not into
insubordination
and deliver us from
the army.
Amen.

The Ballad of the Grenadier

Papa, yesterday in school
a man said, "I'm a grenadier."
And started beating up my friends.
Papa, what's a grenadier?

A grenadier's an ignorant man
who beats up kids to teach them fear.
He cannot love his fellow man.
Papa, what an awful thing
to be a grenadier!

*"Los Pinos" is the Mexican presidential residence.

Ay, ay, ay, ay.

I'll never be a grenadier
Because I live to love and learn.
I'll never go around the world
beating up teachers and pupils in turn.

Ay, ay, ay, ay.

Papa, why does Mexico
have such a bad government, alas?
Why does God make us suffer so
with Cueto, Mendiolea, and Díaz Ordaz?

Ay, ay, ay, ay.

Never will we be grenadiers,
gorillas, and unjust governors.
We'll never go around the world
killing pupils and teachers in turn.

In *Mexico '68: The Students Speak*, trans. Richard Garza et al. (New York: United States Committee for Justice to Latin American Political Prisoners, 1968), 12.

The National Strike Committee

For a Worker/Peasant/Student Alliance (12 September 1968)

Our struggle has laid bare, not only the repressive character of our government, but also the structure of injustice and exploitation on which it rests.

The support that we have received from the popular sectors obliges us to discuss this structure and to let the popular masses know about our point of view on how to transform it, as well as the line of action that students, workers, peasants—in a word, the people as a whole—must take in order to banish from our country once and for all exploitation, poverty, abuse and repression.

Much has been said about the prosperity the country is enjoying. But it has not been pointed out that it is only the prosperity of a privileged minority, which increases its wealth at the expense of the working people. The worker, the peasant, wage earners in general, see how the cost of living increases while wages and income stay fixed or rise more slowly than the prices. Furthermore, increasing numbers of workers are being deprived of the opportunity to work because all of the innovations in industry, in agricultural machinery, etc. are for the benefit of the bosses alone. Through generalized repression the government has turned the organizations (such as the parties and trade unions) of the people into new means of subjugation and exploitation. The independent trade unions have practically disappeared; the peasants' organizations do not defend the interests of the agricultural workers but are instruments of political control in the hands of the corrupt leaders of the official party. Finally, more and more workers have been forced to work in unproductive and underpaid jobs as their only recourse for obtaining enough income to survive.

The government is not the government of all Mexicans; rather its resources are mainly devoted to increasing the privileges of the big bourgeoisie, consisting of the large industrialists, the large merchants and landowners, the bankers and the corrupt politicians of the "revolutionary family."

The PRI [Institutional Revolutionary Party] is a political apparatus which forces the masses to act and vote for its candidates by means of deceit, threats and blackmail. A long time ago it stopped representing any of the popular sectors, which it forces to remain within its ranks for the benefit of the big bourgeoisie.

With the repressions of 1959, those trade unions which used to be controlled by leaders representing the workers ceased being representative in any sense and have become gangs at the service of the bosses and their government.

As time passes, the number of Mexicans who lack education, housing, jobs, etc., increases while, at the same time, part of the national resources are delivered to foreign interests, especially those of the U.S.

The peasants are subjected to more arbitrariness every day. They are exploited not only by the landowner, the money lender, state and private banks, but also by the *ejido* commissariat, trade unions, transportation companies, middle-men, and a whole gamut of corrupt politicians.

These circumstances, and many others too numerous to mention, have led us to the conclusion that we cannot wait any longer. We must begin a general struggle, together with all the workers, in order to demand a minimum of rights that will place us on the road to the final liberation of the Mexican people. The people are our country, not the professional politicians whose only ties with the country are exploitation, treason and crime.

Defense and Improvement of the Standard of Living Through Immediate Wage Increases and Successive Increases Corresponding to Price Rises

The working masses who, by their labor, produce goods and move the machinery that creates all of the wealth, must begin to partake of these riches. For this reason our first issue is *an increase in wages* to a level that would let all workers and their families live decently. But we all know that wage raises are nullified by the rise of prices. Therefore, as an issue complementing the one mentioned above, we propose that a clause should be introduced in workers' contracts that would oblige employers to raise wages in accordance with increases in the cost of living.

Stop Unemployment by Reducing the Hours of Work

It is by exploiting the workers that the employers have become rich and can replace their old equipment with machinery which increases productivity. Therefore, the working people cannot tolerate being thrown on the ash-heap of unemployment once they have been squeezed dry. In order to avoid this, workers must fight so that each technological advance results in a *shorter working day without a reduction of wages*.

Workers' Control to Insure a Just Distribution of Profits

Workers are entitled, by law, to profit-sharing. However, employers dodge this responsibility by fraudulent accounting. The only way to avoid this is by workers' control of production and accounts.

*Win Independent and Democratic Trade Unions. Organize
Committees of Struggle Elected Directly by the Workers*

The employers and the government are using gangster-like groups
in charge of the trade unions to control the workers politically and
to prevent them from fighting for better conditions of living and
work. Therefore, we propose that workers fight for *independent and
democratic trade unions through Committees of Struggle.* This struggle must
side-step the legal trap which forces all the workers' organizations
to be recognized by the government. The Committee of Struggle
must actually represent the workers, must decide upon strikes, stoppages and all other actions for the defense of workers' rights. Workers do not need the approval of the government to stop production
in factories and on farms, for the simple reason that it is not the
government that gets production going. Naturally, the first steps in
this direction must be taken before the bosses, the government, and
their spies catch on. The committees can only come into the open
when they are strong and they can fight a decisive battle against
their enemies.

For a Workers' Federation Based on the Committees of Struggle

If the gangs now in power in the trade unions can maneuver so easily, this is due to the fact that, besides having the support of the
bosses and the government, they are well organized. The workers
must oppose this organization with a revolutionary organization,
based upon the Struggle Committees. The strategic objective in this
direction is the creation of a revolutionary federation of workers,
that is to say, an organization for the workers equivalent to the students' National Strike Committee.

We have already said that the creation of workers' Committees
of Struggle cannot exist in the open at the beginning like the student Committees did. However, their objectives are similar: unite
and organize the workers apart from the puppet organization as a
means of defending their interests.

The way in which the Committees of Struggle must act during
the period in which they cannot operate in the open is by presenting the general points expressed in this program, and others that

they favor, to each section of the factory, branch of industry, etc., where they are active. For this purpose the publication of leaflets and newspapers that would reach all the workers is of the greatest importance.

For the Organization of Peasants' Committees of Struggle

In the countryside, it is also necessary to organize militant committees with basic elements of leadership; however, it is necessary to distinguish between salaried workers and those who own or rent a small piece of land, or belong to an *ejido*. For the former, the same points are valid as for the factory workers, with slight alterations, such as introducing social security for all, etc.

For Easy and Low-Interest Farm Loans

The policy of the government toward the countryside has two basic defects—the funds dedicated to giving credit to the peasants are scarce; in addition, they are distributed very badly: most of the funds disappear through corruption, bribery and chicanery. The small landowners must declare war to the death on those evils. The first demand in this direction is that *state agricultural banks must be managed by the peasants themselves or their representatives, subject to recall when necessary. More funds for the countryside.*

Besides this, the peasants must demand that the state provide more funds for farm loans. Out of 62 billion pesos of the national budget, most is devoted to creating favorable conditions for multiplying the profits of the bosses. The peasants must oppose that policy and demand that at least as much money be devoted to stimulating agricultural development as agriculture contributes to the gross national product, that is to say, a minimum of ten billion pesos annually.

Eliminate the Middle-Men, Creating Struggle Committees of Peasants and Workers to Perform Their Services

One of the most frequent forms of exploitation is that of the middlemen, who buy produce below the guaranteed or market prices. This is often done because these brokers are the only ones who can transport the produce to the shopping centers, for they own the means of transport. The peasants must organize Committees of Struggle together with the workers to take care of services; the strategic objective of these committees should be the elimination of the middle-men through expropriation of the means which they use to exploit the peasants, and the use of those means for the benefit of the workers and peasants themselves.

Fight to Get Back the Lands That Were Taken Away from the Peasants for Water Works and Other Reforms by the Government

It is well known that many politicians and capitalists, clued in on programs for the building of dams, etc., have become rich by buying land fraudulently—with threats, deceit, etc. This land must be rescued for the benefit of the deceived peasants and workers in general. For this reason we propose that *all the lands wrongly acquired should be expropriated with all the installations on them for the benefit of peasants and workers.*

Project

This is the program which we propose to workers and peasants as a starting point towards a nation-wide, long-term, joint struggle. Obviously, it is not the last word and doubtless it must undergo modification that will enrich it with the participation of the workers. However, it can show that our interests have been enlarged in this fight through the contact we have had with the masses of the people and that we are willing to fight in order to fulfill the obligations that we have contracted in the struggle.

We know that the classes in power will scream to high heaven and accuse us of all kinds of things. We don't care. If the government, if the bosses, if those who call themselves patriots and good Christians, truly want to serve the country—that is to say, the large majority of the Mexican people—let them adopt this program in real life, not in speeches.

For our part, this is our answer, on the one hand, to the angry threats of the government and, on the other hand, to the support the people have given us, not only in this movement, but also by giving us the opportunity to study.

If one day our schools are occupied by military force, we will leave for the national battlefield, brandishing this program; and we will not stop under any circumstances, whoever falls and whatever happens.

University City, Mexico
September 12, 1968

In *Mexico '68: The Students Speak*, trans. Richard Garza et al. (New York: United States Committee for Justice to Latin American Political Prisoners, 1968), 25–27.

Abbie Hoffman

Interview (1969)

Many different protest movements converged on the Democratic Party convention in Chicago, 26–29 August 1968. Angry demonstrators demanded civil rights, an end to the Vietnam War, women's rights, economic equality, and other programs. Abbie Hoffman and the "Yippies" (the "Youth International Party") merged these demands with a counter-cultural sensibility that included a public mocking of authority. In Chicago the Yippies attracted extensive attention by nominating a pig for president. Facing federal trial for conspiracy to incite violence as part of the so-called Chicago Eight, Hoffman drew inspiration from Che Guevara and other international figures in his call for a popular revolution against the institutions and culture of established power in the United States.

ABBIE HOFFMAN: If you'd ask me what is going on in this country, I'd say I haven't got the vaguest idea because I don't understand it, you see. The leaders of this country have destroyed it. They've destroyed what I consider to be the destiny of this country and the aims of the founding fathers of the revolution, the American Revolution—I mean I think Thomas Jefferson would vomit over our Vietnam policy.

INTERVIEWER: Do you think we need a revolution every ten years?

HOFFMAN: I think we should aim toward a free society and I mean really *free*—you don't pay. I think not paying is where it's at. I think this society has the technological capabilities to serve the needs of the people in such a fantastic, unbelievably humanistic way that no one would have to work. The machines would do the work or else we could work steadily toward the goal of full unemployment, not full employment—none of those jerk things that even the NAACP is demanding and the administration demands and the Right demands and everybody demands. We're beyond that. We want full unemployment. We want a society of leisure, a society of creative artists in which we're free to do whatever we want, in which we enjoy what we're doing. If you enjoy it, it's not work. Work is something you do for money, for the kids—you know, for the boss, for the machine. I'm never gonna work again ever. You see, I think in fifty years if the whole thing survives—if we get through nuclear war and everything else, including garbage strikes where the garbage piles up so high that you know the whole civilization is being smothered—if we can get through that, we'd *have* this free society of vision. You know twenty or thirty years ago people worked a sixteen-hour workday; now it's eight, and pretty soon it'll be down to four. And the question is how is this society going to deal with leisure, how is it going to deal with abundance? Up to now society, the American system—the American capitalist system, to use a dirty word—has worked on the principles of the industrial revolution. That is, it has been based upon a society of scarcity where there is not enough to go around: therefore some people gotta get more and some people gotta get less and some people gotta go out and work for other people so they can get more. I think the cybernetic revolution allows for a society of abundance in which those kinds of questions become meaningless and the whole concept of property becomes meaningless, and that's what my personal revolution is directed toward. There is something wrong with a civilization where you have to pay a dime to take a shit in the subway. I mean, what're pay toilets about? Like what the fuck is that thing about out there called American Society?

Everybody asks us where our goals are and all that and sometimes we say fuck you and sometimes we clown around and sometimes we'll spell it out in great detail, but nobody asks the leaders of this country what are the goals of this country—like, where the hell is it going? What they *say* is that we're for peace and brotherhood. Well, those kinds of words like peace and brotherhood have no meaning to us. Like after Martin Luther King's death, LBJ goes on TV and says that in the memory of King's name we should be nonviolent. What the fuck is he talking about—is he talking about sit-ins in the Mekong Delta? Is he talking about 'We shall overcome' in Vietnam? No, he isn't talking about that—he's telling the oppressed to get the fuck in the cellar, stay there, and get outta the streets. Well, those days are gone. Nobody is listening to them—it's *in* the streets. That's where we're gonna vote. We're gonna vote heavy. People are into this. You see what the whole hippie movement has done is to focus on the possibility that white people in this country, young white kids, can make their own revolution around their own dreams, their own visions, their own needs, their own aspirations.

There is already an edge in the door. We have an underground press. We have underground newsreels. We have underground theater. We have a whole philosophy. We have a free store around the corner. We give away everything free. We print books; we print poems and we pass them out on the street free. We go around here painting buildings free. We open up communes and have kids live in them free. We're gonna paint the subway stop here free. We're already living in the future—we're living thirty years ahead and, you see, we like it—we like it so much that we're willing to die to defend it and that's where it's at, and that's why we're gonna win.

INTERVIEWER: Who started the Yippies?

HOFFMAN: It was a myth created by the media, not us. What about if we create a myth, program it into the media so that it's always connected to Chicago and August 25th to 30th—come and do your thing—bullshit—everything and anything you want to say, you can do it. Commitment, engagement, Democrats, pigs—the whole thing. All you gotta do is change the "H" in hippie to a "Y" for Yippie and you got it—a new phenomena on the American scene. Well, that's O.K., because the way in which that myth was planned for Chicago, and so for six months you couldn't talk about the Yippies without saying, "Oh yeah— the Yippies are going to Chicago to the Democratic Convention.

So by word of mouth and by using the media, that's how it happened.

INTERVIEWER: But didn't you plan it at a Christmas Eve meeting?

HOFFMAN: So the myth goes. What's a meeting? We've never really had meetings. Three of us sat around and someone said, "Yippie." That was the meeting. "'Yippie,' yeah," we said, "that's great. Yeah, that's good. You say, 'Join the Y'—that's good, we'll steal their symbols. Why—that's our question. Our question is 'Why?' and our slogan will be 'Y'." You know, as long as you can make up a story about it that's exciting, full of shit, mystical, you have to accuse us of going to Chicago to perform magic. And that's out of sight, because that's what it's about. We put out a poster, a jigsaw puzzle of the United States, pointing to Chicago, Yippie, the festival of life, August 25th to 30th, Chicago, music, lights, theater, free, magic, and that was enough. *You* can't understand that. You need three hundred pages, you know, beginning with a capital letter and ending with a period. But young kids don't need that, they don't even want it. Nobody reads books, nobody reads *The New York Times*; we look at movies and watch television.

INTERVIEWER: Well, they read the underground newspaper.

HOFFMAN: But the underground newspaper has a different concept of, let's say, truth, than the "overground" newspapers. The underground newspaper knows that there's no such thing as truth and therefore can have a whole lot of fun. It can talk in terms of myth.

But the cheapest means of communication on the national scale is the national media. I would say that the Yippies spent under $5,000 on Chicago, but ABC, NBC, and CBS must have spent $700,000, you see, so it's like stealing.

We're not very good about money. We had one benefit at a discothèque—at the Electric Circus—one night last February, and we raised about $3,500, but that was about the only money we ever raised, except for some people being on the street, panhandling—whatever. We had a bank account, but we never used it after a month—we really burned that $3,500. We had an office—but no lock on the door after a month. People would come in, pick up the phone, and say, "I'm a Yippie leader." And run down on what it was about. But it didn't matter who they talked to or what was said, because when you deal in the area of myth, it doesn't matter. There's no way it can be distorted, because its life blood is distortion. I mean, you can't even tell the truth about the Yippies—you can't! It's a slogan; it has an exclamation point at the end. There are no real Yippies. Nobody is a Yippie—there are no card-carrying Yippies. The press made up the "Youth International Party," *YIP*, so they could relate to the Yippies in a straight, linear way.

INTERVIEWER: The press did that?

HOFFMAN: Yeah, sure, who the hell talks like that—we don't talk Youth International Party; it's a hoax.

We are very different from the Mobilization. You'll have a lot easier time understanding the National Mobilization to End the War in Vietnam than you will in understanding the Yippies.

INTERVIEWER: That's for sure.

HOFFMAN: When the mobilization sits down to negotiate with the administration, they aren't that different. They understand each other. They all wear suits and ties, they sit down, they talk rationally, they use the same kind of words, the same kind of language, and they want to negotiate a peaceful settlement. The Yippie thing is very different from that—we *don't* use the same kind of words, we *don't* use the same kind of language, we *don't* dress the same. We also don't understand what you're talking about, and you don't understand what we're talking about, and we don't mind that one bit.

INTERVIEWER: You don't want to negotiate—would that be included?

HOFFMAN: We are into revolution and we applied for the permit a long time ago, and that's it. I mean—we are in to win or die.

INTERVIEWER: Revolution by any means necessary?

HOFFMAN: Any means—any means necessary. That's a phrase of great interest to commissions on violence. . . . We will defend ourselves by "any means necessary"—you can say that in different tones, and one time it'll mean laughing and another time fighting. It's not the words that are important, it's the tone and it's the action, really. You have to examine the action—not the words. That's one thing we play on the American psyche—we know the hang-up on words. You know Rap Brown says everybody ought to get a gun. Well, when I hear that I laugh, because I've worked in ghettos and I've worked in the South and every black already has a gun. So, what's he talking about? They all have guns! For all I know, everybody in this country has a gun. So what does it mean—telling people who already have guns, that they ought to get guns? It's a means of raising their revolutionary consciousness because what he's saying is you ought to think about changing the society in which you live and you ought to think about it to the extent that you're willing to risk your life. That's *what* he's saying. That's raising the revolutionary consciousness. In a revolution, you either win or you die, Ché Guevara said, and that's where it's at. I don't know of any of the so-called movement leaders in the country who are not convinced that they're gonna be killed within three or four years. So we are in it to win or die. That's it. There are no doubts about it. We're going to wreck this fuckin' society. If we don't, this society is going to wreck itself anyway, so we might as well have some fun in doing it.

And that's the thing about the underground press, too—it doesn't care what it says, it has fun doing it. It can talk in terms of there will be ten million people in Chicago and Bob Dylan will be climbing the trees and we'll be pulling Hubert Humphrey's pants down, you see. *The New York Times* can't joke about that, you know. *The New York Times* is uninvolving, while the underground media is very involving. Just look at the front page of an underground paper—in terms of layout, in terms of the appeal, underground newspapers look like television commercials.

INTERVIEWER: What about organizing?

HOFFMAN: We operated primarily through the underground press and through our writing and even more in terms of our action. We had to show the people, so we had, for example, a raid on Stony Brook [the State University of New York at Stony Brook, Long Island] after they had the big [drug] raid out there.

So we said, "We're going to have a raid and arrest everybody who's smoking cigarettes and drinkin' booze," and we went out there with rock bands and things in the middle of the morning just like the cops, and went into a whole satirical pun on the way the cops raided that school . . . and that made it . . . got Yippie in the public eye a little.

Then we said, "Well, we need a party!" So on March 21st or 22nd—I guess, the first day of spring, we had a party in Grand Central Station at midnight—we spent $15.00 and had eight thousand people come to our party for no reason at all. We had all these people, playing with balloons and everything, singing on corners and other people pouring in and everybody getting so excited about having this tremendous sense of community. Wow! Everybody turning out at midnight to a party in Grand Central Station, isn't that exciting?

Well, the police responded to that one with an amazing show of force. I must say that I've been in tremendously violent street demonstrations before, both in the North and in the South, and I would say that Grand Central was the goofiest thing I ever encountered—goofier than Chicago!

INTERVIEWER: Who organized that, you and Paul [Krassner] and Jerry [Rubin] or . . . who got the idea and promoted it and started getting people to— Well, somebody must have thought of it first of all?

HOFFMAN: Fuck, that's not the way things happen! It just goes, that's all! People get together and somebody says, "Yeah that's a good idea," and lots of people work on it. I would say five guys and a mimeograph machine could bring down any police force in this country. . . . We had eight thousand people in Grand Central. You see, all we're doing is pinpointing certain feelings—we're naming the day. The energy is already there, and it gathers.

After the parading of the wounded from Grand Central Station, the ACLU came into the picture and wanted to defend people and charge the police with brutality and things went back and forth and then articles started appearing. What does it mean to be a Yippie? What is a Yippie? What is this new phenomenon on the American scene? Is the Yippie a "politicalized hippie?" That's generally the phrase the media used. But people also talked about a "psychedelic revolution" or a "psychedelic left" and stuff like that.

INTERVIEWER: Were these articles prepared by you people?

HOFFMAN: No, they were prepared by *you* people. That was the role of *The New York Times*, and people like that—to analyze what we were about. It was never our role to analyze ourselves. We knew better. We knew we couldn't explain it.

INTERVIEWER: What happened next?

HOFFMAN: Well, we had meetings with New York City officials who were afraid because we planned a sit-in, in tribute to the memory of Martin Luther King, in the mayor's office. Since they were all mourning his loss, we invited President Johnson, Governor Rockefeller, Archbishop Cooke, and the mayor to join us—adopt King's tactics and have this sit-in—because we were not being allowed to have our Yip-out on Easter Sunday. But the City of New York does it a little differently—you put a little pressure on them and they'll come around on most things.

If the Democratic Convention had been held in New York, I think the city would have given us $200,000 and gotten the Beatles to come over and play in the park and everything would have been groovy. That's what I told the Chicago officials to do. Give us some money, let us set up the best festival possible in the park, and nothing will happen. I'd rather dance and listen to music than fight cops in the streets.

INTERVIEWER: Did you put it that way?

HOFFMAN: We put it in all different ways. We can say anything and do anything because it doesn't matter. They're not about to give us the money; they're not about to do what is right.

INTERVIEWER: But you did have the sit-in [in New York]?

HOFFMAN: Yes, we had that little sit-in and we tested the city and the city—

INTERVIEWER: How many people were in the sit-in?

HOFFMAN: We had about thirty. They brought out about eight hundred cops for that event.

INTERVIEWER: Did you see Mayor Lindsay or did you see a representative?

HOFFMAN: A representative. They had no idea at that point, after the Grand Central Station affair, what the hell it all meant. They picked up a leaflet of ours, you know, and they had no idea whether it would mean ten people or ten thousand, so they would be guarding for ten thousand every time we walked around the city. It was kind of exciting in a way. We'd go there with twenty people with bells and flowers and incense. And there would be eight hundred cops with guns.

INTERVIEWER: Did you get a permit at that time for Central Park?

HOFFMAN: I don't know if we actually ever did get a permit. I think we did, but it became clear at that point that the mayor's office called the Parks Department and straightened their heads out and we were allowed to have our music festival and we had it on Easter.

INTERVIEWER: Was it staged to promote Chicago?

HOFFMAN: Anything that had the name Yippie attached to it was to promote Chicago. But it was basically a music festival, just like Grand Central was staged not as a police confrontation event, but as a party.

I'll give you an example of how the media works and how the media is the organizing tool, when you're into myth and organizing through myth. We had two events, two major events before Chicago. We had the Yip-in—which is what we called it—at Grand Central Station, and that was a massacre. They massacred us, no warning, no nothing, and injured two, three hundred people and arrested sixty. I myself got beaten unconscious, you know. Then we had the Yip-out on Easter in Central Park—maybe we had forty thousand, fifty thousand people, fifteen rock bands, flowers out of the sky, a real joyous kind of event, and the police were instructed by the City of New York, which was kind of cool in dealing with us, to keep the fuck out of the park. This I don't think could have happened in Chicago. It might have, who knows? But for that event they kept the police out on the perimeters. If they *had* police there, they were in costume and they didn't look like police. And there were bonfires and people smoked dope and people fucked on the grass and did whatever they wanted. It was a liberated zone. You could do whatever you wanted and no violence happened.

INTERVIEWER: No?

HOFFMAN: No. A month after those two events, you see, it was the Grand Central Station thing that stuck in the nation's mind as being what Yippie was about, not the thing in Central Park, even though there were five times as many people and a lot more of what you would call planning and a lot more money spent. You know, we spent maybe $1,500 on that Central Park thing and $15.00 on Grand Central Station. It's because the media is attracted by violence; it plays it up and what was gonna happen in Chicago—you see a myth in a sense never lies—so Grand Central Station, not Central Park, was a preview of what was gonna happen in Chicago.

Because violence *does* attract your media, and because this is the idea—to get the media, so that you can get people involved. . . .

INTERVIEWER: Is that why you did it—to provoke violence?

HOFFMAN: Hell, no—we didn't ask for *that* kind of media attention! Look, we put out one first call for Chicago only to the underground press. I think we maybe had one press conference before Chicago, and this is *another* example of how it doesn't fit. We had a press conference in the Americana Hotel somewhere along about April, I guess. All the top rock singers, Ginsberg and all this la-de-da about how this was gonna happen and this was gonna happen in Chicago, and it got no coverage—nothing. It was arranged by one of the top publicists in the country. We had all the major media there, and it got no coverage. We asked, "*Why*, man—we did everything right, didn't we?" The reason it didn't was because that wasn't what Chicago was gonna be about. That's my conclusion.

And don't forget we had a series of demonstrations here in New York—when Humphrey would come to town, there would be an antiwar demonstration where people were getting clubbed, brutally clubbed—and people started to realize, that is, hippie types, that you couldn't go to a demonstration without expecting violence. There is no such thing anymore in this country—you've got to expect violence. So at that point they had to say, "Well, are we gonna go to a demonstration or not," and they'd say, "No, we're *not* gonna go," and so they went off up to the hills or someplace. But what happened up in the hills, when they went to develop communes—attempted to really in a sense drop out of society—well, they found they were getting the shit kicked out of them anyway. So you get someone like Timothy Leary, a total pacifist drop-out, a rural kind of guy, saying, "Let's go up to Millbrook and forget about protest—forget about it, it's all dead, your protest is as bad as they are." And he goes up to Mill-brook and opens up a little community and every week the fuck-ing cops are in there raiding the place. Beating up all the people, arresting them on phony charges. You experience this for a while and then you say, "Hey, we gotta fight, we're fightin' for our lives. We can't just drop out, we gotta fight." So people who drifted off to the hills, eventually, through the course of the summer, started to come back, and they ended up in Chicago. If they didn't, they didn't. It didn't matter. Chicago was, in a way, in your head—there were lots of people involved in Chicago who never even went. You didn't have to go. The community is bigger than the numbers that went to Chicago. In January there was a lot of talk about going to Chicago, and Sheriff Joe Woods comes out with "We're going to put them in subterranean mud tunnels," and Daley comes out with his "Shoot to kill" orders, and all that shit. But Woods came on first with their magic. Their magic was forming white vigilante groups and putting us in subterranean mud tunnels underneath the subway system.

In Peter Babcox, Deborah Babcox, and Bob Abel, eds., *The Conspiracy* (New York: Dell Publishing Company, 1969), 43–52.

CIA Report

Restless Youth (September 1968)

At the request of President Lyndon Johnson, in 1968 the Central Intelligence Agency (CIA) conducted a study of protest movements around the world. To the surprise of the president, the CIA found that communists were not behind the unrest. The CIA pointed to a worldwide phenomenon of "restless youth"—highly educated and idealistic young people who were dissatisfied with contem-porary politics. In particular, the CIA argued that students were alienated from modern bureaucratic institutions of power, and drawn to international protest figures, like Mao Zedong and Che Guevara. The CIA not only lamented the se-

rious challenge to authority posed by global protests; it predicted more of the same in the future.

Conclusions

Youthful dissidence, involving students and non-students alike, is a world-wide phenomenon. It is shaped in every instance by local conditions, but nonetheless there are striking similarities, especially in the more advanced countries. As the underdeveloped countries progress, these similarities are likely to become even more wide-spread.

A truly radical concept of industrial society and its institutions prompts much of the dissidence—but it, alone, does not explain the degree to which young agitators have won a wide following in such countries as France, the Federal Republic and the United States.

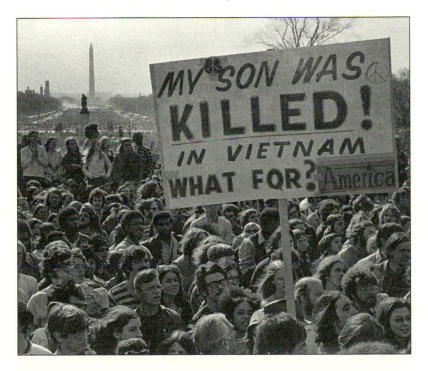

Within the United States large demonstrations against the Vietnam War continued after 1968, reaching a crescendo in the early 1970s.

Some measure of dissidence is traceable to generational conflict, psychic problems, etc. But most owes its dimension to the number of students, a profusion of issues, and skillful leadership techniques.

The proximate causes are rooted in the university; they are chosen for their appeal, for the support they will engender. However, the confidence of the agitators in the likelihood of their being able to expand a limited protest rests—sometimes fragilely—on a growing base of student cynicism with respect to the relevance of social institutions and to the apparent gap between promise and performance.

Perhaps most disturbing of all is the growing belief of the militants—and many less committed young people—in the efficacy of violence as a political device.

The Communists can take little comfort from any of this, even though Moscow and its allies may exact fleeting advantage from the disruption sowed by the dissidents. In the long run, they will have to cope with young people who are alienated by the more oppressive features of Soviet life.

Because of the revolution in communications, the ease of travel, and the evolution of society everywhere, student behavior never again will resemble what it was when education was reserved for the elite. The presence in the universities of thousands of lower- and lower-middle-class students has resulted in an unprecedented demand for relevant instruction. Today's students are a self-conscious group; they communicate effectively with each other outside of any institutional framework, read the same books and savor similar experiences. Increasingly, they have come to recognize what they take to be a community of interests. This view is likely to influence their future political conduct and to shape the demands they make of government.

Preface

Thanks to riots in West Berlin, Paris, and New York and sit-ins in more than twenty other countries in recent months, student activism has caught the attention of the world.

What are the students in New York, Paris, Rome and Buenos Aires trying to tell us? What do they have in common?

Apprenticed to but not yet part of the "System," the activists and malleable fellow students are not restrained by the sanctions which most adults place on themselves. Pragmatic and searching, they refuse to accept many of the premises of an older age; instead, they retreat to gut reaction. Their mode is indignation.

Some of the activists clearly are unwilling to participate in the political process. Their choice of tactics is dictated by a conscious wish to disrupt. A far larger number wish only to reform our social and political institutions so that they will be more responsive, less ponderous.

The optimism of the anarchists is a hallmark of youth. So, too, are the energy and rebelliousness which provide student protest so much of its thrust. The protesters, after all, are adolescents or post-adolescents; the vehemence of protest cannot be understood without some appreciation of the emotional crises attendant on both stages of development.

Some adolescents rebel against their families, bridging the gap between childhood and maturity within the confines of the family; others displace this rebelliousness on to authorities beyond the home—the school, the law, the state. Some, such as those who were active in the early 1960s in the Civil Rights Movement, succeed in doing so in ways that win the approbation of the community. When this occurs the consequences more often than not are constructive—both for society and the individuals involved.

This paper is an attempt to explore the reasons underlying student unrest. Part I examines such questions as motivation, history, leadership and tactics.

Part II consists of a series of country chapters chosen to illustrate the influence of local conditions on the evolution of dissent and the many forms it takes. The chapters on France, West Germany, Italy and the Communist states of Europe—the USSR, Poland and Yu-goslavia—highlight the remarkable parallels between East and West in patterns of dissent. The chapter on the Netherlands suggests some of the ways an enlightened government in cooperation with the universities can anticipate and may be able to defuse student dissent. Those on Africa, India, Iran, Turkey, and Indonesia explore the problem as it is found in emerging states. The chapter on Japan highlights the consequences of mass education and points to the degree to which the political system in Japan has come to accept student activism as a quasi-legitimate expression of legislative opposition. That on China treats the phenomenon of the Red Guards which all too many commentators see as little more than a Maoist version of the western dissidents. The Argentine chapter discusses the effects of the 50-year-old Cordoba Reform on Latin American education and the efforts of the Ongania regime to depoliticize students; that on Brazil has a more current focus.

This paper does not discuss the broader Peace Movement to which organized student groups contribute manpower, the Communist Party/USA, or any parties of the Left—except insofar as they contribute to student dissent. Nor does it deal directly with the Civil Rights Movement, the latter-day current of Black Power or urban riots or violence in American society. These have been the subjects of study by the President's Commission on Civil Disorders and the National Commission on the Causes and Prevention of Violence.

Neither does this paper discuss such symptoms of alienation as the use of drugs, the so-called hippies or teenage runaways, even though all are symptomatic of many of the same problems which fuel organized dissent.

Restless Youth

Student protest is visible, highly vocal, increasingly militant and feared by many to be interconnected world-wide.

In the last few months, it has closed down several great universities, fomented civil strife and altered political careers in more than twenty countries. Indeed, if one accepts Richard Neustadt's definition of power as "the effective influence upon the conduct of others," then Student Power is no longer a chimera. It is a reality which has similar characteristics even though its form may vary from country to country.

Students are an elite and volatile group—to a great degree imbued with an almost mystical faith in the ability of an aroused "people" to generate reform and with a marked distrust of governmental bureaucracy. They have a knack for being among the first to espouse unpopular causes and have been quick to call society to account for its shortcomings.

Student rebelliousness is not a recent phenomenon. It predates the university: it was commonplace in ancient Athens and in imperial Rome. Socrates complained woefully that the students of his time had "bad manners, contempt for authority, disrespect for older people." In the Thirteenth Century students in Paris elected their professors and the illumined texts of the time describe the rampages of medieval English students who burned lecture halls and sacked nearby villages when their wishes were unheeded.

However, it was not until the early Nineteenth Century, following the rise of the nation-state, that students became an important force for social and political change. They were in the forefront of the revolutions in 1848 in Germany and Austria, went "to the people" in Czarist Russia, and to their deaths or exile in 1905. At home and abroad, African and Asian students agitated against colonial regimes during the interwar and post World War II periods.

During the 1950s, aroused students figured in the downfall of Peron in Argentina in 1955 and Perez Jiminez in Venezuela in 1958; students rashly encouraged Imre Nagy and fought Russian tanks in Budapest in October-November 1956, as they seemed prepared to do in behalf of Gomulka during Poland's all too brief "October" of the same year. Rioting Japanese students forced cancellation of President Eisenhower's trip to Tokyo and the ouster of the Kishi Government in 1960. That same year, Korean students were in the van of the anti-Rhee riots in Seoul and in Turkey they took to the streets against Menderes.

In the United States, beginning early in 1960, students supplied much of the manpower and inspiration for the Civil Rights Movement. At first tentatively and then with growing confidence, American students used the sit-in and similar tactics to confront the power structure of the south—appealing for the support of a lethargic but influential public far beyond the confines of Mobile or Birmingham. And they demonstrated to their satisfaction that the tactics of confrontation work; indeed, many came away from Civil Rights with the conviction that *only* confrontation works.

Student activism depends for much of its strength on the way it is regarded by the adult citizenry. In most Western countries, at least, there has long been a feeling that politics is *not* a proper arena for students. This notion has been strengthened by the fact that in

Europe and the United States student movements hitherto have proved transitory and vulnerable to fragmentation.

The incidence in the past of student demonstrations in widely separated places, the Middle East, Japan, or even Latin America did not excite undue concern in the U.S.—even when such outbreaks impinged briefly on American interests, as in the case of President Eisenhower's abortive trip to Tokyo in 1960. They passed unnoticed by all but a few or were dismissed as some kind of seasonal madness.

In many countries, however, student political activism has been a more durable phenomenon and because of its durability has been accommodated in the political process. Argentine students won recognition of their political rights and a role in the administration of the universities in the Cordoba reform of 1918. That reform opened the door to many abuses and is at the root of much of the difficulty which besets Latin American education today, but it has served to sanction student political activity to the extent that participation in campus organizations more often than not constitutes entré to adult careers in government and law. Since World War II, Japanese demonstrations have become so common a tactic of the political opposition that they are taken for granted and occur within guidelines accepted by the public. Japanese student agitators enjoy a quasi-legitimate place in the legislative process. Indonesian students were a bulwark of Sukarno's regime for most of its existence—but turned against him because of his suspected complicity in the attempted Communist coup of 1965. African students are xenophobic; accorded special recognition and privileges, they hunger after more tangible rewards and pose a threat to several governments.

Campus activism may not be the central issue of our times; but none other now excites a greater response. Those who view the dissidents as fledgling conspirators are constrained to blame too permissive parents or lackadaisical teachers. Some point to a general breakdown in public morality for the unease which permeates so many campuses. Others credit the dissidents with reacting to the oppressive demands of an outmoded educational system and to the growing impersonalization of everyday life, to stagnation, to racial injustice. Yet a third group point with alarm to the influence of the mass media, warning that radio and television have a curious "three-dimensional" quality which exposes sham and stimulates discontent. There is no simple explanation.

Leaders + Issues = Followers

The interplay of emotions, ideologies, and attitudes which constitute the motive force behind youthful dissidence is infinitely complex. Those who would lead the dissidents, or stay a step ahead of them, are constrained to identify and exploit issues which promise the support of a wide following. Quite naturally, some issues prove more meaningful and therefore evoke a greater response. Naturally, too, the issues change or are replaced by broader demands as protest develops and a confrontation with authority ensues. At Columbia University, for example, an *ad hoc* protest against an administration decision to erect a much disputed gymnasium was transformed by the effects of outside intervention into an assault on the structure of the university itself. But by far the largest number of students who participated toward the close of the crisis were moved to do so out of indignation over what they regarded as police brutality. A similar evolution of issues and substitution of targets took place during the French disorders in May.

This substitution of issues and broadening of demands has been dubbed "expedient escalationism" by Zbigniew Brzezinski. It often begins with a series of minor confrontations between university authorities and a small band of dissenters whose complaints are limited to some facet of university life. The authorities do not entertain whatever proposals the dissenters are advocating—either because they are too far removed from day-to-day developments within the university to appreciate what is occurring or because they are unsure of their own position and prefer to procrastinate in the hope that time alone will solve the problem. The dissenters, rebuffed, become increasingly vocal and search out allies among other students or, crucially, among faculty members who have their own grievances.

There follows a series of "dress rehearsals," such as attempts to interrupt ROTC exhibitions or to mar faculty convocations in honor of visiting dignitaries. In some instances, the dissenters are turned upon by student critics and are assaulted—as at Nanterre where a rightist clique, the Occident, several times manhandled leftist students. The authorities respond with minor administrative sanctions or do not act at all out of fear of calling attention to a situation going out of their control.

A spontaneous incident, perhaps the arrest of a student away from the university, electrifies the community. A picket line or sit-in follows, and the students seek to negotiate with the authorities. Rather than confront the dissidents directly, however, the authorities welcome the advent of self-appointed middlemen, often disgruntled faculty members. The brokers attempt to clarify the issues and in doing so prolong the crisis.

Under pressure from all sides, the dissidents seek to legitimize their stance by demanding more and more, particularly if authorities dribble out piecemeal concessions which have only a negative impact, thus buttressing the popular view that they have lost the initiative. Reconciliation becomes impossible, and the authorities, after having sought to avoid confrontation, rashly invoke force without regard to its ultimate consequences. Bystanders are involved, sometimes injured, and a cause celebre results.

Sociologists have come to call the process by which more and more participants are drawn into protest *radicalization*. There is little agreement over the dynamics involved—and less evidence that any great number of students remain radicalized once the initial exhilaration of combat is past.

Certain considerations become extremely important to the leader. He must seek to sustain the protest, flexibly moving it to new ground when the occasion permits. To achieve this escalation, he must be prepared to welcome and adjust to the participation of a variety of people—negotiators, the voices of authority, public commentators, etc. Their involvement will tend to broaden the protest, spread its effects, and touch a multiplying number of people— students and non-students alike—each at his own level or point of sensitivity.

In every country the militants are a small minority, but a minority able to weave a strand of vague, inchoate resentments into fulminant protest. The leaders of protest have learned that there is much to protest about. The reasons for this go beyond the revolution in communications or mere leadership techniques. They have to do with the gulf between society's institutions and the people those institutions are designed to serve. Next to the surface almost everywhere are complaints which grow out of the conditions of student life and a demand for university reform. Poor administration-faculty-student relations, inadequate facilities, outmoded curricula, bureaucratic licensing requirements, "sudden death" examinations for the purpose of reducing swollen enrollments—all provide fuel for discontent.

And there are issues which grow out of the image which students have of society—its impersonality, bureaucracy, and the ponderousness of its political dynamics. The real activists view the university as only a proximate cause, the foe close at hand. For them, the real enemy is distant from the scene. It is society organized for efficiency at the expense of the individual, a treadmill that destroys initiative and traps the unwary.

In an era of global stalemate, they find the slogans of the Cold War singularly unconvincing, the resurgence of the 19th Century nation-state in De Gaulle's Fifth Republic anachronistic, and the participation of ruling and opposition parties in coalition governments which sometimes have the parliamentary support of Communists as proof that latter-day politics are a charade.

These attitudes, particularly in Europe, are a consequence of the failure of social and political institutions to accommodate themselves to the remarkable economic strides of the postwar period, the absence of compelling ideological issues, such as those embodied in the 1930s in the Spanish Civil War, and the diminution everywhere of moral authority. Many political parties—for example, the Socialists in Italy, France and Germany, the Anti-Revolutionary Party in the Netherlands, the Republicans and Monarchists in Italy, the Communists in most places—no longer are issue-oriented or responsive to the needs of the constituencies they purport to represent. A younger generation finds government bureaucracy—especially in Italy, France, Spain, Portugal, and the Netherlands—antiquated, cumbersome, and in the hands of a generation that came to power twenty-five years ago and remains committed more to preserving its authority than to utilizing political power to renovate society.

French students bitterly criticize De Gaulle's "arbitrariness," his fascination with nuclear armaments at the expense of badly needed public works, his disregard of public opinion, and the manner in which he stages periodic elections to legitimize his "mandate" and perpetuate what they consider to be one-man rule. And they are no more attracted to De Gaulle's pretensions to national glory, as witness Daniél Cohn-Bendit's rejection in March 1968 of "national flags and frontiers."

Few single issues can impel large numbers of students to demonstrate, although the role of the United States in world affairs, particularly US involvement in Vietnam, is most evocative. It is especially so in the United States where students who are critical of American policy and who regard Selective Service as a means for quashing dissent are distressed by the prospect of being coerced into supporting physically a course of action to which they object on moral grounds.

Abroad, local US involvement and the alleged role of the Central Intelligence Agency provide a backdrop against which to mount a protest over the Vietnam war—the first major conflict in the lifetime of the dissenters. Opposition to American involvement in Southeast Asia and to the North Atlantic Treaty Organization is fueled in Germany, for example, by the Kiesinger government's advocacy of the so-called Emergency Laws and the distrust which many students have of government by coalition. Egyptian students, hypersensitive to the appeals of Arab nationalism, see American participation in a "Zionist conspiracy" aimed at establishing Israeli hegemony in the Middle East and blame the rout of Arab troops by the Israelis in June 1967 on US aid. In Argentina and Brazil students take to the streets against unpopular military regimes which they are convinced are maintained in power through US support. In Panama and Mexico they do so out of resentment over malfeasance or corruption of one-party rule—but always against a backdrop of US involvement.

In Communist countries, anti-American demonstrations can be deceptive; they are hardly a valid manifestation of student dissidence. Anomie nevertheless exists. Russian students resent the heavy-handed attempts of party leaders to bolster a myopic view of history. Dismayed by the revelation of Stalin's perfidy and the fall of Khrushchev, they have been quick to ask whether the Soviet system is at fault. They have turned back in upon themselves, according to most accounts, searching for a new value system grounded in individual worth. Polish and Yugoslav students, far from seeking to overturn the Communist state, hope to nudge it into fulfilling its avowed goals and have rioted against the obstructive tactics of party bureaucrats who bar the advance of a younger and better educated generation.

The children of a generally affluent generation—West or East—are less concerned with matters of economic livelihood or the challenge of building a revolutionary state on the ruins of autocratic rule than were their fathers and some, at least, are deeply engrossed in matters of life-style.

The Student Explosion

As a general observation, student activism has emerged in times of political flux, when social values have been subject to challenge. The mid-1960s are such a time. The concern with which present-day activism is viewed by many is traceable, of course, to the violence which sometimes accompanies it. It also is due to puzzlement over the ultimate objectives of the protesters, who arise out of student bodies drawn from a far wider social base than before, and apprehension over the number of people who might become involved if protest truly is symptomatic of a deeply rooted malaise. There also is a vague feeling that the dissidents are likely to prove more effective with time and the opportunities afforded them by expanding communications.

Next to defense, education is the biggest business of the modern state—and the greatest need of the underdeveloped countries. University populations have more than doubled world-wide in ten years. There are 600,000 students in France and 350,000 in the United Kingdom. The Federal Republic, which has 370,000 in its universities, anticipates 500,000 by 1970. The USSR has 1,900,000 full-time university students. Japan, which like the United States has committed itself to the goal of mass education, has more than one million. There are more than six million Americans enrolled in colleges and universities.

This implosion has strained facilities in all but a few countries; the construction of buildings and the expansion of faculty have not kept pace. Neither has pedagogy made adequate use of modern invention. The situation is especially critical in the great metropolitan universities abroad, e.g., in Paris, Rome, Buenos Aires, Rio, where scores of thousands of students live for long periods of time in hostels and tenements under conditions approaching genuine hardship. At the Sorbonne, for example, more than 100,000 students live in congested quarters and study in obsolescent buildings designed for far fewer than half that number.

More important than antiquated buildings and crowded living conditions, however, has been the failure of university authorities and faculties to modernize administrative techniques, reform curricula to meet the needs of an increasingly technological society, or improve teaching methods. Many courses have little if any relevance to contemporary life. Degree requirements dating back a hundred years force a student to commit to memory great bodies of irrelevant data.

Many of the new generation of European and Latin American and Asian students are from lower- or lower-middle-class families; they have firsthand knowledge of the socioeconomic ills of the day. They arrive at the university with high expectations and an acute appreciation of the type of course content which is likely to prove functional in their lives. All too often the reality does not live up to expectation.

There is an unmistakable correlation between academic discipline and propensity to protest. While it is somewhat misleading to generalize, students enrolled in professional schools, such as Law, Medicine, or Engineering, seldom are found among campus demonstrators. Where there are exceptions, as in parts of Latin America where medicine is regarded as a "liberal" undertaking, the explanation usually can be traced to the effects of emigration on a university faculty or to a significant event in the development of the particular school.

Professional and preprofessional students are vocationally oriented; they are obliged to master a clearly defined body of data and to submit to regular examinations designed to test their progressive skill in applying that data.

The protesters come from what are described as the Liberal Arts—precisely the faculties which have had to absorb the brunt of increasing enrollments and which are hard pressed to maintain any semblance of high standards.

Except in the United States, there is too little information to shed any light on the character, academic standing, etc., of most of the prominent student dissidents. Men like Rudi Dutschke or Karl Dietrich Wolff of West Berlin's *Sozialistische Deutsche Studentenbund* and Daniél Cohn-Bendit of Paris' 22 March Movement are reputed to be better than average students, with considerably more than average oratorical skills. Dutschke, for example, survived the taxing routine of undergraduate study in Germany and was admitted to advanced studies at the Free University.

There are ample data to support the view that some of the best of the students in US universities are involved in protest—and that they often are found at schools judged among the finest in the country. Kennith Keniston, whose books *The Uncommitted* and *The Young Radicals* provide valuable insights into the student psyche, maintains that socially-directed protest requires a special cultural climate, that is, certain distinctive values and views about the effectiveness and the meaning of demonstration and about the wider society. Finally, some historical situations are especially conducive to protest. Keniston believes that there may exist what he terms a "protest-prone personality."

Summarizing a large number of academic studies published since 1965, Keniston notes that almost all student protesters in the United States are outstanding performers in the classroom; the higher the student's grade average, the more likely it is that he will become involved in any given political demonstration. Similarly, students come from families with liberal political values; a disproportionate number report that their parents hold views which are essentially similar to their own and accept or support their activities.

More than 1800 of the 2100 colleges and universities in the United States have reported no significant dissidence. The most serious outbreaks in the United States have occurred in a handful of universities—mostly in the so-called multiversities, which have reputations for arbitrary management, restive faculties, high drop out rates, etc., or in smaller schools where Negro students have sought to improve their lot.

Open communications between administrators and students are critical to the maintenance of the kind of climate which operates against dissidence; so, too, are close student-faculty ties. A restive junior faculty proves an irritant and frequently provides protest with its initial impetus—especially when more senior faculty members abdicate teaching responsibilities.

In much of the world, the real executive authority is vested not in the university but in a government ministry; day-to-day control is entrusted to a political appointee. In Mexico, for example, university rectorship often seems a steppingstone to the governorship of a state. Given the prospect of election to high office in a one-party state at the close of a brief university career, no rector will prove too tolerant of dissident students. Elsewhere, in much of Europe, administrators have little sway over autonomous faculties; rectors are elected for brief terms from among senior faculty and are unlikely to oppose for long their past and future colleagues.

The tenured faculty long have been the autocrats of the academic world. Thanks to government-sponsored research and consultant contracts, private practice in medicine or law, political careers, and a plethora of other outside interests, they have become absentee autocrats. At the University of Rome, for example, a few senior professors appear in class only once or twice a term. None of the law faculty at Lille lives in Lille. Faculty members at Nanterre, outside Paris, commute from homes in the capital and seldom can be found anywhere outside the classroom. When present, many European faculty are unapproachable; they are mandarins. First- and second-year students in the Netherlands are prohibited by custom from addressing professors. The problem is further complicated when, as in the Federal Republic, senior professors because of economic interests or professional jealousy conspire to keep down the number of postgraduate students admitted to teaching positions, and candidates whose progress thus is stymied further swell already large enrollments.

In the United States the compulsion to publish has stimulated increasingly narrow academic specialization and less and less meaningful classroom instruction. Actual teaching all too often is left to graduate assistants or is designed to further some line of esoteric research being pursued by a professor. As David Reisman and Christopher Jencks observe in the recently published *The Academic Revolution*, the inquisitive or sensitive students who hope to find a "visible relationship between knowledge and action, between the questions asked in the classroom and the lives they lead outside it" receive, instead, "pedantry and alienated erudition."

In the Middle East, Japan, Latin America, and even Europe violence has been a hallmark of student dissidence. Protest has grown more militant in the United States because those who speak for it are convinced that docility does not succeed, that over the past several years only violence or the threat of violence has won a respectful hearing. In short, they believe that society is structured in such a way that it can ignore or blunt peaceful protest, but that it abhors interruption and will pay attention to the noisy picket line or raucous demonstration that closes down a vital institution.

Student demonstrations are expressive, rather than directed; they are calculated to dramatize an issue and attract public notice. The demonstration itself becomes the focal point of the action.

This view of the efficacy of confrontation is rooted in the Civil Rights Movement in the United States, where a few hundred activists employed sit-ins and other means to expose to public view regional customs which became an intolerable embarrassment to be remedied under the pressure generated by an aroused public opinion. It has been buttressed by the urban riots of recent years.

Rightly or not, the dissidents sense that latent support for their cause exists and can be galvanized by direct action, that their critical view of society is shared by a far larger number of their age group. In the US, the dissidents have looked without success to the residents of the ghetto; in France with momentary success they found the support of the young workers in the industrial complexes which ring Paris.

It is moot whether television or newsreel coverage of a demonstration or a riot can spark similar outbreaks elsewhere, although several commentators have remarked on the likelihood that a disturbance at Columbia, for example, may embolden dissident students at other schools and cause them to press for relief of their own grievances. French officials found no evidence of significant foreign involvement in the recent Paris riots—but they do cite what they describe as the "grapevine effect" which television coverage of earlier riots in New York and Berlin and other cities had on the mood of the students at Nanterre. It seems likely that the media, by their emphasis on violence, police intervention, etc., add to the intensity and duration of a disturbance. They also tend to evoke sympathy at least on the part of like-minded students elsewhere—sympathy which confirms the belief of the protesters in the probity of their cause.

A student in the US, France, Brazil, or Japan probably does identify with his peers in other countries and is more likely to share their values and feel that their problems are his. Because of the accessibility of foreign-language books and newspapers and the type of *avant-garde* art and films which are so popular in most university communities, there are few, if any, cultural impediments to this kind of identification. Moreover, today's students are highly mobile; they travel within their own countries and abroad, frequently enrolling for study at foreign universities. Many universities have a cosmopolitan character. In the academic year 1967–68, for example, there were 90,000 foreign students registered in American schools and 80,000 Americans studying abroad. In 1966, the last year for which cumulative totals are available, there were more than 100,000 students from the lesser developed countries enrolled in European or US universities. An estimated 10,000 were in the USSR in December 1967.

Theory, Practice and Inspiration

The 1950s, during which many observers were perplexed by the indifference of American university students to political and social issues, witnessed in Europe and then in the United States a rebirth of interest in Marxist social criticism. A conscious effort to construct what since has come to be called "a new politics," this neo-Marxist current was a reaction to political developments of the day—on the international level, to the nuclear arms race, Suez and the Hungarian Revolution, Khrushchev's Secret Speech and the Algerian conflict; and, nationally, to a host of causes. It first found voice in England in *The Universities and Left Review* in 1956, and then in the

United States in 1959 with the University of Wisconsin's *Studies on the Left* and Chicago University's *New University Thought*, in 1960.

Whether in England, France, Japan, West Germany, or the United States, like-minded young people—mostly university-centered—grouped together independently of one another. To date, they have eschewed one creed or one approach. Loosely dubbed the New Left, they have little in common except for their indebtedness to several prominent writers, such as American sociologist C. Wright Mills, Hegelian philosopher Herbert Marcuse, and the late Negro psychiatrist Frantz Fanon, and a few contemporary revolutionary heroes like Mao Tse-tung, Fidel Castro and Ernesto "Che" Guevara. (The term New Left, itself, has little meaning—except as a device to distinguish between today's young radicals and the Communist-Socialist factions of the interwar period. It is taken to mean an amalgam of disparate, amorphous local groups of uncertain or changing leadership and eclectic programs.) The consequence was an amalgam of anarchism, utopian socialism, and an overriding dedication to social involvement.

This intellectual response to the international and domestic crises of the 1950s coincided in time with the emergence of student activism in the United States, i.e., with the first stirring of the Civil Rights Movement. The experience of the Civil Rights Movement electrified the American university community. Nor did its lessons go unnoticed abroad.

In a few countries nearly moribund student organizations were revitalized; in others, where existing organizations clearly were pawns of old-line political parties, new alignments emerged.

Since then, the two currents, neo-Marxist social criticism and student activism, have co-existed in a mutual search for a meaningful program, a lever for overturning social structures. It is easy to belittle their efforts; more difficult to ignore the thrust behind them. Lacking any useful prescriptive advice from the few intellectual mentors whose writings they value, the dissidents have sought to define a political role for students and young intellectuals. The 100,000-member Union Nationale des Etudiants de France, for example, decided that students are "intellectual workers" and entitled as such to recognition by the state. Carl Davidson, an American radical theorist, has argued that students "share many of the social relations and conditions of production with many of the skilled workers of large-scale industry," and are becoming the new working class. Hence, for him, student revolt is "an important historical phenomenon," the "rising of the trainees of the new working class against the alienated and oppressive conditions of production and consumption within corporate capitalism."

Much of the writing of the New Left has an unmistakable improvisational quality about it. The publication recently in France, Italy, and the United States of collections of personal mementos and mimeographed press handouts issued in the course of demonstrations at the Sorbonne, Rome and Columbia make clear that many of the dissidents are concerned most passionately with limited issues of local consequence and have little conception of what they seek once the conflict is broadened.

Exchange of Ideas

Most of the activities of the dissidents, whether in the Communist or Free Worlds, take place not within but against the framework of established student organizations. Such organizational activity and co-ordination as exists among and between dissident groups is conducted out of view of most student organizations and out of operational control of their leaders. The mass of dissident students, whether or not affiliated with existing organizations, does appear to have—like the more radical students in the US—an amorphous and frequently changing, de facto leadership, functioning effectively outside an institutional framework. Such de facto leaders make frequent use of personal contact and may assist one another financially.

Daniel Cohn-Bendit traveled to Amsterdam, Frankfurt, and Berlin—all centers of student radicalism—during the recent French crisis. The now disabled Rudi Dutschke and other West German students have visited Prague. The West Berlin unit of the *Sozialistische Deutsche Studentenbund* reportedly provided what the French have described as a "modest" financial assistance, and German students in Paris served in some kind of liaison capacity between the two organizations during the riots.

These contacts result in little more than an exchange of mutual experience—largely between individuals who may or may not represent the organizations to which they belong. They are brief, frequently public, and held too irregularly to accomplish much. Nevertheless, they do constitute the nucleus of what could become a source of direction.

There may already be some sentiment for formalizing these contacts. In an interview published in the August 1968 issue of *Evergreen Review*, Columbia University's Mark Rudd answered a question about whether there would be "any attempt made to unify all the various national student movements:"

> We're planning a conference for August or September of the revolutionary student movements from France, Germany, and the U.S., possibly Belgium, Japan, Cuba, Vietnam and the others. We want them to come here (which has never happened before) to meet us and see that there is a revolutionary movement here, and more important, so that the U.S. student movement can begin to identify with the international student movement—that's one point we've been very weak on.

The division between the *de jure* and *de facto* student leaderships exists even within Soviet-orbit countries. In Poland, for example, the Polish Students Union (ZSP), a member of the Soviet controlled International Union of Students, is under the leadership of Communist zealots—some of whom hold office in the IUS. Rank-and-file ZSP members have been in the core of "anti-establishment" dissent among Polish youth for years. Various clandestine discussion groups long have existed under a ZSP umbrella; from them have emerged a number of leaders and groups around whom members of different political persuasion have clustered.

The Communists and the Students

There is no convincing evidence of control, manipulation, sponsorship, or significant financial support of student dissidents by any international Communist authority. In fact, the Russians and Chinese have received precious little for the time and money they have spent on cultivating Free World youth. The most vocal of the dissidents have been wary of being caught up in any of the international youth organizations controlled by Moscow. Self-styled Marxists and admirers of Ho Chi Minh, the dissidents are contemptuous of the neanderthal leaderships entrenched in most national Communist parties, including the CP/USA.

The Bloc parties have reacted to student dissidence by harshly suppressing riots in Eastern Europe and expressions of anxiety and dismay at their eruption in the Free World. Underlying these reactions is the unmistakable concern of the ruling Communist parties over the "anarchist" thrust of the students and the lip service they pay to "Maoist" and "extreme leftist" slogans. (There also is a healthy measure of respect for the dialectical skills displayed by the dissidents in debate with party functionaries in the West.) On 30 May, *Pravda*'s Yuri Zhukov denounced Western student rebels as "werewolves" determined to split progressive movements and denounced French student radical Daniél Cohn-Bendit as a "provocateur."

In Western Europe, student dissidents have shaken governments in which national Communist parties have had a stake. Nowhere has this been demonstrably in the interests of over-all Communist policy. Relations between the dissidents and the Communist parties of Western Europe have grown grotesque. In West Berlin students deride the Communists as Stalinists on the one hand and revisionists on the other. Both the illegal German party and the French Communists have been aghast at the antics of the leftist students. The indecisiveness of the French Communist Party during the early stages of the Paris riots and Daniél Cohn-Bendit's antiparty strictures once the Communist-controlled labor unions had reined in their stalwarts and abandoned the students to face the riot police illustrate the dilemma. Cohn-Bendit's impassioned denunciations of the French "Stalinists" were listened to attentively by student dissidents everywhere. The message was clear, threatened by anarchy, bureaucrats of all stripes embrace.

Neither is there evidence that the romantic appeal of Mao Tse Tung has led to significant Chinese influence. The Chinese have from time to time covertly funded sympathetic factions within Communist sponsored youth groups in a number of countries—

exploiting them to embarrass local party leadership and counter pro-Russian propaganda. A few French students under Chinese influence were active in the early days of the disturbances at Nanterre; they soon lost influence, however, and never played a directing role.

The Cubans maintained no such contacts in France or elsewhere in Europe before the outbreak of disturbances, and Cuban personnel abroad shunned participants in the French riots once trouble began. Castro does find favor among the dissidents, who apparently regard him as the embodiment of the student revolutionary. The Cuban leader is determined to counter Russian influence wherever he finds it and welcomes activists anxious to visit Cuba. As a counter to the recent Ninth World Youth Festival in Sofia, the Cubans organized a "Vietnam summer" to attract young European radicals this summer. There is marginal evidence that the Cubans have supplied limited funds to Black Separatists in the United States; there is nothing to corroborate speculation that these monies have found their way to white student activists.

Local Communist parties have gained control of national student organizations in all of South America except Chile, Bolivia, Costa Rica, and Honduras. Nominally accountable to local direction, the leaders of these organizations are likely to prove amenable to Cuban overtures. It remains to be seen, however, whether they will be able to mobilize a following in pursuit of objectives which are in Castro's interest alone and not in the best interest of their memberships.

For years the Russians have funded two instrumentalities for influencing world youth movements, the World Federation of Democratic Youth (WFDY) and the International Union of Students (IUS). Neither organization seems disposed at present to exert control over student dissidents in the Free World and both may prove vulnerable to infection from without. A hard core of the IUS remains responsive to Moscow; nevertheless, the twists and turns of the Cold War and the increasing degree of ideological diversity within Bloc and Free World parties have vitiated the effectiveness of Soviet influence and divested IUS of most of the sway it held over member national organizations in non-Communist countries.

Those who see the IUS from its organizational and operational viewpoint stress the maintenance of Soviet control and point to sporadic efforts by dissidents associated with the IUS to impose some measure of structure within the diffuse mass of students in the non-Communist world. The opposite view is that the IUS is all but dead, that it is split among internal factions and cannot advance the interests of anyone. The truth appears to be that although it is not completely impotent, neither is Russian control over its leadership nor efforts to reinvigorate and expand its efforts relevant to channeling "student power" in support of Moscow's interests.

The leadership of the IUS has attempted without noticeable success to enhance the attractiveness of its propaganda and to attract broader participation in its seminars and meetings. It also has supported the demands of many western students for academic reform.

Lyndon Baines Johnson Presidential Library, National Security File, Files of Walt W. Rostow, Box 13, Folder: Youth and Student Movements, i–vii, 1–23.

Stokely Carmichael

The Pitfalls of Liberalism (January 1969)

During the late 1960s Stokely Carmichael emerged as one of the most eloquent and recognized exponents of "Black Power." He argued that the strategy of mainstream civil rights activists, including the Reverend Dr. Martin Luther King Jr., had reached a dead end because of widespread racist resistance within America. The assassination of King on 4 April 1968, and the ensuing race riots in nearly every major American city, appeared to confirm Carmichael's judgment. He called for the mobilization of organized violence by African-Americans to seize political power, in solidarity with oppressed peoples around the world. Carmichael also demanded a purging of all moderates who, in their opposition to violent revolution, protected established authorities.

Whenever one writes about a problem in the United States, especially concerning the racial atmosphere, the problem written about is usually black people, that they are either extremist, irresponsible, or ideologically naïve.

What we want to do here is to talk about white society, and the liberal segment of white society, because we want to prove the pitfalls of liberalism, that is, the pitfalls of liberals in their political thinking.

Whenever articles are written, whenever political speeches are given, or whenever analyses are made about a situation, it is assumed that certain people of one group, either the left or the right, the rich or the poor, the whites or the blacks, are causing polarization. The fact is that conditions cause polarization, and that certain people can act as catalysts to speed up the polarization; for example, Rap Brown or Huey Newton can be a catalyst for speeding up the polarization of blacks against whites in the United States, but the conditions are already there. George Wallace can speed up the polarization of whites against blacks in America, but again, the conditions are already there.

Many people want to know why, out of the entire white segment of society, we want to criticize the liberals. We have to criticize them because they represent the liaison between both groups, between the oppressed and the oppressor. The liberal tries to become an arbitrator, but he is incapable of solving the problems. He promises the oppressor that he can keep the oppressed under control; that he will stop them from becoming illegal (in this case illegal means violent). At the same time, he promises the oppressed that he will be able to alleviate their suffering—in due time. Historically, of course, we know this is impossible, and our era will not escape history.

The most perturbing question for the liberal is the question of violence. The liberal's initial reaction to violence is to try to convince the oppressed that violence is an incorrect tactic, that violence will not work, that violence never accomplishes anything. The Europeans took America through violence and through violence they established the most powerful country in the world. Through violence they maintain the most powerful country in the world. It is absolutely absurd for one to say that violence never accomplishes anything.

Today power is defined by the amount of violence one can bring against one's enemy—that is how you decide how powerful a country is; power is defined not by the number of people living in a country, it is not based on the amount of resources to be found in that country, it is not based upon the good will of the leaders or the majority of that people. When one talks about a powerful country, one is talking precisely about the amount of violence that that country can heap upon its enemy. We must be clear in our minds about that. Russia is a powerful country, not because there are so many millions of Russians but because Russia has great atomic strength, great atomic power, which of course is violence. America can unleash an infinite amount of violence, and that is the only way one considers America powerful. No one considers Vietnam powerful, because Vietnam cannot unleash the same amount of violence. Yet if one wanted to define power as the ability to do, it seems to me that Vietnam is much more powerful than the United States. But because we have been conditioned by Western thoughts today to equate power with violence, we tend to do that at all times, except when the oppressed begin to equate power with violence— then it becomes an "incorrect" equation.

Most societies in the West are not opposed to violence. The oppressor is only opposed to violence when the oppressed talks about using violence against the oppressor. Then the question of violence is raised as the incorrect means to attain one's ends. Witness, for example, that Britain, France, and the United States have time and time again armed black people to fight their enemies for them. France armed Senegalese in World War II, Britain of course armed Africa and the West Indies, and the United States always armed the Africans living in the United States. But that is only to fight against *their* enemy, and the question of violence is never raised. The only time the United States or England or France will become concerned about the question of violence is when the people whom they armed to kill their enemies will pick up those arms against them. For another example, practically every country in the West today is giving guns either to Nigeria or to Biafra. They do not mind giving those guns to those people as long as they use them to kill each other, but they will never give them guns to kill another white man or to fight another white country.

The way the oppressor tries to stop the oppressed from using violence as a means to attain liberation is to raise ethical or moral questions about violence. I want to state emphatically here that violence in any society is neither moral nor is it ethical. It is neither right nor is it wrong. It is just simply a question of who has the power to legalize violence.

It is not a question of whether it is right to kill or it is wrong to kill; killing goes on. Let me give an example: if I were in Vietnam, if I killed thirty yellow people who were pointed out to me by white Americans as my enemy, I would be given a medal. I would become a hero. I would have killed America's enemy—but America's enemy is not my enemy. If I were to kill thirty white policemen in Washington, D.C., who have been brutalizing my people and who are my enemy, I would get the electric chair. It is simply a question of who has the power to legalize violence. In Vietnam our violence is legalized by white America. In Washington, D.C., my violence is not legalized, because Africans living in Washington, D.C., do not have the power to legalize their violence.

I used that example only to point out that the oppressor never really puts an ethical or moral judgment on violence, except when the oppressed picks up guns against the oppressor. For the oppressor, violence is simply the expedient thing to do.

Is it not violent for a child to go to bed hungry in the richest country in the world? I think that is violent. But that type of violence is so institutionalized that it becomes a part of our way of life. Not only do we accept poverty, we even find it normal. And that again is because the oppressor makes his violence a part of the functioning society. But the violence of the oppressed becomes disruptive. It is disruptive to the ruling circles of a given society. And because it is disruptive it is therefore very easy to recognize, and therefore it becomes the target of all those who in fact do not want to change the society. What we want to do for our people, the oppressed, is to begin to legitimatize violence in their minds. So that for us violence against the oppressor will be expedient. This is very important, because we have all been brainwashed into accepting questions of moral judgment when violence is used against the oppressor.

If I kill in Vietnam I am allowed to go free; it has been legalized for me. It has not been legitimatized in my mind. I must legitimatize it in my own mind, and even though it is legal I may never legitimatize it in my own mind. There are a lot of people who come back from Vietnam, who have killed where killing was legalized, but who still have psychological problems over the fact that they have killed. We must understand, however, that to legitimatize killing in one's mind does not make it legal. For example, I have completely legitimatized in my mind the killing of white policemen who terrorize black communities. However, if I get caught killing a white policeman, I have to go to jail, because I do not as yet have the power to legalize that type of killing. The oppressed must begin to legitimatize that type of violence in the minds of our people, even though it is illegal at this time, and we have to keep striving every chance we get to attain that end.

Now, I think the biggest problem with the white liberal in America, and perhaps the liberal around the world, is that his primary task is to stop confrontation, stop conflicts, *not* to redress grievances, but to stop confrontation. And this is very clear, it must become very, very clear in all our minds. Because once we see what the primary task of the liberal is, then we can see the necessity of not wasting time with him. His primary role is to stop confrontation. Because the liberal assumes a priori that a confrontation is not going to solve the problem. This, of course, is an incorrect assumption. We know that.

We need not waste time showing that this assumption of the liberals is clearly ridiculous. I think that history has shown that confrontation in many cases has resolved quite a number of problems—look at the Russian revolution, the Cuban revolution, the Chinese revolution. In many cases, stopping confrontation really means prolonging suffering.

The liberal is so preoccupied with stopping confrontation that he usually finds himself defending and calling for law and order, the law and order of the oppressor. Confrontation would disrupt the smooth functioning of the society and so the politics of the liberal leads him into a position where he finds himself politically aligned with the oppressor rather than with the oppressed.

The reason the liberal seeks to stop confrontation—and this is the second pitfall of liberalism—is that his role, regardless of what he says, is really to maintain the status quo, rather than to change it. He enjoys economic stability from the status quo and if he fights for change he is risking his economic stability. What the liberal is really saying is that he hopes to bring about justice and economic stability for everyone through reform, that somehow the society will be able to keep expanding without redistributing the wealth.

This leads to the third pitfall of the liberal. The liberal is afraid to alienate anyone, and therefore he is incapable of presenting any clear alternative.

Look at the past presidential campaign in the United States between Nixon, Wallace, and Humphrey. Nixon and Humphrey, because they try to consider themselves some sort of liberals, did not offer any alternatives. But Wallace did, he offered clear alternatives. Because Wallace was not afraid to alienate, he was not afraid to point out who had caused errors in the past, and who should be punished. The liberals are afraid to alienate anyone in society. They paint such a rosy picture of society and they tell us that while things have been bad in the past, somehow they can become good in the future without restructuring society at all.

What the liberal really wants is to bring about change which will not in any way endanger *his* position. The liberal says, "It is a fact that you are poor, and it is a fact that some people are rich; but we can make you rich without affecting those people who are rich." I do not know how poor people are going to get economic security without affecting the rich in a given country, unless one is going to exploit other peoples. I think that if we followed the logic of the liberal to its conclusion we would find that all we can get from it is that in order for a society to become equitable we must begin to exploit other peoples.

Fourth, I do not think that liberals understand the difference between influence and power, and the liberals get confused seeking influence rather than power. The conservatives on the right wing, or the fascists, understand power, though, and they move to consolidate power while the liberal pushes for influence.

Let us examine the period before civil rights legislation in the United States. There was a coalition of the labor movement, the student movement, and the church for the passage of certain civil rights legislation; while these groups formed a broad liberal coalition, and while they were able to exert their influence to get certain legislation passed, they did not have the power to implement the legislation once it became law. After they got certain legislation

passed they had to ask the people whom they were fighting to implement the very things that they had not wanted to implement in
the past. The liberal fights for influence to bring about change, not
for the power to implement the change. If one really wants to
change a society, one does not fight to influence change and then
leave the change to someone else to bring about. If the liberals are
serious they must fight for power and not for influence.

These pitfalls are present in his politics because the liberal is part
of the oppressor. He enjoys the status quo; while he himself may
not be actively oppressing other people, he enjoys the fruits of that
oppression. And he rhetorically tries to claim that he is disgusted
with the system as it is.

While the liberal is part of the oppressor, he is the most powerless segment within that group. Therefore when he seeks to talk
about change, he always confronts the oppressed rather than the
oppressor. He does not seek to influence the oppressor, he seeks to
influence the oppressed. He says to the oppressed, time and time
again, "You don't need guns, you are moving too fast, you are too
radical, you are too extreme." He never says to the oppressor, "You
are too extreme in your treatment of the oppressed," because he is
powerless among the oppressors, even if he is part of that group;
but he has influence, or, at least, he is more powerful than the oppressed, and he enjoys this power by always cautioning, condemning, or certainly trying to direct and lead the movements of the
oppressed.

To keep the oppressed from discovering his pitfalls the liberal
talks about humanism. He talks about individual freedom, about
individual relationships. One cannot talk about human idealism in
a society that is run by fascists. If one wants a society that is in fact
humanistic, one has to ensure that the political entity, the political
state, is one that will allow humanism. And so if one really wants a
state where human idealism is a reality, one has to be able to control the political state. What the liberal has to do is to fight for
power, to go for the political state and then, once the liberal has
done this, he will be able to ensure the type of human idealism in
the society that he always talks about.

Because of the above reasons, because the liberal is incapable of
bringing about the human idealism which he preaches, what usu-

ally happens is that the oppressed whom he has been talking to finally becomes totally disgusted with the liberal and begins to think that the liberal has been sent to the oppressed to misdirect their struggle, to keep them confused so that the oppressor can continue to rule them. So whether the liberal likes it or not, he finds himself being lumped, by the oppressed, with the oppressor—of course he is part of that group. The final confrontation, when it does come about, will of course include the liberal on the side of the oppressor. Therefore if the oppressed really wants a revolutionary change, he has no choice but to rid himself of those liberals in his rank.

In Stokely Carmichael, *Stokely Speaks: Black Power Back to Pan-Africanism* (New York: Random House, 1971), 165–173.

Reactions and Legacies

President Lyndon Johnson, Soviet Ambassador Anatoly Dobrynin, and National Security Council Advisor Walt Rostow

Summary of Their Meeting in the Cabinet Room, Tuesday, August 20, 1968, 8:15 P.M. to 8:42 P.M.

On the night when Soviet bloc tanks crushed the "Prague Spring," Moscow's Ambassador to Washington, D.C., Anatoly Dobrynin, informed President Lyndon Johnson of this military invasion. To Dobrynin's surprise, the president did not condemn Soviet action. Instead, Johnson focused on the prospects for a U.S.-Soviet summit meeting on arms control and superpower cooperation. Popular unrest in the United States, the Soviet Union, and other major countries made the president somewhat desperate for the political prestige and international stability that would come from closer relations among Cold War leaders. Johnson tacitly accepted Soviet brutality against youthful reformers in Czechoslovakia.

The President started off the meeting by asking Ambassador Dobrynin how he had been and asked about Mr. Kosygin. He then told him that he had night before last seen a color movie at the ranch which was very good. The movie was one taken at Glassboro when the President met with Kosygin.

Mr. Dobrynin said that he would have liked to have seen it and the President told him that was good of both Kosygin and of him. The President said it was particularly good when he was talking to the crowd which had assembled outside the house.

Mr. Dobrynin said it was probably the students.

The president said: "And you could have thought he was a . . . "
Mr. Rostow spoke up and said "A campaigner."

The President said: "Well, you would have thought he could be a County Judge of New Jersey, or President of the United States or anybody." Mr. Dobrynin laughed at this statement by the President. The President said it was colorful because the children were in red, blue, and green—different colors. Mr. Dobrynin asked the President if he had ever seen a Youth Parade (he was not sure what the name was) and he said it was a pageant and very colorful and a huge gathering. He said it was an interesting thing to see.

The President told Walt Rostow that Dean Rusk was going to be on television at 9 o'clock and that he ought to watch it.

The President said he had just been down to have his hair cut because he did not have a barber at the ranch, to which Mr. Dobrynin said "Why not?" They both laughed. Mr. Dobrynin then asked the President if he would be at the ranch long. The President had told him he was leaving in the morning for the ranch. He said he would be there unless President Eisenhower died. He said he would have to be there the second day and possibly the third—it's a six day affair. He said on the fifth day, however, they would take him out to Kansas and the President said he did not know whether he would go out there or not. The President said that President Eisenhower had had another attack that day.

Mr. Dobrynin said: "He still has a strong heart because so many heart attacks, and he still survives. It's unbelievable."

The President told Mr. Dobrynin that he (the President) had had one heart attack and he almost did not make it. He said his blood pressure went to zero at once and they counted him out. He said they just thought he was gone.

Mr. Dobrynin said: "This is very dangerous . . . in the old country they used to give some stimulant or something. Otherwise they couldn't do anything. There was no surgery, anything specific. They couldn't do it—especially not at his age. And today, even in my own country, now we have very nice surgeons—but . . . until now there wasn't a single operation."

The President said this was going to open up all new, different and complex problems.

Mr. Dobrynin said: "This is the point."

The President then offered Mr. Dobrynin a Fresca and asked him if he had ever drunk this drink. Mr. Dobrynin said: "No, is it a strong one?"

The President told him that it contained no alcohol and had no calories and Mr. Dobrynin wanted to know how he did it. The President said he had to lose some weight and that he had lost about seven or eight pounds.

Mr. Dobrynin said:

"Now, Mr. President, I have an urgent instruction from my government to tell you about serious business. I will read it."

The President asked him to read a little louder—that he was a little hard of hearing but was so vain he would not wear a hearing aid.

Mr. Dobrynin went on to say:

"Kosygin asked me personally to visit you and to say the following on behalf of my government. I will read this; what I am instructed to say:

'The Government of the Soviet Union considers it necessary to inform, personally, President Johnson about the following. In connection with the further aggravation of the situation which was created by a conspiracy of the external and internal forces of aggression against the existing social order in Czechoslovakia and against the statehood established by the constitution of that government, the government of Czechoslovakia Socialist Republic approached the allied states, the Soviet Union among them, with a request of rendering direct assistance, including the assistance of military forces.

'The Soviet Government repeatedly stated that the events in Czechoslovakia and around it involve vital interests of the Soviet Union and of a number of other states tied by appropriate treaty obligations, and that the threat to the Socialist order in Czechoslovakia constitutes at the same time a threat to the foundations of European peace and world security. In view of this, the Soviet Government and the Governments of the allied countries have taken a joint decision to satisfy the request of the Government of the Czechoslovak Socialist Republic rendering necessary assistance to the Czechoslovak people. Accordingly, the Soviet military units received orders to enter the territory of Czechoslovakia. Of course, they will be withdrawn without delay from the territory of Czechoslovak Socialist Republic as soon as the present threat to the security is eliminated and they come to the conclusion that there is no need in further presence of the allied forces. We would like President Johnson to know that our steps, which are being taken upon the request of the Czechoslovak Government are dictated fully by the concern to strengthen peace and in no degree do they involve state interests of the United States or any other state. We proceed from the fact that the current events should not harm the Soviet-American relations to the development of which the Soviet Government as before attaches great importance.' This is what I was asked to tell you."

The President said:

"I would like to take it and read it and study it and I appreciate very much your bringing it to me and I will review it in the morning with Secretary Rusk and we will be back in touch with you."

Mr. Dobrynin thanked the President.

The President then asked if it were in English and Mr. Dobrynin said it was not, but that he could tell him afterwards if he would like it. The President said that frankly he had missed a word or two here and there. He asked Mr. Rostow how he would summarize it and Mr. Rostow said:

"As I understand it, the Soviet Government informs you, Mr. President, that they and other states have taken a collective decision at the request of the Government of Czechoslovakia to introduce military forces into Czechoslovakia because of a threat defined by the Czech Government; that those forces will remain until the threat to the Czech Government has passed, and be withdrawn. It is the hope of the Soviet Government that this will not interfere with US-Soviet relations and that there is no threat to the United States or to the interests of peace in Europe. In fact, it is stated that these moves should stabilize the peace in Europe."

The President replied:

"Our position with regard to the problem that exists in Czechoslovakia is as represented by Secretary Rusk and I trust that you understand that the position that he explained in detail to you is my view, and the views of this Government, and is the honest and absolutely correct attitude that we have taken. Although I have seen a good many other interpretations and predictions and evaluations, Secretary Rusk, at my instruction, asked you to come in to see him and told you frankly and honestly, looking directly in your eyes, what our position was and you can rely on it.[1]

"I didn't hear the conversation between you and Secretary Rusk but I have such confidence in him that I know he related to you what I asked him to and I don't want there to be any doubt about our attitude."

Mr. Dobrynin said: "No. This message refers to you. I know what you told him to say and it is very clear."

The President asked Mr. Dobrynin what had been done about his announcement and he said they had had no word yet.[2]

The President went on to say:

"Well, I have all these problems about all these folks I have got to talk to beforehand. And I thought I would have them at breakfast at 8:00 o'clock and we'd stay from 8 to 10 at breakfast and I would do it so they wouldn't shout to high heaven that I gave them no information."

Mr. Rostow said that it had been our understanding that the joint announcement would be made at 10 o'clock tomorrow.

The President continued:

"There are four changes. I had to sit down with various people and assure them at 10:00—they would all be in the same room at 10:00 o'clock—but at 10:00, the Soviet Union will say this and we will say this. And I gathered from the announcement that I received that—I think your expression of it when I got off the airplane last night in Detroit—it said that it is acceptable, or there is no objection in Moscow if the American side desires it—if the American side desires it—and announce in the nearest time—I don't know what that means—in the nearest time about the coming visit. Now the language that they suggested, I understand that you and Secretary Rusk had a little adjustment, just a little leeway, about the same thing."

Mr. Dobrynin replied:

"Yes, but you see, Mr. President, sometimes when you make . . . in my impression, the text the Secretary gave me yesterday at

---

[1]Apparently a reference to the Rusk-Dobrynin meeting of July 22; see Document 70.

[2]Reference is to a joint announcement of a visit by President Johnson to the Soviet Union.

midnight, there is no difference really. But the question is, when does the United States, or the President of the United States, Mr. Johnson, wish to continue . . ."

The President said "what we propose is to announce at 10:00 o'clock our time and whatever time it is there—6:00 o'clock their time. Look, while we're at it, I would like to touch a base or two, you see. And in order to touch a base, I have to get people to come in 35 miles to Washington. And I thought I'd do it at the breakfast table, and over breakfast I would say: This is what is going to be said when we finish the breakfast."

Mr. Rostow pointed out that there were two issues that the Presidium would have to set. "The President's suggestion was, raised the question—would things move quicker if we accepted your language. But my guess is you have two issues that have to go to higher authority: One, the exact time of the announcement, and two, the exact language. So that any check-back, there had to be a check-back with Moscow on the time, Mr. President."

Mr. Dobrynin said: "So I will try, Mr. President, to get back tomorrow morning."

The President told him there was no rush, for him to go on and do the best he could.

The President then directed his remarks to Mr. Rostow and said they ought to get their drinks down—that he didn't mind, but he just did not want them to think they all were in there drunk. The President went on to say that Mr. Rayburn used to say that he would never take a drink before the House adjourned in the afternoon because if they had a big fight or something and they had a roll call and he had to get up in the chair, he said just as sure as he did, he would trip his toe and someone would say he is drunk again. They all laughed and the President asked Mr. Dobrynin if he knew Mr. Rayburn and he said, yes, for a long time.

The President said that Mr. Rayburn and his father were deskmates in the Legislature before the President was born.

Mr. Dobrynin said: "That would be in Texas? Now I see."

The President continued:

"The old Capitol that was built was the original Capitol that was destroyed when we were a Republic. You see we were a Republic, an Independent State, before we came in to the Union in 1845. We won our independence in 1856 from Mexico, and from 1836 until 1845, a nine year period, we were an independent Republic."

Mr. Dobrynin asked why it called [*sic*] Lone Star.

The President pointed out that that's the flag—that we had a lone star flag and that we were known as the Lone Star State.

Mr. Dobrynin said: "Did you know the song the Yellow Rose of Texas?"

The President said:

"Yes, that was during the Civil War. One of the better Commanders, the Hood Brigade. My grandfather was a member of it, and they went into battle with the flag flying and the boys singing the Yellow Rose of Texas. It's a good marching hymn. It gets you excited, and so on and so forth."

Mr. Dobrynin asked if we had an official state song or flower. The President replied that we have the bluebonnet as our state flower but he did not know what our state song was. Mr. Rostow laughingly said that if the President didn't know, he certainly didn't.

The President asked Mr. Dobrynin if it was his impression that this meeting be around the first of the month and he replied that was his understanding—the first of the month—the first three days—between the first and the tenth of October.

The President said he had a grandson or a granddaughter that was expected during that period.

Mr. Dobrynin said:

"Ah, you will bring her along . . . But you see, in your case, in America when somebody is born here, he automatically becomes an American citizen. In our case it is not so."

[Here follow comments by the President on his family.]

The President then switched to a more serious note and said there were many subjects that needed to be discussed and that he thought they were very free to do that now and that he thought their meeting in Glassboro was good. He said he enjoyed it very much. He thought it was good for our people and for their people also.

He went on to say:

"I thought the reception they gave Mr. Kosygin was really unusual. Ten years ago you wouldn't have thought that could happen." "I was here ten years ago" Dobrynin said, "so I know how the situation was."

Mr. Dobrynin went on to say:

"For him it was a caution he had no chance to see more than New York and New Jersey. He is very connected with the university. He would like to see for himself, because he is the head of the whole economy of the Soviet Union . . . All the responsibility of dealing with those buildings, dams, those huge dams, factories . . . He said—in New York I would like to see both bad and good sides."

The President said—"We have many misfortunes and lots have problems, but one of the fortunate things that's happened to both countries is that we have been blessed with good men like Thompson in Moscow who tells us what it is without prejudice or without any hatred or without any ambition or personal attempt to satisfy me or our Government. I want you to do the same thing with your people. It would be good for this country and for your country too, if we had men of quality like you and Thompson."

Mr. Dobrynin thanked the President very much.

The President went on to say: "Yes, one Ambassador sometimes can change the fate of the world. And a lot of times Tommy Thompson says to me—well, just a minute."

The President asked Mr. Dobrynin to let us know about the other thing because he wanted to have the breakfast date.

Mr. Dobrynin said: "Thank you very much, and good luck."

Foreign Relations of the United States, 1964–68, Volume 17 (Washington, D.C.: U.S. Government Printing Office), 236–241. Also available on the website for the U.S. State Department Foreign Relations of the United States Series: www.state.gov/ www/about_state/history/vol_xvii/j.html.

John Kenneth Galbraith and Henry Kissinger

Correspondence (2 July 1969–10 October 1970)

Henry Kissinger is one of the most controversial figures to emerge from the late 1960s. Many observers accuse him of prolonging the Vietnam War and committing atrocities in other countries, including Chile, during his years as special assistant for national security affairs and secretary of state, 1969– 1977. At the time, however, he acted with the sympathy of many critics of

American policy. Prominent figures who opposed the actions of the Nixon administration, like John Kenneth Galbraith, saw in Kissinger a smart, hardworking, and capable man protecting reason and order in a time of chaos. Although they later turned against him, diverse thinkers looked to Kissinger for political stability after 1968.

July 2, 1969

Mr. Henry Kissinger
The White House
Washington, D.C.

Dear Henry:

I have tried, with more success than anyone would have thought possible, to be sparing in these last months in my comments on Vietnam. Some special license must surely be allowed people who are working their way out of problems which are not of their own making. While there are a goodly number of things that trouble me there is one which seems to me to justify a word.

The Administration is making a terrible mistake both politically and in terms of national policy in allowing the impression to develop that the South Vietnamese Army is on its way to take over the conflict. I am astonished at the number of people who have come to believe this, partly because it is such a convenient truth and partly because no one in official circles ever says a word to the contrary.

The truth as you and I both know well is that the ARVN is something but not much more than a South American Army. It is vast and largely useless. We have seen so often before, and never more notably than in France in 1940, that such a force, given its uniforms, small arms, tanks and even its ability to march, can look impressive. And as was true of the French Army in 1940, we know how it can disappear overnight. And of course it is an insult to the French Army to speak of the ARVN in these terms. In building up this myth of the ARVN you invite either of two major misfortunes. It will be seen that it can't take over and you will be forced to confess a terrible error, and keep American forces there. Or you will pull out and the army will fade into the trees. You will get credit for not foreseeing a disastrous weakness and collapse. Result: Another error. It is not often the alternatives are so stark and predictable. Only when you agree that this army (and government) has no capacity to defend itself is the country forced to think of the realistic possibilities.

I suppose I would not be so sensitive to the weakness of the army had I not been associated with the problem for so long. When I was there in 1961 for President Kennedy I was solemnly assured that given another six months it would be one of the finest fighting forces since the Spartans.

Faithfully,

John Kenneth Galbraith

JKG:pdm

P.S. I have just seen the Vice-President's speech. This is a disaster. It is impossible that any of us now could successfully counsel moderation.

207 Littauer Center
Harvard University
Cambridge, Massachusetts
May 7, 1970

Mr. Henry Kissinger
The White House
Washington, D.C.

Dear Henry:

This situation is now so bad and will shortly become so ridiculous that I urge you as a personal friend to detach. In some measure you defend it by staying. It is also obvious that your past justification, a considerable one, that you could stop such idiocy has now disappeared. You can be much more effective on the outside helping guide the opposition to this whole trend of events, an opposition which no one can doubt is overwhelming. And of course it will be worse when the strategy of the move becomes known—and it has all to be justified on the basis of a few bags of rice.

There are also the personal aspects of the situation—the exchange of short run influence for long run damage. But these are matters I am reluctant to raise.

Yours faithfully,

John Kenneth Galbraith

JKG:pdm

I know you will take this very seriously. Do follow your conscience and I have no doubt as to where it will lead you.

THE WHITE HOUSE
WASHINGTON

May 27, 1970

Dear Ken:

Your letter meant a lot to me. I wish that we could see each other and talk, about this problem and others. When the immediate crisis has passed, it is important that we be able to heal the wounds it has created and work together on the even deeper ones our country faces. How to do this is one of my principle preoccupations now.

Please do stay in touch.

Warm regards,

Henry A. Kissinger

Professor John Kenneth Galbraith
207 Littauer Center
Harvard University
Cambridge, Massachusetts 02138

June 17, 1970

Dr. Henry Kissinger
The White House
Washington, D.C.

PERSONAL

Dear Henry:

I had some second thoughts about my earlier letter. I guess, everything considered, you had better stay and do your best. As long as we know that you are, we will all be well pleased with you. And don't worry too much about the future.

Yours faithfully,

John Kenneth Galbraith

JKG/adw

THE WHITE HOUSE
WASHINGTON

June 24, 1970

Dear Ken:

Many thanks for your note which was indeed encouraging.

It has been too long since we have talked, and I am pleased that you will be able to come for lunch on Friday, July 10.

Warm regards,

Henry A. Kissinger

Professor John Kenneth Galbraith
207 Littauer Center
Harvard University
Cambridge, Massachusetts 02138

THE WHITE HOUSE
WASHINGTON

October 10, 1970

Dear Ken:

My stay in London proved to be a delightful personal respite from the rigors of official travel, and I particularly welcomed the chance to see you over breakfast on Monday. As usual, your views and counsel were most helpful to me, and I want you to know that I value both your ideas and your friendship. There are all too few people that one can count on for both intellectual stimulation and loyalty.

I am confident that you will enjoy your next few months in England; it looks very tempting indeed to us harassed bureaucrats. I fully expect you to make your usual intellectual splash there as in everywhere you go.

Please keep me posted on your experiences and impressions.

Best regards,

Henry A. Kissinger

The Honorable John K. Galbraith
Faculty of Economics and Politics
Sidgwick Avenue
University of Cambridge
Cambridge, England

John F. Kennedy Presidential Library, Papers of John Kenneth Galbraith, Box 61, Folder: Kissinger, Dr. Henry A., 6/15/66–11/16/70.

Richard Nixon and Mao Zedong

Memorandum of Conversation (21 February 1972)

In February 1972 President Richard Nixon opened U.S. relations with Mao Zedong's government in China. This was a remarkable moment in world history. Since the Chinese Communist Party came to power in 1949, the United States had refused any recognition of its legitimacy. The two governments had engaged in mutual recriminations and frequent military confrontations—in Korea, around Taiwan, in Vietnam, and elsewhere. Nixon and Mao had both frequently expressed frequent hatred of the other's regime. When these two men came together, it signaled a new era. The details of their first conversation reveal that Nixon and Mao sought cooperation not only to improve international relations, but also to build common understandings about the dangers of public disorder in their respective societies. Despite their profound ideological differences, Nixon and Mao found that they had similar domestic problems and similar hopes for political stability in a time of turmoil.

MEMORANDUM

THE WHITE HOUSE

WASHINGTON

February 21, 1972

TOP SECRET/SENSITIVE/
EXCLUSIVELY EYES ONLY

MEMORANDUM OF CONVERSATION

PARTICIPANTS: Chairman Mao Tsetung
Prime Minister Chou En-lai
Wang Hai-jung, Deputy Chief of Protocol
of the Foreign Ministry
Tang Wen-sheng, Interpreter

President Nixon
Henry A. Kissinger, Assistant to the President for National Security Affairs
Winston Lord, National Security Council Staff (Notetaker)

DATE AND TIME: Monday, February 21, 1972—
2:50–3:55 P.M.

PLACE: Chairman Mao's Residence, Peking

(There were opening greetings during which the Chairman welcomed President Nixon, and the President expressed his great pleasure at meeting the Chairman.)

PRESIDENT NIXON: You read a great deal. The Prime Minister said that you read more than he does.

CHAIRMAN MAO: Yesterday in the airplane you put forward a very difficult problem for us. You said that what it is required to talk about are philosophic problems.

PRESIDENT NIXON: I said that because I have read the Chairman's poems and speeches, and I knew he was a professional philosopher. (Chinese laugh.)

CHAIRMAN MAO: (looking at Dr. Kissinger) He is a doctor of philosophy?

PRESIDENT NIXON: He is a doctor of brains.

CHAIRMAN MAO: What about asking him to be the main speaker today?

PRESIDENT NIXON: He is an expert in philosophy.

DR. KISSINGER: I used to assign the Chairman's collective writings to my classes at Harvard.

CHAIRMAN MAO: Those writings of mine aren't anything. There is nothing instructive in what I wrote.

(Looking toward photographers) Now they are trying to interrupt our meeting, our order here.

PRESIDENT NIXON: The Chairman's writings moved a nation and have changed the world.

CHAIRMAN MAO: I haven't been able to change it. I've only been able to change a few places in the vicinity of Peking.

Our common old friend, Generalissimo Chiang Kai-shek, doesn't approve of this. He calls us communist bandits. He recently issued a speech. Have you seen it?

PRESIDENT NIXON: Chiang Kai-shek calls the Chairman a bandit. What does the Chairman call Chiang Kai-shek?

PRIME MINISTER CHOU: Generally speaking we call them Chiang Kai-shek's clique. In the newspapers sometimes we call him a bandit: we are also called bandits in turn. Anyway, we abuse each other.

CHAIRMAN MAO: Actually, the history of our friendship with him is much longer than the history of your friendship with him.

PRESIDENT NIXON: Yes, I know.

CHAIRMAN MAO: We two must not monopolize the whole show. It won't do if we don't let Dr. Kissinger have a say. You have been famous about your trips to China.

DR. KISSINGER: It was the President who set the direction and worked out the plan.

PRESIDENT NIXON: He is a very wise assistant to say it that way. (Mao and Chou laugh.)

CHAIRMAN MAO: He is praising you, saying you are clever in doing so.

PRESIDENT NIXON: He doesn't look like a secret agent. He is the only man in captivity who could go to Paris 12 times and Peking once and no one knew it, except possibly a couple of pretty girls. (Chou laughs.)

DR. KISSINGER: They didn't know it; I used it as a cover.

CHAIRMAN MAO: In Paris?

PRESIDENT NIXON: Anyone who uses pretty girls as a cover must be the greatest diplomat of all time.

CHAIRMAN MAO: So your girls are very often made use of?

PRESIDENT NIXON: His girls, not mine. It would get me into great trouble if I used girls as a cover.

PRIME MINISTER CHOU: (laughs) Especially during elections. (Kissinger laughs.) Dr. Kissinger doesn't run for President because he wasn't born a citizen of the United States.

DR. KISSINGER: Miss Tang is eligible to be President of the United States.

PRESIDENT NIXON: She would be the first woman President. There's our candidate.

CHAIRMAN MAO: It would be very dangerous if you have such a candidate. But let us speak the truth. As for the Democratic Party, if they come into office again, we cannot avoid contacting them.

PRESIDENT NIXON: We understand. We will hope that we don't give you that problem.

CHAIRMAN MAO: Those questions are not questions to be discussed in my place. They should be discussed with the Premier. I discuss the philosophical questions. That is to say, I voted for you during your election. There is an American here called Mr. Frank Coe, and he wrote an article precisely at the time when your country was in havoc, during your last electoral campaign. He said you were going to be elected President. I appreciated that article very much. But now he is against the visit.

PRESIDENT NIXON: When the Chairman says he voted for me, he voted for the lesser of two evils.

CHAIRMAN MAO: I like rightists. People say you are rightists, that the Republican Party is to the right, that Prime Minister Heath is also to the right.

PRESIDENT NIXON: And General DeGaulle.

CHAIRMAN MAO: DeGaulle is a different question. They also say the Christian Democratic Party of West Germany is also to the right. I am comparatively happy when these people on the right come into power.

PRESIDENT NIXON: I think the important thing to note is that in America, at least at this time, those on the right can do what those on the left talk about.

DR. KISSINGER: There is another point, Mr. President. Those on the left are pro-Soviet and would not encourage a move toward the People's Republic, and in fact criticize you on those grounds.

CHAIRMAN MAO: Exactly that. Some are opposing you. In our country also there is a reactionary group which is opposed to our contact with you. The result was that they got on an airplane and fled abroad.

PRIME MINISTER CHOU: Maybe you know this.

CHAIRMAN MAO: Throughout the whole world, the U.S. intelligence reports are comparatively accurate. The next was Japan. As for the Soviet Union, they finally went to dig out the corpses, but they didn't say anything about it.

PRIME MINISTER CHOU: In Outer Mongolia.

PRESIDENT NIXON: We had similar problems recently in the crisis on India-Pakistan. The American left criticized me very heavily for failing to side with India. This was for two reasons: they were pro-India and they were pro-Soviet.

I thought it was important to look at the bigger issue. We could not let a country, no matter how big, gobble up its neighbor. It cost me—I don't say this with sorrow because it was right—it cost me politically, but I think history will record that it was the right thing to do.

CHAIRMAN MAO: As a suggestion, may I suggest that you do a little less briefing? (The President points at Dr. Kissinger and Chou laughs.) Do you think it is good if you brief others on what we talk about our philosophic discussions here?

PRESIDENT NIXON: The Chairman can be sure that whatever we discuss or whatever I and the Prime Minister discuss, nothing goes beyond the room. That is the only way to have conversations at the highest level.

CHAIRMAN MAO: That's good.

PRESIDENT NIXON: For example, I hope to talk with the Prime Minister and later with the Chairman about issues like Taiwan, Vietnam and Korea. I also want to talk about—and this is very sensitive—the future of Japan, the future of the subcontinent, and what India's role will be; and on the broader world scene, the future of US-Soviet relations. Because only if we see the whole picture of the world and the great forces that move the world will we be able to make the right decisions about the immediate and urgent problems that always completely dominate our vision.

CHAIRMAN MAO: All those troublesome problems I don't want to get into very much. I think your topic is better—philosophic questions.

PRESIDENT NIXON: For example, Mr. Chairman, it is interesting to note that most nations would approve of this meeting, but the Soviets disapprove, the Japanese have doubts which they express, and the Indians disapprove. So we must examine why, and determine how our policies should develop to deal with the whole world, as well as the immediate problems such as Korea, Vietnam, and of course, Taiwan.

CHAIRMAN MAO: Yes, I agree.

PRESIDENT NIXON: We, for example, must ask ourselves—again in the confines of this room—why the Soviets have more forces on the border facing you than on the border facing Western Europe. We must ask ourselves, what is the future of Japan? Is it better—here I know we have disagreements—is it better for Japan to be neutral, totally defenseless, or is it better for a time for Japan to have some relations with the United States? The point being—I am talking now in the realm of philosophy—in international relations there are no good choices. One thing is sure—we can leave no vacuums, because they can be filled. The Prime Minister, for example, has pointed out that the United States reaches out its hands and that the Soviet Union reaches out its hands. The question is which danger the People's Republic faces, whether it is the danger of American aggression or Soviet aggression. These are hard questions, but we have to discuss them.

CHAIRMAN MAO: At the present time, the question of aggression from the United States or aggression from China is relatively small; that is, it could be said that this is not a major issue, because the present situation is one in which a state of war does not exist between our two countries. You want to withdraw some of your troops back on your soil; ours do not go abroad.

Therefore, the situation between our two countries is strange because during the past 22 years our ideas have never met in talks. Now the time is less than 10 months since we began playing table tennis; if one counts the time since you put forward your suggestion at Warsaw it is less than two years. Our side also is bureaucratic in dealing with matters. For example, you wanted some exchange of persons on a personal level, things like that; also trade. But rather than deciding that we stuck with our stand that without settling major issues there is nothing to do with smaller issues. I myself persisted in that position. Later on I saw you were right, and we played table tennis. The Prime Minister said this was also after President Nixon came to office.

The former President of Pakistan introduced President Nixon to us. At that time, our Ambassador in Pakistan refused to agree on our having a contact with you. He said it should be compared whether President Johnson or President Nixon would be better. But President Yahya said the two men cannot be compared, that these two men are incomparable. He said that one was like a gangster—he meant President Johnson. I don't know how he got that impression. We on our side were not very happy with that President either. We were not very happy with your former Presidents, beginning from Truman through Johnson. We were not very happy with these Presidents, Truman and Johnson.

In between there were eight years of a Republican President. During that period probably you hadn't thought things out either.

PRIME MINISTER CHOU: The main thing was John Foster Dulles' policy.

CHAIRMAN MAO: He (Chou) also discussed this with Dr. Kissinger before.

PRESIDENT NIXON: But they (gesturing towards Prime Minister Chou and Dr. Kissinger) shook hands. (Chou laughs.)

CHAIRMAN MAO: Do you have anything to say, Doctor?

DR. KISSINGER: Mr. Chairman, the world situation has also changed dramatically during that period. We've had to learn a great deal. We thought all socialist/communist states were the same phenomenon. We didn't understand until the President came into office the different nature of revolution in China and the way revolution had developed in other socialist states.

PRESIDENT NIXON: Mr. Chairman, I am aware of the fact that over a period of years my position with regard to the People's Republic was one that the Chairman and Prime Minister totally disagreed with. What brings us together is a recognition of a new situation in the world and a recognition on our part that what is important is not a nation's internal political philosophy. What is important is its policy toward the rest of the world and toward us. That is why—this point I think can be said to be honest—we have differences. The Prime Minister and Dr. Kissinger discussed these differences.

It also should be said—looking at the two great powers, the United States and China—we know China doesn't threaten the territory of the United States; I think you know the United States has no territorial designs on China. We know China doesn't want to dominate the United States. We believe you too realize the United States doesn't want to dominate the world. Also—maybe you don't believe this, but I do—neither China nor the United States, both great nations, want to dominate the world. Because our attitudes are the same on these two issues, we don't threaten each others' territories.

Therefore, we can find common ground, despite our differences, to build a world structure in which both can be safe to develop in our own ways on our own roads. That cannot be said about some other nations in the world.

CHAIRMAN MAO: Neither do we threaten Japan or South Korea.

PRESIDENT NIXON: Nor any country. Nor do we.

CHAIRMAN MAO: (Checking the time with Chou) Do you think we have covered enough today?

PRESIDENT NIXON: Yes. I would like to say as we finish, Mr. Chairman, we know you and the Prime Minister have taken great risks in inviting us here. For us also it was a difficult decision. But having read some of the Chairman's statements, I know he is one who sees when an opportunity comes, that you must seize the hour and seize the day.

I would also like to say in a personal sense—and this to you Mr. Prime Minister—you do not know me. Since you do not know me, you shouldn't trust me. You will find I never say something I cannot do. And I always will do more than I can say. On this basis I want to have frank talks with the Chairman and, of course, with the Prime Minister.

CHAIRMAN MAO: (Pointing to Dr. Kissinger) "Seize the hour and seize the day." I think that, generally speaking, people like me sound a lot of big cannons. (Chou laughs) That is, things like "the whole world should unite and defeat imperialism, revisionism, and all reactionaries, and establish socialism."

PRESIDENT NIXON: Like me. And bandits.

CHAIRMAN MAO: But perhaps you as an individual may not be among those to be overthrown. They say that he (Dr. Kissinger) is also among those not to be overthrown personally. And if all of you are overthrown we wouldn't have any more friends left.

PRESIDENT NIXON: Mr. Chairman, the Chairman's life is well-known to all of us. He came from a very poor family to the top of the most populous nation in the world, a great nation.

My background is not so well known. I also came from a very poor family, and to the top of a very great nation. History has brought us together. The question is whether we, with different philosophies, but both with feet on the ground, and having come from the people, can make a breakthrough that will serve not just China and America, but the whole world in the years ahead. And that is why we are here.

CHAIRMAN MAO: Your book, "The Six Crises," is not a bad book.

PRESIDENT NIXON: He (Mao) reads too much.

CHAIRMAN MAO: Too little. I don't know much about the United States. I must ask you to send some teachers here, mainly teachers of history and geography.

PRESIDENT NIXON: That's good, the best.

CHAIRMAN MAO: That's what I said to Mr. Edgar Snow, the correspondent who passed away a few days ago.

PRESIDENT NIXON: That was very sad.

CHAIRMAN MAO: Yes, indeed.

It is alright to talk well and also alright if there are no agreements, because what use is there if we stand in deadlock? Why is it that we must be able to reach results? People will say . . . if we fail the first time, then people will talk why are we not able to succeed the first time? The only reason would be that we have taken the wrong road. What will they say if we succeed the second time?

(There were then some closing pleasantries. The Chairman said he was not well. President Nixon responded that he looked good. The Chairman said that appearances were deceiving. After handshakes and more pictures, Prime Minister Chou then escorted the President out of the residence.)

National Security Archive, George Washington University, www2.gwu.edu/~nsarchiv/NSAEBB/NSAEBB19/05-01.htm

U.S. Department of State Bulletin

Basic Principles of Relations Between the United States of America and the Union of Soviet Socialist Republics (29 May 1972)

Richard Nixon was the first U.S. president to visit the Soviet Union since World War II. His May 1972 trip announced a new era of "détente" between the superpowers, codified in their agreement on "Basic Principles." In this document, the two governments pledged themselves to conflict avoidance, arms control, mutual consultation, increased economic and cultural cooperation, and "noninterference in internal affairs." The Basic Principles did not include any language about human rights or social justice. They also reaffirmed the dominance of the two superpowers across a broad range of international issues. Détente, in these terms, promised a more peaceful world, but one where domestic calls for political and social change had little influence. Soviet and American leaders saw the Basic Principles as an important mechanism for maintaining their authority and silencing domestic critics.

Text of Basic Principles, May 29

Basic Principles of Relations Between the United States of America and the Union of Soviet Socialist Republics

The United States of America and the Union of Soviet Socialist Republics,

Guided by their obligations under the Charter of the United Nations and by a desire to strengthen peaceful relations with each other and to place these relations on the firmest possible basis,

Aware of the need to make every effort to remove the threat of war and to create conditions which promote the reduction of tensions in the world and the strengthening of universal security and international cooperation,

Believing that the improvement of US-Soviet relations and their mutually advantageous development in such areas as economics, science and culture, will meet these objectives and contribute to better mutual understanding and business-like cooperation, without in any way prejudicing the interests of third countries,

Conscious that these objectives reflect the interests of the peoples of both countries,

Have agreed as follows:

First. They will proceed from the common determination that in the nuclear age there is no alternative to conducting their mutual relations on the basis of peaceful coexistence. Differences in ideology and in the social systems of the USA and the USSR are not obstacles to the bilateral development of normal relations based on the principles of sovereignty, equality, non-interference in internal affairs and mutual advantage.

Second. The USA and the USSR attach major importance to preventing the development of situations capable of causing a dangerous exacerbation of their relations. Therefore, they will do their utmost to avoid military confrontations and to prevent the outbreak of nuclear war. They will always exercise restraint in their mutual relations, and will be prepared to negotiate and settle differences by peaceful means. Discussions and negotiations on outstanding issues will be conducted in a spirit of reciprocity, mutual accommodation and mutual benefit.

Both sides recognize that efforts to obtain unilateral advantage at the expense of the other, directly or indirectly, are inconsistent with these objectives. The prerequisites for maintaining and strengthening peaceful relations between the USA and the USSR are the recognition of the security interests of the Parties based on the principle of equality and the renunciation of the use or threat of force.

Third. The USA and the USSR have a special responsibility, as do other countries which are permanent members of the United Nations Security Council, to do everything in their power so that conflicts or situations will not arise which would serve to increase international tensions. Accordingly, they will seek to promote conditions in which all countries will live in peace and security and will not be subject to outside interference in their internal affairs.

Fourth. The USA and the USSR intend to widen the juridical basis of their mutual relations and to exert the necessary efforts so that bilateral agreements which they have concluded and multilateral treaties and agreements to which they are jointly parties are faithfully implemented.

Fifth. The USA and the USSR reaffirm their readiness to continue the practice of exchanging views on problems of mutual interest and, when necessary, to conduct such exchanges at the highest level, including meetings between leaders of the two countries.

The two governments welcome and will facilitate an increase in productive contacts between representatives of the legislative bodies of the two countries.

Sixth. The Parties will continue their efforts to limit armaments on a bilateral as well as on a multilateral basis. They will continue to make special efforts to limit strategic armaments. Whenever possible, they will conclude concrete agreements aimed at achieving these purposes.

The USA and the USSR regard as the ultimate objective of their efforts the achievement of general and complete disarmament and the establishment of an effective system of international security in accordance with the purposes and principles of the United Nations.

Seventh. The USA and the USSR regard commercial and economic ties as an important and necessary element in the strengthening of their bilateral relations and thus will actively promote the growth of such ties. They will facilitate cooperation between the relevant organizations and enterprises of the two countries and the conclusion of appropriate agreements and contracts, including long-term ones.

The two countries will contribute to the improvement of maritime and air communications between them.

Eighth. The two sides consider it timely and useful to develop mutual contacts and cooperation in the fields of science and technology. Where suitable, the USA and the USSR will conclude appropriate agreements dealing with concrete cooperation in these fields.

Ninth. The two sides reaffirm their intention to deepen cultural ties with one another and to encourage fuller familiarization with each other's cultural values. They will promote improved conditions for cultural exchanges and tourism.

Tenth. The USA and the USSR will seek to ensure that their ties and cooperation in all the above-mentioned fields and in any others in their mutual interest are built on a firm and long-term basis. To give a permanent character to these efforts, they will establish in all fields where this is feasible joint commissions or other joint bodies.

Eleventh. The USA and the USSR make no claim for themselves and would not recognize the claims of anyone else to any special rights or advantages in world affairs. They recognize the sovereign equality of all states.

The development of US-Soviet relations is not directed against third countries and their interests.

Twelfth. The basic principles set forth in this document do not affect any obligations with respect to other countries earlier assumed by the USA and the USSR.

Moscow, *May 29, 1972*

For the United States of America	For the Union of Soviet Socialist Republics
RICHARD NIXON	LEONID I. BREZHNEV
President of the United States of America	General Secretary of the Central Committee, CPSU

U.S. Department of State Bulletin, Vol. 66 (26 June 1972), 898–899.

U.S. National Security Council

Memorandum of Conversation (6 November 1970)

On 4 September 1970 the Popular Action Front Party in Chile received 36.3 percent of the vote in national elections. This was more than any other party. According to custom, the party's leader, Salvador Allende Gossens, would become the Chilean president. The United States had long provided aid to Allende's opponents, fearful that he would allow communist influence to grow in Chile. American policy makers were especially anxious about Allende's personal ties to Cuban leader, Fidel Castro. The Nixon administration initially attempted to prevent Allende from becoming president, and then sought to force him from power. This included a multifaceted strategy of economic pressures, propaganda, and covert funding for a coup. On 11 September 1973 General Augusto Pinochet, operating with financial support from the U.S. government, overthrew Allende. Pinochet established dictatorial rule and began a brutal campaign to murder his opponents in Chile and across the region. Thousands of men and women, including two residing in the United States, died. Critics blamed the Nixon administration for bringing this violent government to power, because of excessive fears about communist influence and popular opinion in Chile under Allende. They also condemned officials like Henry Kissinger for allowing Pinochet to violate human rights without reprisal. Chile became a focus of con-

tention for social activists in the 1970s, and many members of the U.S. government (including Richard Bloomfield, the author of the 11 July 1975 paper) who shared the sentiments of Kissinger's critics.

MEMORANDUM

THE WHITE HOUSE
WASHINGTON

MEMORANDUM OF CONVERSATION—
NSC MEETING—CHILE (NSSM 97)

PARTICIPANTS:
The President
The Vice President
Secretary of State William P. Rogers
Secretary of Defense Melvin Laird
Director of Emergency Preparedness
   George A. Lincoln
Attorney General John N. Mitchell
General William Westmoreland, Acting
   Chairman, Joint Chiefs of Staff
Director of Central Intelligence Richard Helms
Under Secretary of State John N. Irwin II
Deputy Assistant Secretary of State
   Robert A. Hurwitch
Assistant to the President for National
   Security Affairs Henry A. Kissinger
General Alexander M. Haig, NSC Staff
Mr. Arnold Nachmanoff, NSC Staff
Col. Richard T. Kennedy, NSC Staff

PLACE: The Cabinet Room
DATE & TIME: Friday—November 6, 1970
                9:40 a.m.

THE PRESIDENT opened the meeting by asking Director Helms to brief.

DIRECTOR HELMS read from the briefing paper which is attached at Tab A. THE PRESIDENT interrupted to review what Director

Helms said about the makeup of the Allende Cabinet. [See page 9]
He wished to emphasize the degree to which the Cabinet ministries
were controlled by Marxists.

The President then asked Dr. Kissinger to brief.

DR. KISSINGER: All of the agencies are agreed that Allende will try
to create a socialist State. As for our response to this, the SRG
came up with four options. But really basically it amounts to two
choices: (1) seek a modus vivendi with the Allende Government,
or (2) adopt a posture of overt and frank hostility. In between is
a third possibility: adopt what is in fact a hostile posture but not
from an overt stance, that is, to move in hostility from a low-key
posture.

A modus vivendi has the risk that he will consolidate his position and then move ahead against us. A posture of overt hostility gives strength to his appeal of nationalism and may not work
anyway. As for in between—the problem is that he will know we
are working against him and he can expose us anyway even
though we maintain a correct and cool posture.

All of these options have advantages and disadvantages. There
is no clear choice.

SECRETARY ROGERS: Dr. Kissinger has spelled it out well. There
is general agreement that he will move quickly to bring his
program into effect and consolidate his position. We are also
in agreement that it is not necessary to make a final decision
now.

Private business and the Latin American countries believe
that we have done the right things up to now. If we have to be
hostile, we want to do it right and bring him down. A stance of
public hostility would give us trouble in Latin America. We can
put an economic squeeze on him. He has requested a debt
rescheduling soon—we can be tough. We can bring his downfall
perhaps without being counterproductive.

The Christian Democratic Foreign Minister thinks we are doing the right thing. He sees two possibilities: that his economic
troubles will generate significant public dissatisfaction, or second, that his difficulties will become so great that there will be
military moves against him. I think the U.S. military should keep

in contact with their Chilean colleagues and try to strengthen our position in Chile.

We have severe limitations on what we can do. A strong public posture will only strengthen his hand. We must make each decision in the future carefully in a way that harms him most but without too much of a public posture which would only be counterproductive.

SECRETARY LAIRD: I agree with Bill Rogers. We have to do everything we can to hurt him and bring him down, but we must retain an outward posture that is correct. We must take hard actions but not publicize them. We must increase our military contacts. We must put pressure on him economically. He is in the weakest position now that he will be in; we want to prevent his consolidation.

MOORER [to Rogers]:   What is the reaction of the Congress?

SECRETARY ROGERS: There is very little, but if he consolidates his position the criticism will build up. Attitudes are therefore favorable to our policy.

MOORER: What would be the reaction if he resorts to expropriation later, after we have given more aid?

SECRETARY ROGERS: We shouldn't give any more credit guarantees. We should do everything we can to show hostility without publicizing it.

VICE PRESIDENT: China and USSR are watching our approach to Argentina. If we show undue interest before anything happens; for example if we sell F-4s to Argentina, it could trigger massive support to Chile from the USSR and China. We should act principally inside Chile.

DIRECTOR LINCOLN: Copper accounts for 80% of Chile's exports. They are expanding production rapidly. Other producers (Zambia, Australia, etc.) are also going up in production. So there could be a price decline in the future, with an adverse economic impact in Chile. They blame us. We have a stockpile. If we are adopting a hostile posture, maybe we have to increase the stockpile or alternatively to sell if the market eases in the future.

THE PRESIDENT: I want something in a week on how we can sell from the stockpile. Now we can do it. Cutting the stockpile would hurt Chile and also save on the budget.

DIRECTOR LINCOLN: We'll do this. We've been studying this on a
   priority basis.

THE PRESIDENT: This is very important—will it hurt anyone else?
   I want State and Defense and everyone to study it. It could be
   the most important thing we can do.

DIRECTOR LINCOLN: The law says we can't sell from the stockpile
   unless we do it to stabilize the price. The copper price is down in
   the world market. We've already sold 50 million tons before the
   prices dropped.

SECRETARY ROGERS: Can we help others build up their production, to help our friends?

THE PRESIDENT: We should do this if we can.

DIRECTOR LINCOLN: If we sell anything too fast it will destabilize
   the price. Most things don't sell fast.

MR. IRWIN: The problem is how to bring about his downfall. I
   would question our capability to do it. Internal forces in Chile
   are the only way. The question is how best to influence the internal forces to create the conditions for change. He will need to
   consolidate his position and probably he will move slowly for the
   sake of respectability as he moves. It will be soon that dissatisfaction begins. As he tries to consolidate he will inevitably have
   strains. If we move too quickly in opposition to him we will help
   him consolidate quickly. As we move to consider specific issues
   either overt or covert, we should be hostile only if we can be sure
   it will have a significant effect on the internal forces there in a
   way that will hurt Allende and prevent his consolidation. This
   may mean we may have to do things we would not want to do—
   it depends on the effects on the internal situation in Chile. Graham Martin would like to see us move along as we have.

THE PRESIDENT: It is all a matter of degree. If Chile moves as we
   expect and is able to get away with it—our public posture is important here—it gives courage to others who are sitting on the
   fence in Latin America. Let's not think about what the really
   democratic countries in Latin America say—the game is in
   Brazil and Argentina. We could have moves under the surface
   which bring over time the same thing.

   I will never agree with the policy of downgrading the military in Latin America. They are power centers subject to our
   influence. The others (the intellectuals) are not subject to our

influence. We want to give them some help. Brazil and Argentina particularly. Build them up with consultation. I want Defense to move on this. We'll go for more in the budget if necessary.

Our main concern in Chile is the prospect that he can consolidate himself and the picture projected to the world will be his success. A publicly correct approach is right. Privately we must get the message to Allende and others that we oppose him. I want to see more of them; Brazil has more people than France or England combined. If we let the potential leaders in South America think they can move like Chile and have it both ways, we will be in trouble. I want to work on this and on the military relations—put in more money. On the economic side we want [*sic*] give him cold Turkey. Make sure that EXIM and the international organizations toughen up. If Allende can make it with Russian and Chinese help, so be it—but we do not want it to be with our help, either real or apparent.

We'll be very cool and very correct, but doing those things which will be a real message to Allende and others.

This is not the same as Europe—with Tito and Ceaucescu—where we have to get along and no change is possible. Latin America is not gone, and we want to keep it. Our Cuban policy must not be changed. It costs the Russians a lot; we want it to continue to cost. Chile is gone too—he isn't going to mellow. Don't have any illusions—he won't change. If there is any way we can hurt him whether by government or private business—I want them to know our policy is negative. There should be no guarantees. Cut back existing guarantees if it's possible.

No impression should be permitted in Latin America that they can get away with this, that it's safe to go this way. All over the world it's too much the fashion to kick us around. We are not sensitive but our reactions must be coldly proper. We cannot fail to show our displeasure. We can't put up with "Give Americans hell but pray they don't go away." There must be times when we should and must react, not because we want to hurt them but to show we can't be kicked around.

The new Latin politicians are a new breed. They use anti-Americanism to get power and then they try to cozy up. Maybe it would be different if they thought we wouldn't be there.

We must be proper on the surface with Allende, but otherwise we will be tough. He is not going to change; only self-interest will affect him.

In Peter Kornbluh, *The Pinochet File: A Declassified Dossier on Atrocity and Accountability* (New York: New Press, 2003), 116–120.

U.S. Department of State

Memorandum (11 July 1975)

July 11, 1975

TO: ARA: Mr. William D. Rogers
          APA: Ambassador Hewsen Ryan

FROM: ARA/PLC: Richard J. Bloomfield

SUBJ: Ambassador Popper's Policy Paper.

The Ambassador characterizes our present stance as one of "disapproval" (p. 20 and p. 21). But the image is otherwise, at least as far as the Executive Branch is concerned:

—We are solicitous about Chile's debt problem and deploy our diplomacy to promote a debt rescheduling.
—We use our influence in the IFIS to assure that Chilean loans are not held up.
—We vote against or abstain on resolutions in international organizations that condemn the GOC's human rights record.
—We assure the GOC that we want to sell it arms and that we regret Congressional restrictions.

How would the Junta ever get the impression that the USG "disapproves"? As the old saying goes, actions speak louder than words.

The Ambassador says that any stronger signs of our (read Executive Branch) disapproval would not improve the human rights situation (which I am willing to concede). Conclusion: We must provide economic and military assistance; in fact by page 25, we are worrying about our responsibilities for making the Junta's economic program a success. Why? Because "preventing the re-emergence of a Chilean Government essentially hostile to us (p. 22) is our chief interest and the human rights problem is secondary."

This argument overlooks the possibility that the human rights problem in Chile may not be "secondary" but may be a major U.S. interest in the present domestic and international context. In the minds of the world at large, we are closely associated with this *junta*, ergo with fascists and torturers. This is the way it is perceived by a vocal and increasingly numerous element in Congress whose support we need for other aspects of our Latin American policy (e.g. Panama) and, indeed, for our foreign policy in general. It is one more reason why much of the youth of the country is alienated from their government and its foreign policy. Chile is just the latest example for a lot of people in this country of the United States not being true to its values.

This is not the emotionalism of a bleeding heart. The Secretary himself has said that no foreign policy will be successful if it is carried in the minds of a few and the hearts of none. Our current Chile policy comes perilously close to fitting that description.

The need to "live with" the absence of human rights in Chile in order to prevent the re-emergence of a hostile government is, to my mind, a distinctly secondary consideration. We survived a hostile government in Chile in the recent past. It is really a bizarre world when the globe's greatest superpower has to worry about the hostility of the dagger-pointed-at-the-heart-of-Antartica.

The specific objectives in human rights that Ambassador Popper sets out on page 21 are fine. The problem is that we will not achieve them without turning the screws harder and taking the risks that entails.

cc: Ambassador Popper
      c/o Mr. Karkashian:ARA/BC

In Peter Kornbluh, *The Pinochet File: A Declassified Dossier on Atrocity and Accountability* (New York: New Press, 2003), 254–255.

Ronald Reagan

Vietnam II (30 November 1976)

More than any other figure in American politics, Ronald Reagan capitalized on the international turmoil of the late 1960s. Then governor of California, he emerged as a national political figure who spoke to the anger and dislocation of many Americans. He condemned the intellectual and media elites who had allegedly forgotten the country's inherited ideals in the midst of the Vietnam War and the riots across the nation's cities. Through radio and television he spoke to ordinary Americans about the need for a return to basic beliefs in patriotism, anti-communism, and fair play. He promised to renew the American dream and make the nation stand tall again overseas. This message carried Reagan to the White House in 1980. He was both a product of the global revolutions of 1968 and a reaction against them.

Vietnam II
November 30, 1976

Hypocrisy is doing well in the town of Babel on the Hudson and not too bad in the editorial enclaves of some of our leading journals. I'll be right back.

A few days ago I spoke about our negotiations with the North Vietnamese. ~~aggressors who Having wantonly & cold bloodedly violated every condition of the *Paris* Peace Accords~~ They ~~now~~ are arrogantly demanding that we kick in with about $3 Bil. ~~If we do so~~ *after which* they say they may possibly give us an accounting of our men still missing ~~in Vietnam~~ *in action.*

In the meantime the U.S. has twice vetoed the N. Vietnam application for membership in the United Nations. For doing so our govt. is being soundly criticized not only by the small in size, large of mouth 3rd world nations in the U.N. ~~by~~ but by ~~our~~ a great many of our own newspapers.

One powerful Eastern paper contends our veto violated ~~one of~~ a "basic rule of the U.N.—the principle of universal membership by all legit. govts." ~~Now by any standard that charge is based on a false premise. First of all t~~ There is no such U.N. principle or concept as universal membership. The charter welcomes nations ~~that~~ which have renounced force of arms as a means of settling disputes. Article 4 states: "Membership in the U.N. is open to all peace loving states which accept the obligations contained in the present charter and are able & willing to carry out those obligations." ~~One of those obligations is, "to solve international problems of a humanitarian character."~~

~~But~~ And what about that line, "legit. govts."? If someone invades your home carrying a big club, subdues you, & locks you in a closet & squats in your living room does he become the legit. owner of your home?

The N. Vietnamese conquered S. Vietnam by force of arms. *This was no civil war.* They have been ~~civil~~ separate nations for 2000 yrs. Now they hold a *nation* captive just as the Soviet U. holds the countries of Central & Eastern Europe captive.

During all the long years of war N.V.N. fuzzed up the issue by claiming U.S. presence in V.N. was the cause of their mil. activity. Their claims were echoed by many papers who now find fault with our UN Vetos. Alright we are no longer in V.N. therefore what reason can the N. Vietnamese have for the mil. occupation of S.VN?

How loud would the editorials objections be if the govts. of S.Korea & the Repub. of China on Taiwan were sending out patrol boats to machine gun makeshift rafts & boats carrying refugees who were trying to escape from those countries? We have learned the N. Vietnamese are doing just that to the conquered people of S.V.N.

We express concern that human rights are being denied to some in Rhodesia, S. Africa & Chilé. But where are the indignant voices protesting the hundreds of thousands of S. Vietnamese, & Laotians & Cambodians who are dying of torture & starvation in ~~cam~~ N. Vietnams concentration camps?

If there is any principle or honor left at all in the U.N. & for that matter in a number of newsrooms shouldn't N.V.N. be told it will be welcome in the U.N. when it has withdrawn to its own borders; when it has once again allowed the S. Vietnamese to govern themselves; when true peace among friendly neighbors has been restored to S.E. Asia and when they've given us an accounting of our men missing in action? We in turn will *THEN* keep our pledge to repair the ravages of war in all their countries. ~~This is R.R. Thanks for listening~~ But that is the only basis upon which there can be any talk of normalizing relations. This is RR Thanks for listening.

In Kiron K. Skinner, Annelise Anderson, and Martin Anderson, eds., *Reagan, in His Own Hand* (New York: Simon and Schuster, 2001), 134–135.

Ronald Reagan

Blind on the Left (20 February 1978)

Why is it so many people ⚡ alert to any threat from the right are incapable of seeing danger from the left? A remarkable woman who understood this is gone & will be missed.

I'll be right back.

A number of years ago when a concerted, organized effort was made to subvert the motion picture industry ~~& make sure~~ *to a communist* propaganda tool I asked a question which is still unanswered. The question *was* why is it that the many defectors from communism, domestic or International make so little impression on those ~~whose liberalism~~ who had no trouble seeing the menace of Nazism & Fascism. Now ~~let me make it plain~~ for the record—I take 2nd to no one in my detestation of Adolph Hitler & everything he represented. As a matter of fact I'm still mad at the Kaiser. But there are others in the world today as evil as Hitler & guilty of the same brutal, inhuman deeds. When a defector—sometimes one who held ~~high~~ a *fairly high* ~~position~~ *ranks* in the Soviet social order or even a domestic communist party member now dis-illusioned wants to tell us the reason for their defection or dis-illusionment they are dismissed by many liberals as no longer a credible source. And yet very often those same liberals will accept as gospel the complaints of an American who disavows patriotism and proclaims from podium & printed page—"What's wrong with America."

I was reminded of all this not long ago when a very remarkable woman *in Wash. D.C.* died just a few days short of her 80th birth-

Soviet general secretary Mikhail Gorbachev and U.S. president Ronald Reagan were deeply influenced by the global revolutions of 1968. They came together in a shared desire to revise the dominant Cold War ideologies in their societies.

day. It would be impossible to count the lives she touched in Eng. where she was born, in China, Japan, the Soviet U. & here in her adopted home the U.S.

~~In~~ She once described herself as a "premature anti-communist. I told the truth about communism long before the world was prepared to hear it." And Freda Utley knew the truth about communism because as an idealistic young woman in the 1920's she accepted communism. In fact she married a Russian & went to live in Moscow.

After he was taken away by ⚡ Stalin's secret police she came out of Russia and wrote a book "The Dream We Lost," in which she said: "The just & the unjust enter through the same *revolving* door & the stream pressing in with great expectations is matched or exceeded by the crowd of the disillusioned getting out."

But many of the intellectuals didn't want to hear what she had to say. She had impressive academic credentials ~~but~~ when she came to the U.S. but publishers and the academy closed doors against her. She understood all too well;. ~~s~~She had tried communism & learned it's ~~falsehood~~ FALSENESS. She said only those "who have never fully committed themselves to the communist Cause" can continue to believe in it. Her book "The China Story" which told of how the Reds were taking over became a bestseller—after China was lost.

It is bone chilling now to read that Soviet defector Oleg Glagolev former consultant to the Kremlin on strategic arms is telling our govt. Russia has the cruise missile already deployed in submarines off our coasts. Is anyone *REALLY* listening?

This is RR Thanks for listening.

In Kiron K. Skinner, Annelise Anderson, and Martin Anderson, eds., *Reagan, in His Own Hand* (New York: Simon and Schuster, 2001), 136–139.

Charter 77–Declaration (1 January 1977)

After 1968, dissidents within Czechoslovakia and other Soviet bloc states confronted renewed repression. Although détente allowed government authorities to crack down on domestic detractors with little international reprisal, it also encouraged growing global attention to common principles. The Helsinki Final Act, signed by the leaders of thirty-five states (including the United States and the Soviet Union) on 1 August 1975, called for both the protection of the political status quo in Europe and universal recognition of human rights. In January 1977 a group of 230 Czechoslovak citizens used this language of human rights to organize an informal network that would mobilize for political change and hold the government publicly accountable for its frequent brutalities. Despite attempts to smother it, Charter 77 became a foundation for the dissident activism that destroyed communist authority a decade later. In this sense, Charter 77 carried the ideals of 1968 forward to 1989.

In the Czechoslovak Collection of Laws, no. 120 of 13 October 1976, texts were published of the International Covenant on Civil and Political Rights, and of the International Covenant on Economic, Social and Cultural Rights, which were signed on behalf of our Republic in 1968, were confirmed at Helsinki in 1975 and came into force in our country on 23 March 1976. From that date our citizens have the right, and our state the duty, to abide by them.

The human rights and freedoms underwritten by these covenants constitute important assets of civilised life for which many progressive movements have striven throughout history and whose codification could greatly contribute to the development of a humane society.

We accordingly welcome the Czechoslovak Socialist Republic's accession to those agreements.

Their publication, however, serves as an urgent reminder of the extent to which basic human rights in our country exist, regrettably, on paper only.

The right to freedom of expression, for example, guaranteed by article 19 of the first-mentioned covenant, is in our case purely illusory. Tens of thousands of our citizens are prevented from working in their own fields for the sole reason that they hold views differing from official ones, and are discriminated against and harassed in all kinds of ways by the authorities and public organisations. Deprived as they are of any means to defend themselves, they become victims of a virtual apartheid.

Hundreds of thousands of other citizens are denied that 'freedom from fear' mentioned in the preamble to the first covenant, being condemned to live in constant danger of unemployment or other penalties if they voice their own opinions.

In violation of article 13 of the second-mentioned covenant, guaranteeing everyone the right to education, countless young people are prevented from studying because of their own views or even their parents'. Innumerable citizens live in fear that their own or their children's right to education may be withdrawn if they should ever speak up in accordance with their convictions. Any exercise of the right to 'seek, receive and impart information and ideas of all kinds, regardless of frontiers, either orally, in writing or in print' or 'in the form of art,' specified in article 19, para. 2 of the first covenant, is punished by extrajudicial or even judicial sanctions, often in the form of criminal charges as in the recent trial of young musicians.

Freedom of public expression is repressed by the centralised control of all the communications media and of publishing and cultural institutions. No philosophical, political or scientific view or artistic expression that departs ever so slightly from the narrow bounds of official ideology or aesthetics is allowed to be published; no open criticism can be made of abnormal social phenomena; no public defence is possible against false and insulting charges made in official propaganda; the legal protection against 'attacks on honour and reputation' clearly guaranteed by article 17 of the first covenant is in practice non-existent; false accusations cannot be rebutted and any attempt to secure compensation or correction through the courts is futile; no open debate is allowed in the domain of thought and art. Many scholars, writers, artists and others are penalised for having legally published or expressed, years ago, opinions which are condemned by those who hold political power today.

Freedom of religious confession, emphatically guaranteed by article 18 of the first covenant, is systematically curtailed by arbitrary official action; by interference with the activity of churchmen, who are constantly threatened by the refusal of the state to permit them the exercise of their functions, or by the withdrawal of such permission; by financial or other measures against those who express their religious faith in word or action; by constraints on religious training and so forth.

One instrument for the curtailment or, in many cases, complete elimination of many civic rights is the system by which all national institutions and organisations are in effect subject to political directives from the apparatus of the ruling party and to decisions made by powerful individuals. The constitution of the Republic, its laws and other legal norms do not regulate the form or content, the issuing or application of such decisions; they are often only given out verbally, unknown to the public at large and beyond its powers to check; their originators are responsible to no one but themselves and their own hierarchy; yet they have a decisive impact on the actions of the law-making and executive organs of government, and of justice, of the trade unions, interest groups and all other organisations, of the other political parties, enterprises, factories, institutions, offices, schools, and so on, for whom these instructions have precedence even before the law.

Where organisations or individual citizens, in the interpretation of their rights and duties, come into conflict with such directives, they cannot have recourse to any non-party authority, since none such exists. This constitutes, of course, a serious limitation of the right ensuing from articles 21 and 22 of the first-mentioned covenant, which provides for freedom of association and forbids any restriction on its exercise, from article 25 on the equal right to take part in the conduct of public affairs, and from article 26 stipulating equal protection by the law without discrimination. This state of affairs likewise prevents workers and others from exercising the unrestricted right to establish trade unions and other organisations to protect their economic and social interests, and from freely enjoying the right to strike provided for in para. 1 of article 8 in the second-mentioned covenant.

Further civic rights, including the explicit prohibition of 'arbitrary interference with privacy, family, home or correspondence' (article 17 of the first covenant), are seriously vitiated by the various forms of interference in the private life of citizens exercised by the Ministry of the Interior, for example, by bugging telephones and houses, opening mail, following personal movements, searching homes, setting up networks of neighbourhood informers (often recruited by illicit threats or promises) and in other ways. The ministry frequently interferes in employers' decisions, instigates acts of discrimination by authorities and organisations, brings weight to bear on the organs of justice and even orchestrates propaganda campaigns in the media. This activity is governed by no law and, being clandestine, affords the citizen no chance to defend himself.

In cases of prosecution on political grounds the investigative and judicial organs violate the rights of those charged and of those defending them, as guaranteed by article 14 of the first covenant and indeed by Czechoslovak law. The prison treatment of those sentenced in such cases is an affront to human dignity and a menace to their health, being aimed at breaking their morale.

Paragraph 2, article 12 of the first covenant, guaranteeing every citizen the right to leave the country, is consistently violated, or under the pretence of 'defence of national security' is subjected to various unjustifiable conditions (para. 3). The granting of entry visas to foreigners is also handled arbitrarily, and many are unable to visit Czechoslovakia merely because of professional or personal contacts with those of our citizens who are subject to discrimination.

Some of our people—either in private, at their places of work or by the only feasible public channel, the foreign media—have drawn attention to the systematic violation of human rights and democratic freedoms and demanded amends in specific cases. But their pleas have remained largely ignored or been made grounds for police investigation.

Responsibility for the maintenance of civic rights in our country naturally devolves in the first place on the political and state authorities. Yet, not only on them: everyone bears his share of responsibility for the conditions that prevail and accordingly also for the observance of legally enshrined agreements, binding upon all citizens as well as upon governments. It is this sense of co-responsibility, our belief in the meaning of voluntary citizens' involvement and the general need to give it new and more effective expression that led us to the idea of creating Charter 77, whose inception we today publicly announce.

Charter 77 is a free informal, open community of people of different convictions, different faiths and different professions united by the will to strive, individually and collectively, for the respect of civic and human rights in our own country and throughout the world—rights accorded to all men by the two mentioned international covenants, by the Final Act of the Helsinki conference and by numerous other international documents opposing war, violence and social or spiritual oppression, and which are comprehensively laid down in the United Nations Universal Declaration of Human Rights.

Charter 77 springs from a background of friendship and solidarity among people who share our concern for those ideals that have inspired, and continue to inspire, their lives and their work.

Charter 77 is not an organisation; it has no rules, permanent bodies or formal membership. It embraces everyone who agrees with its ideas, participates in its work, and supports it. It does not form the basis for any oppositional political activity. Like many similar citizen initiatives in various countries, West and East, it seeks to promote the general public interest. It does not aim, then, to set out its own programmes for political or social reforms or changes, but within its own sphere of activity it wishes to conduct a constructive dialogue with the political and state authorities, particularly by drawing attention to various individual cases where human and civil rights are violated, by preparing documentation and suggesting solutions, by submitting other proposals of a more general character aimed at reinforcing such rights and their guarantees, and by acting as a mediator in various conflict situations which may lead to injustice and so forth.

By its symbolic name Charter 77 denotes that it has come into being at the start of a year proclaimed as the Year of Political Prisoners—a year in which a conference in Belgrade is due to review the implementation of the obligations assumed at Helsinki.

As signatories, we hereby authorise Professor Dr Jan Patočka, Václav Havel and Professor Jiří Hájek to act as the spokesmen for the Charter. These spokesmen are endowed with full authority to represent it *vis-à-vis* state and other bodies, and the public at home and abroad, and their signatures attest the authenticity of documents issued by the Charter. They will have us, and others who join us, as their co-workers, taking part in any needful negotiations, shouldering particular tasks and sharing every responsibility.

We believe that Charter 77 will help to enable all the citizens of Czechoslovakia to work and live as free human beings.

In H. Gordon Skilling, *Charter 77 and Human Rights in Czechoslovakia* (London: George Allen & Unwin, 1981), 209–212.

Mikhail Gorbachev

Excerpt from Memoirs

Mikhail Gorbachev, the last Soviet leader, came of age in the shadow of 1968. He had hoped that the reforms in Czechoslovakia and throughout the Soviet bloc during the 1960s would build a more humane communist society. The brutal repression of the Prague Spring and other dissident movements extinguished this hope, at least temporarily. When he came to power as general secretary in 1985, Gorbachev began to formulate his own reform agenda, deeply influenced by the activism of the late 1960s. He thought explicitly about 1968 when, in 1989, he confronted movements to dismantle communist authority throughout Eastern Europe. Unwilling to renounce his own reform ideals and exhibit the brutality of his predecessors, Gorbachev chose to allow the former satellite states freedom from Soviet rule. Gorbachev's memories of 1968 help explain why he did not intervene in 1989.

The Defeat of the Reformers

The spirit of reform kindled in the 1950s and 1960s was strong and dynamic; the need for changes in so many spheres of social life was only too obvious. Brezhnev was forced to maneouvre skilfully between different Politburo factions and to disguise carefully his own conservative views. Both the March 1965 plenum on agriculture and the September plenum on economic incentives to increase industrial productivity were essentially progressive and aimed at reforming the existing system of economic management.

Yet the decisions taken at these meetings were never implemented. An ambiguous situation developed: while the press heatedly discussed all kinds of projects and published articles by economists and publicists, the resurrected ministries were 'quietly doing their job,' tightening the screws of bureaucratic centralism. Local authorities viewed all innovations with scepticism: 'Up there in Moscow all they do is talk, while we have to do the job and fulfil the plan.' The so-called Barakov case was a striking illustration of this attitude. It happened in Stavropol, before my nomination as Second Secretary of the krai committee.

I knew Innokenty Barakov quite well. He was energetic, had an independent mind and was probably too impulsive. He was friendly with the reformist economist Lisichkin and an ardent exponent of the latter's ideas. Nobody objected as long as Barakov—whether in private or in public—spoke only of the need for 'easing' the state plan and expanding the rights of the kolkhozes to allows them to sell their produce freely. But things took a serious turn when he tried to implement these ideas in his Georgievsk district.

As head of the district agricultural department, Barakov stopped forcing the farms to fulfil rigid plans, leaving the initiative to them. In those days, the krai committee perceived this as an open assault upon the entire 'system.' Barakov was first summoned to a bureau meeting and warned, then on 21 January 1967 he was relieved of his duties.

I had not attended that meeting, but I learned that Barakov was accused of committing 'grave errors in a number of his pronouncements on fundamental political issues.' It was further pointed out that his 'insistent, confusing statements' about the right of the kolkhozes and sovkhozes to sell their produce on the free market and to strengthen their economies by any means and methods 'caused objective harm to the education of the cadres in the spirit of responsibility toward the implementation of Party and government decisions. Failing to fulfil the state plan for the sale of grain and other products, some kolkhozes had permitted the free marketing of their produce . . .'

Yefremov—who had a fine nose for sensing which way the wind was blowing—decided that it was high time for 'our organization to present its views nationally.' On 13 September 1967 the Central Committee agricultural newspaper, *Selskaya Zhizn*, published an article entitled 'Contrary to facts,' signed by Yefremov and other krai party workers. The article attacked Gennady Lisichkin's essay 'After two years,' which had appeared in the journal *Novy Mir* in February 1967.

Lisichkin was accused of 'making absurd, unrealistic suggestions, such as free trade in kolkhoz and sovkhoz produce, the abolition of planned state purchases of produce paid in kind . . . disregarding the principle of socialist planning based on the maximum levels already achieved.' But the main charge was that by 'trying to substantiate his economic recommendations, which are both theoretically confused and not adapted to real life, Lisichkin distorts and juggles with facts drawn from the life and work of the kolkhozes and sovkhozes of Stavropol krai.'

Barakov's fate made the future appear rather ominous. That was the time when the decisions of the March 1965 Central Committee plenum—which had spurred the quest for new solutions in agriculture—were supposed to be implemented. You might have expected that the 'Kosygin reforms' would serve as an additional impetus for this quest. Alas, as in industry, changes in agriculture were not to exceed the clearly defined limits. Barakov's and Lisichkin's suggestions went further—and, therefore, the 'Barakov case' demonstrated the urgent need for changes and bore testimony to the system's immediate sharp reaction to the mere possibility of such changes. It was a hard lesson for me.

In the early summer of 1967, I met Zdenek Mlynar, an old friend from Moscow University. He worked at the State and Law Institute of the Czechoslovak Academy of Sciences and had come to Moscow to discuss proposals for planned political reforms. His speech met a cool reception in Moscow academic circles. Subsequently he visited Georgia and came to Stavropol to spend a few days with us.

I have already mentioned that we lived in a two-room flat on the fourth floor. This was our first self-contained home and we liked it. Zdenek inspected it rather critically. Apparently, by Czechoslovak standards, it was rather modest for a Party committee secretary of a capital city. Zdenek asked me about the situation in our country and our krai and about our life. He described the latest developments in Czechoslovakia in detail, telling us how Novotny's authority was dwindling. From what he said, I realized that Czechoslovakia was on the verge of major upheaval.

A few months later I read in a newspaper that Mlynar had been appointed to the Central Committee of the Czechoslovak Communist Party. He was one of the authors of the famous 'Action programme of the Czechoslovak CP' and an active participant in the 'Prague Spring.' I wrote him a letter, but waited in vain for an answer. From hints dropped by the head of the krai KGB, who was also a member of the krai committee bureau, I understood that my letter had landed in a different postbox.

We received only biased reports about the 1968 events in Prague. All information was under strict and total control, and this news, obviously, even more so. The events—I mean the entry of armed forces—started on 21 August, only days after I had been elected second secretary. Since Yefremov was away, I chaired the meetings of the krai committee bureau. Leonid Nikolaevich telephoned me before the meeting which had been called to discuss the Politburo communiqué on the invasion by Warsaw Pact troops. He informed me about the deliberations of the Central Committee and outlined his own suggestions. The bureau then adopted a resolution approving the 'decisive and timely measures taken in defence of socialist achievements in the CSSR' (Czechoslovakia). The krai committee expressed its support for the Central Committee, although, quite frankly, one had to wonder about the purpose of the invasion and whether it was excessive.

Guided by these and similar thoughts, I was trying to grasp the underlying causes of many grievous phenomena in our domestic and foreign policies. Patently reaction was on the move. After 21 August ideological 'streamlining' and the harsh suppression of the smallest display of dissent were the order of the day. The Central Committee demanded that local authorities should take decisive ideological measures—the struggle against dissent was intensified all over the country.

In early 1969 F. B. Sadykov, the acting head of the faculty of philosophy at the Stavropol agricultural institute, published a book with the krai publishing house under the title *Unity of the People and Contradictions of Socialism*. It had been written earlier—on the wave of hopes and expectations aroused by Khrushchev's and also Kosygin's reforms. The manuscript of the book was discussed at the faculty a year before its publication. Sadykov had brought it to Moscow—had even shown it to someone in the Central Committee apparatus and published an article in the journal *Voprosy Filosofii* (*Problems of Philosophy*).

Basically, Sadykov had formulated a number of ideas which began to be implemented during the period of perestroika. But that was still over fifteen years ahead. And by 1969 ideas half-heartedly accepted a few years earlier were considered 'subversive.'

Moscow sent word: 'Severe criticism necessary.' At the krai committee bureau meeting held on 13 May, we reviewed the 'grave errors contained in the book by F. B. Sadykov, assistant professor at the faculty of philosophy of the Stavropol agricultural institute.' We really tore him to pieces. Yes, this was a real execution. Our leading 'ideologist,' Likhota, demanded Sadykov's expulsion from the Party. Yefremov did not support the motion. My speech was highly critical. Sadykov was severely reprimanded and dismissed as faculty head. Soon afterwards he left Stavropol for Ufa, if I remember correctly.

I was deeply affected by what had happened to Barakov and Sadykov. I knew both of them personally as intelligent, thoughtful people. I had qualms of conscience about the cruel and undeserved punishment meted out to them.

The reformist spirit was dying before our very eyes. The implementation of sensible, intelligent decisions taken at the 1965–7 Central Committee plenums came to a standstill. The 'Kosygin reform' was losing its impetus. Letters written by the specialists and scientists were carefully stored away in the archive cellars. The events in Czechoslovakia had practically put an end to all subsequent quests for ways and means to transform the existing system of economic management.

It was the beginning of 'the period of stagnation.'

Facing Up to History

In the late 1970s, Poland had found itself in a grave crisis, one that Moscow considered the result of weakness and indecision on the part of the Polish leadership. In fact, the situation was much more serious than that. The imposition of a socio-political model alien to Poland—albeit greatly altered and partially adapted to national conditions—had run into opposition from the populace, including a significant portion of the working class. At first the discontent was of a passive nature and found an outlet in jokes about the authorities. As the years passed, however, it mounted, and there were explosions of social and political unrest, each more powerful than the last (1953, 1970, 1979). To top it all, the country recklessly amassed a colossal hard currency debt to the West. Poland was essentially the first to enter the stage that could be called the general crisis of socialism. State institutions found themselves on the brink of paralysis, and the country was literally one step away from total chaos and national disaster.

Under these conditions, the opposition, Solidarity, which had gathered momentum, advanced a programme for a self-governing Rzeczpospolita, which the orthodox leadership of the Polish United Workers' Party, to say nothing of the CPSU and the other ruling parties of the Socialist community, saw, with some reason, as an agenda for dispensing with the existing system and deserting the Warsaw Pact for NATO. The Soviet leadership feverishly sought a solution between what were to them two equally unacceptable positions: the acceptance of chaos in Poland and the ensuing break-up of the entire Socialist camp; or armed intervention. The opinion that both positions were unacceptable predominated. Nonetheless, our troops, our tank columns along the border with Poland, and even a rather powerful northern group of Soviet troops stationed in Poland—all these could be put in motion, given extreme circumstances.

In this situation, Wojciech Jaruzelski, who had replaced S. Kania as First Secretary of the PUWP Central Committee in October 1981, weighed the various possible courses of events, all of which were obviously negative, and decided on what he considered the lesser evil: martial law was declared on the night of 12 December 1981. This was more an administrative-political measure than a military one, although it was prepared for and implemented by the army and the police.

In the face of the West's blockade of the Jaruzelski regime, the substantial material and financial assistance to Poland from the USSR, East Germany, Czechoslovakia, and several other countries had a stabilizing effect. The Soviet Union allocated about US $2 billion and several billion rubles to the Poles, and supported them in later years as well. Our troops were categorically prohibited from interfering in events, and they behaved themselves irreproachably.

In addition to help, however, Jaruzelski was pestered with advice and suggestions as to whom to avoid and whom to rely on. The quality of this advice can be judged from the fact that the most unflattering characterizations concerned, for instance, such a distinguished figure as Mieczyslaw Rakowski. After martial law was imposed, Moscow and East Berlin transparently hinted that it was time to act more decisively and not to permit any spinelessness or liberalism. Politely but firmly, Jaruzelski deflected attempts to foist a line of conduct on him, and he followed his own course, calculated to calm the situation, placate the nation, and gradually transform the political system. But, as he later told me, he was naturally forced to reckon with the country's real dependence on Moscow.

Martial law under Jaruzelski did not put an end to the reforms; in its own way, it facilitated them. Polish reformers took advantage of the newly instituted law and order in the country not to turn back but, on the contrary, to rally all the healthy forces of society that supported political pluralism and a market economy.

In the first half of the 1980s the situation in Poland substantially mirrored ours, but when it came to economic reforms the Poles were clearly ahead of us. We were just beginning to understand the essence of what was going on in Poland and Hungary. Real understanding did not come until 1985–6.

The alienation between the two countries and the two peoples that had grown up in the late 1970s and early 1980s had to be overcome. To no small degree this feeling was the result of the activities of the Politburo's Special Commission on Poland, which Suslov headed for a long time. The Commission and its apparatus kept constant tabs on the course of Polish events, issuing assessments and recommendations to the Politburo, ministries, departments, and public organizations. A *cordon sanitaire* was erected around striking, rebellious, stormy Poland: all contacts were frozen or sharply curtailed.

Right up to the mid-1980s, reports reaching Moscow from Warsaw would frequently have even a phrase like 'Socialist renewal'— which was the official policy of the PUWP—crossed out! The fear of the 'Polish contagion' overshadowed even the obvious fact that a Polish society isolated from contacts with its neighbour to the East was left prey to those circles in the West that were taking advantage of the situation to promote anti-Soviet and anti-Russian moods.

On Jaruzelski's initiative, and supported by reformers in the PUWP and CPSU leadership, preparations began on a document whose goal was to promote rapprochement and co-operation between the two countries. The result was the 'Declaration on Soviet-Polish Co-operation in Ideology, Science, and Culture.'

Naturally, the document is not free of the ideological overtones of the period, but many of its ideas are still relevant. It was then that the go-ahead was given for revitalizing and significantly expanding contacts among sociologists, writers, journalists, scholars, cultural figures, and the creative intelligentsia and the youth of both countries. This effort on the part of the democratic circles in Polish and Soviet society to meet each other halfway helped to dispel the feelings of mutual suspicion, dislike, and fear that reactionary elements in our country and in Poland were stoking.

'History,' this document said, 'should not be an object of ideological speculation or grounds for igniting nationalistic passions.' But we could put history behind us only if we were prepared to face the most painful episodes of the past.

After Jaruzelski's visit to Moscow in 1987, the work of the joint commission of Soviet and Polish historians, abandoned in 1974, was revived. We needed the whole truth about the Soviet-Polish war of 1920, Stalin's punishment of the Polish Communist Party, and especially the Katyn massacre, the most painful point of all for the Poles.

The creation of a commission of Polish and Soviet historians had significantly stimulated the activities of our researchers, who included N. S. Lebedeva, V. S. Parsadanova, and Ye. N. Zorya. They did not abandon their search even when the situation seemed absolutely hopeless. Now we know why those searches had reached an impasse: the documents had been destroyed on the orders of the former leadership of the KGB, when it had been run by A. Shelepin. The archive documents found by the group testified circumstantially but convincingly to the direct culpability of Beria, Merkulov, and their assistants for the crime in the Katyn forest. I stated this publicly, handing over the documents to Jaruzelski on 13 April 1990.

A TASS statement on 13 April 1990 expressed the Soviet Union's profound regret in connection with the Katyn tragedy, stating that it represented one of the most heinous crimes of Stalinism. As for the other documents referring to the Katyn massacre, I remember two files that were shown to me by Boldin on the eve of my visit to Poland. It was, however, a random set of documents meant to confirm the conclusions of Academician Burdenko's commission under Stalin. We found the document that directly implicated those truly to blame for the massacre only in December 1991, a few days before I stepped down as President of the Soviet Union. It was then that the archive staff were able to convince Revenko, the director of the President's staff, to make sure I looked at one file kept in a special archive. The draft of my final speech as President was then being typed. I was totally preoccupied by this and other matters.

Nonetheless, Revenko continued to insist and handed me the file on the eve of my meeting with Yeltsin, in the course of which it had been agreed that I would hand over affairs to him. I opened the file. In it there was a memorandum from Beria concerning the fate of the Polish servicemen and representatives of other groups in Polish society who were being detained in several camps. The memorandum ended with a recommendation that all the interned Poles should be executed. This last part was marked off and above it was written in Stalin's blue pencil: 'Resolution of the Politburo.' And the signatures: 'In favour—Stalin, Molotov, Voroshilov.' It took my breath away to read this hellish paper, which condemned to death thousands of people at a single stroke. I put the file in my safe and then took it out again in the course of my conversation with Yeltism, when we had reached the point of signing the document about the transfer of the special Central Committee archive (which held one or two thousand so-called special files containing documents of special importance). I showed Yeltsin the document and read it to him in Yakovlev's presence, and we agreed on its transfer to the Poles.

'But now,' I said, 'this is your mission, Boris Nikolaevich.'

There was another paper in the file as well, written and signed in Shelepin's hand when he was Chairman of the KGB. Addressed to Khrushchev, it proposed the destruction of all documents connected with the NKVD's actions to eliminate the Polish servicemen.

It seemed to me that, just as it was essential for us to understand our own history, so, in establishing new relationships with our allies, it was important to clear away the débris of the past by admitting our often grievous mistakes. On a visit to Yugoslavia, for example, I felt it necessary to admit that the interruption in the good relations between our countries had been the Soviet leadership's fault, and that the resulting conflict had inflicted great damage on Yugoslavia, the Soviet Union, and the cause of socialism. Then came the words that appeared throughout the press and were met with applause in the Skupstina: 'I felt it was essential to talk today about this so that no wariness, suspicion, mistrust or resentment remained. As history shows, these can easily arise in relations between peoples and are very hard to overcome afterwards. This is essential also in order to emphasize the significance of the conclusions that we have drawn from the lessons of the past, and in order to build our relations firmly and rigorously on a basis of full equal rights, independence, and mutual respect.'

At the time of my official visit to Czechoslovakia in April 1987 I was often asked how I assessed the events of 1968. This was the hardest question for me. I found it extremely awkward to repeat the positions agreed upon in the Politburo before my visit to people who—I felt this—were drawn to me in all sincerity. Never had I experienced the kind of internal division I did at that moment.

The question of re-assessing the events of 1968 was being raised there with increasing frequency and intensity. Half a million people who had been excluded from the Czechoslovak Communist Party could not forget the fact that they and their loved ones were cut off from political and social life, that they had been humiliated, ostracized, and some even forced to leave their homeland. The reformers of the Prague Spring greeted our perestroika with enthusiasm and demanded changes in their own land as well.

In an interview, Zdenek Mlynar, my friend and fellow student at Moscow University, said: 'In the Soviet Union they are doing what we did in Prague in the spring of 1968, perhaps acting more radically. But Gorbachev is General Secretary and I am still in exile.'

The Czechoslovak leadership was well aware that the principal players in the Prague Spring were attempting to make overtures to us. If the Soviet Union repudiated the events of 1968, this would deal a tremendous blow to the Czechoslovak Communist Party. Therefore they did all they could to bolster our 'fighting spirit,' sending us various statements to prove the historical correctness of the August action, which, they said, saved socialism, drove back imperialism, and thereby averted a world war.

The paradox consisted in the fact that both sides proceeded from a common point of departure. They assumed that the fate of Czechoslovakia had to be decided in Moscow. They simply could not believe that we truly had no intention of interfering in the affairs of other countries, that we intended to put into practice the principle proclaimed in the documents of the Socialist community and the Communist movement, according to which each Party was independent and responsible to its own people.

I cannot come to a full stop in my discussion of relations between Moscow and Prague without relating one more meeting.

On 21 May 1990 Alexander Dubcek, Chairman of the Federal Assembly of the Czech and Slovak Federal Republic (as it was called at the time), walked into the presidential office in the Kremlin, next to the hall where the all-powerful Politburo once convened. The last time he had come (or, rather, had been brought) to Moscow had been nearly twenty-two years before, in August 1968. Then he was forty-six years old and was First Secretary of the Czechoslovak Communist Party Central Committee, and it seemed as if his career was over for good. Relatively soon thereafter, following a brief sojourn as Ambassador to Turkey, he was excluded from the Party and sent into political oblivion under the surveillance of the secret police.

And here was Dubcek walking towards me with his invariable, somewhat shy smile, older but still quite slim. He walked with his arms opened slightly in friendly greeting. We met warmly, and Dubcek's eyes were wet.

Mikhail Gorbachev, *Memoirs* (New York: Doubleday, 1995), 80–83, 478–483.

Interpretations

Paul Berman

The Dream of a New Society

Paul Berman, an independent journalist, reflects on the role of utopian visions in the global revolutions of 1968. He points to the power of ideals in motivating people for action, and also blinding them to limits and costs. He argues that although the utopianism of the 1960s had many grave shortcomings, it evolved over the course of the next two decades into an effective program for social and political reform. Of course, all former 1960s activists did not take the same intellectual path.

In the years around 1968, a utopian exhilaration swept across the student universe and across several adult universes as well, and almost everyone in my own circle of friends and classmates was caught up in it. The exhilaration was partly a fury against some well-known social injustices, and against some injustices that had always remained hidden. Partly it was a belief, hard to remember today (except in a cartoon version), that a superior new society was already coming into existence. And it was the belief that we ourselves—the teenage revolutionaries, freaks, hippies, and students, together with our friends and leaders who were five or ten years older and our allies around the world—stood at the heart of a new society.

The exhilaration was brought on by circumstances close to hand—by the activities of two or three tiny left-wing organizations, by several strong personalities whom we loved to deplore, by chance happenings that could just as easily have turned out differently. But it was brought on, most of all, by a confluence of very large events. Four enormous revolutions were roiling the world at that one moment, each of those revolutions different in nature and purpose from the others, each of them far too huge and unprecedented for anyone, no matter how old and experienced, to comprehend at the time. And from each of those revolutions, and from the combination of all four, radiated an intense excitement, which came beaming down on us and on people like ourselves in scattered university towns all over the world.

Our own student uprisings, the building occupations, marches, strikes, battles with the police, the insurrections that were sexual, feminist, and gay, the bursts of ecological passion, the noisy entrance of the first mass group of African-American students into the previously segregated American universities, the slightly crazy effort to raise insubordination into a culture, to eat, dress, smoke, dance differently—all of that counted as merely one of those simultaneous revolutions. It was a political insurrection, but also an insurrection in middle-class customs (a phrase we would have loathed). Revolution Number Two was closely related—a cousin, let us say, of the insurrection in customs. It was an uprising in the zone of the spirit (that phrase we would have liked). In San Francisco and in hippie districts around the country, a handful of adventurous souls were gathering up bits and pieces of Buddhism, Beat poetry, transcendentalism, Mexican folklore, psychedelic mind expansions, and God knows what else, and were funneling those many random oddities into a vague new sensibility, with results that were much less than a religion—something half-hearted, provisional. Yet the half-hearted thing managed to be trembly with expectation, therefore contagious.

The nameless new sensibility spread into the world of rock and roll, which no one would have predicted. And the music, too, proved to be contagious, not just in the United States. No small affair! But the biggest event in the zone of the spirit was going on deep within the Catholic Church. The middle 1960s had been an age of Vatican theological reform, and the reforms went lapping one upon the other until, by that same 1968, the bishops of Latin America were convening at Medellín, Colombia, to give their ecclesiastic blessing to several of the insights of liberation theology. Which was hard to believe. But not every impossibility fails to occur. And so, among the sober Catholics as among the anti-sober freaks and rockers, all kinds of rebellions were strangely afoot, and in several places around the world the conservative instincts of long ago appeared to be sinking into the past, and some crucial flaw in the human personality seemed to be correcting itself before our eyes, and the revolution in the zone of the spirit was nothing you could dismiss.

Revolutions Three and Four were strictly this-worldly. The most violent of all, the worldwide revolution against Western imperialism, was by 1968 reaching a gory climax. Communist dictatorships (another phrase that might not have set too well, except among us left-wing libertarians) had taken over Cuba and half of Vietnam and were spreading outward to no one knew where. The National Liberation Front of South Vietnam launched its Tet Offensive in the early weeks of 1968, in spite of every claim by the American generals that nothing of the sort could possibly occur. And the impression arose that Marxist-Leninist liberation movements were capable of triumphing in every faraway peasant land, and the superpower of the West could do nothing about it, and the high-tech madness of Western civilization had met its nemesis. That was Revolution Number Three.

In Communist Czechoslovakia during several months of 1968 (and, earlier in the sixties, in the inner debates and schisms of Communist Parties and left-wing youth movements all over Western Europe, the United States, Mexico, and elsewhere), the fourth revolution, this one *against* the dictatorships of the left, was meanwhile entering a first, tentative phase. The possibility that left-wing movements might actively turn against Soviet Communism and that Soviet-style tyrannies might be resisted and overthrown was suddenly, in Prague, a reality—for a little while. Communism's defeat became, for the first time, imaginable—even if no one could picture what would happen next. Obviously, Revolutions Three and Four were badly at odds. One of those revolutions was spreading the totalitarianism of Europe to the former colonies; the other was undermining the totalitarianism of Europe. One was peaking; the other, just getting under way.

But the late sixties and early seventies were years of war and panic, and in the noise and confusion the aspirations from each of those very large political revolutions were somehow projected onto the other, and opposites began to look the same. The effort to throw off the dead weight of totalitarianism (Revolution Number Four) was considered to be in some fashion a goal of Communism's spread into the tropics and the Southern Hemisphere (Revolution Number Three). Imaginary panoramas deployed across the world. The vision that was espoused by the democratic reformers in Czechoslovakia and their supporters and by people with still more libertarian views all over the radical left in the Western countries— the dream of a genuine socialism, uncorrupted, untyrannical, de-Stalinized, ultra-democratic—was pictured even by people who should have known better as flesh-and-blood reality, anyway a lively possibility for the future, in Cuba, in China, and in embattled Vietnam. The dismal old choice between a democratic civilization in the West that appeared to have lost its soul to capitalism and a Soviet civilization in the East that had surely lost its soul to bureaucracy (such was our understanding of the cold war) seemed finally to be a thing of the past. And the new alternative for mankind was thought to be upon us.

It was going to be a society of direct democracy, in a fashion that might be rustic (Third World style), sophisticated (Czechoslovak style), anarchist (workers' council style), or countercultural (hippie style), but admirable in any case. It was going to be a socialism of the poor countries and of their friends around the world, neither Stalinist nor liberal. A worldwide shift in power from the elites to the masses. A society of individual liberty (as per the revolution in middle-class customs). A society of spiritual grandeur (as per the revolution in the zone of the spirit). Something soulful. A moral advance. And in the glow of that very grand and utopian idea, a thousand disparate events from around the world—the student uprisings, the hippie experiments, the religious transformations, the rise of Communism in some places and the first sign of its fall in other places, the Black Power movement, and onward through feminism and every insurrectionary impulse of the age—seemed to merge into a single tide. And the tide swept forward, unstoppable, all-powerful. It was the new society coming into being. That was the source of our exhilaration. Or if the new society seemed, even at the time, more figurative than literal (though some people took everything literally enough), and if the world revolution seemed less than certain, the exhilaration was authentic even so. For something useful was bound to come of those many uprisings. Maybe not a revolution in the major sense; but a revolution in the minor sense. Maybe not an entirely new society; but not the rickety old social system that already existed, either.

Such was the spirit of 1968. It led to a very peculiar aftermath, visible and invisible, during the next decades. In the United States and a number of other countries the cultural half of the old rebellions went on to enjoy a fair amount of success, in a toned-down version. The minor revolution took place. Fashions and customs that were once considered shocking shocked no longer. There were political advances. The barriers that had blocked the paths of women and all sorts of minority groups became a little lower. And because of the prestige that accrued to those achievements, something odd took place in the universities and a few of the bohemian neighborhoods. Rebellions in the '68 style became a kind of ritual, year after year.

Always there were new groups of left-wingers or avant-gardists plotting ever more novel uprisings on behalf of identity politics and a dozen other causes. And always there were the hot red faces of indignant reactionaries, putting up a bitter resistance; always a little circle of left-wing fanatics astounding the world by proclaiming a conversion to right-wing fanaticism; always a conservative politician shaking a wily fist at the odious sixties and gliding to victory at the polls. It was the Battle of Gettysburg in nonstop reenactment. That was 1968's visible aftermath. It endured into the 1990s. And because the culture wars and the endless insurrections attracted a lot of attention, the many combatants on the right and the left could flatter themselves into supposing that issues as grave as those of an earlier moment were still in dispute, and the shape of society was going to depend on the outcome, and 1968 was forever.

The culture wars did have their importance, sometimes. Yet 1968 was not forever. For beneath those wars, something bigger and deeper, 1968's invisible aftermath, was all the while going on. The invisible aftermath was an undertow of analysis and self-criticism among the rebels themselves. The undertow pulled steadily at the old left-wing political ideas, and one by one drew them out to sea, where they quietly drowned. And where the old ideas had been, newer thoughts silently bobbed to the surface. The new ideas came in different versions in different countries, which made it hard to recognize that, all over the world, an entire generation was going through the same political transformation. There was a French version (which got its shaky start in the movement known as New Philosophy); an Eastern Bloc version (in which the student socialists from 1968 evolved, in the course of their prison terms, into liberal human rights dissidents); a United States version (intellectually muddled, as is our wont, with everyone claiming not to have changed any opinions at all); and a Latin American version (slower and more begrudging than elsewhere, if only because in Latin America the leftism of the student movement resulted in guerrilla wars, which are not like culture wars, and the martyrdom was staggering, and martyrs impede thought). Yet everywhere the drift was more or less the same.

In place of the old aspirations for direct democracy and revolutionary socialism you could begin to see a much livelier appreciation of liberal democracy, social-democratic style (for some of us) or free-market style (for some lamentable others), but committed to Western-style political institutions in either case. Sometimes the old animosity for the United States dropped away. Sometimes there was even a bit of enthusiasm for America's culture and political traditions, which was quite a novel development. Naturally, the rise of the new ideas in what had been the precincts of the radical left around the world did not cause everybody to jump for joy. In the remote Peruvian Andes straight into the 1990s whole villages clung to a Maoism from long ago, and in the big American universities and a few other places that had gotten stuck in the past still other people clung to a variety of antique doctrines about U.S. imperialism and bourgeois democracy and the evils of Western civilization. And to everyone who still adhered to the leftist fundamentals, the fading away of the old revolutionary aspiration was a dismal thing to behold, and the entire trajectory from leftist to liberal was pathetic, and events have gone steadily downhill since 1968.

But then, what does it mean—"revolutionary"? World history is not the theater of happiness, Hegel said; yet every so often comes a joke. No sooner did the old ideas about a left-wing revolution drop away than, beginning in 1989, to universal astonishment, the forgotten genie from 1968, a world revolution, flew out from a bottle. Half of Europe was suddenly on the barricades, together with any number of countries in Asia, Africa, and Latin America. Everyone watched with intense interest to discover if the old left-wing radicalism was by any chance going to revive, and the new kind of socialism appear, and the workers' councils make their bid for power. But, no. In one insurrectionary country after another in 1989 and for a few years after, the vanguard of the late-twentieth-century revolution turned out to be adventurous persons who called themselves (sometimes sincerely!) liberal and democratic and seemed to be, some of them, moderately fond of the United States, too. In the modern age, nothing is more revolutionary than what only yesterday seemed the height of reaction. And in the bright light of the democratic revolutions, the student uprisings of the years around 1968 began suddenly to look, in retrospect, a little different than they had in the past.

Suddenly it was obvious that those long-ago utopian efforts to change the shape of the world were a young people's rehearsal, preparatory to adult events that only came later. Suddenly it was obvious that the authentic political revolution of our era was now, not then; liberal and democratic, not radical leftist in the '68 style; real, not imaginary. Here and there the leaders of the revolutions of '89—a Václav Havel in Czechoslovakia, an Adam Michnik in Poland—turned out to be the same heroic persons, now adult liberals, who as young radicals had helped lead the movements of '68, just to show the relation of one uprising to the next. And with the liberal revolutions breaking out in sundry regions from the Baltic Sea to South Africa during the entire period from 1989 to 1994, the old hope of reorganizing the world on a drastically new and infinitely more democratic basis, the universal project, the grand aspiration for the poor and the downtrodden, *that* hope, the forbidden utopian dream, once again seemed, in its newly liberal and anti-grandiose version—well, thinkable. Once again there was a feeling that all over the world several main principles of a good society (a liberal democratic political system, a functioning market, free trade unions, a commitment to open debate and rational ways of thinking—to name a few) had at last been discovered. Again history seemed to be advancing in a definite direction. And again, just as had happened after the insurrections of circa 1968 in different parts of the world, came a scarlet wave of spectacular disasters, the ethnic massacres and the gangster tyrannies.

So what are we to think—we, the twice-revolutionary, who have seen worldwide political hopes rise and fall, rise and fall, two times in a short generation? Are we to conclude that the idea of progress is the enemy of progress and that revolutionary exhilaration is drunkenness and folly, to be avoided at all cost? Or are we to conclude that better societies do sometimes arise, and are arising even now because of the liberal passions that spread around the world in 1989 (sometimes with a remoter origin in the student movements of the past), and that a confidence in historical progress may have its justifications still, even if no one can feel too cheery about it? Or should we merely conclude that an endless oscillation from one of those views to the other is our modern fate?

The radical exhilarations of circa 1968; the awkward modulation from revolutionary leftism to liberal democracy on the part of rebellious-minded people around the world; the outbreak of a new and different revolutionary exhilaration in 1989; finally the unresolvable debate about world history and the idea of progress: those have been the four main stations in the political journey of the generation that came of age in the student rebellions of the past. It is a tale of two utopias—and of two reconsiderations.

In *A Tale of Two Utopias: The Political Journey of the Generation of 1968* (New York: W. W. Norton, 1996), 7–18.

Arthur Marwick

The Consummation of a Cultural Revolution

Arthur Marwick, a social historian who resides in Great Britain, focuses on the cultural side of 1968. He describes how the global revolutions of the period transformed everyday behavior. Societies generally became more informal, more open to nontraditional lifestyles, and more youth-centered. Personal freedoms expanded and deference to authority diminished. Marwick argues that the troubling political legacies of 1968 should not blind us to the positive cultural changes rooted in this era.

During the long period in which I was writing this book, I took part in a radio discussion on the sixties. The academic (not a historian!) chairing the discussion put to me the suggestion that 'the sixties was a dry run for the nineties.' Behind such a notion lies the metaphysical assumption that there is some immanent presence or process which divides the flux of human affairs and the developments and changes in human societies into periods, each with some purposive identity. A 'dry run' is the dried-up bed of a river. In the remark just quoted, it is being used as a metaphor—a very dead metaphor, in fact a cliché—to make the suggestion that in some way the sixties was a 'try-out,' or 'rehearsal,' for the nineties. As I started, so I finish: resort to the sloppy clichés of everyday conversation does not make for clear, rigorous history, nor does the belief that periods have some intrinsic existence, as distinct from being merely the products of the analytical methodology of historians. Were my interests in economic history, diplomatic history, the history of political institutions, or, indeed, the history of the Third World, I would not feel that anything particularly important or unique happened between 1958 and 1974. It is because I am interested in what happens to majorities, rather than minorities, because I am a social and cultural historian, and because I am a historian of the West, that I do feel that the years 1958 to 1974 form a period, as self-contained as a period can ever be; that is to say, I believe that 1958 to 1959 was a point of change, that in the

years which followed the manifold activities and developments
which took place are integrated together by certain distinctive and,
in some cases, unique characteristics, and that another point of
change is apparent by 1974. As these things go, it is reasonable, I
would argue, to apply the term 'cultural revolution' to this period,
though only if we evacuate from both adjective and noun any
Marxist implications of violent confrontation or of one discrete
and integrated culture totally replacing another. If we prefer the
route of semantic caution, then 'social and cultural transformation'
will do very well. The period 'integrated by distinctive, and even
unique, characteristics' does not exactly coincide with the decade
1960–69, but there is no problem about referring to it as 'the sixties,' especially if we keep in mind the fruitful concept of 'the long
sixties.'

The flabby phrase about the sixties being a 'dry run' for the
nineties would seem to be suggesting, not so much that in the
nineties there was a return to the practices and values of the sixties,
but that in the nineties these practices and values reappeared in a
perfected form. At once, one must comment that any notion that
the practices and values of the sixties disappeared during some
intervening period, in consequence (the implication usually is) of
the reactionary policies and new moral piety associated with the
administrations of President Ronald Reagan and Prime Minister
Margaret Thatcher, is quite mistaken. The sixties was a time of en-
trepreneuralism and private enterprise, a time of the creation and
satisfaction of new consumer needs, a time of expansion in the
service and entertainment industries. Such developments anticipated aspects of 'Thatcherism' (an international phenomenon),
rather than being antithetical to them. More critically, those elements of sixties lifestyles which Reagan and Thatcher detested continued to be present during the seventies and were very evident
throughout the eighties. All the statistical evidence suggests that
permissive attitudes and permissive behaviour continued to spread
at accelerating rates, with only the utterly unforeseen occurrence of
AIDS to bring any kind of caution; single-parent families prolifer-
ated, the term 'husband' and 'wife' became almost quaint, giving
place to 'lover' and 'partner.' It took a long time in coming, but by
the mid-nineties topless sunbathing was evident even on some Italian beaches. The appearance, also, of moralistic crusades simply

testifies to the strength of the by now well-established behaviour patterns which the crusades, vainly, hoped to eliminate. The cultural revolution, in short, had continuous, uninterrupted, and lasting consequences.

The essence of the cultural revolution was its involvement of vast numbers of ordinary people: from peasant families in rural Italy getting the basics of civilized living to black children in the ghettos of the American South being admitted for the first time to properly equipped schools; from paraplegics whose needs as integrated members of the community were for the first time being recognized, to women everywhere freed from the confinements of the feminine mystique; from Italian, French, British, and American workers with freshly negotiated wages and conditions of employment to young people in once-dreary provincial cities, now provided with boutiques and discos. All sections of society (workers, blacks, women, provincials) hitherto ignored became visible. At the beginning of the decade, in America, what hit the headlines with respect to segregated housing was the right of whites to safeguard the value of their properties; by the end of the decade what was discussed in the newspapers was the intrinsic unfairness of racial discrimination in housing. Everywhere, as we saw, there was a growth both in state action and voluntary action aimed at the ordinary problems of social welfare. At the same time people gained power to make decisions for themselves. Life became more varied and enjoyable. With less rigid conceptions of marriage and new opportunities for divorce, with changing attitudes to fashion and to education, with the abandonment of comfortable fictions about the nature of beauty and the arrival of informal, body-hugging clothing, there was a healthier openness to ordinary living, less need for lies, fewer cover-ups—literally in the case of female sunbathers no longer constrained to go through incredible contortions in endeavouring to combine maximum exposure to the sun with minimum outrage to public pudicity. The testimony that the new universal language of rock was genuinely liberating, and not just for the young, is overwhelming.

It is important not to exaggerate the extent of change, or its novelty. Not everything in the sixties that I have picked out to discuss was entirely new; what was new was that so many things happened at once. Much of what was done in the sixties was downright stupid:

I referred at the start to the Great Marxisant Fallacy, and we have seen that there was much pointless violence in pursuit of a revolution that was never there to be grasped. Faith in drugs as the key to a better society was mindless, self-deluding, and destructive; many other counter-cultural activities owed far more to self-indulgence than to serious protest against established ways of doing things. The desire to silence pompous, hidebound males and to give voices to females and oppressed minorities was entirely laudable; unfortunately, even before the decade was out there were intimations of what small minds were later to turn into the sour prescriptiveness which the right, with less than the usual exaggeration, denounced as 'political correctness.' But if we are looking at what was not done, or what was done badly, then we have to turn to those in authority, those who had the power to make a difference. That is why it is absurd to accuse, as latter-day right-wing revisionists and turncoat radicals have done, anti-war extremists of prolonging the Vietnam war; the protesters gave witness as conscience dictated, and in the end they won. Governments often did badly on domestic issues as well. In all countries housing policies were misguided, and sometimes downright inadequate. Environmental protection began late, and too many disasters were allowed to happen. But this *was* an area in which ordinary people had taken action, and *did* make a difference. So, above all, in civil rights. The greatest advances in race relations as between the beginning and the end of my long sixties were made in the United States. As we have seen, great trenches of white prejudice remained, while militant black separatism did nothing to further peaceful and just accommodation.

Of course, the issue of the proper relations between two different races had existed since the foundation of the United States. It only began to become truly significant in Britain and France in the sixties, when, also, the question of the treatment in north and central Italy of southern immigrants became pressing; only at the very end of our period did blacks begin to arrive from the territories in the Horn of Africa that Italy under Mussolini had once tried to conquer. Only then, too, did the rights of American Indians begin to be recognized, particularly after the generally peaceful occupation of the deserted former penitentiary on Alcatraz Island, San Francisco Bay, by about thirty American Indians, mainly local students, with some children, from 20 November 1969 to 11 June 1971. Addressing Congress on 9 July 1970, President Nixon spoke some measured, indeed progressive words, referring to 'aggression, broken agreements, intermittent remorse and prolonged failure,' and proposing a wide-ranging programme to give American Indians dignity and control over their own lives.[1] Putting things another way: it was in the sixties that an important stage was passed in the passage to our contemporary world made up of multicultural societies—a process caused not by deliberate human agency but by the great demographic movements of our time. The question which has to be asked about individuals, groups, and governments in the sixties is: what did they do to foster or to frustrate the advance of multiculturalism? The counter-cultural and movement groups, with their genuine celebration of the colour, the variety, and the mutual stimulus to be found in a multicultural society, score well. So do some of the liberal Democrats in America, politicians like Roy Jenkins in Britain, and some Hollywood film-makers. Those who advocated segregation, discrimination, or separatism (including Enoch Powell and Toni Morrison) were the unseeing and distinctive members of their time.

Of the sixteen characteristics of the sixties I outlined in Chapter 1, this one is probably the most contentious. But some readers, perhaps, are still unpersuaded by my concept of 'measured judgement.' Let me quote from the autobiography of the leader of the radical socialist group SDS, Tom Hayden. Hayden and many others suffered grievously at the hands of the most reactionary elements in the 'justice' system, George Jackson most atrociously of all. In the following couple of sentences Hayden is wittingly making the case that he and his fellow-protesters were basically right (I do not demur); unwittingly he brings out that deep within the American system as it developed during the sixties, there was measured judgement:

It was remarkable that during these several years of political trials on conspiracy charges, the federal government failed to win against

[1] Troy Johnson, Joane Nagel, and Duane Champagne (eds.), *American Indian Activism: Alcatraz to the Longest Walk* (Urbana, Ill., 1997). For the Nixon speech, see the chapter by John Garvey and Troy Johnson, 'The Government and the Indians: the American Indian Occupation of Alcatraz Island, 1969–71,' 167.

any of the sixty-five conspiracy defendents. Such defendents as the Harrisburg Seven, the Camden Seventeen, and the Gainesville Eight always managed to win, either before juries or appeals courts, a dramatic difference from the McCarthy era, only fifteen years before.[2]

Testimony on sexual liberation in the sixties is less supportive than we have sometimes been led to believe of the position that liberation was purely for males to exploit females. The new freedom for girls and women was real, though so also was a strong determination among males to exploit new opportunities to the full. Even so, male chauvinism had its positive consequences in providing a stimulus to the nascent women's liberation movement. Feminist ideas, never monolithic in any case, have since gone through a number of phases, including some very extreme ones. Self-evidently, discrimination against women has not yet ended, but it would be a sour commentator indeed who would not concede that a movement initiated in the sixties has resulted at the end of the second millennium in more humane and balanced relationships between the sexes than ever existed previously.

There was no economic revolution, no political revolution, no advent of the proletariat to power, no classless society, no destruction of mainstream culture, no obliteration of language. The gospel according to Marcuse was that, since the mass of the ordinary workers were so content with the boons of consumer society that they had no interest in revolution, the revolutionary forces would have to come from the outcast and deprived, including in particular racial minorities—not, in other words, from the working class but from the under-class—and the revolutionary leadership would have to come from the student activists. But why have a revolution? If the majority are already contented, would it not be better to concentrate in a systematic and pragmatic way on raising the living standards of the minority, and thus abolishing the under-class? What possible reason, anyway, was there for believing that even if a revolution could be carried out it would bring anything but further misery to the lowest class of people? Governments with their

[2]Tom Hayden, *Reunion: A Memoir* (New York, 1988), 452.

welfare policies actually achieved far more for the under-class than did the Movement or the New Left. But not nearly enough. And with market economies rampant in later decades, the under-class greatly expanded. Revolution was never the answer. Nor were badly conceived and badly applied welfare schemes. Not so much unfinished business as business for which neither the radicals nor the apostles of measured judgement had found effective answers.

Democratic institutions survived, if somewhat fitfully, in Italy, where special problems (identified in Chapter 2) were never resolved. But the Italian people became more self-aware during the sixties, more responsible for their own destinies. The seventies was a time of violence and terrorism, but there was enough confidence, enough resilience among the people for democratic Italy to survive. Austerity measures in the mid-nineties, designed to equip Italy for European Monetary Union, have stripped the workers of many of the gains they made at the end of the sixties. For all that, Italy remains a freer, more affluent, more joyful society than it was in the fifties. That stands across the four countries. Today, in all four countries, the proportion of the disadvantaged is growing all the time, and too much power is still held by too few people. But it is senseless to dismiss the developments of the sixties because they did not have revolutionary consequences. It is perfectly true that many of the most spectacular features—the music of the Beatles, the fashion of Mary Quant, the art of Andy Warhol—were thoroughly implicated with the profit-making commercialism of the time, but suggestions that they averted revolution by lulling people into a false contentment are absurd; what they did do was to contribute their mite to the people's liberation.

After the end of the sixties, despite the economic crisis of 1973–4, living conditions for most people continued to improve. However, I would not want to claim that the sixties have been followed by an irreversible upward trend in material circumstances. The world economy has been much more unstable than seemed likely in the sixties; 'globalization' has meant that developments anywhere in the world can threaten the job security of people in the West. Without question, global economic stability was indispensable to the happy circumstances of the sixties; but no recipes for permanent economic success were produced then. As I have said, there is certainly no case to be made that people in the sixties were somehow more moral, more unselfish, or more far-sighted than people in any other age: circumstances were different, though, given the favourable circumstances, people did show extraordinary energy, imagination, and critical awareness directed at their own society. A vital factor was the existence, and expansion, of the liberal and progressive element within the structures of authority, who practised measured judgement. That was what gave the societies of the sixties much of their unique quality: gone was the stuffy conservatism of previous decades, while the radical, divisive, philistine conservatism of Reagan and Thatcher was yet to come. Yet, whatever the political changes, the consequences of what happened in the sixties were long-lasting: the sixties cultural revolution in effect established the enduring cultural values and social behaviour for the rest of the century. This had been no transient time of ecstasy and excess, fit only for nostalgia or contempt. I began this short concluding chapter carping at someone else's cliché. But now, in making my closing pronouncements on the sixties, I cannot improve upon these two clichés: there has been nothing quite like it; nothing would ever be quite the same again.

In *The Sixties: Cultural Revolution in Britain, France, Italy, and the United States, c. 1958–c. 1974* (Oxford: Oxford University Press, 1998), 801–806.

Jeremi Suri

Power and Protest

Jeremi Suri, a historian born after 1968, examines the intersection of Cold War diplomacy and social activism during the period. He argues that the contradiction between idealistic claims and stagnant politics among state leaders triggered domestic contention across societies. Fearful of the challenges they now faced at home, Cold War policy makers collaborated to ensure international stability and repress domestic change. Confronting this repression, social activists adopted self-

defeating positions of extreme radicalization and political disengagement. For Suri, the global revolutions of 1968 mark a lost opportunity to build more consensual and effective global politics.

The 1960s came to a close with diplomacy and domestic politics oddly frozen in place. These were the conservative consequences that, paradoxically, followed from radical social upheaval. Stability did not arise naturally during this period. It was artificially enforced by the besieged leaders of the largest states.[1]

The decade began when John Kennedy, Nikita Khrushchev, Charles de Gaulle, and Mao Zedong pursued a charismatic kind of politics. Appealing to what they recognized as widespread unease with the territorial divisions and nuclear dangers of the Cold War, these men promised an era of unprecedented achievements: Kennedy would conquer new frontiers, Khrushchev would build real-existing communism, de Gaulle would restore French *grandeur*, and Mao would guide China in a great industrial leap ahead of Europe. An expanding cohort of men and women entered universities convinced that with enlightened leadership they would change the world.

This optimism quickly soured. Youthful citizens expected too much in a world still dominated by nuclear dangers, Cold War divisions, and large bureaucratic institutions. The muscular rhetoric of charismatic leaders encouraged unrealistic hopes that far exceeded practical capabilities. This contradiction between rhetoric and capabilities explains the disjunction that emerged between public persona and private policy in each state. Leaders continued to promise their citizens more than ever before, but time and again they accepted compromises—in Berlin, Cuba, Algeria, and the aftermath of the Great Leap Forward—that rejected the aggressiveness of their rhetoric.

---

[1]Historians have made similar arguments about the periods following World Wars I and II. See Arno J. Mayer, *Politics and Diplomacy of Peacemaking: Containment and Counterrevolution at Versailles, 1918–1919* (New York, 1967), 3–30; Charles S. Maier, *Recasting Bourgeois Europe: Stabilization in France, Germany, and Italy in the Decade after World War I* (Princeton, 1988), 481–594; idem, *In Search of Stability: Explorations in Historical Political Economy* (Cambridge, 1987), 261–273.

Vietnam was the exception that proved the rule. In this corner of Southeast Asia, John Kennedy and Lyndon Johnson believed they had to press for communist containment and economic development as proof that they really meant what they said. Vietnam appeared deceptively "safe" for the muscle flexing that charismatic leaders needed to impress young and ambitious citizens. This was hardly the first time that Americans, fearful of political and social stagnation, had displayed their "manliness" through war.[2]

Leaders in Washington did not have a monopoly on this kind of self-defeating behavior. Their counterparts in Moscow and Beijing pursued their own interventions in Vietnam. Mao also embarked on a ruinous "Cultural Revolution" that sought to purge China of the "counterrevolutionary" influences deposited on the mainland by the United States and the Soviet Union. By the end of the decade Chinese and Soviet assertiveness brought these communist states to the point of war. Leaders in both countries turned to the United States, West Germany, and other capitalist adversaries for assistance in repairing the damage of their overheated rhetoric.

Throughout this period, young men and women grew visibly more violent in nearly every society. Adopting the "language of dissent" popularized by a series of authors, students accused their elders of hypocrisy and corruption. Leaders were delegitimized by their own rhetoric. They did not conquer new frontiers, build real-existing communism, restore national *grandeur*, or achieve any great industrial leaps. Around universities, young men and women assembled to criticize and attack authorities. This was true even in the repressive communist states, where *kompanii* and Red Guard meetings became sites for organized rebellion.

By 1968 rebellion produced revolution. Young men and women took to the streets, smashing symbols of government legitimacy. In Berkeley, Washington, D.C., and other American cities mobs blocked buildings, burned streets, and fought with the state's armed police and military forces. In West Berlin and Paris students built barricades and engaged in street battles with police. In Prague men

---

[2]See Kristin L. Hoganson, *Fighting for American Manhood: How Gender Politics Provoked the Spanish-American and Philippine-American Wars* (New Haven, 1998); Emily S. Rosenberg, *Financial Missionaries to the World: The Politics and Culture of Dollar Diplomacy, 1900–1930* (Cambridge, Mass., 1999); John Milton Cooper Jr., *The Warrior and the Priest: Woodrow Wilson and Theodore Roosevelt* (Cambridge, Mass., 1983).

and women demonstrated for freedom and independence from Soviet intervention. In Wuhan young Red Guards seized weapons
from the army and used them against their elders. This was a truly
"global disruption" that threatened leaders everywhere.

Detente was a reaction to these troubling circumstances. Willy
Brandt, Richard Nixon, and Leonid Brezhnev abandoned the muscular rhetoric and charismatic politics of their predecessors. Mao
Zedong reincarnated himself as an opponent of the Cultural Revolution he had initially launched. Despite their ideological differences, these men colluded to stabilize their societies and preserve
their authority. They refrained from challenging one another as
they had throughout the Cold War. They used obsessive secrecy to
insulate their activities from domestic attack. They pursued arms
control and trade to furnish new resources for domestic needs.
Most significant, they collaborated to bolster their respective images. The summits and agreements of the period made the leaders
appear indispensable. To challenge Brandt, Nixon, Brezhnev, or
Mao was to undermine new steps toward international "peace."
The promise of detente became a stick with which to beat domestic critics.

In place of the charismatic politics that characterized the early
part of the decade, leaders now practiced profoundly conservative
politics. Detente preserved stability at the cost of progressive
change. It made the sacrifices of the Cold War appear "normal,"
and it further isolated policymakers from their publics. In this way,
detente contributed to the pervasive skepticism of our "postmodern" age.

People of all kinds are now looking beyond the boundaries of the
nation-state to understand the world around them. The end of the
Cold War, the Internet, and the economic turbulence of the 1990s
have raised public awareness about "globalization." Environmental
and human rights activism has drawn attention to common interests across cultures. Most shocking, the terrorist attacks of 11
September 2001 and the subsequent "war on terrorism" have encouraged a sense of shared danger among the members of diverse
societies.

To help us comprehend what it means to think globally, scholars
have begun to conceptualize history in these terms as well. By

examining how states, peoples, and cultures interacted with one another in the past, we surely gain some leverage on understanding the present. To see globalization as a historic phenomenon is to recognize that the new technologies of our day are not necessarily the primary forces behind the interdependence of economies, the interpenetration of cultures, and, perhaps most worrying, the internationalization of terrorism. Studying the 1960s and detente in global terms reveals how ideas, institutions, and personalities transcended national boundaries before the Internet or the "war on terrorism."

The Cold War, more than anything else, created a remarkable conjuncture among societies in the 1960s. Nuclear dangers elicited common fears of annihilation. International competition contributed to the growth of state-run bureaucracies. This trend was especially robust in universities, which in nearly every society expanded to accommodate both a larger population of young citizens and state demands for more advanced technical training. Cold War rhetoric about capitalism and communism promoted rising expectations that, by the late 1960s, produced a common sense of disillusionment among culturally diverse men and women.

To see the period in these terms, and detente's function as counterrevolution, requires a global perspective that looks across national boundaries and within societies at the same time. It demands attention to various kinds of relationships: social, cultural, political, and diplomatic. Isolating one kind of interaction from another simply recasts the parochialism of national history over a wider geographic terrain. Understanding moments of global conjuncture such as the 1960s requires an international history that treats power as both *multicultural* and *multidimensional*. This approach involves following the interactions of ideas, institutions, and personalities at many levels. It also leads to an examination of how policies such as detente evolved from truly diverse, and often unintended, influences.

Many social reforms grew out of the 1960s, especially with regard to race and gender relations in the United States and Western Europe. These accomplishments, however, pale in comparison with the extensive ambitions voiced by reformers at the time. Poverty, despite the writings of John Kenneth Galbraith and Michael Harrington, remains prevalent on city streets and in rural communities throughout the wealthiest nations. The gap between the richest and poorest states also remains large, and has probably grown since the 1960s.[3]

Communism has collapsed in the Soviet Union and Eastern Europe, but citizens in many societies are still deprived of an effective political voice. They suffer from the kind of isolation that angered dissidents and protesters decades earlier. Unrepresentative international bodies such as the European Union and the World Trade Organization worsen this "democratic deficit," even in the most democratic states. Demonstrations against these international institutions have evoked images somewhat similar to those of the 1960s: young men and women marching, organized groups staging sit-ins, and mobs vandalizing city streets.[4]

Detente constrained political and economic reform in the last quarter of the twentieth century. Cooperation among the leaders of the largest states discouraged creative policymaking and risk-taking. Quite the contrary, triangular diplomacy and Ostpolitik emphasized political predictability. Extensive coordination among a tiny group of men excluded most advocates of change. Political institutions, as a consequence, grew more rigid. Boundaries for authority, both national and international, were also fortified.

The history of globalization is, in this sense, intimately connected with detente. International institutions continue to embody the conservative inclinations of leaders. They are generally opaque, elitist, and dominated by the largest states. They have important public influence, but they remain creatures of national governments. Detente protected a state-centered world and forestalled hopes for the creation of truly independent international authorities.

---

[3] See Arthur Marwick, *The Sixties: Cultural Revolution in Britain, France, Italy, and the United States, c. 1958–c. 1974* (Oxford, 1998), 801–806; William Julius Wilson, *The Truly Disadvantaged: The Inner City, the Underclass, and Public Policy* (Chicago, 1987), 20–62; Paul Kennedy, *Preparing for the Twenty-first Century* (New York, 1993), 193–227.

[4] See Fritz W. Scharpf, *Governing in Europe: Effective and Democratic?* (Oxford, 1999), 6–42, 187–204; Philippe C. Schmitter, *How to Democratize the European Union . . . and Why Bother?* (Lanham, Md., 2000), 1–19.

The excesses of the 1960s discredited political idealism. As a consequence, many societies suffer from what one writer calls "diminishing expectations." "Personal preoccupations" have replaced collective engagement and common purpose. Christopher Lasch has defined this as the "culture of narcissism" that emerged from the "turmoil of the sixties" and continues to characterize a world in which politics lack popular meaning. "Having no hope of improving their lives in any of the ways that matter," Lasch has written, "people have convinced themselves that what matters is . . . to live for yourself, not for your predecessors or posterity." Detente encouraged narcissism among leaders and citizens, especially in Europe and the United States.[5]

This narcissism has infected relations among states and societies. Since the 1960s leaders have generally failed to build popular consensus for their foreign policies. Even after 11 September 2001 government deliberations have remained highly centralized and secretive. President George W. Bush and his counterparts in Europe, the Middle East, and other regions have spoken of a "moral crusade," but they have done little to engage citizens on fundamental issues. No leader has seriously asked his or her constituents to think about why people turn to terrorism. Nor has any figure of authority articulated a vision for how citizens can cooperate to improve global conditions. Most troubling, governments have deployed force at home and abroad with the worthy intention of preventing future terrorism, but also with little public discussion about infringements on individual liberties. Like their predecessors in the late 1960s, leaders have protected stability at the cost of liberty.

Terrorist threats might justify this calculation. It is, however, a decision that requires public discussion, not elite dictate. The history of the 1960s and detente warns that stability without consensus prohibits progress. Anger and resentment fester, moving from traditional institutions to other, often more belligerent, venues. To some extent, this process has encouraged bursts of "home-grown" violence in Europe and North America since the early 1970s. It

[5]Christopher Lasch, *The Culture of Narcissism: American Life in an Age of Diminishing Expectations* (New York, 1978), 3–7, 31–51.

has also produced militant behavior among men and women, frequently from the Arab world, who feel dispossessed by globalization. Although many of the claims articulated by terrorists are illegitimate, we must take seriously their alienation from the processes of economic growth, political democratization, and cultural recognition. The anger that fuels terrorism has deep roots in past policies, both domestic and international, that have excluded many people from a personal stake in the existing order.

Moralistic rhetoric and isolated policymaking, though sometimes necessary, will not reintegrate the dispossessed into a world of global markets, democratizing states, and Hollywood movies. Combining force with consensus-building efforts, both at home and abroad, appears much more likely to turn people away from terrorism. Residents of different societies need not agree on all issues to recognize that they share a common fate. They need not enjoy similar lifestyles to understand that they benefit from peaceful trade and cooperation. The leaders of the largest states must work to show, in actions and in words, that their foreign policies reflect the concerns of international citizens, not just national constituents or national "interests."

Building consensus, of course, is difficult and sometimes impossible. It can also inspire violent counterreactions. That said, alternative approaches to stability without consensus are far worse. Detente failed to satisfy citizens, it prolonged Cold War sacrifices, and it created festering resentments. Contemporary policies that advocate isolated decisionmaking appear little better. Foreign policy is also social policy. We will never build a better world until leaders and citizens recognize this simple truism and work together in the use of force and the pursuit of peace.

In *Power and Protest: Global Revolution and the Rise of Détente* (Cambridge, Mass.: Harvard University Press, 2003), 260–265.

SUPPLEMENTARY BIBLIOGRAPHY

Memoirs

Ayers, William. *Fugitive Days* (Boston: Beacon Press, 2001).

Brandt, Willy. *People and Politics: The Years 1960–1975*, trans. J. Maxwell Brownjohn (Boston: Little, Brown, 1976).

Dobrynin, Anatoly. *In Confidence: Moscow's Ambassador to America's Six Cold War Presidents* (New York: Random House, 1995).

Fraser, Ronald, et al. *1968: A Student Generation in Revolt* (London: Chatto and Windus, 1988).

Gitlin, Todd. *The Sixties: Years of Hope, Days of Rage* (New York: Bantam Books, 1987).

Gorbachev, Mikhail. *Memoirs* (New York: Doubleday, 1995).

Grimaud, Maurice. *En mai, fais ce qu'il te plaît: le préfet de police de mai 68 parle* (Paris: Éditions Stock, 1977).

Hayden, Tom. *Reunion: A Memoir* (New York: Random House, 1998).

Johnson, Lyndon. *The Vantage Point: Perspectives of the Presidency, 1963–1969* (New York: Holt, Rinehart, and Winston, 1971).

Khrushchev, Nikita. *Khrushchev Remembers*, ed. and trans. Strobe Talbott (Boston: Little, Brown, 1970).

Kissinger, Henry. *White House Years* (Boston: Little, Brown, 1979).

Kun, Miklós. *Prague Spring–Prague Fall: Blank Spots of 1968*, trans. Hajnal Csatorday (Budapest: Akadémiai Kiadó, 1999).

324

Li Zhisui. *The Private Life of Chairman Mao*, trans. Tai Hung-chao (New York: Random House, 1994).

McNamara, Robert S., with Brian VanDeMark. *In Retrospect: The Tragedy and Lessons of Vietnam* (New York: Random House, 1995).

Massu, Jacques. *Baden 68* (Paris: Plon, 1983).

Nixon, Richard. *RN: The Memoirs of Richard Nixon* (New York: Grosset and Dunlap, 1978).

Poniatowska, Elena. *Massacre in Mexico*, trans., Helen R. Lane (Columbia, MO: University of Missouri Press, 1992, reprint edition).

Books

Anderson, Jon Lee. *Che Guevara: A Revolutionary Life* (New York: Grove Press, 1997).

Andrew, John A., III. *The Other Side of the Sixties: Young Americans for Freedom and the Rise of Conservative Politics* (New Brunswick, NJ: Rutgers University Press, 1997).

Berman, Paul. *A Tale of Two Utopias: The Political Journey of the Generation of 1968* (New York: W. W. Norton, 1996).

Blum, John Morton. *Years of Discord: American Politics and Society, 1961–74* (New York: W. W. Norton, 1991).

Brigham, Robert K. *Guerilla Diplomacy: The NLF's Foreign Relations and the Viet Nam War* (Ithaca, NY: Cornell University Press, 1999).

Bundy, William. *A Tangled Web: The Making of Foreign Policy in the Nixon Presidency* (New York: Hill and Wang, 1998).

Buzzanco, Robert. *Masters of War: Military Dissent and Politics in the Vietnam Era* (New York: Cambridge University Press, 1996).

Carson, Clayborne. *In Struggle: SNCC and the Black Awakening of the 1960s* (Cambridge, MA: Harvard University Press, 1981).

Chan, Anita. *Children of Mao: Personality Development and Political Activism in the Red Guard Generation* (Seattle: University of Washington Press, 1985).

Connelly, Matthew James. *A Diplomatic Revolution: Algeria's Fight for Independence and the Origins of the Post–Cold War Era* (New York: Oxford University Press, 2002).

DeBenedetti, Charles, with Charles Chatfield. *An American Ordeal: The Antiwar Movement of the Vietnam Era* (Syracuse, NY: Syracuse University Press, 1990).

Duiker, William J. *Ho Chi Minh* (New York: Hyperion, 2000).

Fink, Carole, Phillip Gassert, and Detlef Junker, eds. *1968: The World Transformed* (New York: Cambridge University Press, 1998).

Gaiduk, Ilya V. *The Soviet Union and the Vietnam War* (Chicago: Ivan R. Dee, 1996).

Gavin, Francis J. *Gold, Dollars, and Power: The Politics of International Monetary Relations, 1958–1971* (Chapel Hill, NC: University of North Carolina Press, 2004).

Goines, David Lance. *The Free Speech Movement: Coming of Age in the 1960s* (Berkeley, CA: Ten Speed Press, 1993).

Golan, Galia. *The Czechoslovak Reform Movement: Communism in Crisis, 1962–1968* (New York: Cambridge University Press, 1971).

Hersh, Seymour M. *My Lai 4: A Report on the Massacre and Its Aftermath* (New York: Random House, 1970).

Hilderbrand, Klaus. *Von Erhard zur Großen Koalition, 1963–1969* (Stuttgart: Deutsche Verlags-Anstalt, 1984).

Isserman, Maurice, and Michael Kazin. *America Divided: The Civil War of the 1960s* (New York: Oxford University Press, 2000).

Kaiser, David. *American Tragedy: Kennedy, Johnson, and the Origins of the Vietnam War* (Cambridge, MA: Harvard University Press, 2000).

Katsiaficas, George. *The Imagination of the New Left: A Global Analysis of 1968* (Boston: South End Press, 1987).

Kusin, Vladamir V. *The Intellectual Origins of the Prague Spring: The Development of Reformist Ideas in Czechoslovakia, 1956–1967* (New York: Cambridge University Press, 1971).

Marwick, Arthur. *The Sixties: Cultural Revolution in Britain, France, Italy, and the United States, c. 1958–c. 1974* (Oxford: Oxford University Press, 1998).

Miller, James. *Demoracy Is in the Streets: From Port Huron to the Siege of Chicago* (New York: Simon and Schuster, 1987).

Peck, Abe. *Uncovering the Sixties: The Life and Times of the Underground Press* (New York: Pantheon Books, 1985).

Rioux, Lucien, and René Backmann. *L'Explosion de Mai: 11 mai 1968, Histoire complète des evénements* (Paris: Robert Laffont, 1968).

Rosen, Stanley. *The Role of the Sent-Down Youth in the Chinese Cultural Revolution: The Case of Guangzhou* (Berkeley, CA: University of California Center for Chinese Studies, 1981).

Rossinow, Doug. *The Politics of Authenticity: Liberalism, Christianity, and New Left America* (New York: Columbia University Press, 1998).

Roszak, Theodore. *The Making of a Counter Culture: Reflections on the Technocratic Society and Youthful Opposition* (Garden City, NY: Doubleday, 1969).

Sarotte, M. E. *Dealing with the Devil: East Germany, Détente, and Ostpolitik, 1969–1973* (Chapel Hill, NC: University of North Carolina Press, 2001).

Schwartz, Thomas Alan. *Lyndon Johnson and Europe: In the Shadow of Vietnam* (Cambridge, MA: Harvard University Press, 2003).

Smith, Ralph B. *An International History of the Vietnam War*, Volumes 1–3 (London: Macmillan, 1983–91).

Suri, Jeremi. *Power and Protest: Global Revolution and the Rise of Détente* (Cambridge, MA: Harvard University Press, 2003).

Suri, Jeremi. *Henry Kissinger and the American Century* (Cambridge, MA: Harvard University Press, 2007).

Varon, Jeremy. *Bringing the War Home: The Weather Underground, the Red Army Faction, and Revolutionary Violence in the Sixties and Seventies* (Berkeley, CA: University of California Press, 2004).

Wang, Shaoguan. *Failure of Charisma: The Cultural Revolution in Wuhan* (New York: Oxford University Press, 1995).

Williams, Kieran. *The Prague Spring and Its Aftermath: Czechoslovak Politics, 1968–1970* (New York: Cambridge University Press, 1997).

Articles and Essays

Anderson, David L. "What Really Happened?" in idem, ed., *Facing My Lai: Moving Beyond the Massacre* (Lawrence: University Press of Kansas, 1998), 1–17.

Chen, Jian. "China's Involvement in the Vietnam War, 1964–1969," *China Quarterly* 142 (June 1995), 356–87.

Collins, Robert M. "The Economic Crisis of 1968 and the Waning of the 'American Century,'" *American Historical Review* 101 (April 1966), 396–422.

Cornils, Ingo. "'The Struggle Continues': Rudi Dutschke's Long March," in Gerald J. DeGroot, ed. *Student Protest: The Sixties and After* (New York: Longman, 1988).

Eisler, Jerzy. "March 1968 in Poland," in Carole Fink, Phillip Gassert, and Detlef Junker, eds. *1968: The World Transformed* (New York: Cambridge University Press, 1998), 237–51.

Glazer, Nathan. "What Happened at Berkeley," reprinted in idem, *Remembering the Answers: Essays on the American Student Revolt* (New York: Basic Books, 1970), 71–99.

Habermas, Jürgen. "Student Protest in the Federal Republic of Germany," reprinted in idem, *Toward a Rational Society: Student Protest, Science, and Politics*, trans. Jeremy J. Shapiro (Boston: Beacon Press, 1970).

Isserman, Maurice. "You Don't Need a Weatherman but a Post-man Can Be Helpful," in Melvin Small and William D. Hoover, eds. *Give Peace a Chance: Exploring the Vietnam Antiwar Movement* (Syracuse, NY: Syracuse University Press, 1992), 28–34.

Kramer, Mark. "Ukraine and the Soviet-Czechoslovak Crisis of 1968 (Part 1): New Evidence from the Diary of Petro Shelest," *Cold War International History Project Bulletin* 10 (March 1998), 234–47.

Nelson, Keith L. "Nixon, Kissinger, and the Domestic Side of Dé-tente," in Patrick M. Morgan and Keith L. Nelson, eds. *Re-Viewing the Cold War: Domestic Factors and Foreign Policy in the East-West Confrontation* (Westport, CT: Praeger, 2000), 127–48.

Suri, Jeremi. "The Cultural Contradictions of Cold War Educa-tion: The Case of West Berlin," *Cold War History* 4 (April 2004), 1–20.

———. "Lyndon Johnson and the Global Disruption of 1968," in Mitchell B. Lerner, ed. *Looking Back at LBJ: White House Politics in a New Light* (Lawrence: University Press of Kansas, 2005), 53–77.

Wall, Irwin. "The United States, Algeria, and the Fall of the Fourth Republic," *Diplomatic History* 18 (Winter 1994), 489–511.

CREDITS

Berman, Paul: from *A Tale of Two Utopias: The Political Journey of the Generation of 1968* © 1996 by Paul Berman. Reprinted by permission of W. W. Norton & Company, Inc.

Brezhnev, Leonid: "Transcript of Leonid Brezhnev's Telephone Conversation with Alexander Dubček, August 13, 1968," translated by Mark Kramer, Joy Moss, and Ruth Tosek, © 1998 by The Prague Spring Foundation. Reprinted by permission of Central European University Press.

Carmichael, Stokely: from *Stokely Speaks: Black Power Back to Pan-Africanism* © 1965, 1971 by Stokely Carmichael. Reprinted by permission of Random House, Inc.

Cohn-Bendit, Daniel: "Interviewed by Jean-Paul Sartre" from "The French Student Revolt" by Daniel Cohn-Bendit, Jean-Pierre Duteuil, Alain Geismar, and Jacques Sauvageot. Copyright Editions du Seuil, 1968. Translation copyright 1968 by Jonathan Cape Limited and Hill and Wang, Inc.

Deng Tuo, "The Kingly Way and the Tyrannical Way," 25 February 1962, translated by Timothy Cheek in the journal, *Chinese Law and Government: The Politics of Cultural Reform: Deng Tuo and the Retooling of Chinese Marxism* (Winter 1983–84, Vol XVI, No. 4). Reprinted by permission of M. E. Sharp, Inc.

Dutschke, Rudi. "The Students and the Revolution, Speech in Uppsala, 7th March 1968" translated by Patricia Howard (*The London Bulletin*, No. 6, Autumn 1968). Reprinted by permission of the Bertrand Russell Peace Foundation.

330

Marwick, Arthur: from *The Sixties: Cultural Revolution in Britain, France, Italy, and the United States, c. 1958–c. 1974*, © 1998. Reprinted by permission of Oxford University Press.

National Liberation for South Vietnam: "Ten Point Manifesto" © 1960 translated by Robert K. Brigham. Reprinted by permission of Cornell University Press.

National Strike Committee: "For a Worker/Peasant/Student Alliance," from *Mexico '68, The Students Speak*, translated by Richard Garza, Bobby Ortiz, Nell Salm, Linda Wetter, Maria Jose. Reprinted by permission of the Bertrand Russell Archive.

Sakharov, Andrei: *Vospominaniya*, reprinted by permission of Chekhov Publishing Group. Translated by Richard Lourie © 1990 by Alfred A. Knopf, a division of Random House Inc. Used by permission of Alfred A. Knopf, a division of Random House, Inc.

Strike Committee of the Faculty of Philosophy and Letters of University of Mexico: "The Mexican Student Movement: Its Meaning and Perspectives" from *Mexico '68: The Students Speak*, translated by Richard Garza, Bobby Ortiz, Nell Salm, Linda Wetter, Maria Jose. Reprinted by permission of the Bertrand Russell Archive.

Suri, Jeremi: from *Power and Protest: Global Revolution and the Rise of Détente* © 2003 by the President and Fellows of Harvard College. Reprinted by permission of Harvard University Press.

Vaculík, Ludvík: "Two Thousand Words to Workers, Farmers, Scientists, Artists, and Everyone," 27 June 1968, from *The Party and the People* (London: Allen Lane and Penguin Press, 1973) pp. 261–68 by permission of Allen Lane and Penguin Press and reprinted with permission of St. Martin's Press.

Young Americans for Freedom: "The Sharon Statement," © 2003 by the Young Americans for Freedom. Reprinted by permission of the Young Americans for Freedom.

Zedong, Mao: "Talk to the Leaders of the Centre." 21 July 1966, translated by John Chinnery and Tieyun. © 1974 by Pantheon Books. Reprinted by permission of Random House, Inc.

INDEX

Academic Revolution, The (Reisman and Jencks), 231
Action programme of the Czechoslovak CP, 292
activists, xxiii
    feminist, xix–xx
    see also civil rights movement; demonstrations; Paris student uprising; student protest
Adenauer, Konrad, 132
affluent society, Marcuse on, 72–73, 73, 77, 79, 80
    as affluent warfare state, 77–78
Africa
    Congo
        Guevara in, 61–71
        Marcuse on, 73
        and Cuban revolutionaries, 61
        MLK on independence in, 11–12
African Dream, The: The Diaries of the Revolutionary War in the Congo (Guevara), 61–71
Agnew, Spiro (Vice President), 273
AIDS, 310
Alcatraz Island, occupation of, 312–13
Alexandrov, Anatoly, 117
Allende Gossens, Salvador, xxi, 272, 274, 277
    see also Chile
Amalrik, Andrei, 108
American Golden Age, SDS on, 41
American Indians, rights of, 312–13
Andropov, Yuri, 98, 107, 117
antiballistic missile (ABM) systems, Sakharov on, 87
Antonov, Oleg, 99
apathy, SDS on (*Port Huron Statement*), 48

Argentina
    in meeting on Chile policy, 275, 276–77
    student protest in, 221, 222, 226
"Armageddon between the sexes," Friedan on, 142, 158
arms limitation or control, 319
    in U.S.-Soviet "Basic Principles," 270–71
arms race, and SDS on academia (*Port Huron Statement*), 49
"As Breathing and Consciousness Return" (Solzhenitsyn), 117n
authoritarianism, retreat of, xx
authoritarian personality, Dutschke on, 121–22
authority
    liberal and progressive element in, 316
    student attitudes from diminishing of, 225
    youth culture against, xii
automation
    and Cohn-Bendit on education, 140
    Kennedy on, 29
    Marcuse on, 80, 81

Babitsky, Konstantin, 114, 118n
Bachman, Josef, 118
Baikal, Lake, Sakharov on protection of, 98–102
Ballad of the Grenadier, The (Mexican student poem), 199–200
Ban Gu, 39
Barakov, Innokenty, 290–92, 294
"Basic Principles of Relations Between the United States of America and the Union of Soviet Socialist Republics," xx, 268–72

Beatles, 315
beatniks, Marcuse on, 79
Beria, Lavrenty, 7, 297
Berlin
    and Dutschke in West Berlin, 118, 122,
        125, 128 (*see also* Dutschke, Rudi)
    riots in (and Nanterre students), 232
    students vs. Communists in West
        Berlin, 236
Bil'ak (Czech leader), 182
Bill of Rights for Women, Friedan on,
    144–45, 148, 156, 157–58
Black, Shirley Temple, 152
Black Panthers, xvii
"Black Power" movement 238, 304
blacks (Negroes)
    Friedan on, 142, 152, 154
    MLK on rising consciousness of, 10–18
black separatism, 312
    and Cubans, 237
Bliss, Mrs. Ray, 148
Bloomfield, Richard, 273, 278
Bogoraz, Larisa, 98, 114, 118n
Boldin (Soviet official), 298
Born, Max, 112
bourgeois view of history, Dutschke on,
    128–29
Brandt, Willy, 131, 319
Brazil
    in meeting on Chile policy, 276–77
    student protest in, 226
Brezhnev, Leonid
    in conversation with Dubček (Prague
        Spring), 166–84
    and Czechoslovakian reform, 166
    and détente, 319
    "Basic Principles" on, xx, 272
    and reform forces, 290
    and Sakharov, 95, 101, 107, 114
    and student protest, xviii
    and Trapeznikov, 106
Britain, *see* United Kingdom
Brodsky, Joseph, 103
Brooks, Mary, 147
Brown, Rap, 211, 239
Brzezinski, Zbigniew, 223
Buckley, William F. Jr., 32
Bukovsky, Vladimir, 95
Burdenko (Soviet Academician), 298

bureaucracy
    academic (SDS), 49
    Soviet-style, 304
    students against, 220, 225, 227
bureaucratic centralism, Gorbachev on,
    290
Bush, George W., 322
Butler, Paul, 26

Camacho, Manuel Avila, 194
Cambodia
    human rights denied in, 281
    U.S. bombing of, xxi
Camden Seventeen, 314
capitalism
    contradictions of (Mexican economy),
        197
    Dutschke on, 119, 122–23, 128
    see also economic system (Western);
        market economy
Cárdenas, Lázaro, 194
Carmichael, Stokely, 238
    The Pitfalls of Liberalism, 238–45
Castro, Fidel, xxi, 61, 67, 130–31, 233,
    237, 272
Catholicism and Catholic Church
    in Kennedy's acceptance speech, 26–27
    reform of, 302–3
Ceaucescu, Nicolae, 277
Černik (Czech official), 168, 170, 172,
    176, 181
Chamaleso (Congolese revolutionary),
    68
Charter 77 declaration, xxii, 284–89
chauvinism, retreat of, xx
Chervonenko (Communist official), 178,
    184
Chiang Kai-shek, 261
Chicago, University of, *New University
    Thought*, 233
Chile, 272
    human rights denied in, 281
    U.S. policy toward, xxi, 272–79
    and Kissinger, 254, 272, 274
China
    Cultural Revolution in, xvii–xviii, 36,
        83–85, 318
    Dutschke on, 131
    Mao as opponent of, 319

Red Guards of, xiii, xviii, 83, 220, 318, 319
and democratic vision of socialism, 304
and Deng Tuo on Kingly Way and Tyrannical Way, 35–40
"Great Leap Forward" in, 35, 317
repression in, xiv
vs. Soviet Union, 318
and U.S. policy toward Argentina, 275, 277
U.S. relations with, 259–60
China Story, The (Utley), 284
Chou En-Lai, with Mao and Nixon, 260, 261, 262, 263, 265–66, 267
Christian religion, and colonialism (Fanon), 24
Churchill, Winston, 28
CIA (Central Intelligence Agency)
and 1968 global revolutions, xvii
Restless Youth report of, xii, 216–38
Čierna nad Tisou meeting (Prague Spring), 167, 170, 171, 172, 173, 174, 175, 176, 177, 178, 179, 180, 181, 183
Cisař (Czech official), 174, 177, 179
citizenship participation, students' disregard of (SDS), 48
civil rights, advances in, 312
Civil Rights Act (1964), 157
Civil Rights Act, Title 7, 157
civil rights movement
in CIA report, 219, 221, 233
and confrontation, 221, 231
and LBJ's message to Congress, 50–60
and Martin Luther King Jr., 10
The Rising Tide of Racial Consciousness, 10–18
Selma march, 50, 51, 55, 58
Coe, Frank, 262
Cohn-Bendit, Daniel
achievement of as student, 229
French students' solidarity with, 190
vs. national glory, 226
Pravda's denunciation of, 236
Sartre's interview with, 132–41
on "Stalinists," 236
travels of, 234

Cold War, xiv
détente in, xx–xxii, xxiii, 268–72, 319, 323 (*see also* détente in Cold War)
Dutschke on, 125
end of, 319
and Gorbachev, xiv
international interdependence as result of, 320
and Kennedy, 25
lack of hope over, xvi
Marcuse on, 72
and 1960s leadership, 317
and Reagan, xxii
and Sakharov, 86
in SDS *Port Huron Statement*, 41
and Soviet-funded youth organizations, 237–38
and Soviet repression in Czechoslovakia, xix
and Stalin's death, 1
and student dissidents (CIA report), 225
student revolutionaries' view of, 304
summits and agreements of, 319
superpower force on periphery of, xxi
college, *see* education; students; universities
colonialism
Fanon on, 19, 20–25
in NLF Manifesto, 34
SDS on revolution against, 41–42
Columbia University, student uprising at, 223
emulation of, 231
Comintern, and Hitler, 89–90
Committees of Struggle, in Mexican call for worker/peasant/student alliance, 203–4, 205
Communism and Communists
and CIA report on protest, 216, 218, 235–38
vs. New Left, 233
collapse of, 321
independence of each Party as principle of, 300
in Kennedy's acceptance speech, 28, 31
and MLK on racial discrimination, 13
Mexican Communist Party, 194
Mexican student protests attributed to, 186, 187, 190, 191

Communism and Communists (*continued*)
  and Paris student strike, 133, 236
  Reagan on, 282–83
  and Russian student protests, 226
  and student activists' view of politics,
    225
  and U.S. intervention in Chile, 272
  Utley on, 283–84
  Vaculík on, 159, 160–61, 163
  and Vietnam, 303
  YAF on threat of, 33
  see also Marxist thought
Confrontation
  liberals opposed to (Carmichael), 242
  student belief in (CIA report), 221
  and civil rights movement, 231
Congo
  Guevara's revolutionary efforts in,
    61–71
  Marcuse on, 73
Conquest, Robert, 92
consensus building, need for, 322–23
Constitution (U.S.), Young Americans for
    Freedom on, 33
convergence (West-Soviet)
  dissidents' belief in, xix
  Sakharov on, 86, 102, 104
    Soviet official's attack on, 109
  Solzhenitsyn on, 116
Cooke, Archbishop, 213
Cordoba reform (Argentina, 1918), 222
Corona del Rosal, Alfonso, 191, 195
counter-culture, 304, 12
Cuban Revolution, 303
  and democratic vision of socialism, 304
  Mexican students celebrate, 186
  and student dissidents, 237
Cueto (Mexican student poem), 198–99
cult of an individual or personality
  and Khrushchev on Stalin, 8
  in Sakharov's *Reflections*, 109
cultural exchanges, in U.S.-Soviet "Basic
    Principles," 271
cultural revolution
  1968 revolutions as, xxii–xxiii, 309–16
  and economic conditions, 315–16
  and Italy, 315
  and underclass as revolutionary
    force, 314–15

Cultural Revolution (China), xvii–xviii,
    36, 83, 318
  Dutschke on, 131
  Mao as opponent of, 319
  Mao's talk to leaders on, 83–85
  Red Guards in, xiii, xviii, 83, 220, 318,
    319
"culture of narcissism," 322
culture wars, 305
cybernetic revolution
  Hoffman on, 207
  see also automation
Czechoslovakia
  and Charter 77 declaration, 284–89
  Czech-Slovak federation in, 172–73
  dissidents in, xix
  in Gorbachev's memoir, 299–300
  Prague Spring in, 102–3, 166–84, 303,
    318–19 (*see also* Prague Spring)
  "socialism with a human face" in, xiv,
    158

Daley, Richard J., 216
Daniel, Yuli, 95, 98, 103, 113
"Danny the Red," *see* Cohn-Bendit,
    Daniel
Dar es Salaam, Che Guevara in, 64, 67,
    68
Davidson, Carl, 233–34
decolonization
  Fanon as exponent of, 18–25
  and revolution in Africa, 61
Delone, Vadim, 114, 118n
democracy
  in Czechoslovakia (Vaculík), 164
  LBJ on, 52
  and 1968 aftermath, 306, 307–8
  participatory (SDS), 46–47
  Sakharov for, 104
  as revolutionaries' vision, 304
  SDS on (*Port Huron Statement*), 46–47
democratic centralism, Khrushchev on, 8
"democratic deficit," 321
Democratic Party National convention
    (1968), demonstrations at, 206,
    208, 213, 216
demonstrations
  anti-Vietnam War, 215, 217
  in Communist countries, 226

at Democratic Party Convention
(1968), 206, 208, 213, 216
as focal point of protest (CIA report),
231
against international institutions, 321
Keniston on requirements for, 229
by Mexican students, 186–90, 191
Mexico's prohibition of, 191
in Soviet Union (Sakharov), 93–94, 95
against invasion of Czechoslovakia,
114, 115–16, 117
see also civil rights movement; sit-ins;
student protest
Deng Tuo, 35–36
The Kingly Way and the Tyrannical Way,
35–40
depersonalization, SDS on (*Port Huron
Statement*), 44
and object of violence, 47
Destruction of Nature, The (Komarov), 98–99
détente in Cold War, xx–xxii, xxiii, 319, 323
and "Basic Principles," 268–72
as counterrevolution, 320, 321
and globalization, 321
and government repression, xx, 284
Diaz Ordaz, Gustavo, 184, 186, 187,
192, 192–93, 193, 195, 200
"diminishing expectations," 322
Dirksen, Everett, 148
disarmament, in U.S.-Soviet "Basic
Principles," 271
dissidents (dissidence)
CIA on, 217–38
and Eastern Bloc student socialists, 306
Sakharov's intervention for, 95–96
in Soviet-bloc states, xix, xxii
repression of, 284
Soviet laws for prosecution of, 90–91
Dobrovolsky, Alexei, 95
Dobrynin, Anatoly, in conversation with
LBJ and Rostow, 247–54
Dream We Lost, The (Utley), 284
Drell, Sidney, 87
Dremlyuga, Vladimir, 114, 118n
Drugs, faith in, 312
Dubček, Alexander, 300
in conversation with Brezhnev (Prague
Spring), 166–84
and Sakharov on Soviet invasion, 114

Dulles, John Foster, 265
Dutschke, Rudi, 118
achievement of as student, 229
The Students and the Revolution, 118–32
travels of, 234
Duvalier, François, and Dutschke, 131
Dylan, Bob, 211

Eastern bloc, *see* Soviet bloc
Echeverria, Luis, 191, 195
economic freedom, and political freedom
(YAF), 33
economic system (Western)
Dutschke on, 119
Hoffman on abundance of, 206–7
Marcuse on, 73
of Mexico, 192–93, 194, 197, 201
call for changes in, 202–3
SDS on (*Port Huron Statement*), 46–47
see also capitalism; socialism; work
economic system, global, 315–16
economic system (Soviet), reforms
attempted in, 290, 291–92, 294
economic system (Czech), Vaculík on,
162, 163–64
education
Cohn-Bendit on, 139–40
Dutschke on role of, 126–27
growth of, 227
see also students; universities
Efimov, Boris, 107
Egypt, student protest in, 226
Ehrenburg, Ilya, 90
Eisenhower, Dwight D.
imminent death of, 248
Kennedy on, 27
trip to Tokyo canceled (1960), 221,
222
and women, 151
environmental problems, Sakharov's
involvement with, 98–99
and Lake Baikal, 98–102
Equal Employment Opportunity
Commission, and sex
discrimination, 157
Equal Rights Amendment, 145, 146,
156, 157
Eros and Civilization (Marcuse), Political
Preface of, 72–82

Esenin-Volpin, Alexander, 93
European Monetary Union, and Italian
     austerity measures, 315
European Union, and "democratic
     deficit," 321
Evergreen Review, 235

Fainberg, Viktor, 114, 118*n*
Fanon, Frantz, xvi, 18, 233
     on violence, xvii, 18–25
farm loans, demand for (Mexico), 204
fascism
     Carmichael on, 243, 244
     Dutschke on, 121, 122
     see also neo-fascism
feminine mystique, 150, 151, 311
     as natural purity mystique, 152
Feminine Mystique, The (Friedan), xix, 141
feminism
     Betty Friedan on, 141–58
     natural purity mystique as
          perversion of, 152
     phases of, 314
     in revolutionaries' vision, 304
feminist activists, xix–xx
foreign policy
     as social policy, 323
     YAF on, 33
For a Worker/Peasant/Student Alliance
     (National Strike Committee,
     Mexico), 200–206
France
     New Philosophy in, 306
     number of students in, 227
     and race relations, 312
Frankel, Charles, 150
freedom
     Marcuse on, 74
     YAF on indivisibility of, 33
freedom of expression
     Charter 77 on, 285–86
     Sakharov for, 104
     Vaculík on, 162
freedom of the press, Vaculík for, 165
Free Speech Movement at Berkeley,
     Marcuse on, 79
French, Eleanor Clark, 146
Friedan, Betty, xix–xx, 141–42
     on politics of sex, 142–58

Fritchey, Clayton, 151
Fronte de Force, Congo, and Guevara's
     Congolese expedition, 71
Furness, Betty, 143

Gainesville Eight, 314
Galanskov, Yuri, 95, 103
Galbraith, John Kenneth, 255, 321
Gandhi, Mahatma, MLK on, 14, 15
Gaulle, Charles de, xviii, 317
     and Fanon on colonialism, 24
     and French women, 151–52
     in Mao-Nixon conversation, 263
     and students, 225, 226
Gbenye (Congolese revolutionary), 64, 65
Geilikman, Boris, 88, 90
Ginsberg, Allen, 215
Ginzburg, Alexander, 95, 103
Ginzburg, Eugenia, 92, 106
Ginzburg, Vitaly, 88, 96
Glagolev, Oleg, 284
glasnost (public disclosure), and Sakharov
     on dissent, 92
Glassboro summit meeting, 247, 253
globalization, 319–20
     and détente, 321
     and dispossessed as militants, 323
     threat from, 315
global revolutions of 1968, xiii, 307–8,
     318–19
     aftermath of, 305, 310–11, 312–14,
          315–16
     conservative politics, 316, 319, 321
     culture wars, 305
     disillusionment, 317–18, 320
     in Italy, 315
     leftist-to-liberal transformation, 305–7
     and 1968 seen as rehearsal, 307
     CIA on, xvii (*see also* student protest)
     as cultural revolution, xxii–xxiii,
          309–16
     and economic conditions, 315–16
     and Italy, 315
     and underclass as revolutionary
          force, 314–15
     and détente, xx–xxii, 319 (*see also*
          détente in Cold War)
     as four revolutions, 302, 304
     against conventional customs, 302

of new sensibility, 302–3
    against totalitarian Left, 303, 304
    against Western imperialism, 303, 304
    living history of, xxiii
    as lost opportunity, 317
    origins of, xv–xvii
    and personal attitudes vs. new
        institutions, xxii
    reactions to and legacies of, xx–xxii
    and sobering reversals, 308
    as unexpected, xi
    utopian visions in, xxii, 75, 301, 302,
        304–5
    see also 1960s
Gnedin, Evgeny, 106
Goethe, Johann Wolfgang von, and
    Sakharov, 105
Gomulka, Wladyslaw, 221
Gorbachev, Mikhail, xiv, xxii, 290
    Memoirs of, 290–300
    with Reagan, 283
Gorbanevskaya,, Natasha, 114
Grand Central Station, Hoffman on
    party in, 212–13, 214
"grapevine effect," 232
"Great Leap Forward" in China, 35, 317
Great Marxist Fallacy, 312
Great Proletarian Cultural Revolution, see
    Cultural Revolution (China)
"great society," LBJ's vision of, 50
Great Terror, The (Conquest), 92
Grigorenko, Pyotr, 111
guerrilla warfare, Marcuse on, 76, 78
Guevara, Ernesto "Che," xvi, xviii, 61
    Congo diaries of, 61–71
    and Dutschke, 118
    and Hoffman, 206, 211
    and student protestors (CIA report),
        216, 233
Gulag Archipelago, The (Solzhenitsyn), 116
guns, Hoffman on prevalence of, 211

Haig, Alexander A., 273
Haiti, and Dutschke, 131
Hájek, Jiří, 289
Harding, Warren G., 151
Harrington, Michael, 321
Harrower, Tina, 148
Havel, Václav, 289, 307

Hayden, Tom, 313
Heath, Edward, 263
Heckler, Margaret, 148
Hegel, G. W. F., 307
Helms, Richard, 273–74
Helsinki Final Act, 284, 285, 288
Henri, Ernst (Semyon Rostovsky), 88–90,
    95, 97
Hicks, Louise Day, 152
Hidalgo, Father, 189
hippie movement or hipsters, 304
    Hoffman on, 208 (see also Yippies)
    Marcuse on, 79
historical progress, confidence in, 308
history, x
    Dutschke on, 128–29
    of globalization, 321
    in global terms, 319–20
    Hegel on, 307
    of 1960s, 322
    of 1968 global revolutions, xxiii
    of Soviet-Polish relations, 297–98
    of Texas (LBJ on), 252–53
Hitler, Adolf, and Comintern, 89–90
Hitler Over Europe? (Rostovsky), 90
Ho Chi Minh, 236
Hoffman, Abbie, 206
    interview with, 206–16
human relationships, SDS on (Port Huron
    Statement), 45
human rights
    Charter 77 on, 284–89
    and Chilean junta, 278–79
    and LBJ on voting rights, 54
    Kennedy on, 29
    and Reagan on Vietnam, 281
    Sakharov on abuses of, 91
human rights movement (Soviet Union),
    103
Humphrey, Hubert, 26, 150, 154, 156,
    157, 211, 215, 243
Hungarian uprising (1956), 232
    students in, 221
Hungary, reforms in, 296
Hurwitch, Robert A., 273

idealism
    Carmichael on, 244
    as discredited, 322

imperialism, American (Yankee)
  Guevara on, 63, 66
  and Kabila, 64
  worldwide revolution against, 303
India, in Nixon-Mao conversation, 263,
    264
individualism, SDS on (*Port Huron
    Statement*), 45–46
Indonesia, student activism in, 222
industrial society, and CIA on youthful
    dissidence, xii–xiii, 217
Institutional Revolutionary Party (PRI),
    Mexico, 184, 191, 195, 201
international authorities, détente as
    forestalling hopes for, 321
International Union of Students (IUS),
    235, 237–38
International Vietnam Congress, 118
Internet, and globalization, 319
Ioffe, Boris, 91
Iran (Persia), and Dutschke, 131
Irwin, John N. II, 273, 276
Italy, in aftermath of revolutions, 315

Jackson, George, 313
Japan
  in Nixon-Mao meeting, 264
  number of students in, 227
  student protest in, 221, 222
Jaruzelski, Wojciech, 295–96, 297
Jeanette Rankin Brigade, 151–52
Jefferson, Thomas, and Vietnam policy
    (Hoffman), 206
Jencks, Christopher, 231
Jenkins, Roy, 313
Jiminez, Perez, 221
Johnson, Ladybird, 143–44, 150
Johnson, Lyndon (LBJ), xviii, xxi, 50
  and CIA report on youthful dissidence,
    216
  civil-rights message of, 50–60
  in conversation (Prague Spring) with
    Dobrynin and Rostow, 247–54
  as Kennedy running mate, 26
  and MLK's death, 208
  in Nixon-Mao conversation, 265, 266
  and Vietnam War, 318
  and women, 143, 150
  Yippie sit-in invitation for, 213

Johnson Administration, and sex
    discrimination, 157
Journey into the Whirlwind (Ginzburg), 92

Kabila, Laurent, 64, 65, 67, 68, 69
Kamenev, Lev, 5–6
Kania, S., 295
Kanza (Congolese revolutionary), 64, 65
Kapitsa, Pyotr, 88
Katyn massacre, 297–98
Keldysh, Mstislav, 101
Keniston, Kenneth, 229
Kennedy, John F., xvi, 25, 317
  nomination acceptance address of
    (1960), 25–32
  sex appeal of, 151
  and Vietnam War, 318
  and South Vietnam army, 256
Kennedy, Richard T., 273
Kennedy, Robert, 154, 156
Kerensky, Aleksandr, 6
Keyserling, Mary, 157
Khachaturova, Tamara, 115
Khan, Yahya, 265
Khariton (Soviet official), 106–7, 108, 110
Khaustov, Viktor, 95
Khrushchev, Nikita, xvi, 1, 317
  fall of, 226–27
  Kirov murder commission established
    by, 93
  reforms of, 293
  20th Party Congress Speech (anti-Stalin,
    1956), 1–10, 232
Kiesinger, Kurt Georg, xiii, 131
Kiesinger government, 226
Kigoma, Tanzania, 64, 69
King, Coretta, 150
King, Martin Luther Jr., xvi, 10
  assassination of, 208, 238
  and Carmichael, 238
  The Rising Tide of Racial Consciousness,
    10–18
  tribute to (Hoffman), 213
Kingly Way and the Tyrannical Way, The
    (Deng Tuo), 35–40
Kirillin, Vladimir, 96
Kirov, Sergei, 93
Kissinger, Henry, xxi, 254–55
  and Chile, 272, 273, 274

Galbraith correspondence with, 255–59
    with Nixon and Mao, 260, 261, 262,
    263, 266, 267
Kolmogorov, Andrei, 89
Komarov, Boris, 98–99
Koones, Sarah, 155
Kosygin, Alexei, 88, 101, 247, 249,
    253–54
"Kosygin reforms," 292, 293, 294
Krassner, Paul, 212
Kriegel (Czech official), 174, 177, 179,
    179–80
Ku Klux Klan, MLK on, 12
Kurganov, Professor, 117
Kuznetsov, Viktor, 93
Ky, Nguyen Cao, and Dutschke, 131

labor unions, see unions
Laird, Melvin, 273, 275
"language of dissent," 318
Laotians, human rights denied to, 281
Lasch, Christopher, 322
Lashkova, Vera, 95, 103
Latin America (South America)
    Communist-controlled student
        organizations in, 237
    in deliberation on U.S. Chile policy,
        277
    guerrilla wars in, 306
    repression in, xiv
"law and order"
    demands for, xviii–xix
    LBJ on respect for, 57
    liberals' call for (Carmichael), 242
    women at Republican convention for,
        149
Leary, Timothy, 215–16
Lebedeva, N. S., 297
Lenárt (Czech official), 168
Lenin, V. I.
    Khrushchev on, 1, 2, 4–9
    popularity of as author, 111
    Solzhenitsyn on, 116
Leontovich, Mikhail, 88, 98
Let History Judge (Medvedev), 92–93
liberal democracy, as aftermath of 1968
    revolutions, 306, 307–8
liberalism and liberals
    Carmichael on, 238–45

MLK on, 13–14
    in Mexico, 195
    and Sakharov's Reflections, 111
    SDS on (Port Huron Statement), 43
    and Stalin, 90
liberation theology, 302–3
lifestyle, and 1960s activism, xxiii
Lifshitz, Ilya, 96
Likhota (Soviet official), 294
Lincoln, Abraham, LBJ's appeal to, 55
Lincoln, George A., 273, 275, 276
Lindsay, John, 213
Lisichkin, Gennady, 291, 291–92
Little Rock, civil rights movement in,
    12
Litvinov, Pavel, 114, 118n
Liu Xiang, 36–37
Lloyd George, David, 31
López Mateos, Adolfo, 192
Lord, Winston, 260
Lowell, Robert, 146
Lusia, 104–5

"machine, the"
    Marcuse on revolt against, 76
    Eugene McCarthy against (Friedan),
        145
"Make love, not war," Marcuse on, 79
Malyarov, Mikhail, 98
Manicheanism, and Fanon on colonists'
    picture of natives, 18, 23–24
Maoism
    in Peruvian Andes, 306
    of student dissidents, 236
Mao Zedong, xiii, xx, 317
    in conversation with Nixon, 260–68
    and Cultural Revolution, xvii–xviii, 83,
        318
    as opponent, 319
    Talk to Leaders of the Centre (1966),
        83–85
    and "Great Leap Forward," 35
    popularity of as author, 111
    and student protestors (CIA report),
        216, 236
Marchenko, Anatoly, 113
Marcuse, Herbert, xvi, 72–82, 233
    and Dutschke, 118
Marwick on, 314

market economy
    and Marcuse on repressive system,
        81
    YAF espousal of, 33
    see also capitalism; economic system
Martin, Graham, 276
Marxist-Leninist liberation movements,
    303
Marxist thought
    and Dutschke
        on Left in Fifties, 122
        on revolutionary organization, 129
    and Fanon on colonialism, 22
    Great Marxist Fallacy, 312
    Marcuse on, 75–76
    rebirth of interest in, 232
    and Sakharov, 105
    see also Communism and Communists
Masengo (Congolese revolutionary), 68
material circumstances, upward trend in,
    315
mathematics, Sakharov on teaching of,
    89
Mauriac, François, 24
Mbili (Cuban revolutionary), 67
McCarthy, Eugene, 145, 156
McCarthy (Joseph) period
    and court victories of protesters, 314
    SDS on (*Port Huron Statement*), 47
meaning
    pre-1960s lack of, xvi
    SDS on
        as human goal, 45
        work lacking in, 41
measured judgment, 313–14, 315, 316
media
    and Hippies (Hoffman), 209, 214
    New York Times, 108, 209, 211, 213
    and student protest (CIA report),
        222–23, 231–32
    underground press, 209, 211, 215
    and violence (Hoffman), 215
    see also samizdat
Medvedev, Alexander, 92
Medvedev, Roy, 92–93, 97, 98, 102, 103,
    106
Medvedev, Zhores, 92, 105
Merkulov (Soviet authority), 297
Merman, Ethel, 143

Mexican student poems, 198–200
Mexico, 184–85
    economic and political developments
        in, 192–95, 201
    protests and violence in (summer
        1968), 185–92
    revolution against leftist dictatorships
        in, 303
    student movement in, 184, 195–97 in
        CIA report, 226
    "Tlatelolco Massacre" in, 184, 185
    university governance in, 230
    worker/peasant/student alliance called
        for in, 200–206
Mezhirov, Alexander, 105
Michnik, Adam, 307
Millbrook, Leary community in, 216
Mills, C. Wright, 233
Mitchell, John N., 273
Mitoudidi (Congolese revolutionary), 68
Mlynar, Zdenek, 292, 299
Moja, Comandante (Cuban
        revolutionary), 67
Molotov, V. M., 298
Montgomery, Alabama, civil rights
        movement in, 12
Moorer, 275
moral authority
    student attitudes from diminishing of,
        225
    see also authority
moral strength
    Kennedy on slippage in, 29
    and YAF on government interference,
        33
Morrison, Toni, 313
"Movement," and under-class, 315
Mulele (Congolese revolutionary), 64
multicultural societies, progress toward
        (Marwick), 313
My Country and the World (Sakharov), 87
My Testimony (Marchenko), 113
myth(s)
    moral language as (SDS), 43
    Yippies as (Hoffman), 208, 210, 214

NAACP, 207
Nachmanoff, Arnold, 273
Nagy, Imre, 221

Nanterre
  faculty members at, 230
  student uprising in, 224, 237 (*see also* Paris student uprising)
  and "grapevine effect," 232
"narcissism," détente as encouraging, 322
National Commission on the Causes and Prevention of Violence, 220
national liberation, Fanon on, 18
National Liberation Front for South Vietnam (NLF), xvii, 303
  Manifesto of (1960), 34–35
National Mobilization to End the War in Vietnam, 210
National Strike Committee (Mexico), *For a Worker/Peasant/Student Alliance,* 200–206
NATO (North Atlantic Treaty Organization)
  Dutschke against, 127, 131
  Poland's jump to feared, 295
  and student protest (CIA report), 226
Nazarov, Anatoly, 112, 112n
neo-colonialism
  and Che Guevara, 61–62, 66
  Marcuse on, 79
"neo-conservative" writers, x
neo-fascism, 118
  Dutschke on, 118, 119, 121–22
Neustadt, Richard, 220
New Frontier of Kennedy, 25, 30, 31
New Left, xv, xvi, 234
  CIA report on, 233
  Students for a Democratic Society as, 40
  and under-class, 315
New Philosophy, 306
New Politics, 143, 147, 149, 150, 154, 156, 232
New Right, xv
  Young Americans for Freedom, 32
Newton, Huey, 239
New University Thought, 233
New York City, Hoffman on Yippie events in, 212–15
New York Times
  Hoffman on, 209, 211, 213
  and Sakharov's *Reflections,* 108

Ngo Dinh Diem, 34
Nietzsche, Friedrich, 74–75
Nikolaevich, Leonid, 293
Nikolsky, Nikolai, 99
1960s
  accomplishments of, 312, 315, 316, 320
  and relations between sexes, 314
  close of, 317, 319
  experiences of, x
  national focus of, xi
  as historical dividing line, xii
  partisan perspectives on, x
  rhetoric vs. capabilities in, 317, 318, 320–21
1968, global revolutions of, *see* global revolutions of 1968
Nixon, Richard, xx, xxi, 268, 319
  and American Indians, 313
  anti-crime stance of, 149
  "Basic Principles" signed by, 272
  and Carmichael on liberals, 243
  and Chile, 273–74, 275–278
  in conversation with Mao, 260–68
  Kennedy on, 27, 28, 29
  and sex appeal, 151
  and women, 151, 154, 156
Nixon administration, and Pinochet government, 272
non-Marxist social criticism, 233
nonviolent resistance, MLK on, 14, 17
"normalcy," Kennedy on, 31
North Atlantic Treaty Organization, *see* NATO
Novotny, Antonin, 292
NOW, Friedan at conference of, 144
nuclear research, Sakharov in, 86
nuclear warfare
  Sakharov on, 87–88, 102, 104, 111
  and U.S.-Soviet "Basic Principles," 269–70

Oak and the Calf, The (Solzhenitsyn), 116
Olympic Games in Mexico City (1968), 184, 190–91
One-Dimensional Man (Marcuse), 74
organized labor, *see* unions
Orlov (paper-industry minister), 99, 100
overdeveloped countries, Marcuse on, 77

Pakistan, in Nixon-Mao conversation, 263
Panama
    student protest in, 226
    and U.S. policy, 279
Paris Commune, and Mao, 83
Paris student uprising (1968), 132
    Cohn-Bendit interview on, 133–41
    and Communists, 236, 237
    and Nanterre, 224, 237 (see also Nanterre)
Parsadanova, V. S., 297
participatory democracy, SDS on (Port Huron Statement), 46–47
party politics, see political parties
paternalistic assumptions, 1960s attacks on, xii
Patočka, Jan, 289
Pavlenkov, Vladlen, 112, 112n
peaceful coexistence, 269
peasants, organization of (Mexico), 204
Pelikán (Czech official), 168, 174, 177
perestroika, 293, 299
permissiveness, 310
permissiveness, rejection of, see "law and order"
Peron, Juan, 221
Persia, and Dutschke, 131
personhood
    correction of flaw in, 303
    Dutschke on, 127
"peaceful coexistence," xx, xxi
"people power," xviii
Peterson, Elly, 148
Peterson, Esther, 157
Petryanov-Sokolov, Igor, 99, 100
Pinochet, Augusto, 272
Pire, Georges, 112
planned obsolescence, Marcuse on, 73
Plisetskaya, Maya, 88
Poland
    Communist student leadership in, 235
    in Gorbachev's memoirs
        and Katyn massacre, 297–98
        Solidarity crisis, 294–97
    student protest in, 227
    students in 1956 uprising in, 221
polarization, 239
police brutality, student protest over, 223

"political correctness," 312
political freedom, and economic freedom (YAF), 33
political idealism, as discredited, 322
political language of early 1960s, xvii
    see also "language of dissent"
political parties
    in Cohn-Bendit interview, 132
    Dutschke on, 126
    Solzhenitsyn on, 117
    student attitudes toward (CIA report), 225
    see also party politics
"polymorphous sexuality," Marcuse on, 75
Ponomarev, Sergei, 112, 112n
Popper, Karl (Ambassador), 278, 279
Poremsky, Vladimir, 112
Port Huron Statement (SDS, 1962), xv–xvi, 40–50
"postmodern" age, 319
poverty
    continued prevalence of, 320–21
    in LBJ's message to Congress, 56, 59
    and Kennedy's New Frontier, 30
    in Marcuse's critique, 74
Powell, Enoch, 313
power, Carmichael on, 243–44
Power and Protest (Suri), xxiii
Prague Spring, xxi, 102–3, 303, 318–19
    Brezhnev-Dubček conversation on, 166–84
    in Gorbachev's memoirs, 292–93
    issue of Soviet intervention in, 110
    Soviet repression of, xix, xxi, 112–13, 166
        attempts at repudiation of, 299–300
        demonstrations against, 114, 115–16, 117
        and Gorbachev, 290, 293
        LBJ's tacit acceptance of, 247–52
    Vaculík on, 158–165
    vision of, 304
Prayer to a gorilla (Mexican student poem), 199
President's Commission on Civil Disorders, 220
press (newspapers)
    underground, 209, 211, 215
    see also media

PRI (Institutional Revolutionary Party),
Mexico, 184, 191, 195, 201
Price, Margaret, 147
Priest, Ivy Baker, 149
progress, confidence in, 308
proletarian internationalism, and Che
Guevara on foreign
revolutionaries, 61
protest, *see* civil rights movement;
demonstrations; Paris student
uprising; student protest
"protest-prone personality'" (Keniston),
229

Quant, Mary, 315

race relations
advances in, 311, 312
and Fanon on decolonization, 18–25
LBJ on, 50–60
Martin Luther King Jr. on, 10–18
in SDS critique, 40–41
racism, 1960s attacks on, xii, xx
radicalization, 224, 316–17
Rakowski, Mieczyslaw, 296
Rayburn, Sam, 252
Reagan, Ronald, xxii, 280, 310, 316
on Communism, 282–83
emotional appeal of to women, 149
and Gorbachev, 283
on Vietnam War, 280–82
Reality Principle, Marcuse's version of,
75
Red Army Faction (West Germany), xvii
Red Guards (China), xiii, xviii, 83, 220,
318, 319
*Reflections on Progress, Peaceful Coexistence, and
Intellectual Freedom* (Sakharov), 96,
97, 102, 104–12
reform
and Brezhnev on Czechoslovakia, 166
of Catholic Church, 302–3
of Czechoslovak Party (Sakharov), 112
Dutschke on, 129
of Polish economy, 296
of Soviet economy (Gorbachev), 290,
291–92, 294
from student uprising (Cohn-Bendit),
135–36

of university (Cohn-Bendit), 123,
138–39, 140
reform-repression dualism, xiii–xiv
Reisman, David, 231
religion
and uprising of spirit, 302
see also Catholicism and Catholic
Church
repression
and détente, xx, 284
nation-to-nation differences in, xiii–xiv
of Prague Spring, xix, xxi, 112–13, 166
attempts at repudiation of, 299–300
demonstrations against, 114,
115–16, 117
and Gorbachev, 290, 293
LBJ's tacit acceptance of, 247–52
in Soviet bloc, 284
in Soviet Union, xiv, xix
in Western democracies, xiii–xiv
and Marcuse on affluent society,
80–81
see also "law and order"
Restless Youth (CIA report), 216–38
Reve, Karel van het, 108
Revenko (Soviet official), 298
revolution
advocates of, xvi
and Carmichael on moderates, 238
Cohn-Bendit on, 134, 136–37
and "material demands," 139
Dutschke's call for, 125, 129–32
vs. evolution (Sakharov), 105
and Che Guevara in Congo, 61–71
Hoffman on, 210
and Mao on Cultural Revolution, 84
Marcuse on, 75
Marwick's view of, 314
and solidarity with wretched of
earth, 76
Paris student uprising as threat of, 132
see also global revolutions of 1968
"revolutionary vanguard" theory, Cohn-
Bendit on, 136–37
Rhodesia, human rights denied in
(Reagan), 281
riots, in CIA report, 231
Rising Tide of Racial Consciousness, The
(King), 10–18

Rockefeller, Nelson, 154, 156, 213
rock and roll music, 302, 311
Rogers, William P., 273, 274–75, 275,
    276, 278
Rogozin (cellulose specialist), 99
Roosevelt, Franklin D.
    in LBJ's message to Congress, 60
    Kennedy's appeal to, 27–28
Rossiter, Cal, 155–56
Rostovsky, Semyon, 89–90
    see also Henri, Ernst
Rostow, Walt, in conversation with LBJ
    and Dobrynin, 247–54
Rubin, Jerry, 212
Rudd, Mark, 235
Rusk, Dean, 248, 250
Ryan, Hewsen, 278

Sadykov, F. B., 293–94
Sakharov, Andrei, xix, 86
    Memoirs of, 86–117
Sakharaov, Klava, 94, 103, 111
samizdat
    for officials, 97
    and Sakharov, 92, 107
        for Reflections, 111
    Skurlatov document as, 94
Sartre, Jean-Paul (Cohn-Bendit
    interview), 132–41
Savio, Mario, 128
Schlesinger, Arthur Jr., 146
science
    Dutschke on, 120–21, 125
    and Kennedy's New Frontier, 30
    in U.S.-Soviet cooperation in ("Basic
        Principles"), 271
"science of human relations," Marcuse
    on, 72
SDI (Strategic Defense Initiative),
    Sakharov talk on, 87
Seeger, Nika Satter, 187
Selma march, 50, 51, 55, 58
"separate but equal" facilities, Supreme
    Court decision against, 11
sex discrimination
    as diminished, 314
    Friedan on, 142, 146
    and "Armageddon between the
        sexes," 142, 158
    Humphrey's opposition to, 157

sexual liberation, 314
Shakhmagonov, Fyodor, 114–15
Shang Yang, 38
Sharon Statement (Young Americans for
    Freedom), 32–33
Shelepen, A., 297, 298
Sholokhov, Mikhail, 95, 115
Sierra, Javier Barros (Rector of National
    University), 189, 190, 195
Sima Qian (Chinese historian), 38
Sinyavsky, Andrei, 95, 98, 103
sit-ins
    and CIA report on dissidence, 218
    by southern students (MLK on), 12,
        15–16, 17
Six Crises, The (Nixon), 267
"68 generation," xi–xii
    see also global revolutions of 1968
Skurlatov, Valery, 94
Slavsky, Efim, 96, 100, 108–10, 116
Smrkovský (Czech official), 114, 170,
    172, 176
Snow, Edgar, 268
social change, radical demands for, xvi–xvii
Social Democracy, Comintern's view of
    vs. Hitler, 89–90
social engineering, Marcuse on, 72
socialism
    in aftermath of 1968 revolutions, 306
    in Czechoslovakia (Vaculík), 161, 165
    general crisis of (Gorbachev), 295
    and Mao on Cultural Revolution, 84,
        85
    reformers' dream of, 304
    Sakharov vs. Born on, 112
    SDS (Port Huron Statement) on, 43
    Solzhenitsyn on, 116
"socialism with a human face," in
    Czechoslovakia, xiv
    and Prague Spring, 158
    Sakharov on, 103
Socrates, on faults of students, 221
Solidarity, 295
Solzhenitsyn, Alexander, 105, 111, 115–17
soul force, MLK on, 15
Soumaliot (Congolese revolutionary), 64,
    65
South Africa
    human rights denied in, 281
    Marcuse on, 73

South America, see Latin America
South Korea
  in Mao-Nixon conversation, 266
  student protest in, 221
South Vietnam, xxi
  see also Vietnam War
Soviet bloc
  bureaucracy as dominating, 304
  and Charter 77 declaration, 284
  dissidents in, xix, xxii
  and Khrushchev's denunciation of
    Stalin, 1
  and student dissidence, 236
  student socialists evolved into liberal
    dissidents in, 306, 307
  see also Czechoslovakia; Poland
Soviet-Polish war (1920), 297
Soviet Union (USSR)
  and "Basic Principles" of relations
    with U.S., xx, 268–72
  vs. China, 318
  and Cuba (Nixon), 277
  dissidents in, xiii, xix
    and anti-dissident laws, 90–91
    repression of, xiv
  and Khrushchev's anti-Stalin speech,
    1–10, 232
  in Nixon-Mao meeting, 264
  number of students in, 227
  "period of stagnation" in, 294
  "Prague Spring" suppressed by, xix,
    xxi, 112–13, 166
  attempts at repudiation of, 299–300
  demonstration against, 114, 115–16,
    117
  and Gorbachev, 290, 293
  LBJ's tacit acceptance of, 247–52
  and Reagan, xxii
    with Gorbachev, 283
  and revolution against dictatorships of
    left, 303
  and U.S. policy toward Argentina, 275,
    277
Spanish Civil War, 225
spirit of 1968, 305
spontaneity, Cohn-Bendit on, 132, 137
Springer concern, Dutschke on, 131
Stalin, Josef, 1
  and Hitler, 90
  and Katyn massacre, 298

Khrushchev's speech denouncing,
    1–10, 232
  Medvedev book on, 92–93, 106
  and Polish Communist Party, 297
  Sakharov opposes rehabilitation of,
    88–89, 104
  Solzhenitsyn on, 116
  and student protest (CIA report), 226
Stalinism
  and Katyn massacre, 297–98
  Prague Spring attacks on Soviet
    leaders for, 169
  SDS on, 44
  and West Berlin students on
    Communism, 236
Stevenson, Adlai, 25, 26
Strauss, Franz-Josef, and Dutschke, 131
student movement, Cohn-Bendit on, 138
  and workers, 134–35
student movement (China), Mao on, 84
student movement (Mexico), 184, 195–97
  in worker/peasant/student alliance,
    200–206
student movement (U.S.), women
    empowered in, 155
student poems, Mexican, 198–200
student protest
  CIA on, 220–23
  and Communists, 235–38
  and faculties, 230–31
  intellectual inspiration for, 232–34
  international contacts within, 234–35
  motivations behind, 223, 224–27
  process of, 223–24
  social and demographic context of,
    227–32
  and violence, 231 (see also violence)
  as against conventional custom, 302
  as new sensibility, 302–3
  retrospective view of, 307
  see also demonstrations; civil rights
    movement; Paris student uprising
students
  alienation of (Bloomfield), 279
  and CIA on dissidence, 218
    historical view of, 221
  international identification of, 232
  in Mexican protests, 185–92
  problematic definition of (Cohn-Bendit
    interview), 140–41

students (*continued*)
  SDS on (*Port Huron Statement*), 47–50
  see also education; universities
Students for a Democratic Society, xv, 40
  and Hayden, 313
  Port Huron Statement, 40–50
Students and the Revolution, The (Dutschke),
  118–32
student uprising (Paris 1968), *see* Paris
  student uprising
Studies on the Left, 233
suffragette leaders, 151
Suslov, Mikhail, 97, 296
Svetlichny, Ivan, 95
Svoboda (Czech official), 170
Swedish society, Dutschke on, 127–28,
  131–32
Symington, Stuart, 26

Taiwan, in Mao-Nixon conversation, 264
Tamm, Igor, 102
Tang Wen-sheng, 260
Tanzania, and Che Guevara's Congolese
  venture, 63, 64, 69
television, and Hoffman, 209, 211
terrorism
  alienation as source of, 323
  failure to seek explanation for, 322
  individual liberties sacrificed in fight
    for, 322
terrorist attacks of 11 September, 319
Tet Offensive, 303
Texas history, LBJ to Dobrynin on,
  252–53
Thatcher, Margaret, 310, 316
thermonuclear warfare
  Sakharov on, 87–88, 102, 104, 111
  and U.S.-Soviet "Basic Principles,"
    269–70
Thieu, Nguyen Van, and Dutschke, 131
Thompson, Tommy, 254
Title 7, Civil Rights Act, 157
Tito, 277
"Tlatelolco Massacre," Mexico, 184, 185
tourism, in U.S.-Soviet "Basic Principles,"
  271
Trapeznikov, Sergei, 106
Trotskyites
  Khrushchev on, 2–3, 6
  and Mexican protest accusations, 190

Truman, Harry S., 26, 60, 265
Tshombe, Moise-Kapenda, 66
Tsirkov, 96
Tuchman, Jessie, 155
Turkey, student protest in, 221
Tverdokhlebov, Andrei, 95

Ulbricht, Walter, 166–67
Uncommitted, The (Keniston), 229
under-class, 314–15
underdeveloped countries, and worldwide dissidence, 217
underground press, 209, 211, 215
Union Nationale des Etudiants de France
  (UNEF), 140, 233
unions (organized labor)
  and equal opportunity for women, 156
  Marcuse on, 79, 81–82
  in Mexico, 201, 203
  in 1989 vision, 308
  and Paris student uprising (1968), 132
  Cohn-Bendit on, 133
Union of Soviet Socialist Republics, *see*
  Soviet Union
United Kingdom (Britain)
  number of students in, 227
  and racial relations, 312
United Nations
  North Vietnam membership
    application to, 280–81
  in U.S.-Soviet "Basic Principles," 269,
    270
United Nations Universal Declaration of
  Human Rights, Charter 77
  appeal to, 288
United States
  in aftermath of 1968 revolutions, 306
  and "Basic Principles" of relations
    with USSR, 268–72
  Black Panthers in, xvii
  and Chile, xxi
  China's relations with, 259–60
  and Chinese-Soviet conflict, 318
  Marcuse's condemnation of, 72
  on ghettos of, 73
  in NLF Manifesto, 34
  and proving "manliness" through war,
    318, 318n
  race relations in (Marwick), 312
  Reagan as president of, xxii

SDS critique of, 40–42 (*see also Port Huron Statement*)
student protestors in, 229
and violence, 231
university faculty in, 230–231
and Vietnam War, xxi
see also civil rights movement
Unity of the People and Contradictions of Socialism (Sadykov), 293
universities
and CIA on dissidence, 218, 219
in Cohn-Bendit interview, 135–36, 138, 140
cosmopolitan character of, 232
Dutschke on, 119–21, 123, 128
expansion of, 320
rebellions as yearly rituals in, 305
SDS critique of (*Port Huron Statement*), 43, 48–50
student discontent with (CIA report), 225
unsatisfactory conditions in (CIA report), 228
see also education; students
Universities and Left Review, The, 232
University of Mexico, statement of strike committee at, 184–197
University of West Berlin, Dutschke at, 122 (*see also* Berlin; Dutschke, Rudi)
University of Wisconsin, *Studies on the Left*, 233
"urban guerrillas," xviii
USSR, see Soviet Union
Utley, Freda, 283–84
utopia and utopianism
Marcuse on, 75
and 1989 liberal revolutions, 307–8
of 1960s, xxii, 301–2, 304–5
SDS on decline of, 42, 44

Vaculík, Ludvík, xix, 102, 158–65
Vallejo, Demetrio, 194
values
in Fanon's view of colonial encounter, 23, 24–25
SDS on (*Port Huron Statement*), 43–47
Vietnam
Communist takeover in (North), 303

and democratic vision of socialism, 304
and South Vietnam army, 256
Vietnam War, xxi
anti-war extremists accused of prolonging, 312
and containment policy, 318
demonstrations against, 215, 217, 226
Dutschke on, 127, 131
Friedan's protest against, 144
and Kissinger, 254
in correspondence with Galbraith, 255–59
Marcuse on, 72, 73, 78
and NLF Manifesto, 34–35
Reagan on, 280–82
and science (Dutschke), 125
Tet Offensive, 303
women's vote on, 154
violence
and Carmichael, 238
on liberals, 239–42
emergence of, xviii
Fanon's advocacy of, xvii, 18–25
"home-grown," 322
increasing belief in (CIA report), 218
LBJ against, 57, 58
MLK against, 14–15
Marcuse on, 79
and Marcuse's followers, 72
media attracted by (Hoffman), 215
pointless, 312
of police against hippies (Hoffman), 212, 214, 215–16
Republican women on use of (Friedan), 149
SDS rejection of (*Port Huron Statement*), 47
and student dissidence (CIA report), 231
Volkov, Oleg, 99
Voroshilov, Kliment, 298
voting rights, LBJ on, 52–54
Voting Rights Act (1965), 50
Vuchetich, Evgeny, 114–15

Wallace, George, 149, 239, 243
Wang Hai-jung, 260
Warhol, Andy, 315

war on poverty, and women, 150
"war on terrorism," 319
"we shall overcome"
  LBJ's affirmation of, 55
  Marcuse's affirmation of, 78
West Berlin, *see* Berlin
Western democracies
  economic systems of (*see also*
      capitalism; work)
    Dutschke on, 119
    Hoffman on abundance of, 206–7
    Marcuse on, 73
    SDS on (*Port Huron Statement*), 46–47
  repression in, xiii–xiv
    and Marcuse on affluent society,
        80–81
West Germany
  and Kiesinger on protests, xiii
  number of students in, 227
  Red Army Faction in, xvii
  student-protest issues in, 226
Westmoreland, William, 273
White Citizens Councils, MLK on, 12
Wilson, Harold, 133
Wilson, Woodrow, 30, 151
Wolff, Karl Dietrich, 229
"woman power," 144, 147, 150
women
  Bill of Rights for (Friedan), 144–45,
      148, 156, 157–58
  and natural purity mystique (Friedan),
      152–53
  new independence of, 153–54
  oppression of, 149–50
  in politics, 142–43, 144, 150–52, 153
    in Friedan's experience, 145–48
    and New Politics, 154–56
    and sexual timidity, 149
    and politics of sex discrimination,
        156–58
  see also feminine mystique; feminism
Women Strike for Peace, 151–52
Woods, Joe, 216
work
  Hoffman on, 207

Marcuse on, 80
schizophrenic character structure from
    (Dutschke), 130
SDS on (*Port Huron Statement*), 41,
    46–47
in simultaneous workstudy system,
    141
see also at economic system
worker/peasant/student alliance,
    National Strike Committee
    (Mexico) call for, 200–206
World Federation of Democratic Youth
    (WFDY), 237
World Trade Organization, and
    "democratic deficit," 321

Yakir, Pyotr, 92
Yakovlev (Soviet official), 298
"Yankee imperialism," Che Guevara on,
    63
Yasnov, Mikhail, 91
Year of Political Prisoners, 289
Yefremov (Soviet official), 291, 293,
    294
Yeltsin, Boris, 298
Yippies ("Youth International Party"),
    206, 209–10, 212, 214
  origin of, 208–9
Young Americans for Freedom, 32
  Sharon Statement of, 32–33
Young Radicals, The (Keniston), 229
youth culture, xii
youthful rebellion, worldwide differences
    in, xiii
Yugoslavia
  in Gorbachev's memoir, 299
  student protest in, 227

Zeldovich, Yakov, 92, 96
Zhavoronkov, Nikolai, 100, 101
Zhivlyuk, Yuri, 94–95, 102, 103, 104,
    106, 114
Zhukov, Yuri, 236
Zinoviev, Grigory, 5–6
Zorya, Ye. N., 297